Looking back at English Electric Locomotives

Strathwood

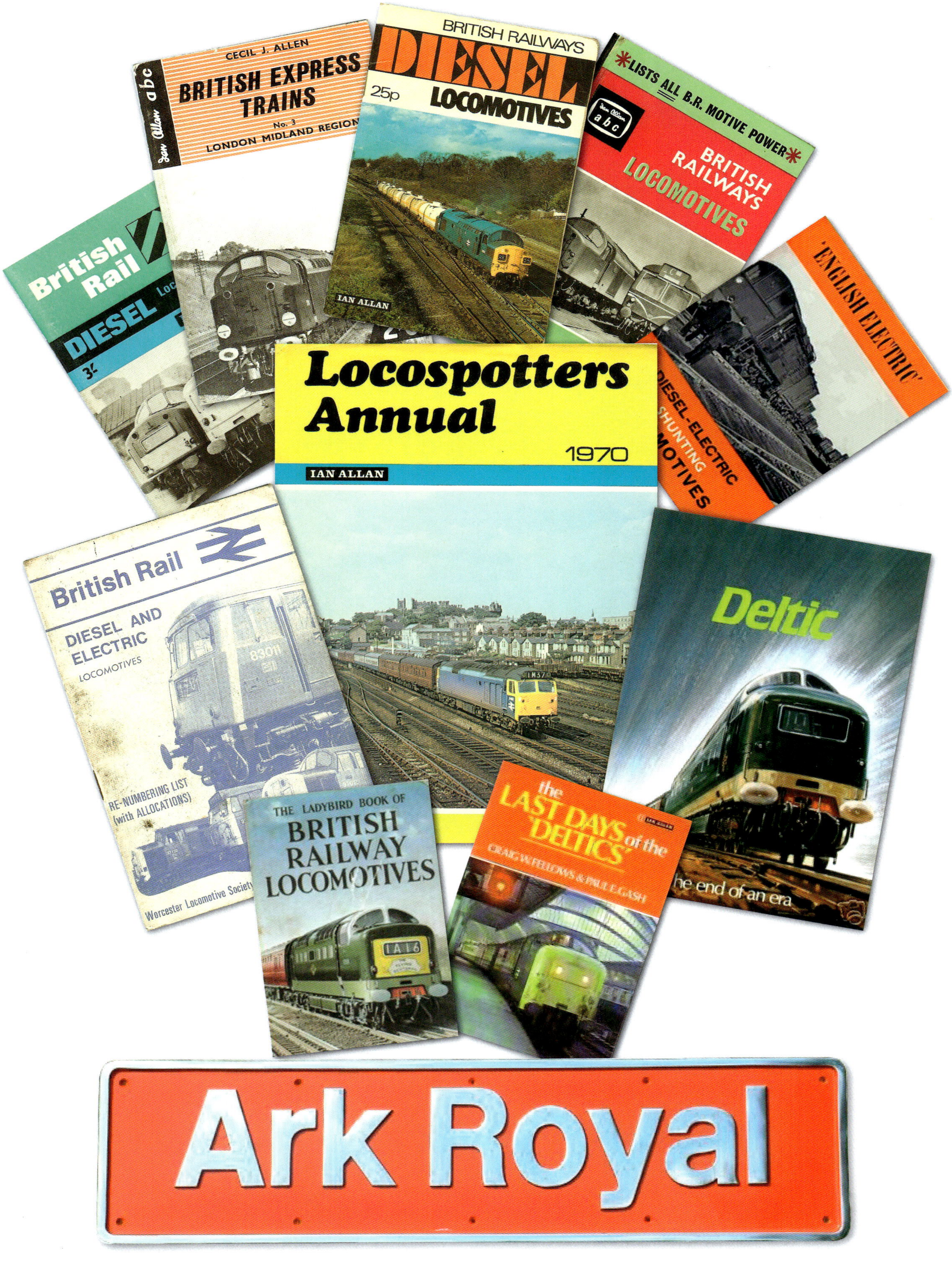
CECIL J. ALLEN
BRITISH EXPRESS TRAINS
No. 3
LONDON MIDLAND REGION
Ian Allan abc
BRITISH RAILWAYS
DIESEL
LOCOMOTIVES
25p
IAN ALLAN
LISTS ALL B.R. MOTIVE POWER
Ian Allan abc
BRITISH RAILWAYS LOCOMOTIVES
British Rail
DIESEL
3/-
'ENGLISH ELECTRIC'
DIESEL-ELECTRIC SHUNTING LOCOMOTIVES
Locospotters Annual
1970
IAN ALLAN
British Rail
DIESEL AND ELECTRIC
LOCOMOTIVES
RE-NUMBERING LIST (with ALLOCATIONS)
Worcester Locomotive Society
Deltic
the end of an era
THE LADYBIRD BOOK OF
BRITISH RAILWAY LOCOMOTIVES
the LAST DAYS of the 'DELTICS'
CRAIG W. FELLOWS & PAUL E. GASH
Ark Royal

Looking back at English Electric Locomotives

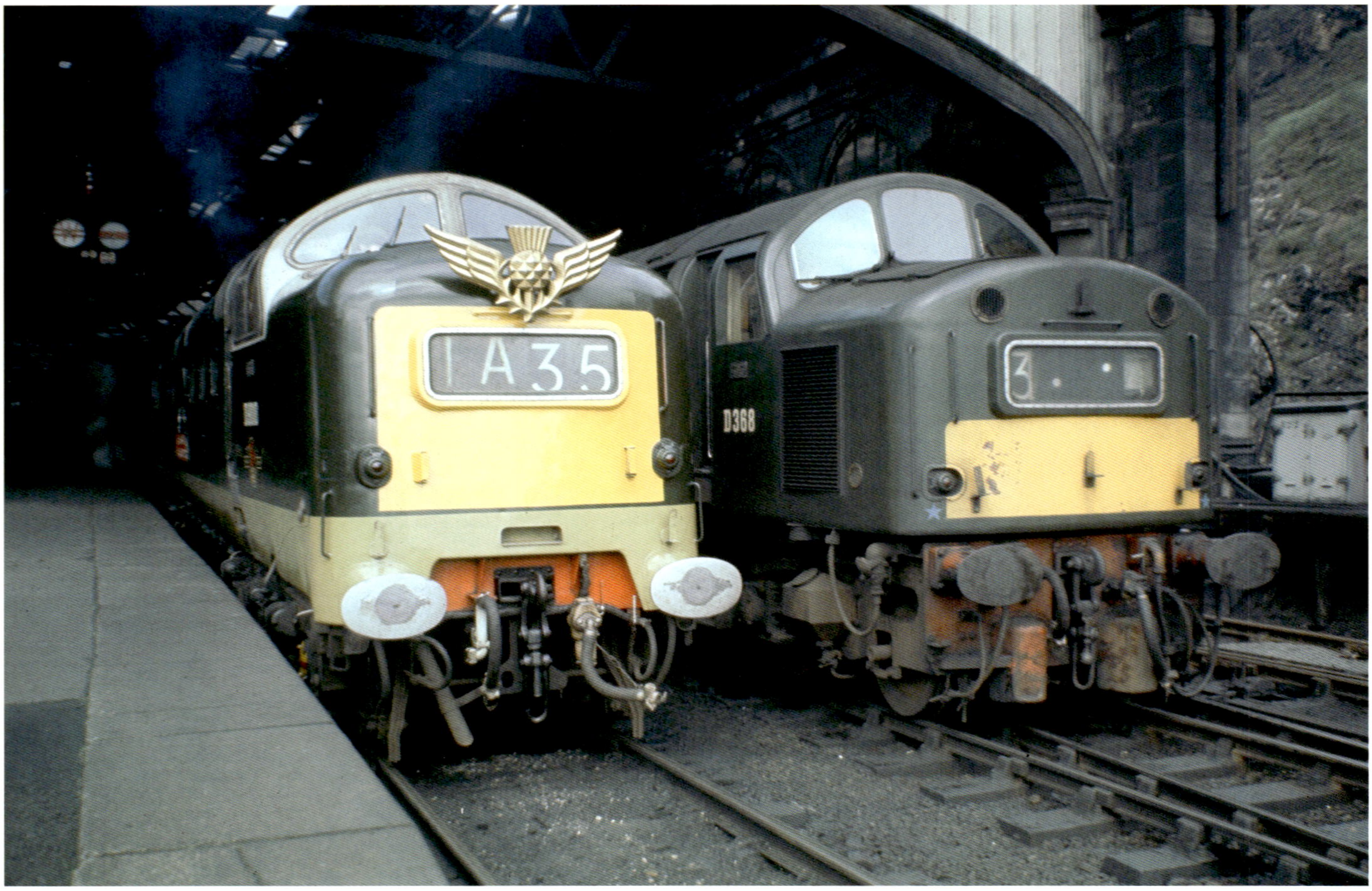

Adorned with a splendid winged thistle for the southbound Flying Scotsman service from Edinburgh Waverley around 1966 is Deltic D9010 The King's Own Scottish Borderer. Alongside is a more work weary D368 allocated to 64B Haymarket. ***Strathwood Library Collection***

Kevin Derrick

Strathwood

Looking back at English Electric Locomotives

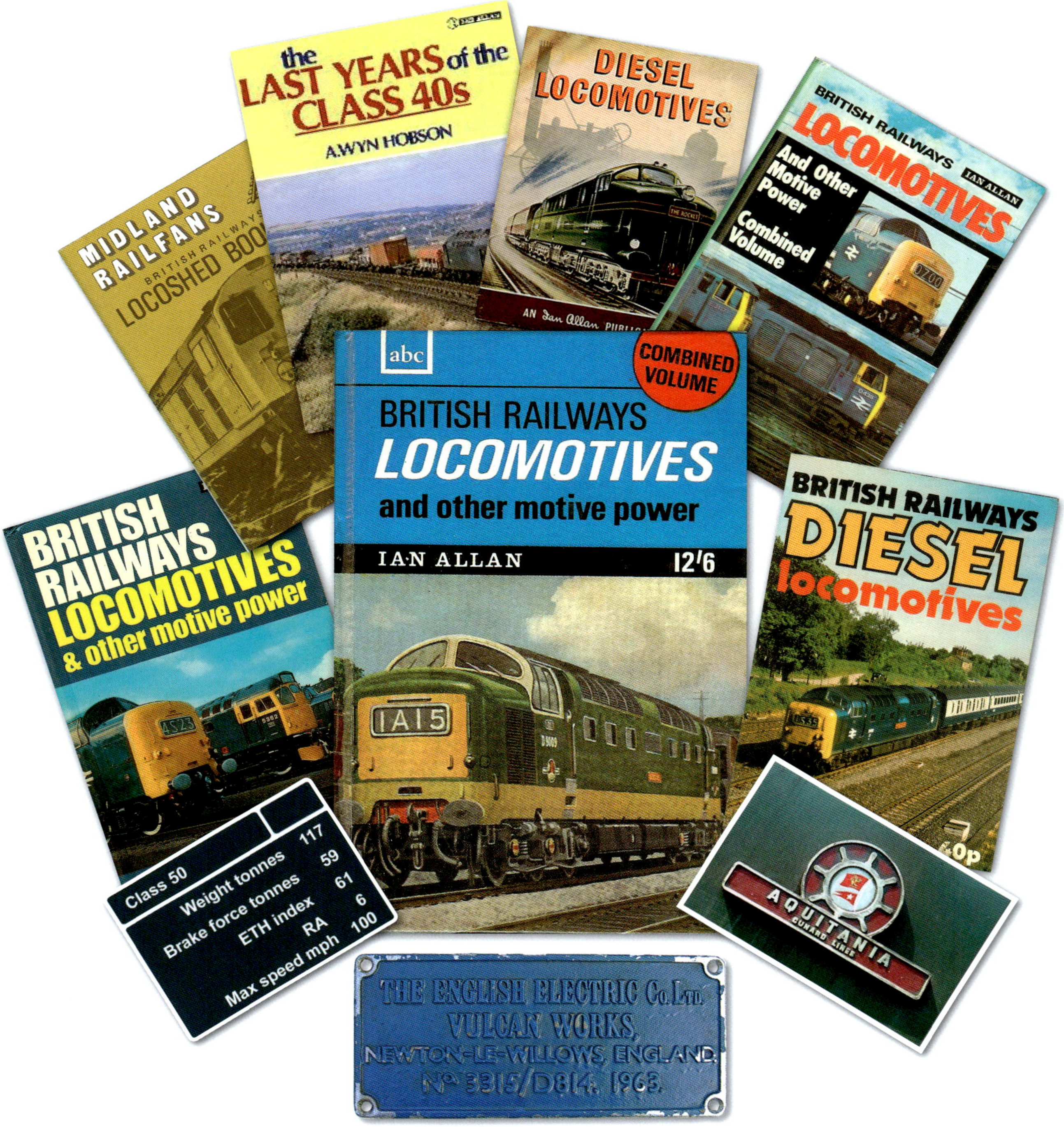

First published 2009

ISBN 1-905276-22-2
ISBN 978-1-905276-22-6

Published by Strathwood Ltd, Glenavon House, Kinchurdy Road,
Boat of Garten, Inverness-shire, PH24 3BP. Tel 01479 831139

Contents **Page**

Introduction....6

Those Big Napier Engines....7

Baby Deltics....14

Whistlers....18

Hoovers for Hire....25

Twenties, Choppers or Dominoes....34

Growlers Galore....53

Mainline and Shunting Genesis....66

New for Old....72

Things Electric....75

Scrappers....77

Into the Darkness....80

Specials....87

Mix and Match....90

Photographic Archive....96

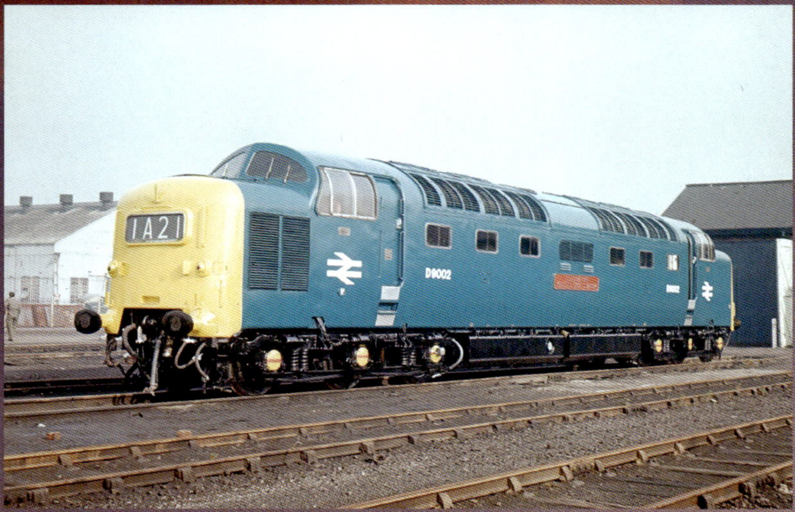

Introduction

The English Electric Company was perhaps best placed to make the most of the potential for orders as a result of the 1955 Modernisation Plan. The company had demonstrated the viability of its products within not only the LMS order for Co-Cos 10000 and 10001, but also two further versions for the Southern Region as 1Co-Co1 with 10201/2 and the more powerful 10203. All four of the pre-nationalisation companies had placed orders for similar designs of 0-6-0 diesel shunters utilising English Electric power plants. Thus the company should have had the edge on the competition in the chase for much needed government funded construction contracts in the aftermath of a world war. Indeed versions of these same engines were being sold to other railways around the world, before the contracts for pilot locomotives were awarded by British Railways.

Whilst other designs were tried in the various categories it seems that English Electric may be judged in hindsight to have won the battle of the shunters fairly conclusively, also seeing off opposition from British Thomson Houston, North British and Clayton for the Type One contracts, but not before much public money was wasted in the process. The Type Two situation did not go very well with the choice of the Napier Deltic engines, although the company kept some faith and rebuilt the locomotives in the hope perhaps that it might win further favour with Type Three and Type Four contracts.

When it came to the Type Three business, Beyer Peacock had been successful on the Western Region with the Hymeks, whilst the Southern Region opted for the Birmingham Railway Carriage & Wagon Company's design. The field was thrown open when both of these companies suffered financial problems, resulting in repeat orders for what would become 309 Class 37s.

The battle for the valuable Type Four contracts was not so clear cut as we saw in the volume on Sulzer powered locomotives along with competition from further hydraulic designs. Although DP2 was put up to combat the lack of power and weight critic's had piled onto what became Class 40s, it was only the lease arrangement that allowed British Rail to proceed with the Class 50s For what was only conceived at the time as a stop gap until full electrification of the WCML. In the end the Class 50s did for the Western's Class 52s, and the spare Class 37s drafted in to the region finished off the Hymeks too.

Returning to the Type Two category a windfall came upon the company with the engine fatigue problems encountered in the Brush built locomotives which were equipped with Mirlees engines, and a chance to do a deal to fit two hundred and sixty three new English Electric power plants.

It cannot be overstated just how important the prototype DELTIC was to both the company and to the other British builders of locomotives as it was marketed as the world's most powerful diesel locomotive and no doubt provided a flagship for the salesmen seeking orders from railways who were impressed by this British built machine. Even if they ordered more modest locomotives for their own requirements, it must have helped to keep the American General Motors and General Electric designs to a minimum within Europe and the British Empire. Ultimately the battle was lost but we all enjoyed it while we had many of our favourites in everyday service on British Railways.

The Looking Back at series continues to develop to give broader overviews of various designs and specific classes, with the emphasis upon the service years rather than preservation, together with what we hope is an easy to read style, not getting bogged down with too much technical detail that may only concern a small number of readers.. So sit back and enjoy this first delve into English Electric Locomotives.

Kevin Derrick
Boat of Garten 2009

Above: Fresh into blue is D9002 The King's Own Yorkshire Light Infantry outside Doncaster Works in October 1966, the first Deltic into blue livery and among the first locomotives in the country into this then new livery. ***Strathwood Library Collection***

This page; The distinctive profiles of a Class 37s 37087 and 37026 near Ormside descend on the Settle & Carlisle at sunset on 4 May 1996. ***Late Pete Walton/Sid Steadman***

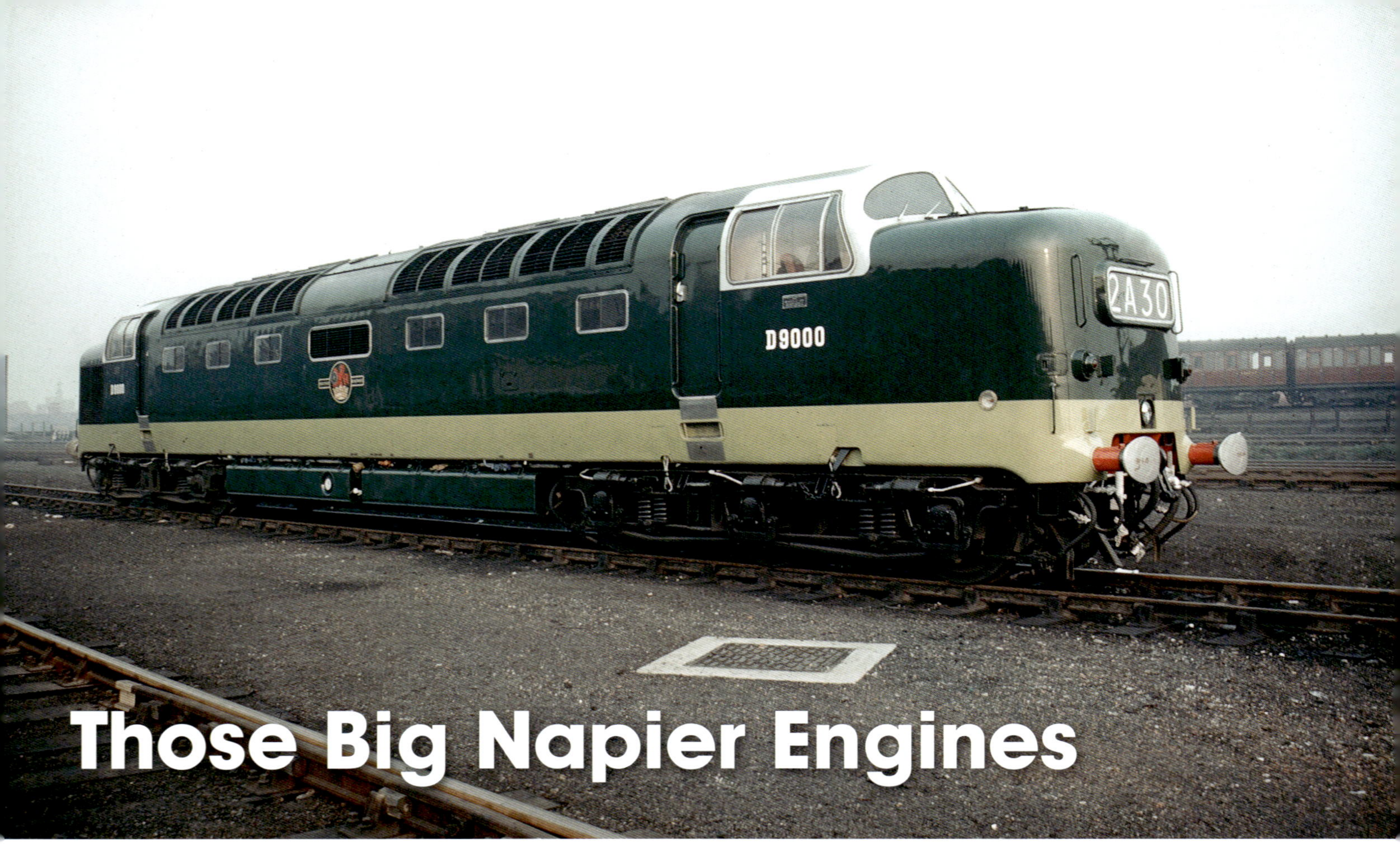

Those Big Napier Engines

On the last day of February in 1961 D9000 ran light engine from Vulcan Foundry, Newton-Le-Willows, to Doncaster Works for acceptance trials into service and was allocated to 64B, Haymarket depot in Edinburgh. Delivery of the Deltic locomotives was heavily delayed due to various factors. However, D9000's introduction was further delayed due to the addition of an experimental flashing headlight fitted to both ends above the buffer beams as seen here. The locomotive was noted with the flashing light on test around the Hadley Wood area on 10 March whilst running light engine from Finsbury Park to Doncaster. Experiments were however abandoned and the light was later removed during August 1961. ***Strathwood Library Collection***

Seen at York in early August 1961 was D9009 Alycidon. The locomotive had been delivered from English Electric's works at Vulcan Foundry and named on 21 July 1961 at Doncaster Works without ceremony, (in honour of the racehorse owned by the 17th Earl of Derby, who won The Ascot Gold Cup, Goodwood Cup, Corporation Stakes and Doncaster Cup. "ALYCIDON" was sire to "MELD"). ***Richard Sinclair Collection***

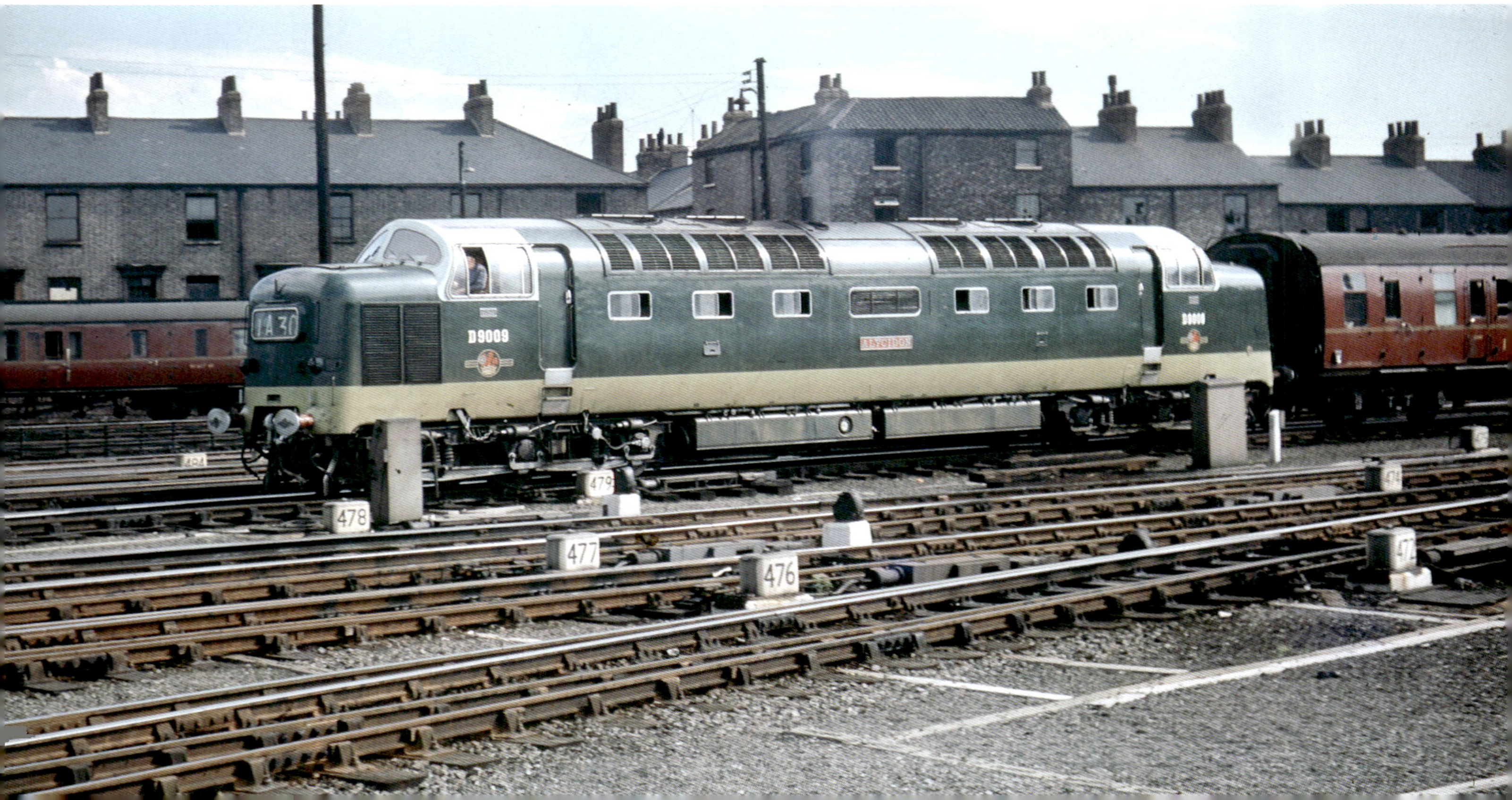

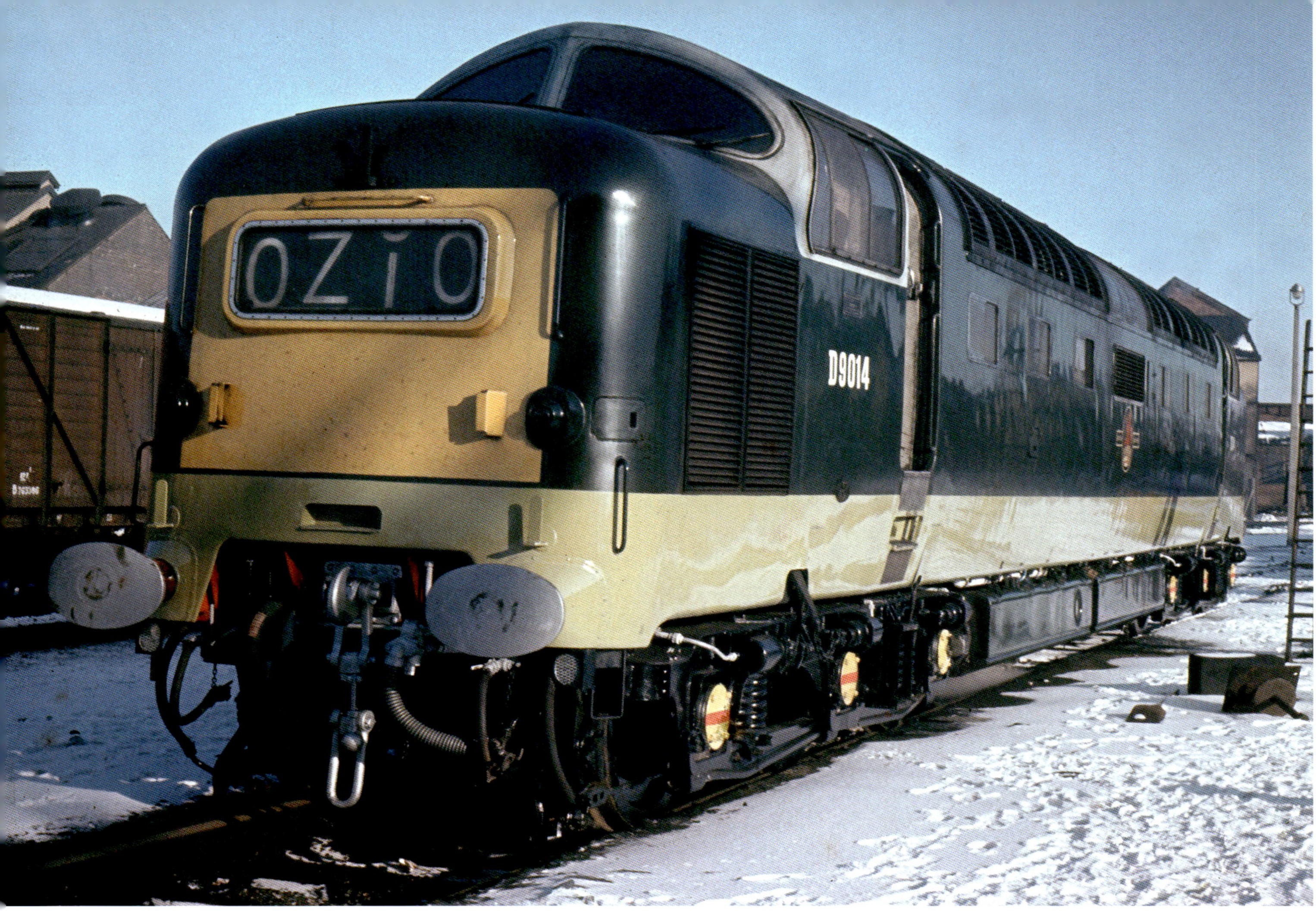

Service Deltic number fifteen D9014 had entered service on 29 September 1961 and was based at 52A Gateshead. She was back on Doncaster Works after a light snow fall in December 1962. The following October saw the locomotive named in a ceremony at Darlington, with the nameplates fitted where the original British Railways larger style of emblem was affixed to the engine's flanks. The name The Duke of Wellington's Regt (West Riding) was previously carried by LMS Royal Scot No. 46145. ***Strathwood Library Collection***

Standing by the former Test House at Doncaster Works in September 1965 having just been named as Royal Highland Fusilier at Glasgow Central on the eleventh of the month. ***Strathwood Library Collection***

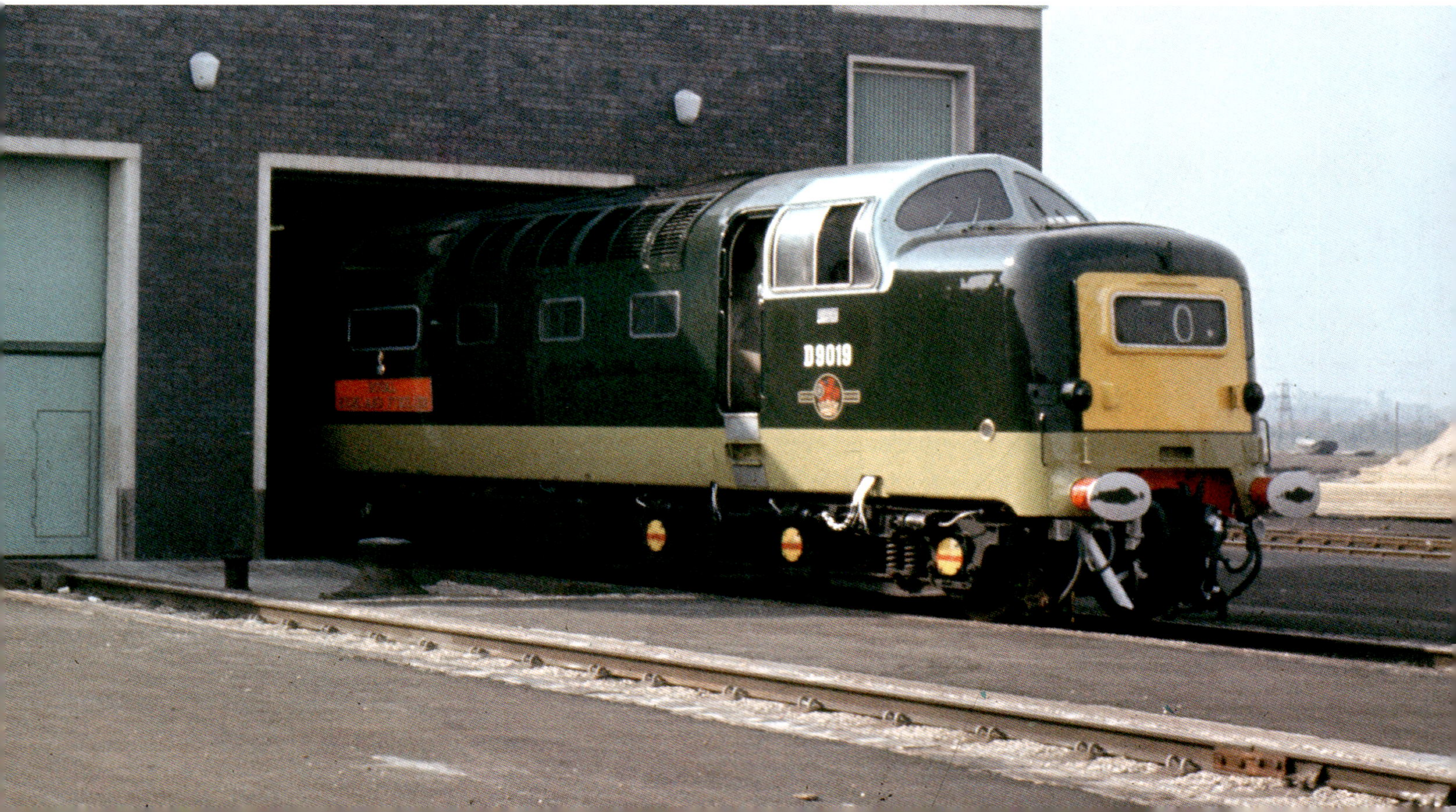

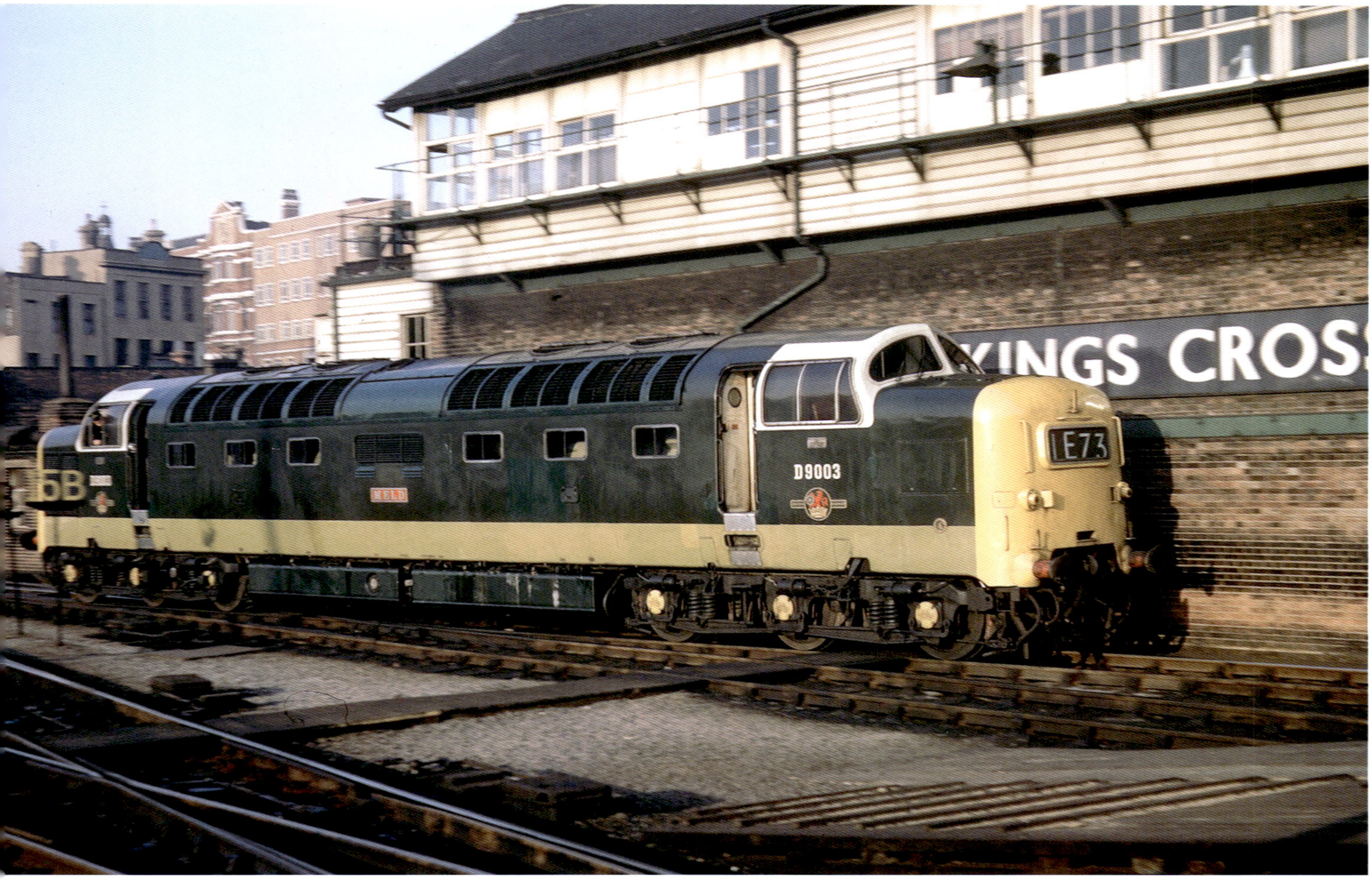

The first two of the class to receive full yellow ends were D9010 The King's Own Scottish Borderer and D9003 Meld in December 1966. Our cameraman recorded the racehorse Deltic at Kings Cross the following March. ***Michael Beaton***

Released from Doncaster Works after general repair, with full yellow ends applied D9003 & D9010 were out-shopped the same day, 23 December 1966, as they were the first to be so treated after D9002 had already been given a full repaint two months earlier into blue. It is also possible that the new Inter City arrows were applied at this stage, as opposed to the Lion & Wheel emblems. D9010 was the only Deltic locomotive to carry green livery and Double-Arrows. Half yellow fronts still rule in this view at Kings Cross on the other engines stabled early in 1967. ***Win Wall/Strathwood Library Collection***

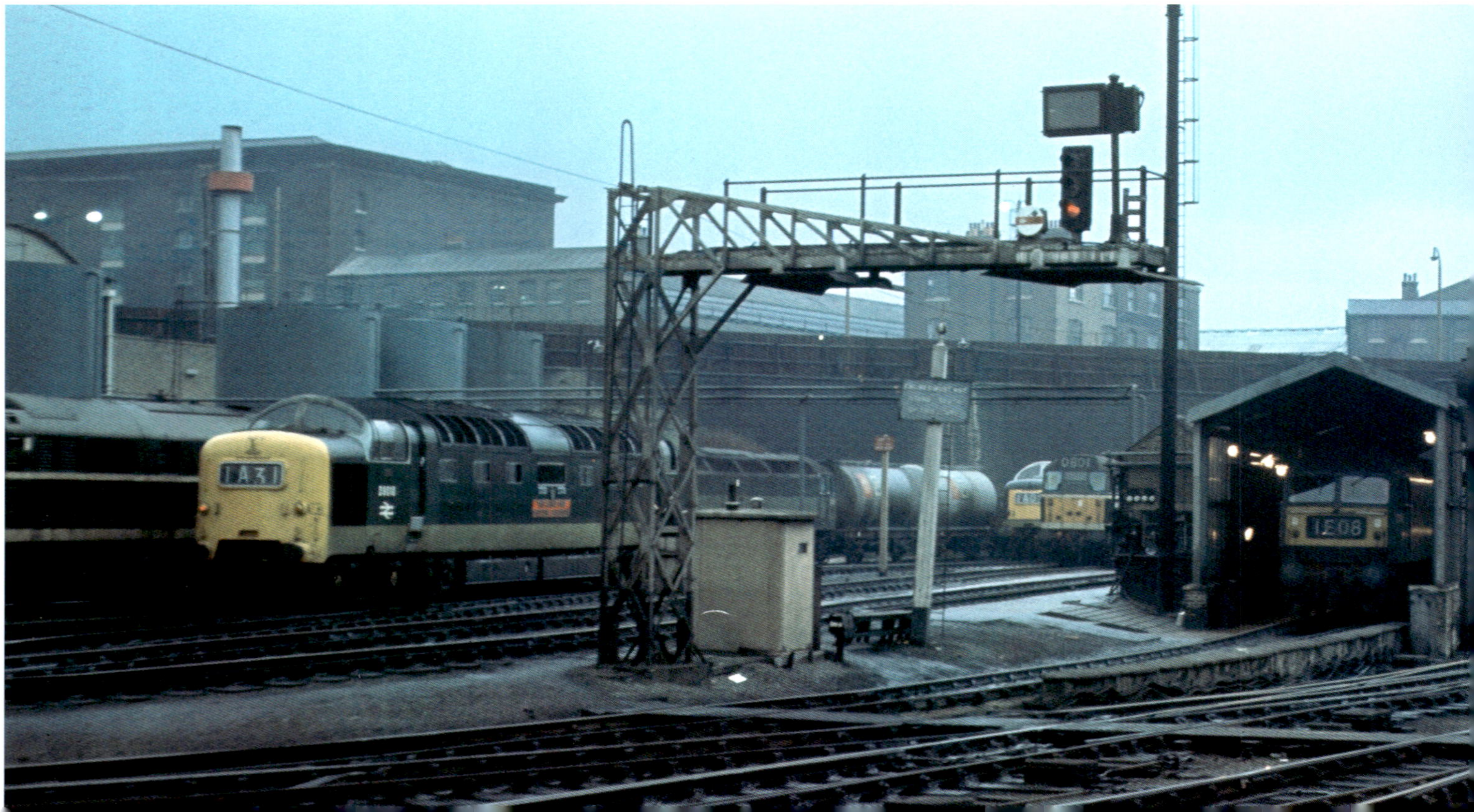

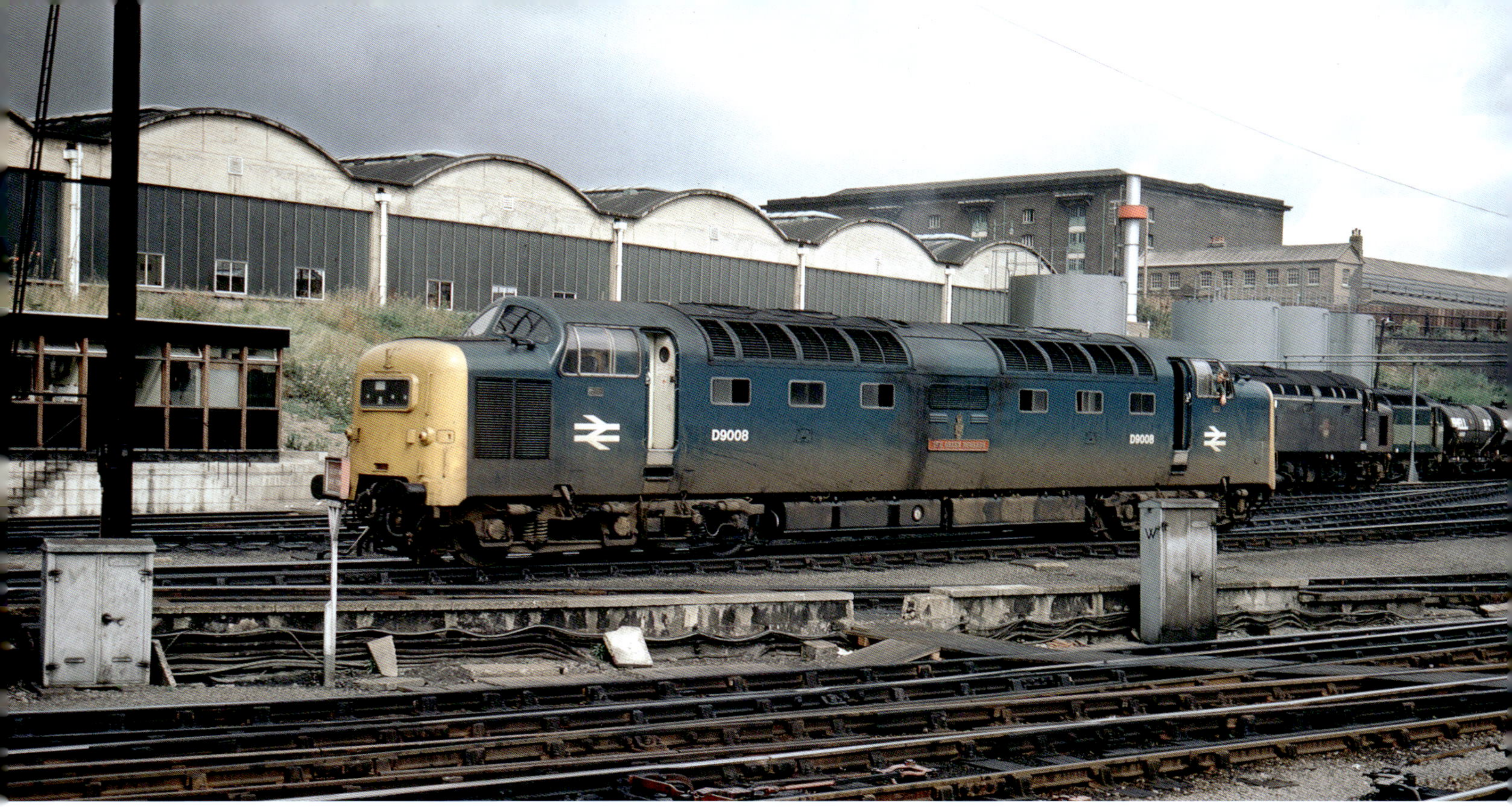

Again seen on the much lamented stabling point at Kings Cross on 12 August 1967 was D9008 The Green Howards. Released from Doncaster Works after general repair, in blue livery on 1 July six weeks previously. The nameplates were lowered to accommodate the fitting of regimental crests at this time. ***Frank Hornby***

Well turned out at Askham on 23 October 1976 was 55020 Nimbus. Less than eighteen months later on 30 March 1978 this Deltic was sent out on the 6E05 Oxford - Newcastle (parcels), from York - this was the locomotives final working and was undertaken whilst restricted to one power unit. Nimbus required shopping at Doncaster Works for power unit exchange. However, due to industrial action by Doncaster employees 55020 was instead held by Gateshead depot staff and was heavily robbed of spares for the rest of the fleet, finally being dispatched to Doncaster on the 26 April 1978. Unfortunately repairs were never sanctioned, and on 18 December 1979 this once fine locomotive was withdrawn from Eastern Region operating stock. ***Ian Harrison***

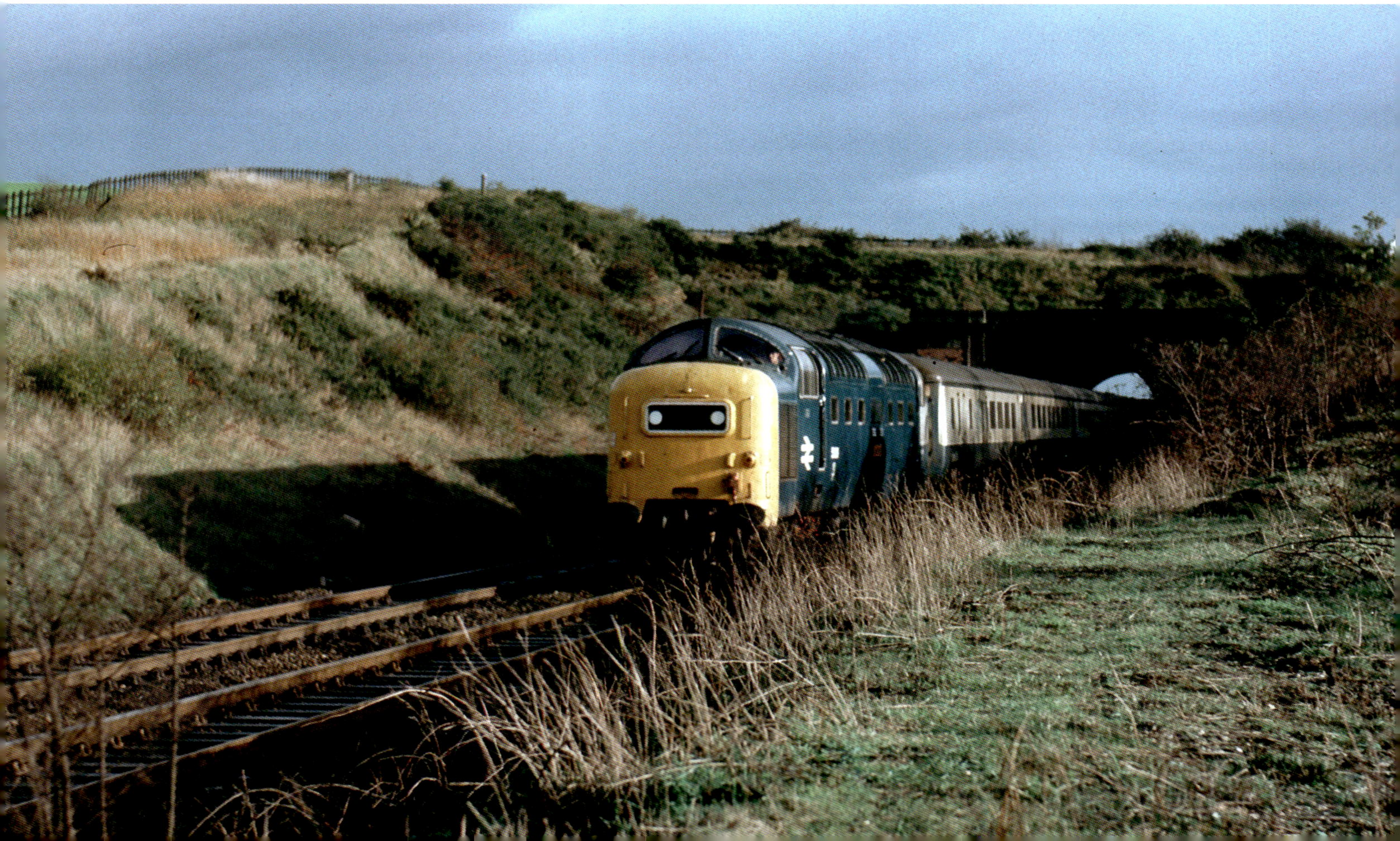

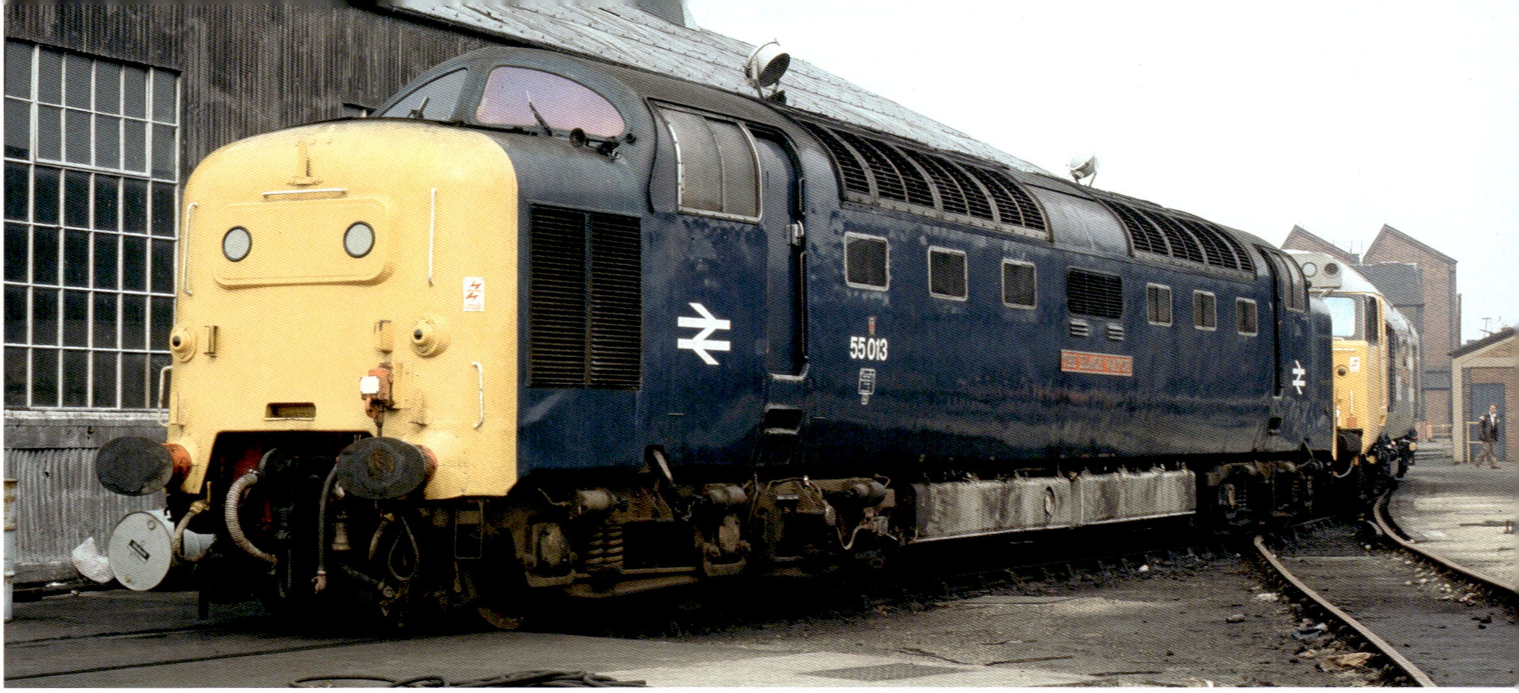

Now with the former headcode panelled over and fitted with opaque marker lights outside Doncaster Works was 55013 The Black Watch with Class 50 favourite 50035 Ark Royal standing behind on Sunday 29 March 1981. ***Colin Whitbread***

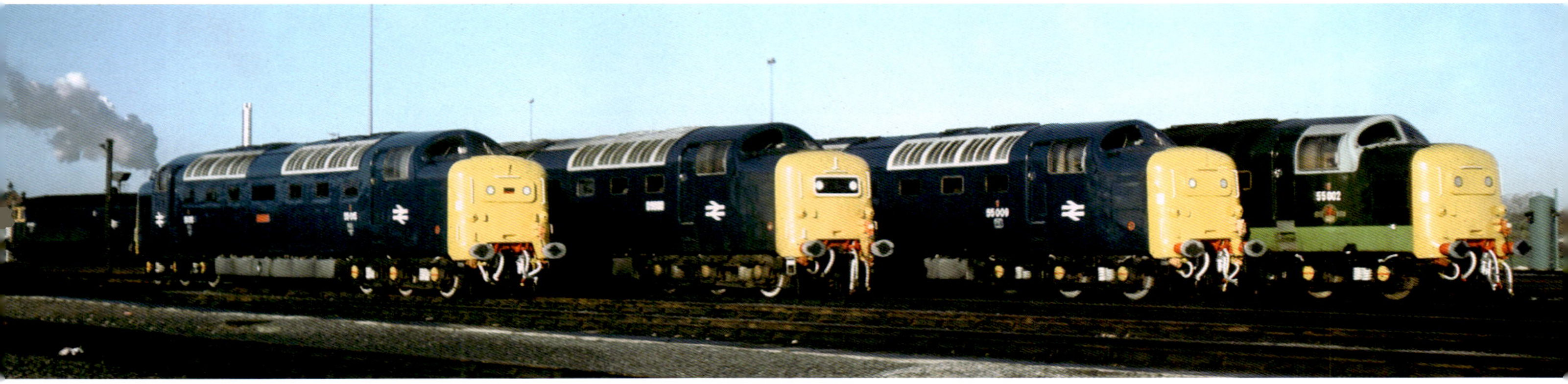

Lined up at York on 5 November 1981 are 55015 Tulyar, 55022 Royal Scots Grey, 55009 Alycidon and 55002 The King's Own Yorkshire Light Infantry, all taken into preservation shortly afterwards. ***Strathwood Library Collection***

Below: Showing some of Finsbury Park depot's customising is 55007 Pinza on the 12.34 Hull to Kings Cross on 10 April 1981 at Hadley Wood. ***Colin Whitbread***

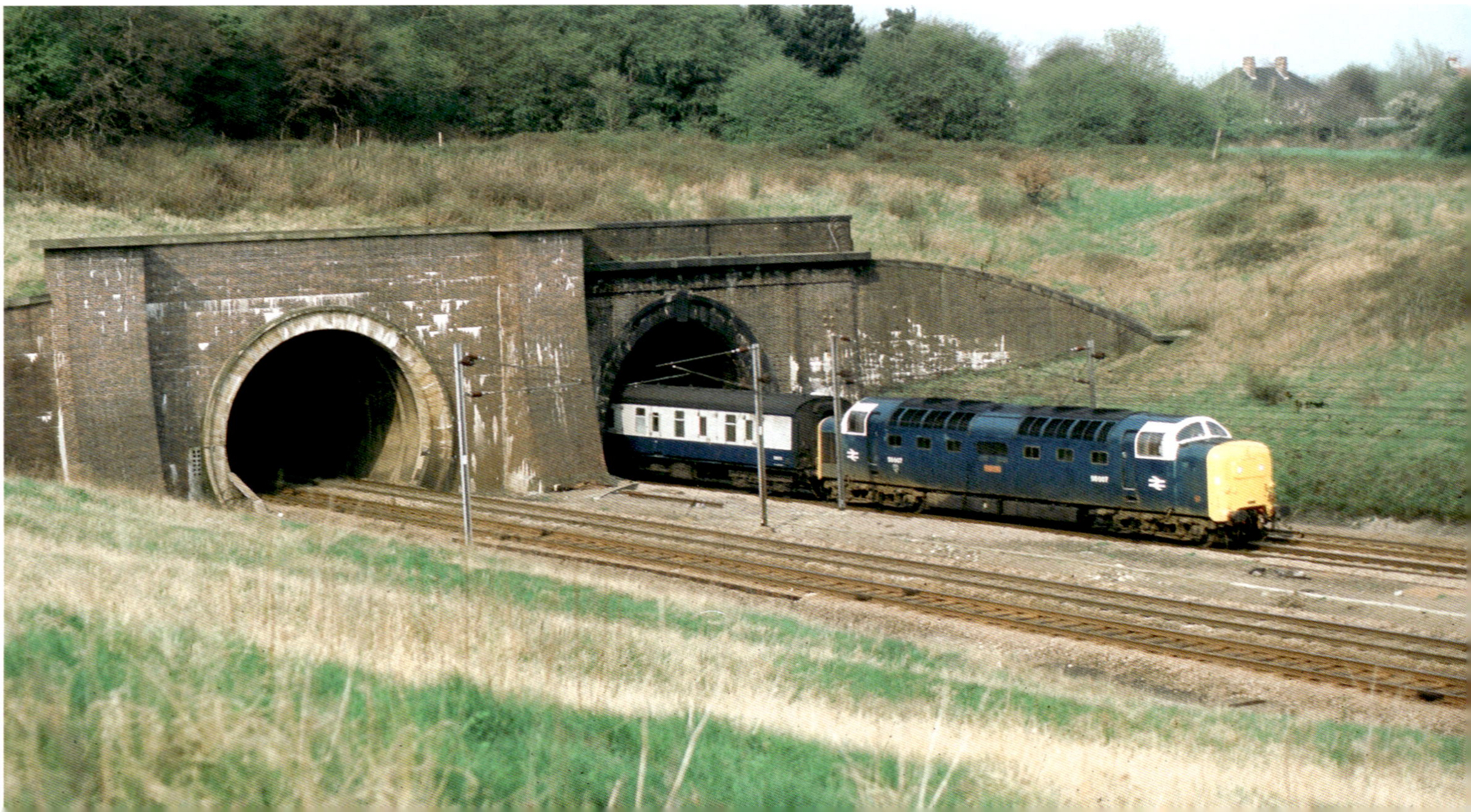

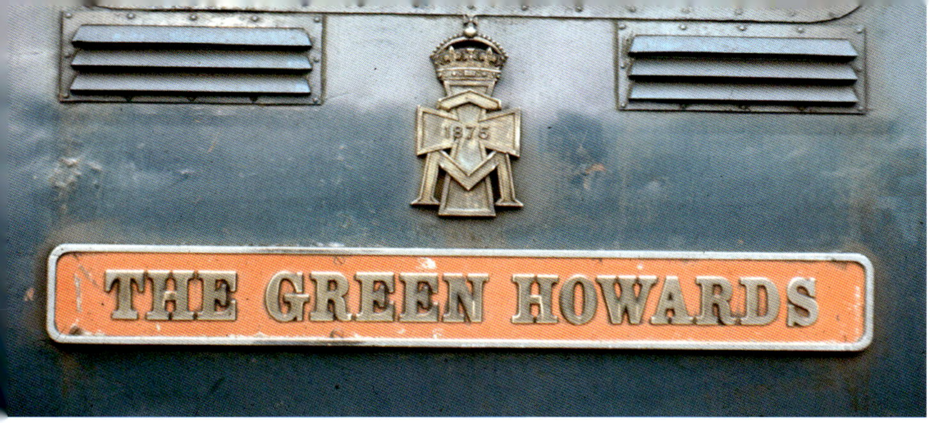

The nameplates fitted to 55008 The Green Howards along with 55005, 55011, 55014 and 55017 had rounded edges and were cast in brass and chromed. ***Matthew Hall***

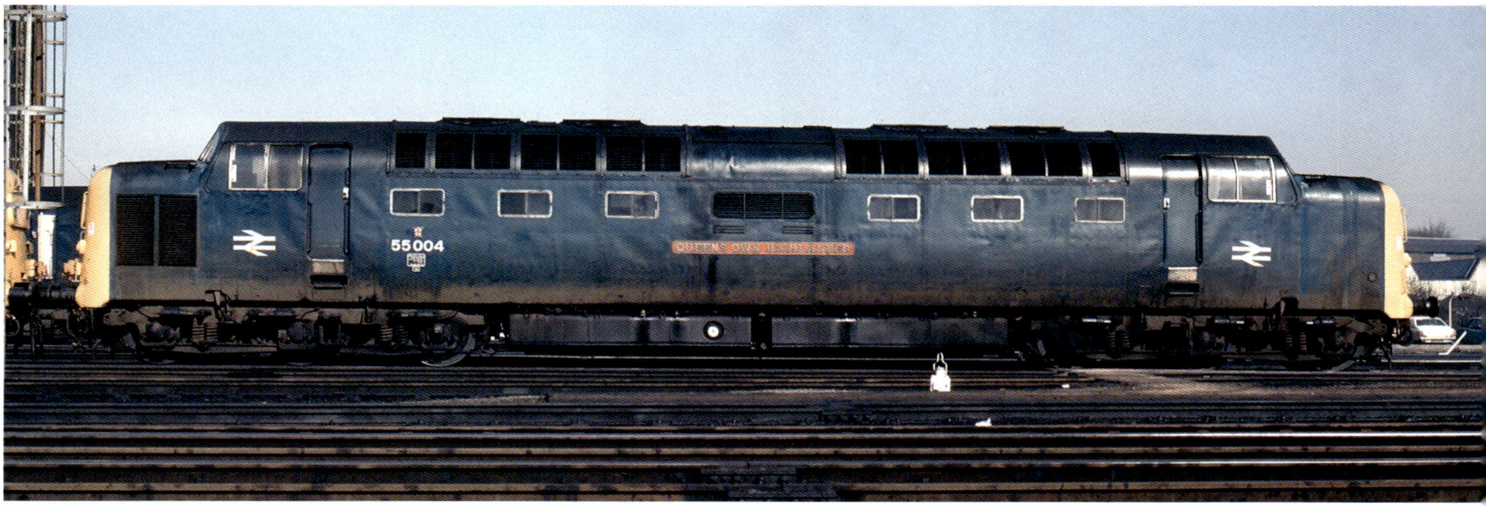

Put back into traffic after an extended period out of traffic 55004 Queen's Own Highlander had lost the regimental crests which had been previously carried when seen at Haymarket on 5 April 1980. ***Sid Steadman***

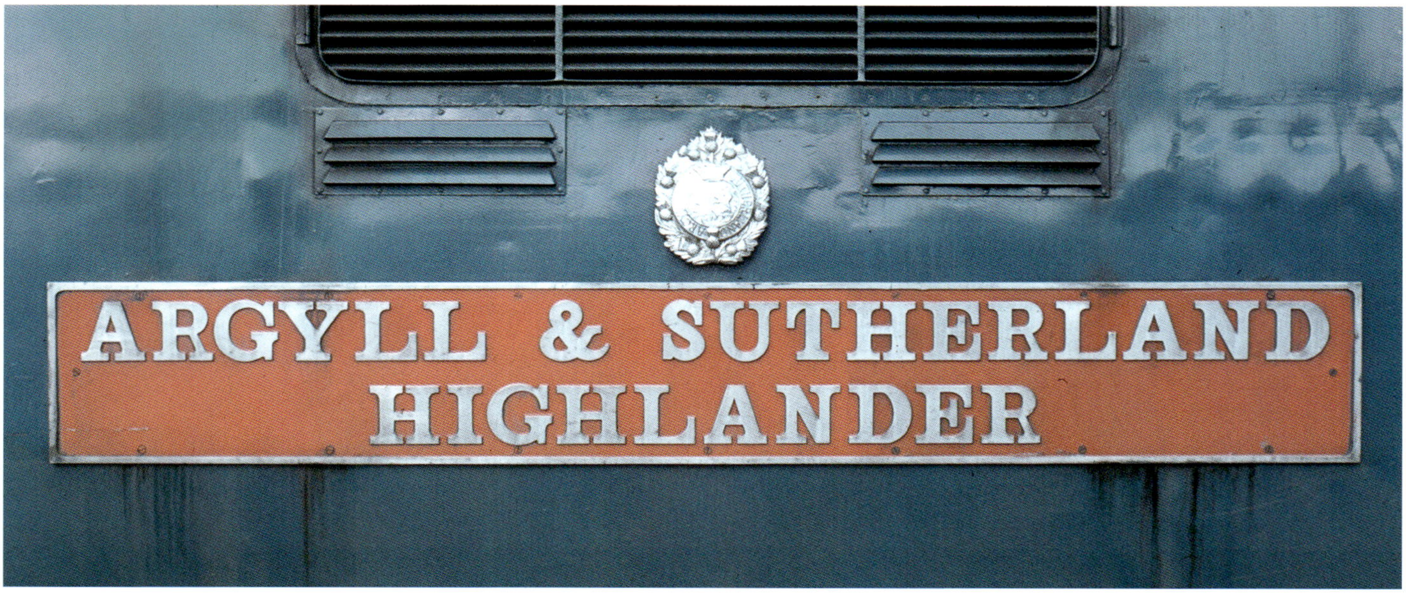

In 1977 55021 Argyll and Sutherland Highlander still proudly carried her crests. ***Strathwood Library Collection***

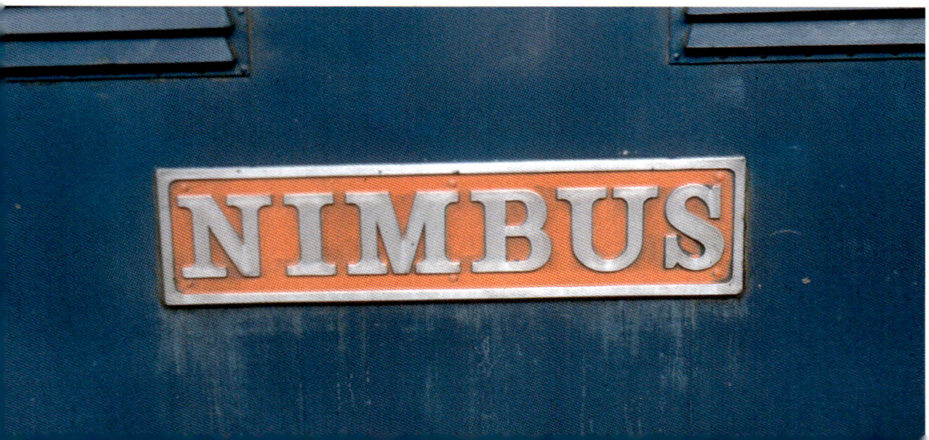

Combinations of cleaning agents and rainfall have left alloy stains on the paintwork off the nameplates fitted to 55020 Nimbus in October 1977. ***David T Williams***

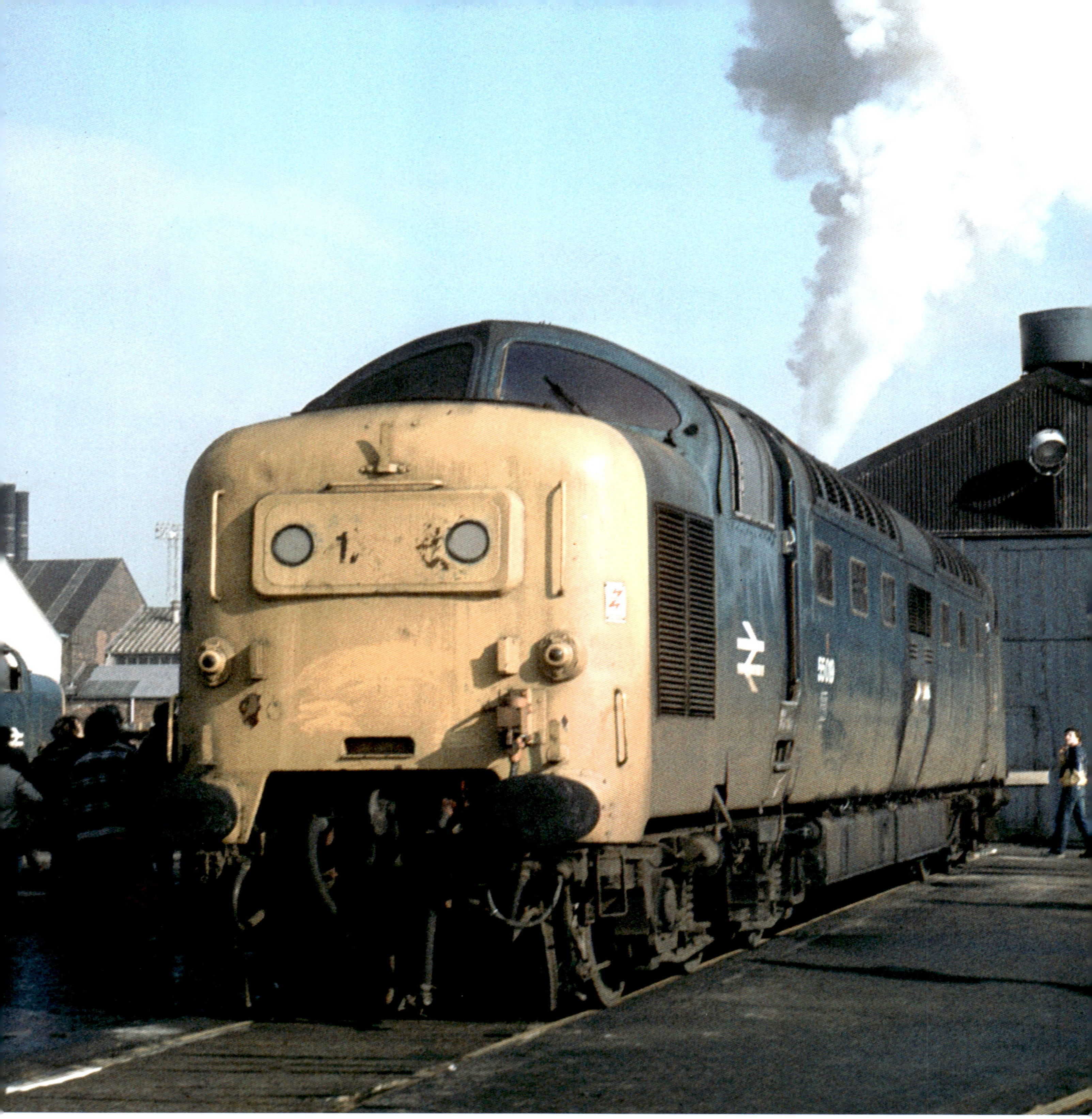

Unprecedented crowds turned out for the Deltic Open Day at Doncaster Works on 27 February 1982 in the winter sunshine. All the surviving class members were present around the works. Although the nameplates had been removed the heart of 55019 Royal Highland Fusilier was brought back to life when one of the engines was fired up to the joy of the assembled crowd of admirers. This Deltic had been based at York since May 1979 working until the end on the last day of 1981. The locomotive arrived at the works here on 4 January 1982 and was put into storage pending interest from The Deltic Preservation Society. Fortunately a sale was agreed and after handing over £16,550 and 19 pence excluding VAT on 20 August 1982 a move was arranged to the North Yorkshire Moors Railway, making a debut on enthusiasts' trains two days later. ***Steve Ireland***

Baby Deltics

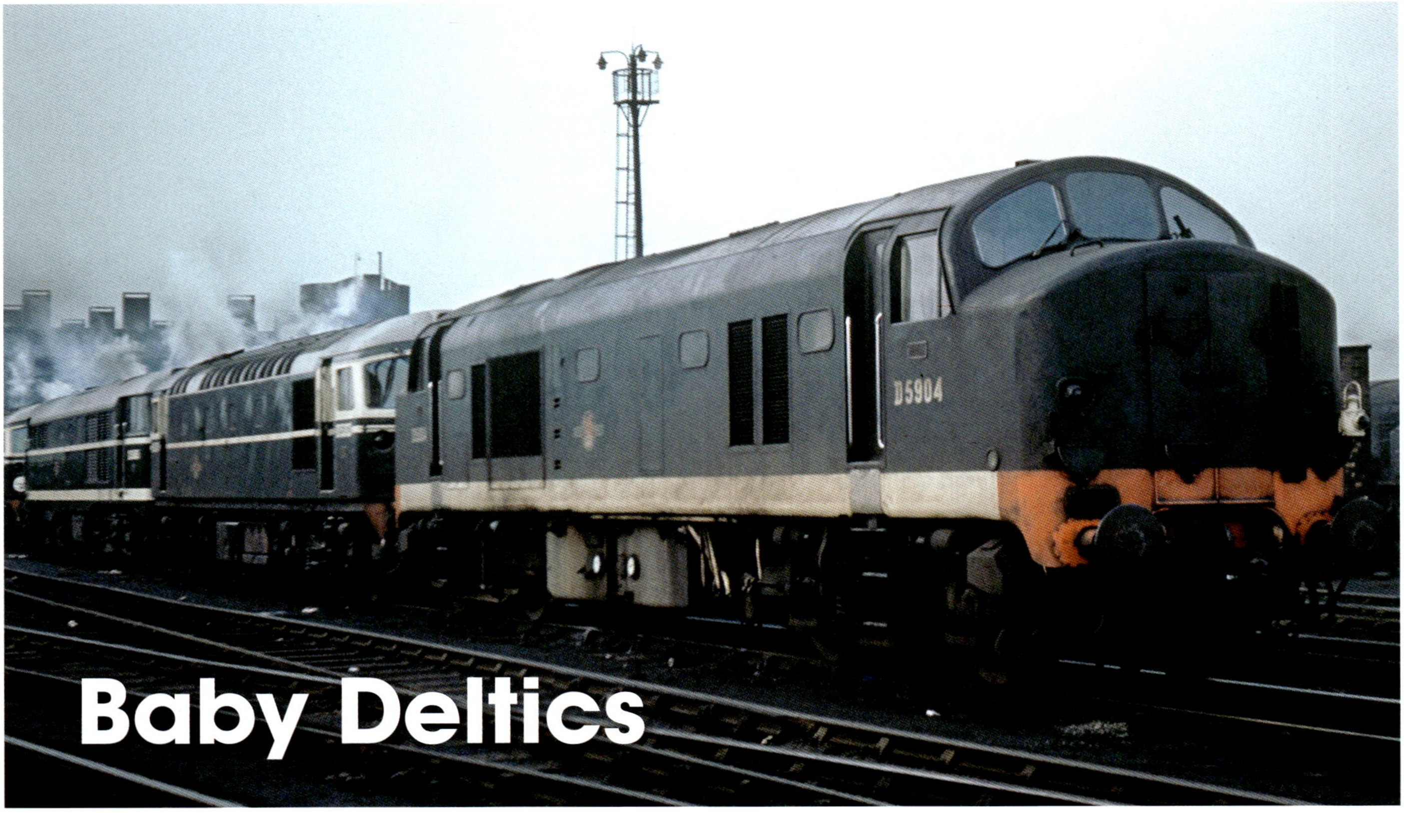

Built in 1959 the Baby Deltics, so named due to their size and use of a single Napier power unit per loco instead of two as in the larger Type 5 Deltic locomotives, the class (later designated class 23) was prone to problems and failure. The power units used in the Bo-Bo locomotives were 1100hp Napier Deltic T9-29 engines, not those used in the larger Co-Co locomotives, and gave persistent problems with crankshaft seizures. Standing at Hornsey on 19 March 1960 was D5904. ***Frank Hornby***

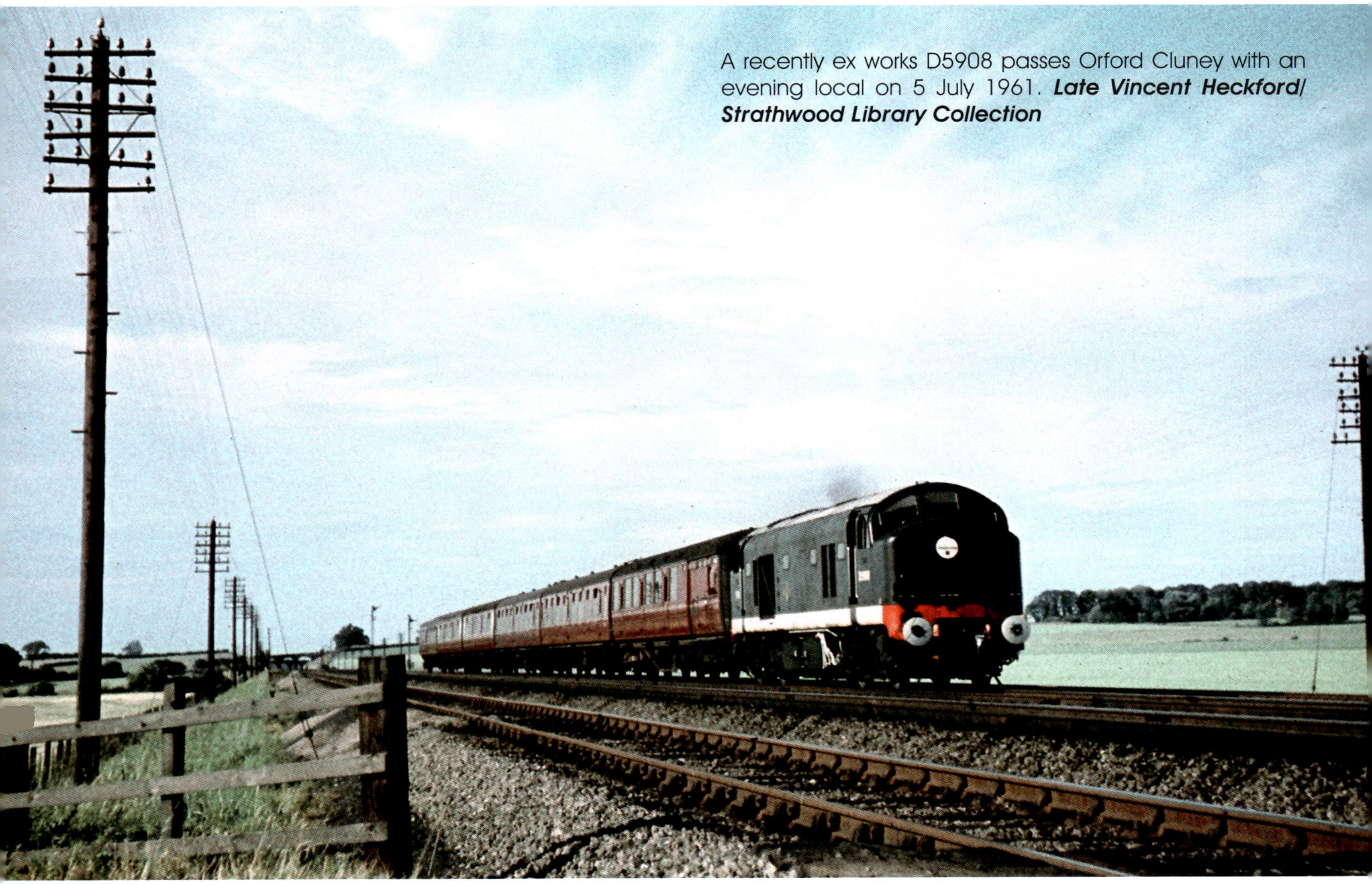

A recently ex works D5908 passes Orford Cluney with an evening local on 5 July 1961. ***Late Vincent Heckford/ Strathwood Library Collection***

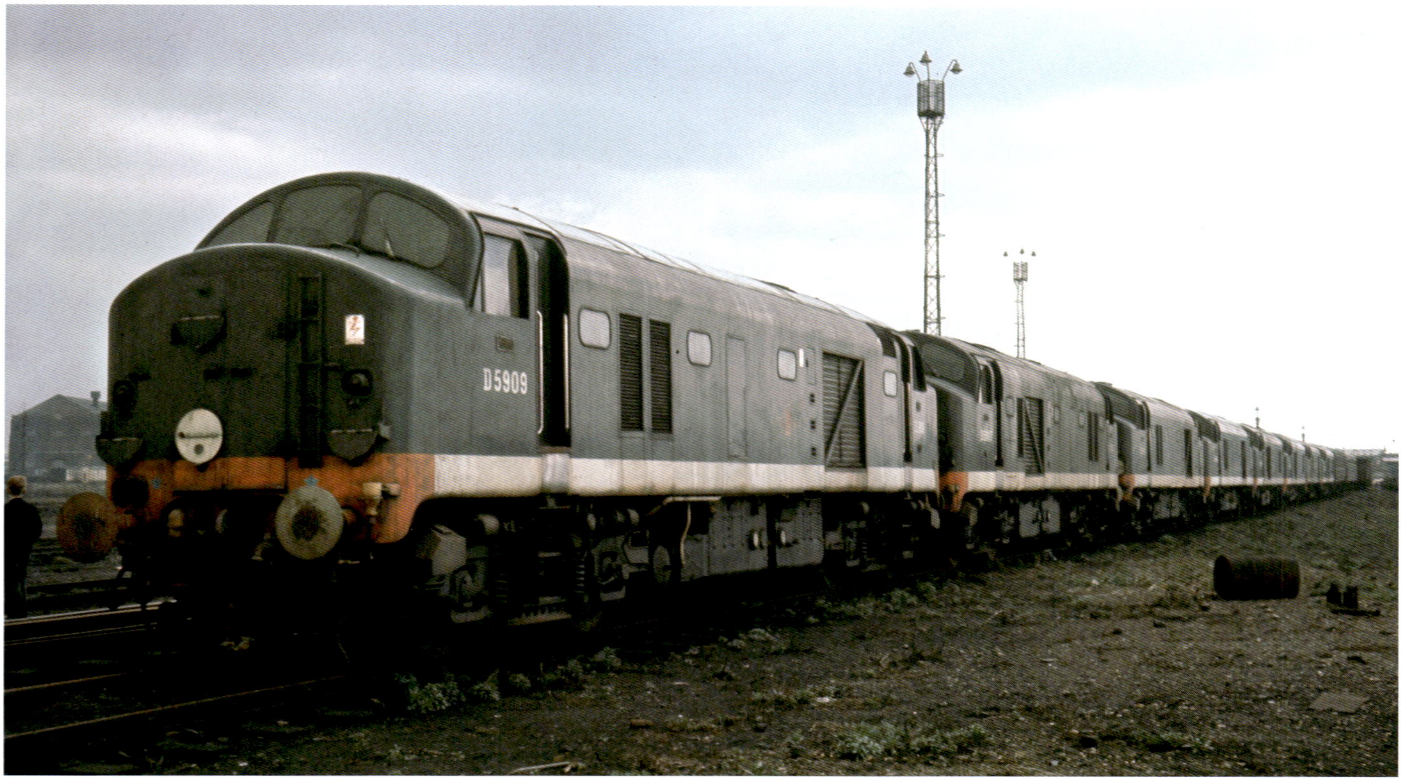

The class was also overweight when first built and this held up acceptance by British Railways who refused to take delivery. The weight problems continued into service and the locomotives were restricted in use, finding themselves banned from certain routes. As consistent failure continued the locomotives were steadily stored at Stratford and by 1962 only four of the ten built were left in service. All ten were finally stored when the last of the class still remaining in service, D5905, eventually succumbed to failure in June 1963. All the locomotives were moved to Doncaster Works in July 1963 and then onto Vulcan Foundry for refurbishment. This was the line up at Stratford in May 1963 led by D5909. ***Richard Sinclair Collection***

The first locomotive back into service was D5904 in July 1964 with them all back in traffic by June 1965. Two more of the now refurbished locomotives are seen with D5904 at Kings Cross in 1966. ***Len Smith***

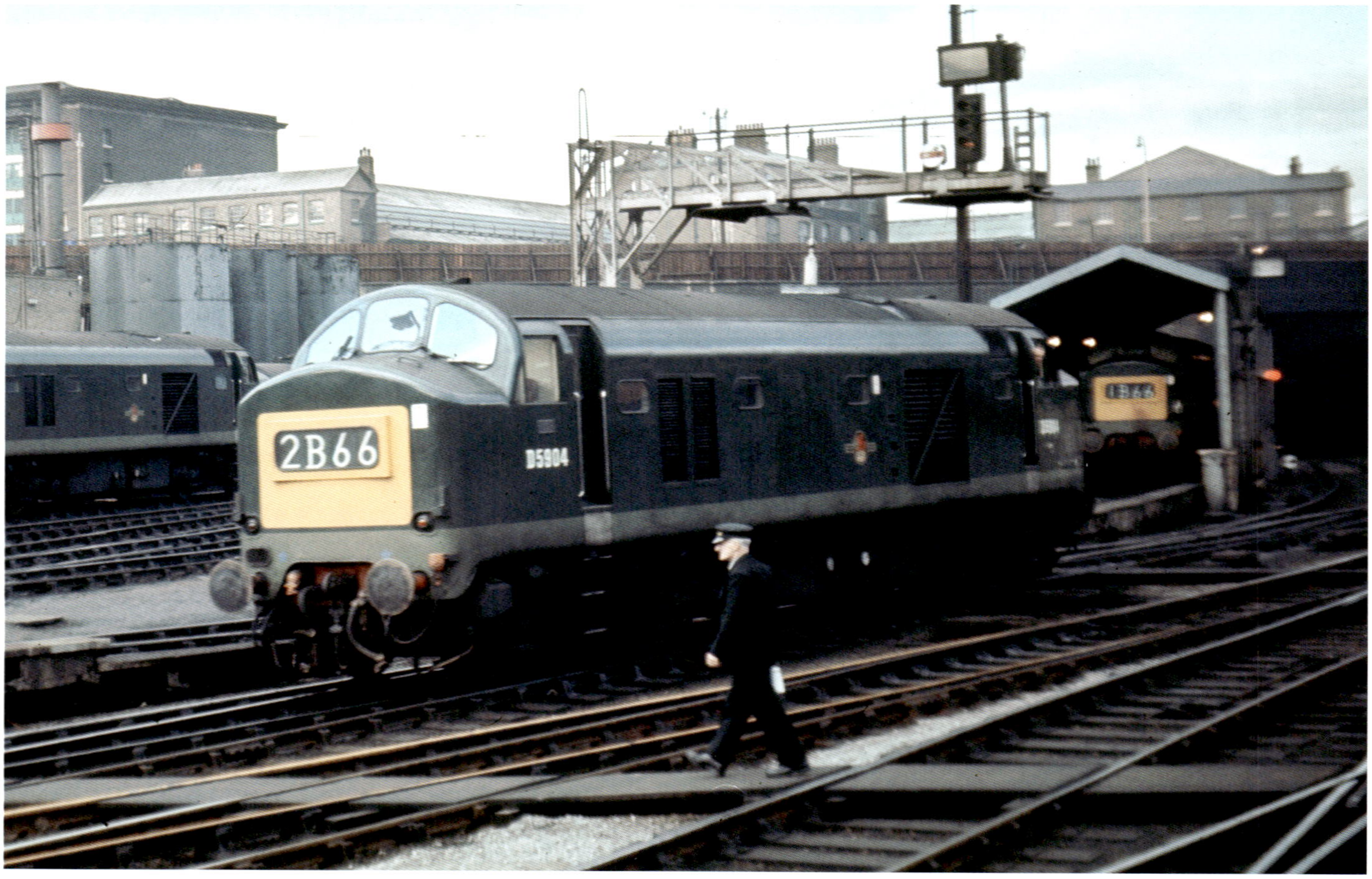

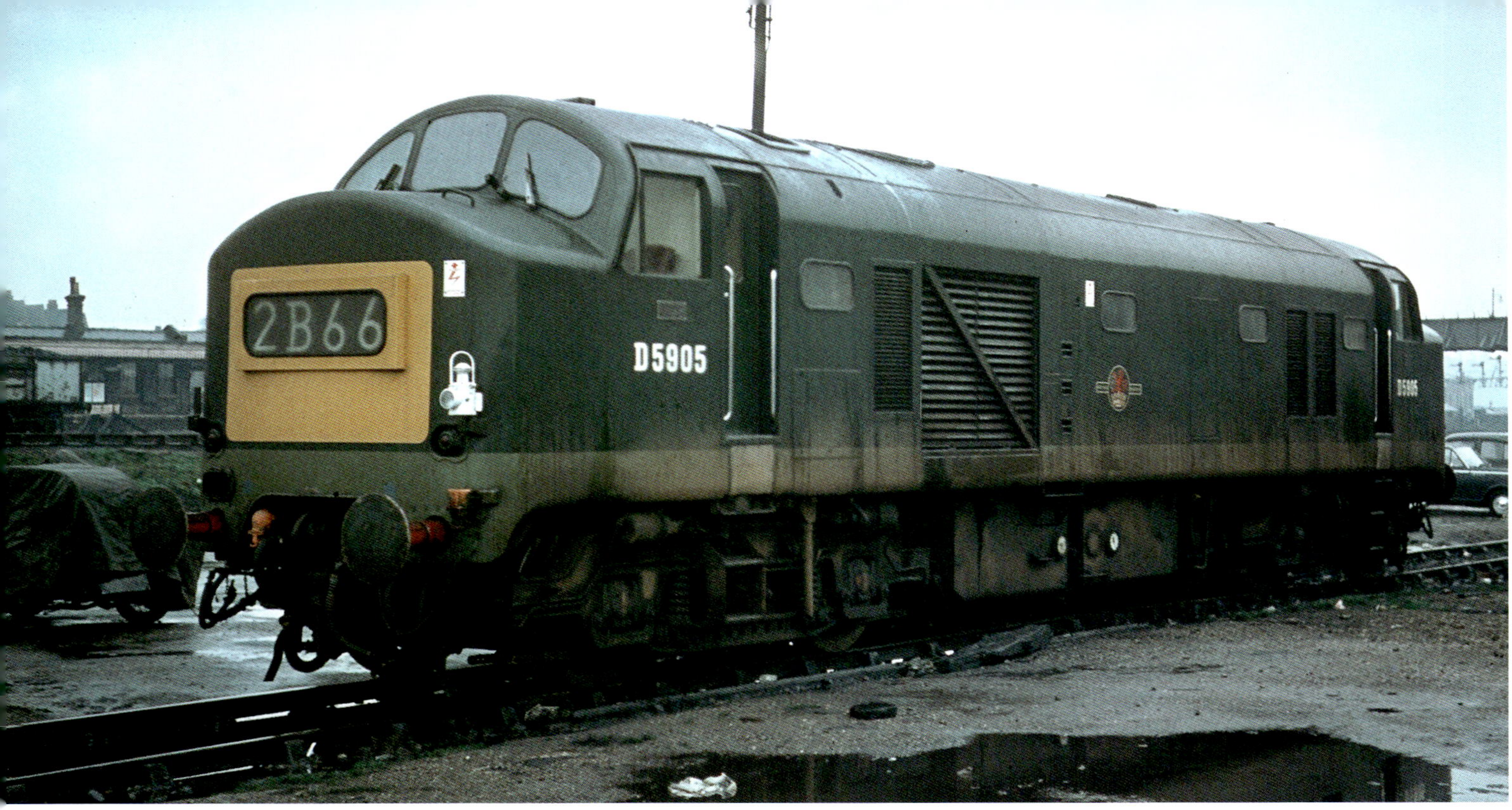

Out of service in the rain at Ferme Park in 1965 was D5905.
Richard Sinclair Collection

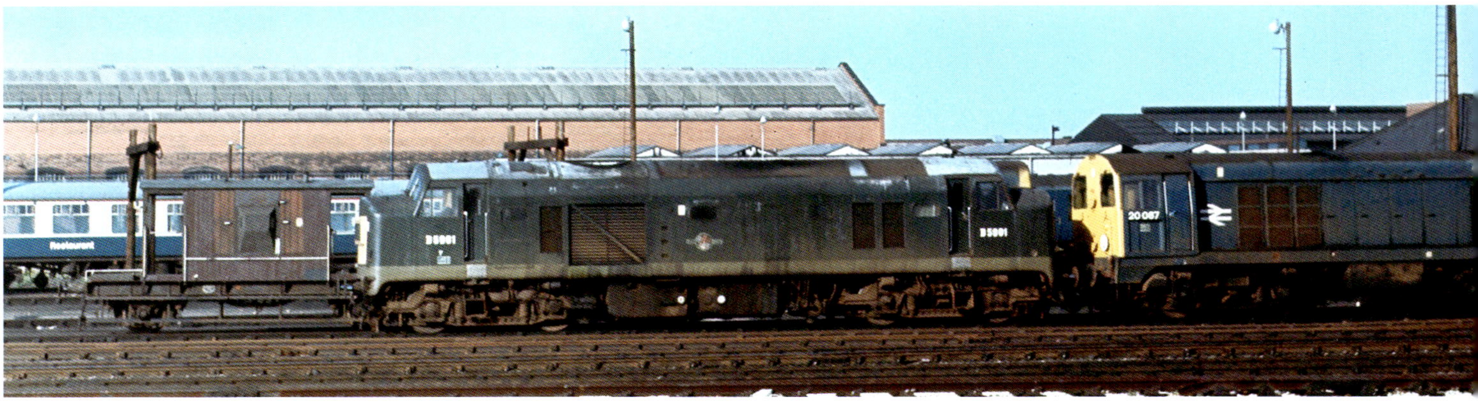

One of the Class 23s, D5901 was taken into departmental stock and based at Derby where we see it stabled with a Class 20 on 15 July 1974. This last surviving Baby Deltic was condemned in November 1975 and cut up at Doncaster Works in February 1977. ***Ian James***

Below: Withdrawn on 9 March 1969, D5908 was stored variously at Hornsey, Finsbury Park and Stratford as here before going to Bescot on 6 October 1969 thence to George Cohen's scrap yard at Kettering on 14 January 1970 and cut up three days later. ***Neil Snuggs***

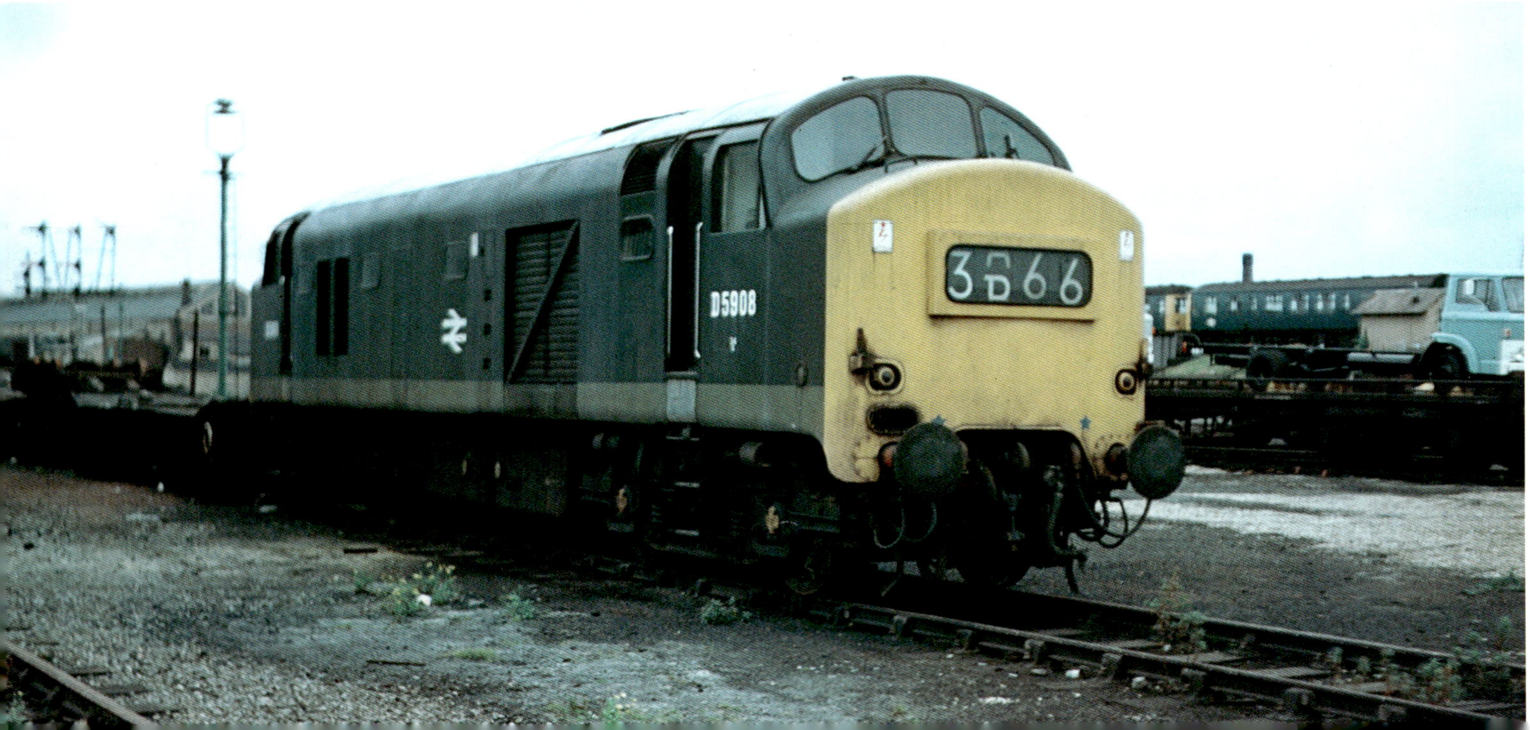

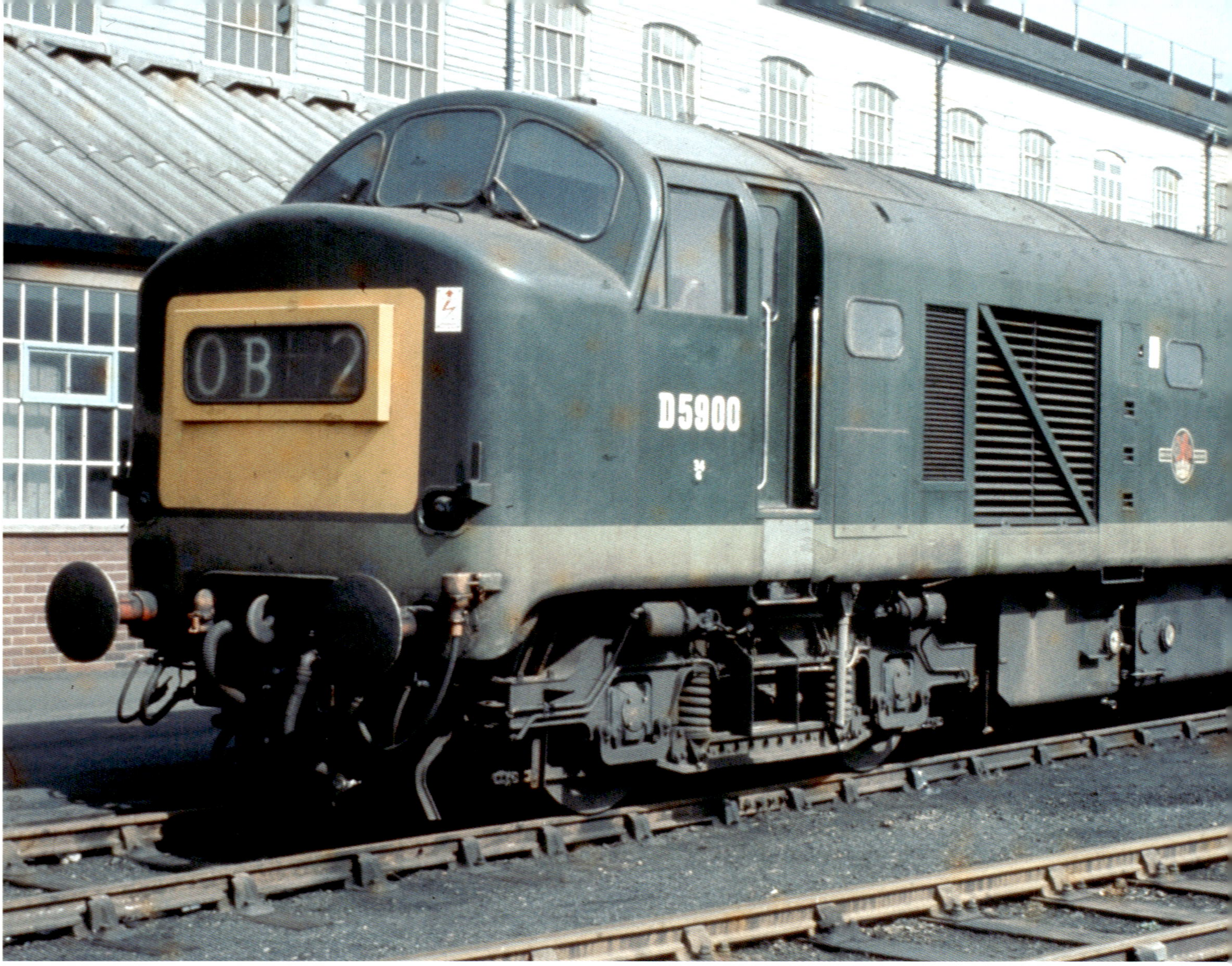

In April 1968 D5900 found itself at Doncaster Works for attention before a brief return to service, being withdrawn on 30 December that year. ***Strathwood Library Collection***

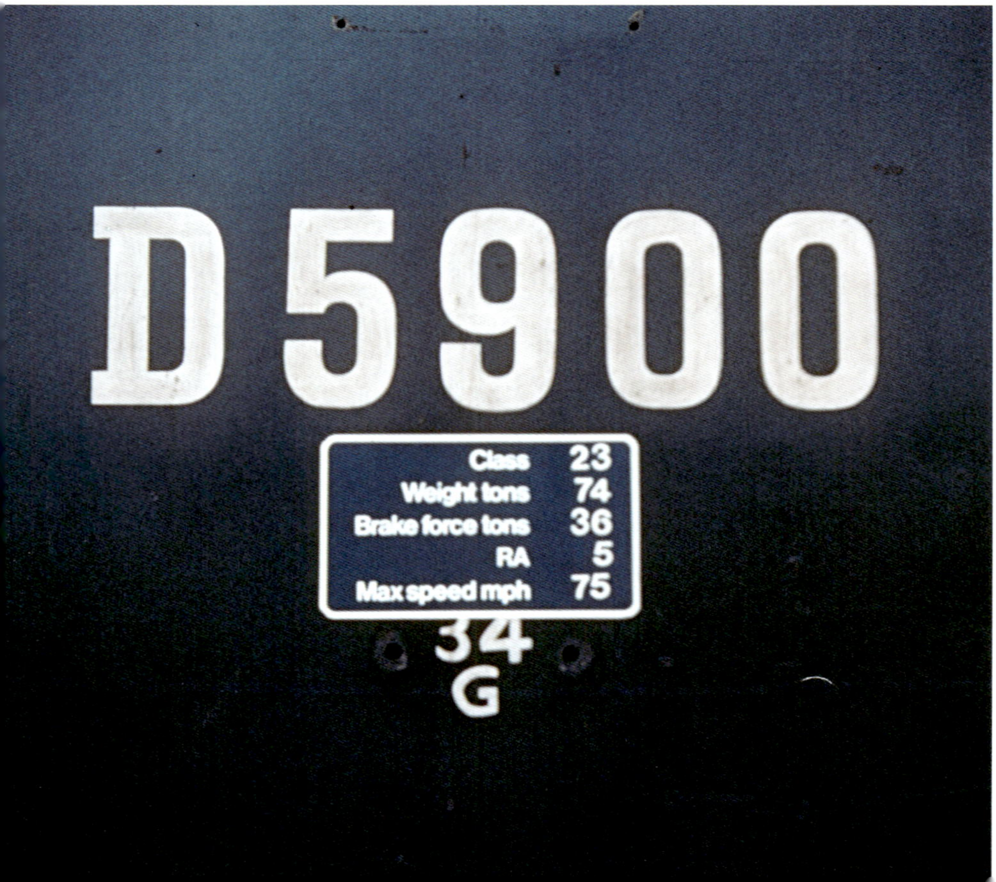

Sent for storage at Stratford until February 1969 where our cameraman recorded the recently affixed data panel sticker before further moves to Hornsey and Finsbury Park until a sale was made to Cohen's of Kettering in July 1969, with cutting up taking place the following month. ***John Ferneyhaugh***

Whistlers

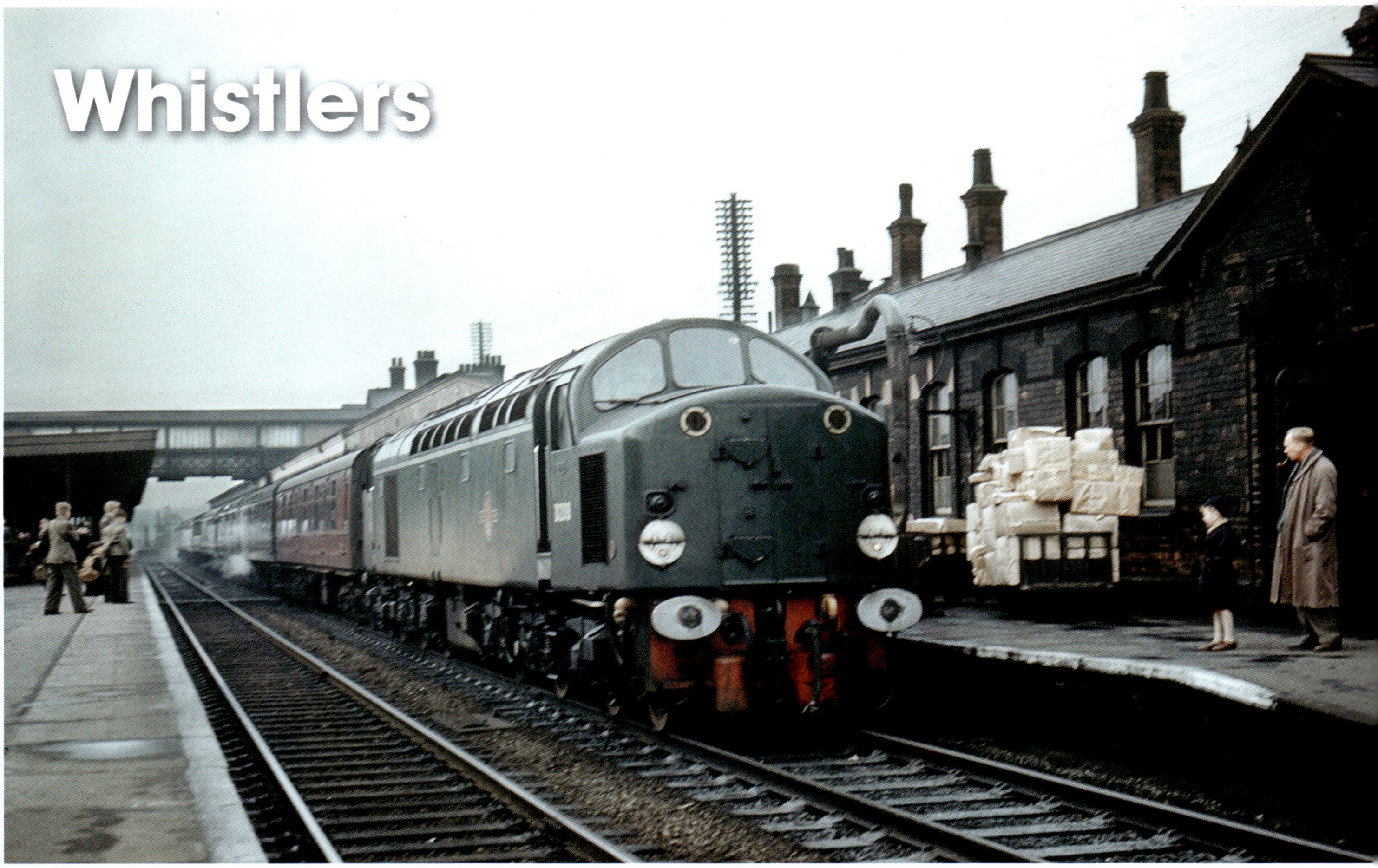

That distinctive engine note has caught the attention of several people on the platforms at Grantham as D209 arrives with an up express on 12 March 1960. ***Frank Hornby***

Split headcode fitted D340 pulls up at Macclesfield with The Comet in May 1961. Numbers D324 to D345 were delivered in this format of all over green and twin route indicator boxes. ***Strathwood Library Collection***

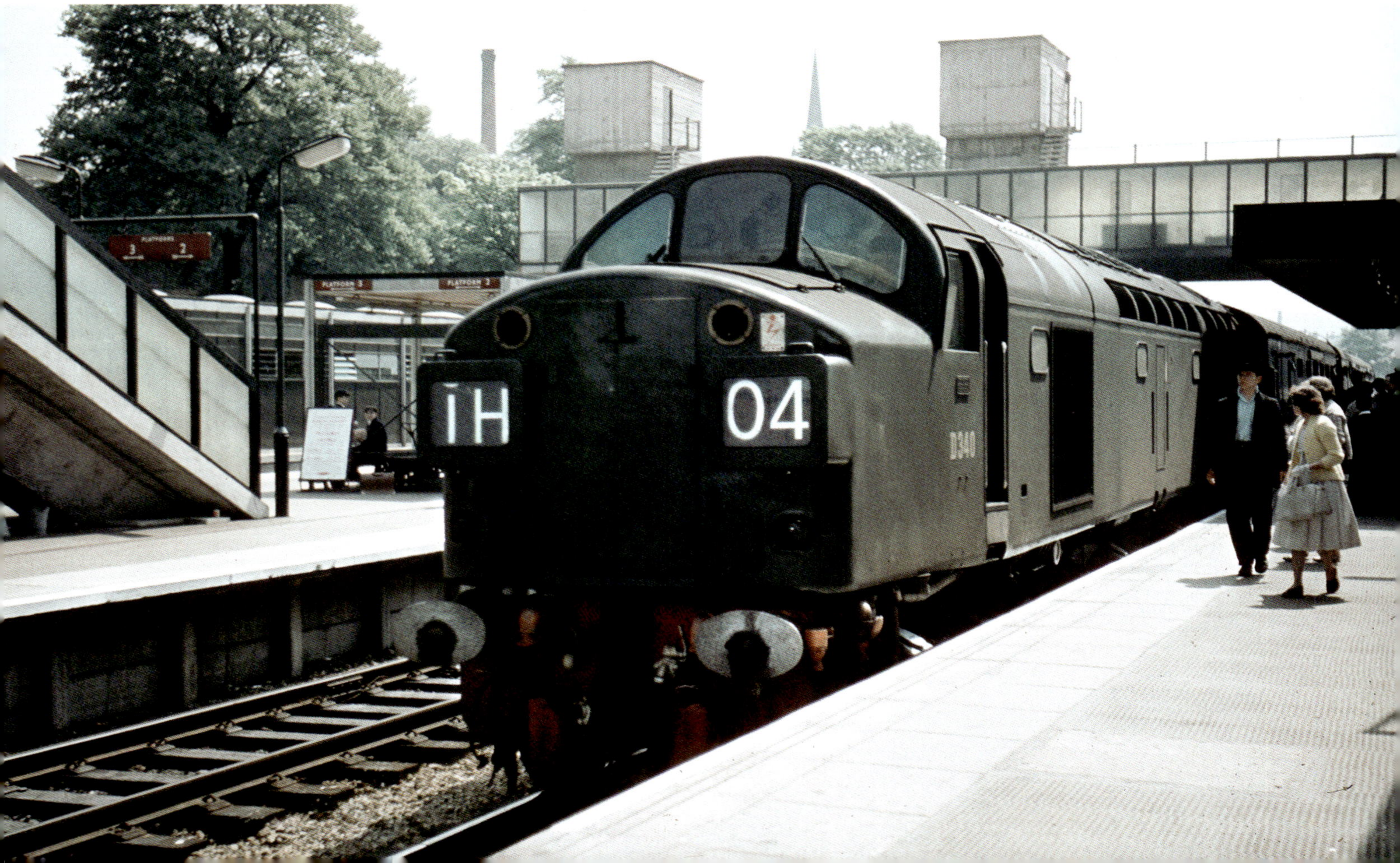

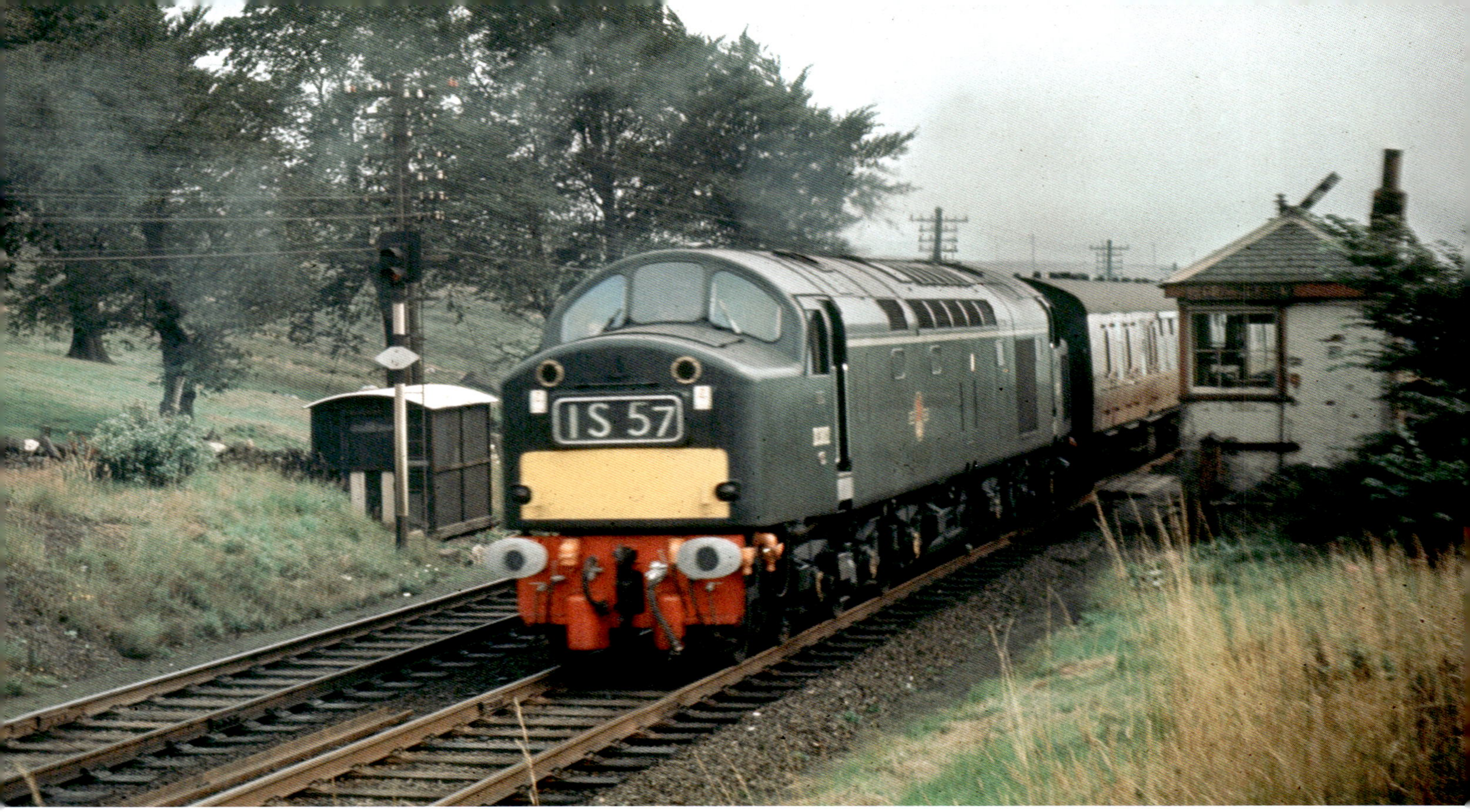

Delivered to 1B Camden on 17 March 1962, D382 still had fresh paintwork showing at Scout Green in April 1962. ***Len Smith***

One of the original pilot batch of engines was D205 which has just been out shopped from Doncaster Works in a fresh coat of paint in late 1962 after four years in traffic. ***Strathwood Library Collection***

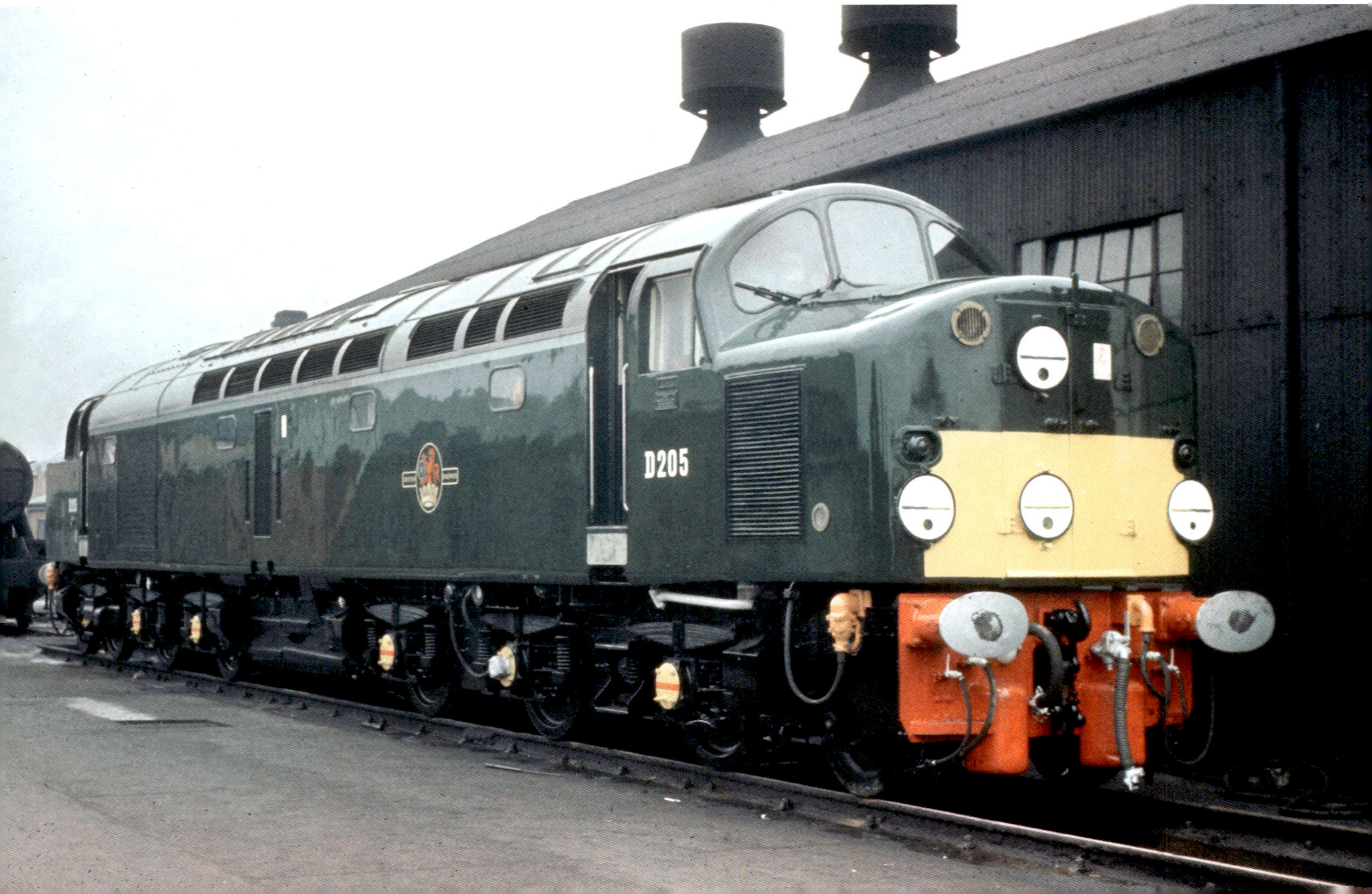

Just over two years into its twenty year working career was D373 at Beattock on 20 July 1964 as the driver throttles up through the station for the climb ahead. ***Richard Icke***

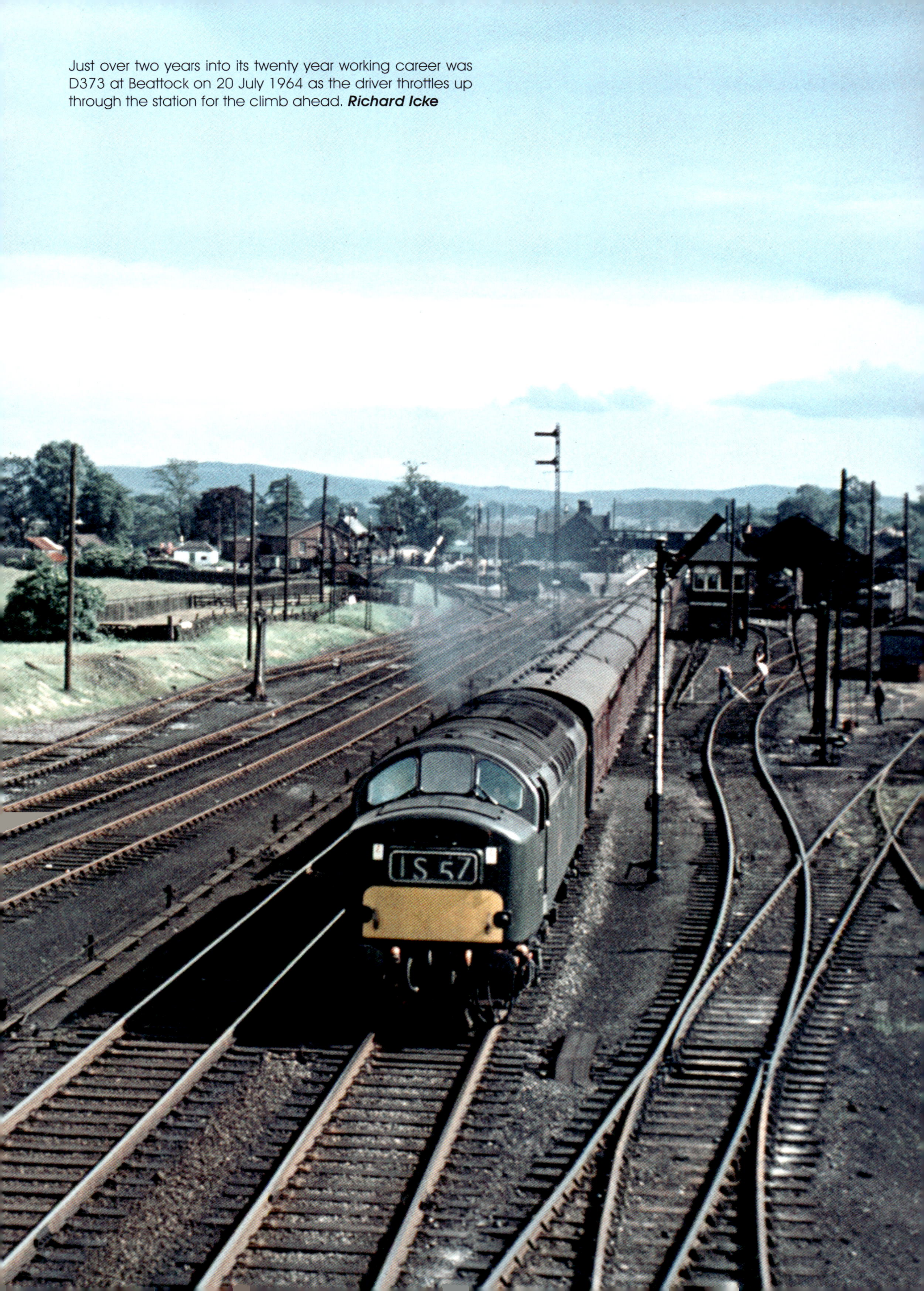

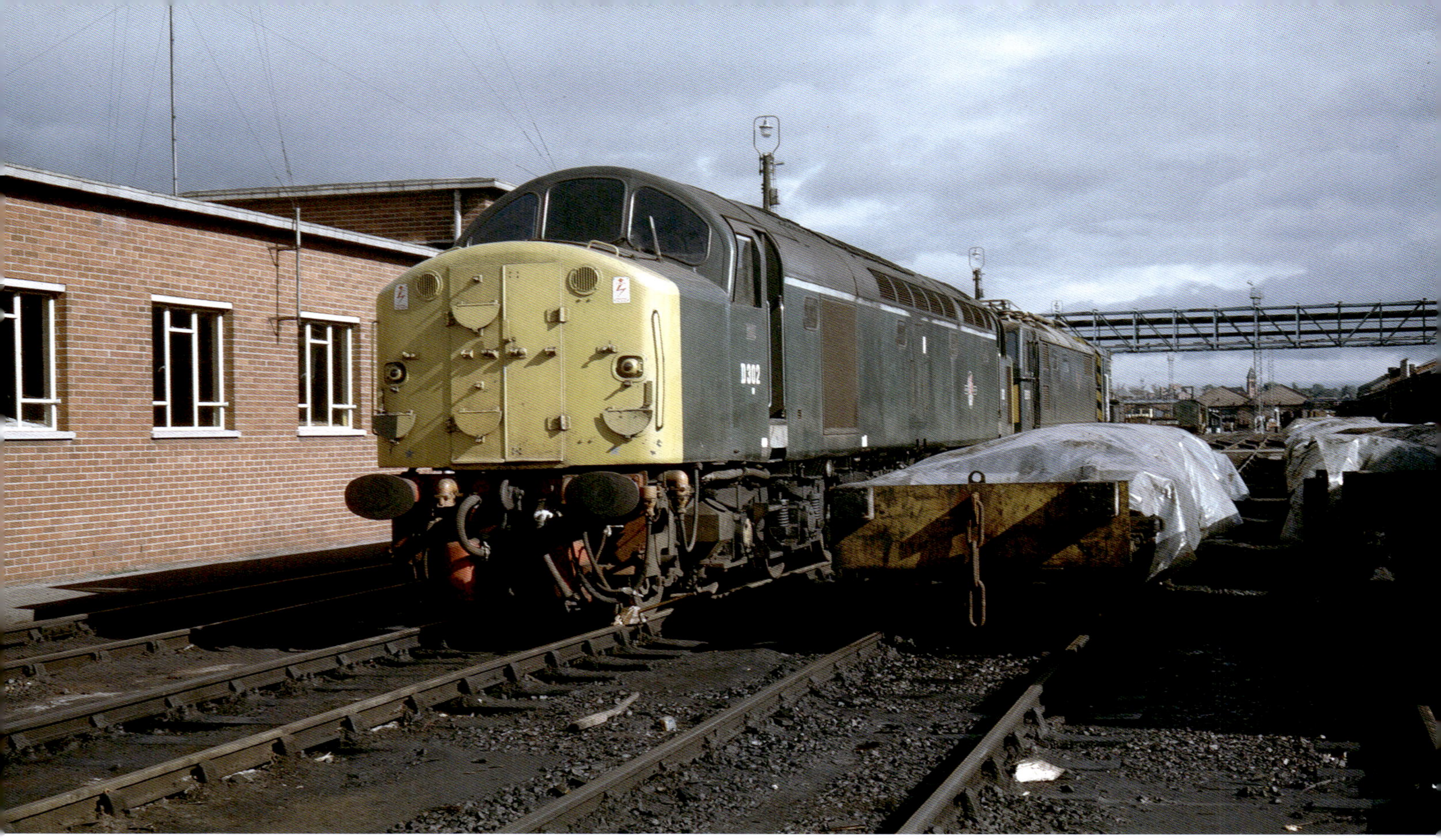

Stabled among the transition bogies at Crewe Works during a society visit on 21 September 1969 was D302, which was part of the D09 Manchester Division pool of locomotives at the time. ***Frank Hornby***

Although Crewe had turned out a few Class 40s in 1967 in the new blue livery, a policy of patching up paintwork ensured that green locomotives would survive for some time. One such engine was D367 still looking very smart with a shabbier looking Clayton 8510 nearby at Haymarket on 24 May 1970. ***Strathwood Library Collection***

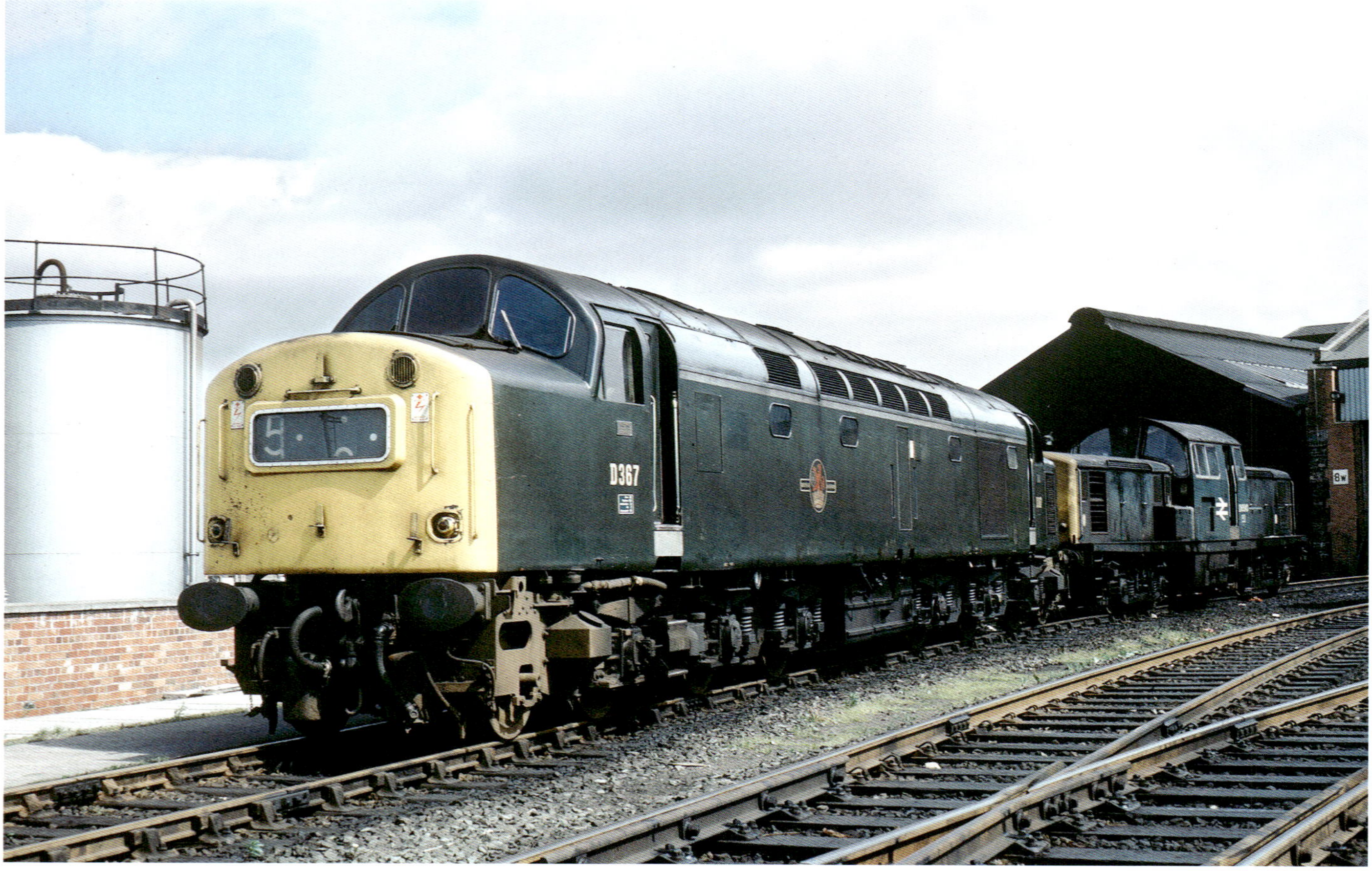

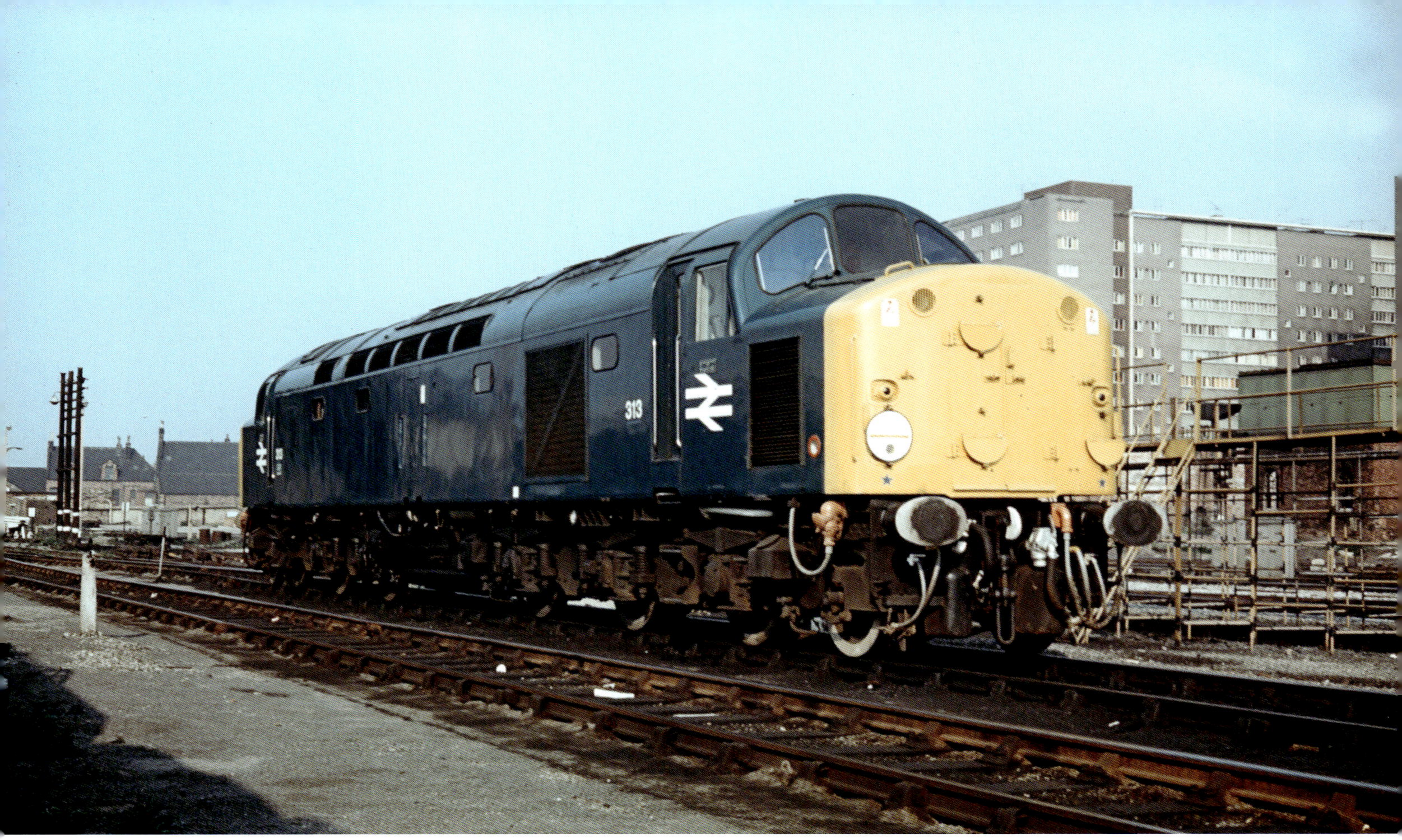

Some locomotives would arrive on works beyond a quick patch up. One of those must have been 313 seen at Gateshead on 20 May 1972, looking smart in a recently applied coat of blue paint. ***Frank Hornby***

One example of a scruffy green Class 40 was renumbered 40171 at Reddish, taking in the sunshine outside the depot during 1975. ***Nev Sloper***

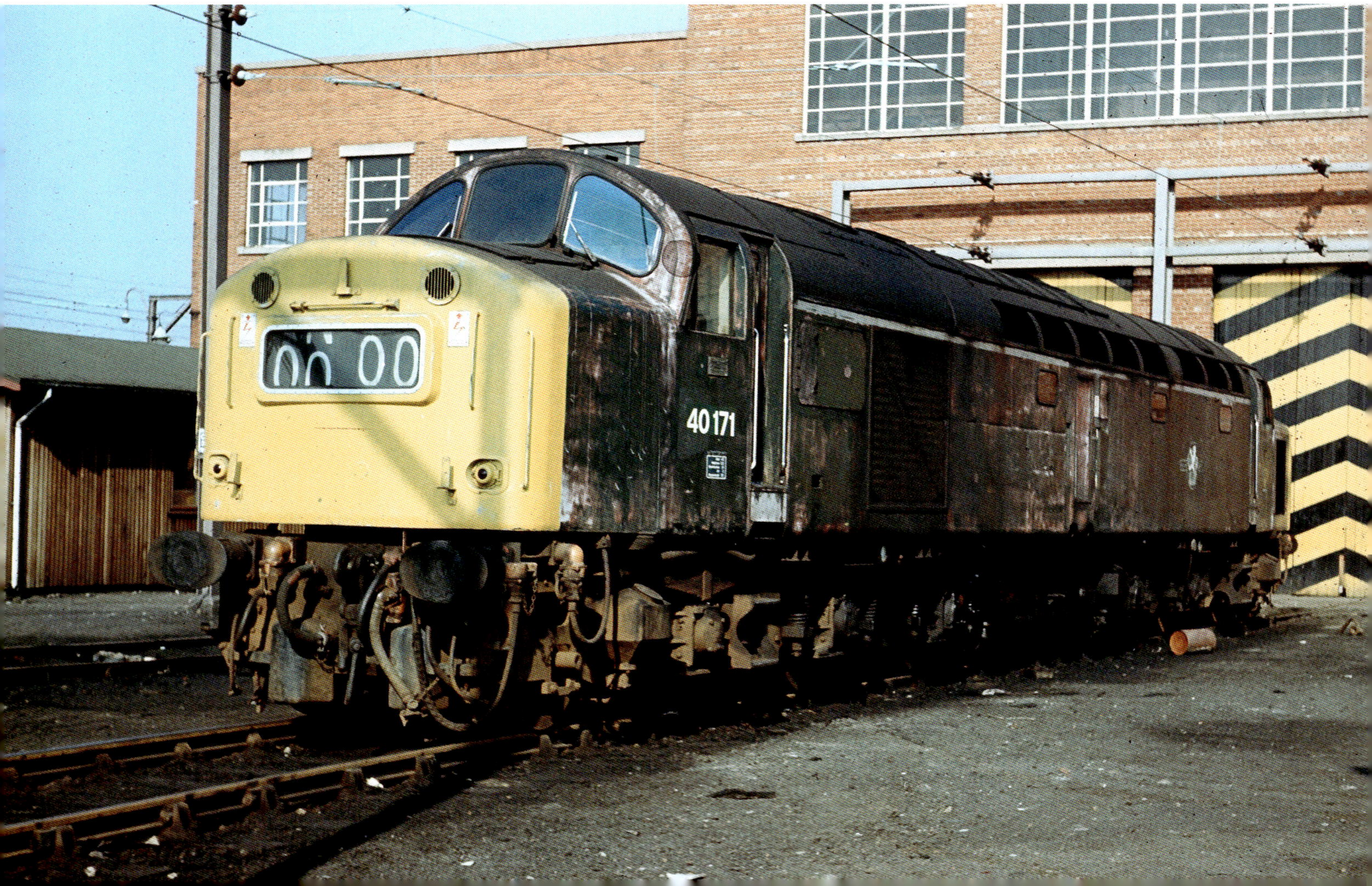

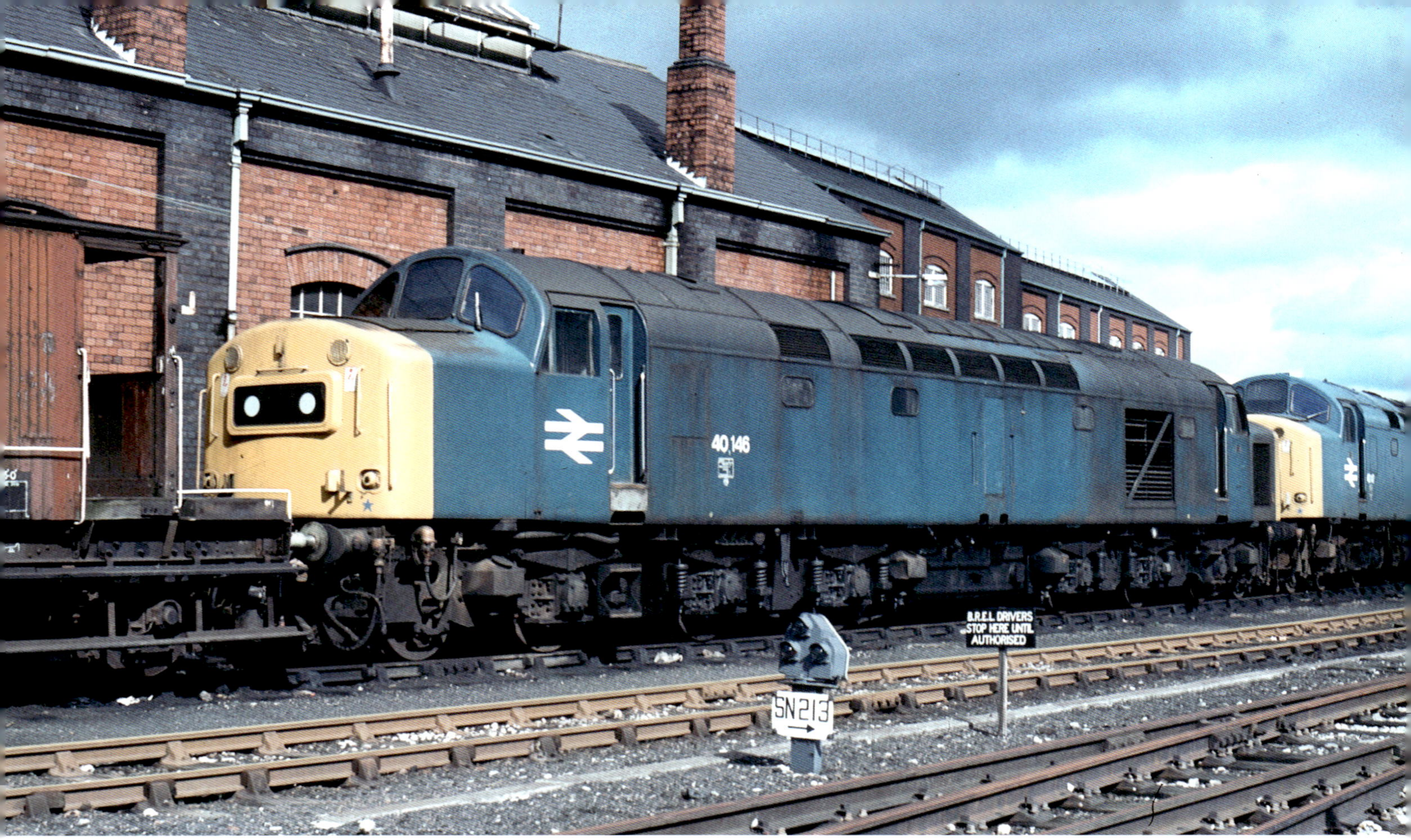

Swindon was perhaps an unlikely place to find large numbers of Class 40s. However as means of keeping the workforce busy in salvaging useful parts and cutting locomotives a good number of the class made a final pilgrimage to the Works here. One example was 40146 which had journeyed with a classmate and a brake van during a visit on 20 March 1981. ***Steve Ireland***

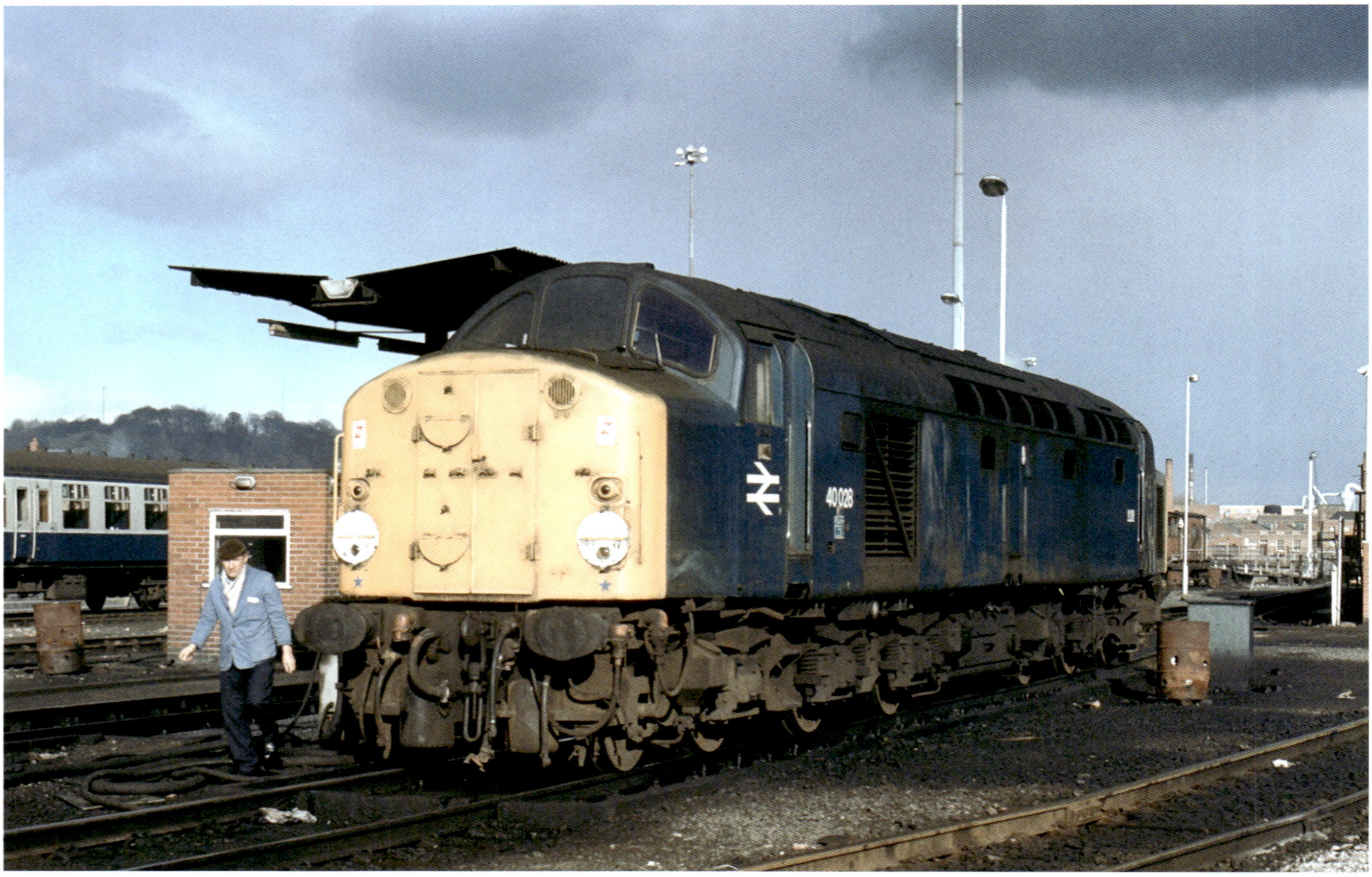

It was the namers of course that attracted a lot of interest at this time such as 40028 which had long since lost its Samaria nameplates when photographed at Nottingham in April 1984. ***Steve Ireland***

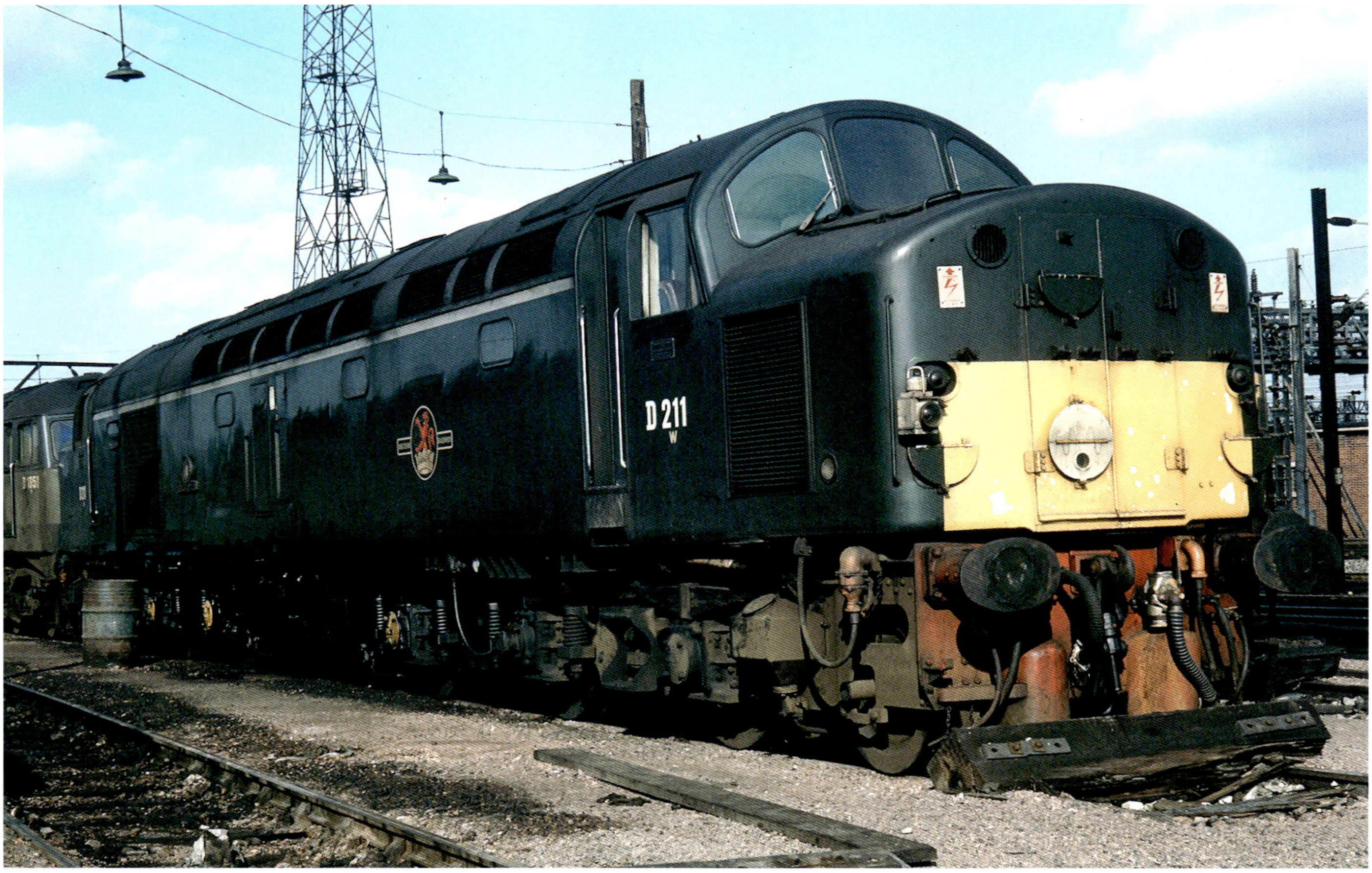

Still resplendent with those distinctive nameplates was D211 Mauretania, standing on the stabling point that existed for a short time after the closure of Crewe North steam sheds on 5 March 1967. ***Frank Hornby***

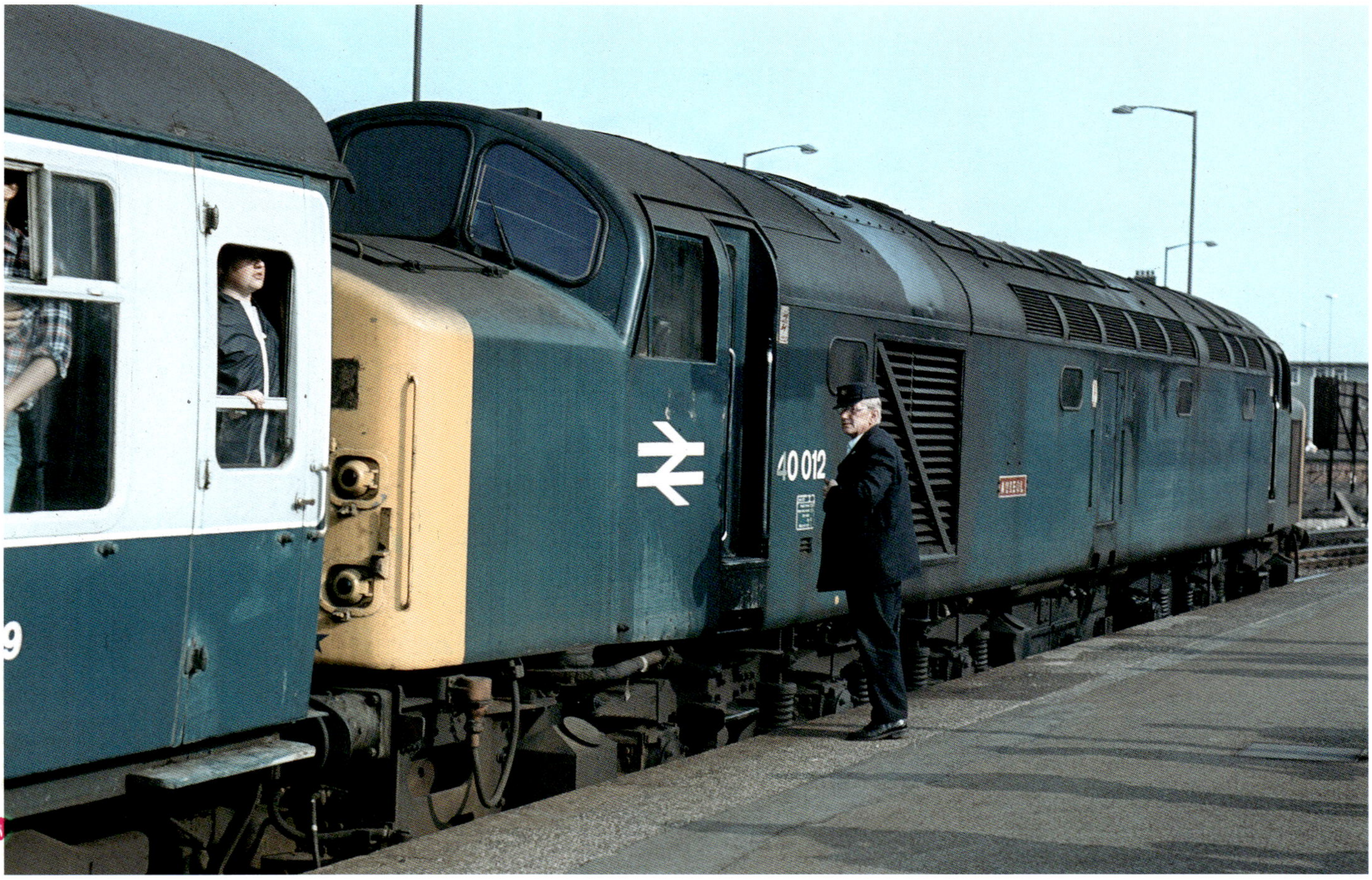

Some years after the last of the nameplates had disappeared from the class members, enthusiastic staff began repainting some with their former names once more. One such machine was 40012 Aureol awaiting the right away at Sheffield Midland in August 1984. ***Steve Ireland***

Hoovers for Hire

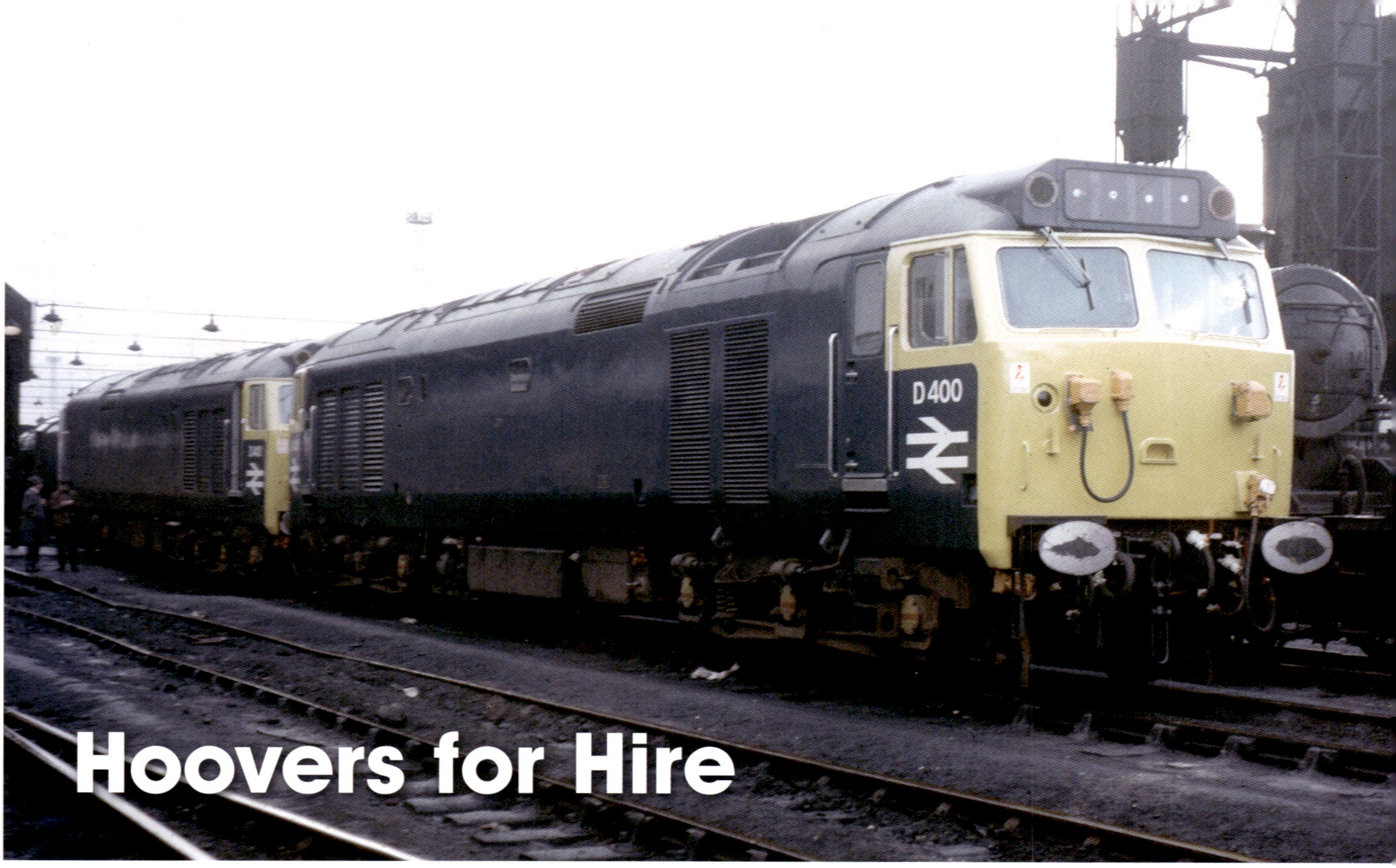

A fairly radical approach really for British Rail to embark on a lease agreement with English Electric in 1967 which saw ultimately fifty Class 50s taken into service. The first pair seen here D400 and D401, were delivered with multiple control equipment which was coded at the time as an orange square when seen at Crewe South on 29 October 1967. ***Strathwood Library Collection***

Although all of the class would eventually be so fitted for double heading on the difficult route from Crewe north to Glasgow, the remainder were delivered without the jumper cables in place as seen on D406 at Crewe on 30 March 1969. ***Frank Hornby***

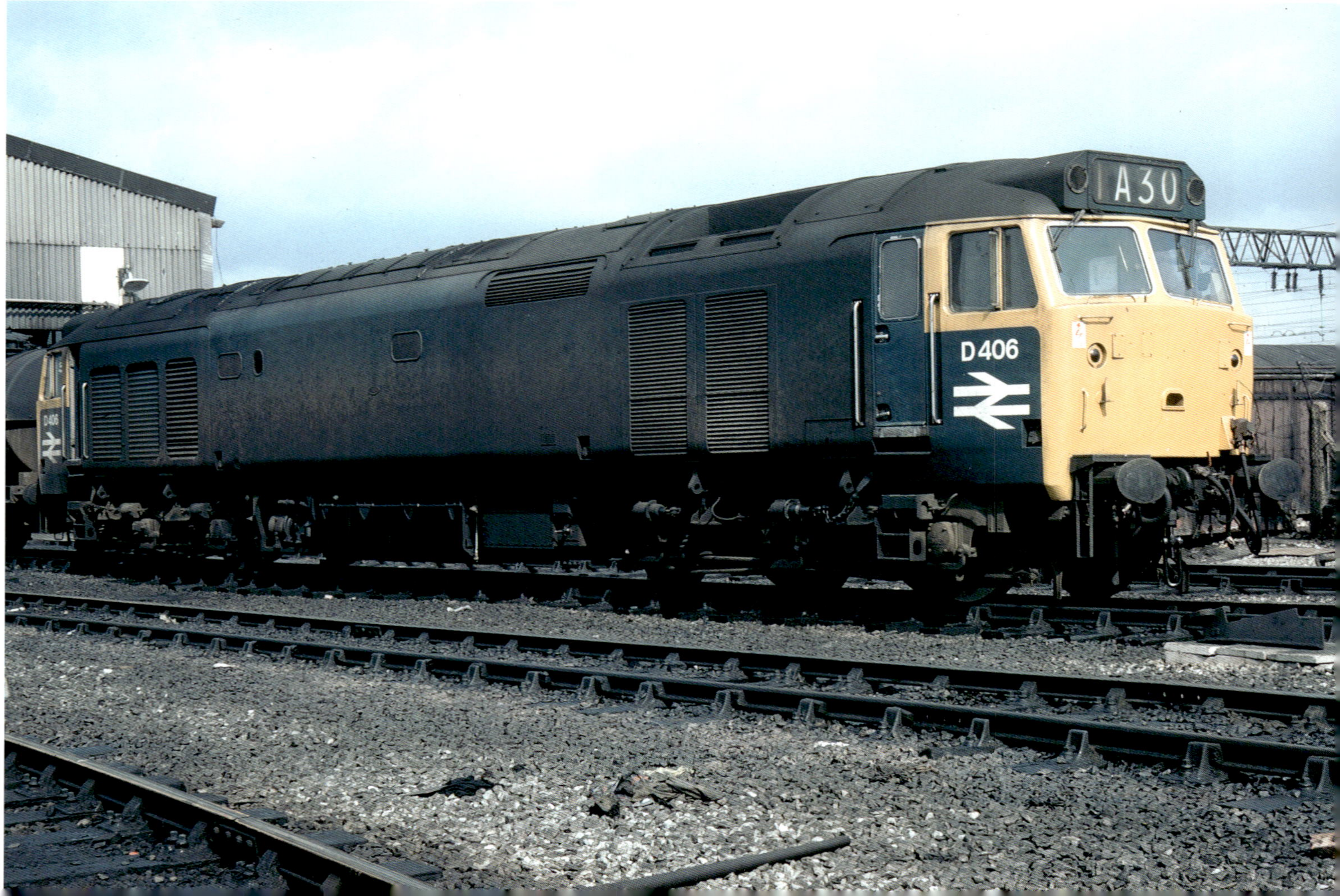

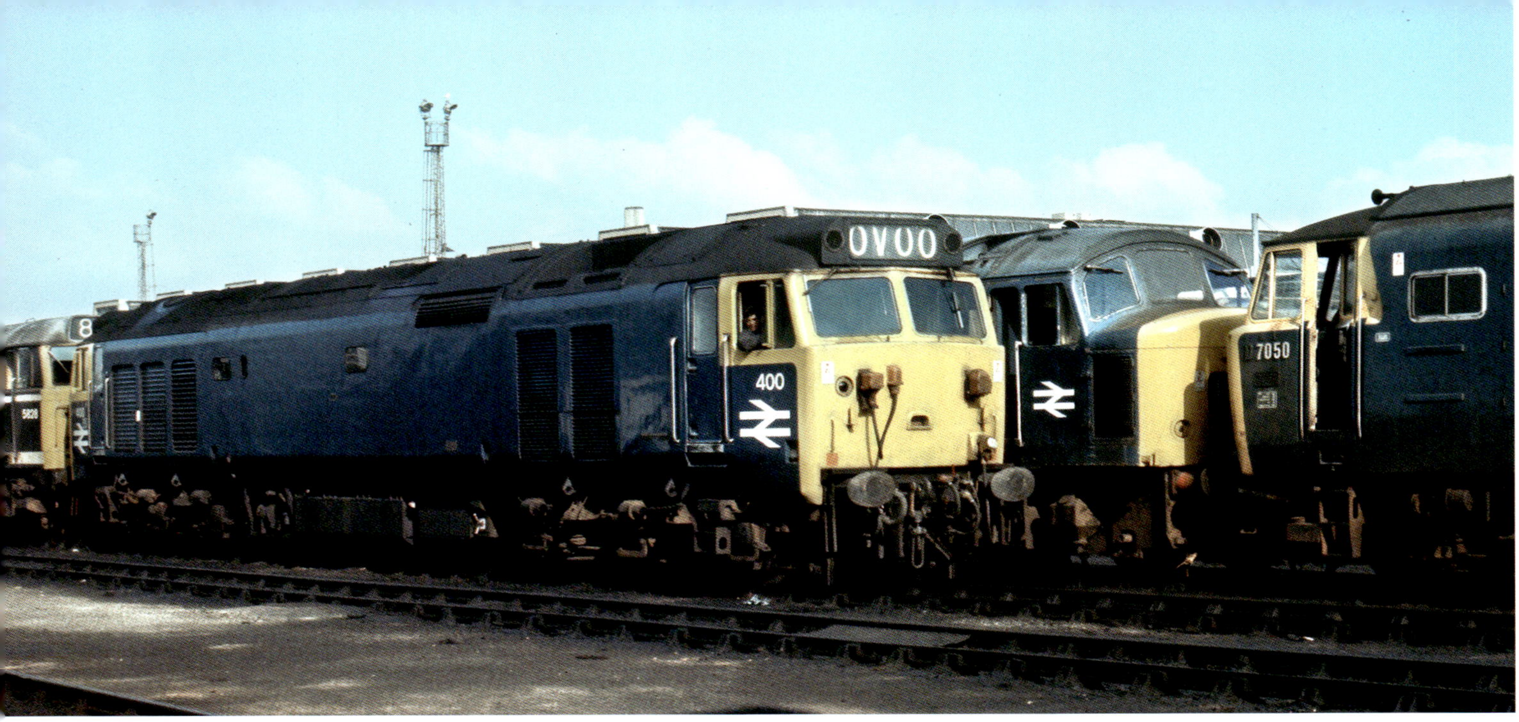

Electrification work on the West Coast Main line was well in hand by October 1972 and further use would need to be found for the Class 50s. At the time the Western Region was engaged on the wholesale slaughter of Warships and Hymeks from its books and would soon begin on the Westerns as well. To fill the void created 400 was first to move from the London Midland Region and is seen just twenty four hours after arrival on its new region at Bath Road on 15 October 1972. ***Roger Griffiths***

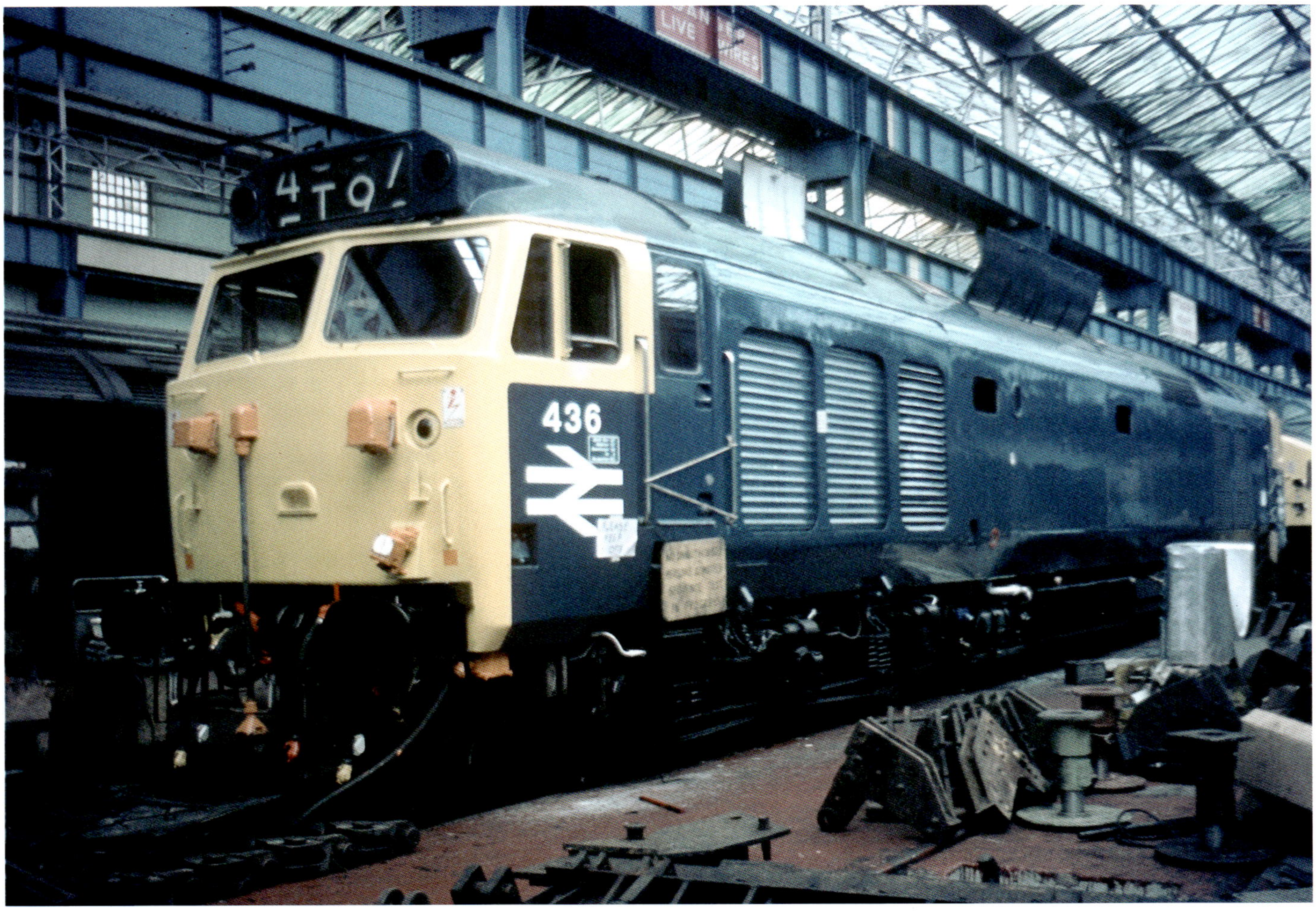

Thought to be the last Class 50 out shopped from Crewe from overhaul before the up take of the TOPS numbers, was 436 undergoing tests at Crewe in 1972. ***Steve Ireland***

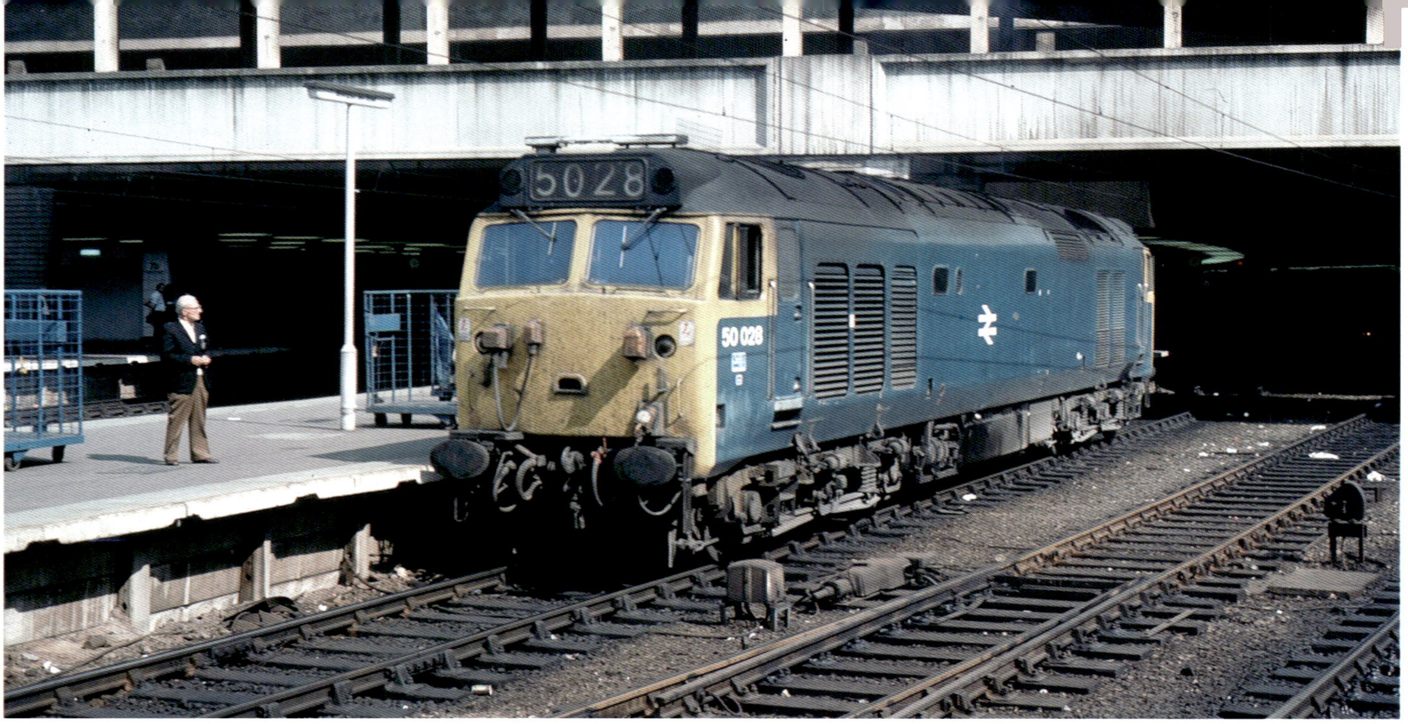

The Hoovers as they were nicknamed came across piecemeal and enjoyed several years service on the Western Region before the advent of naming after warships, such as 50028 in September 1976 at New Street. ***David T Williams***

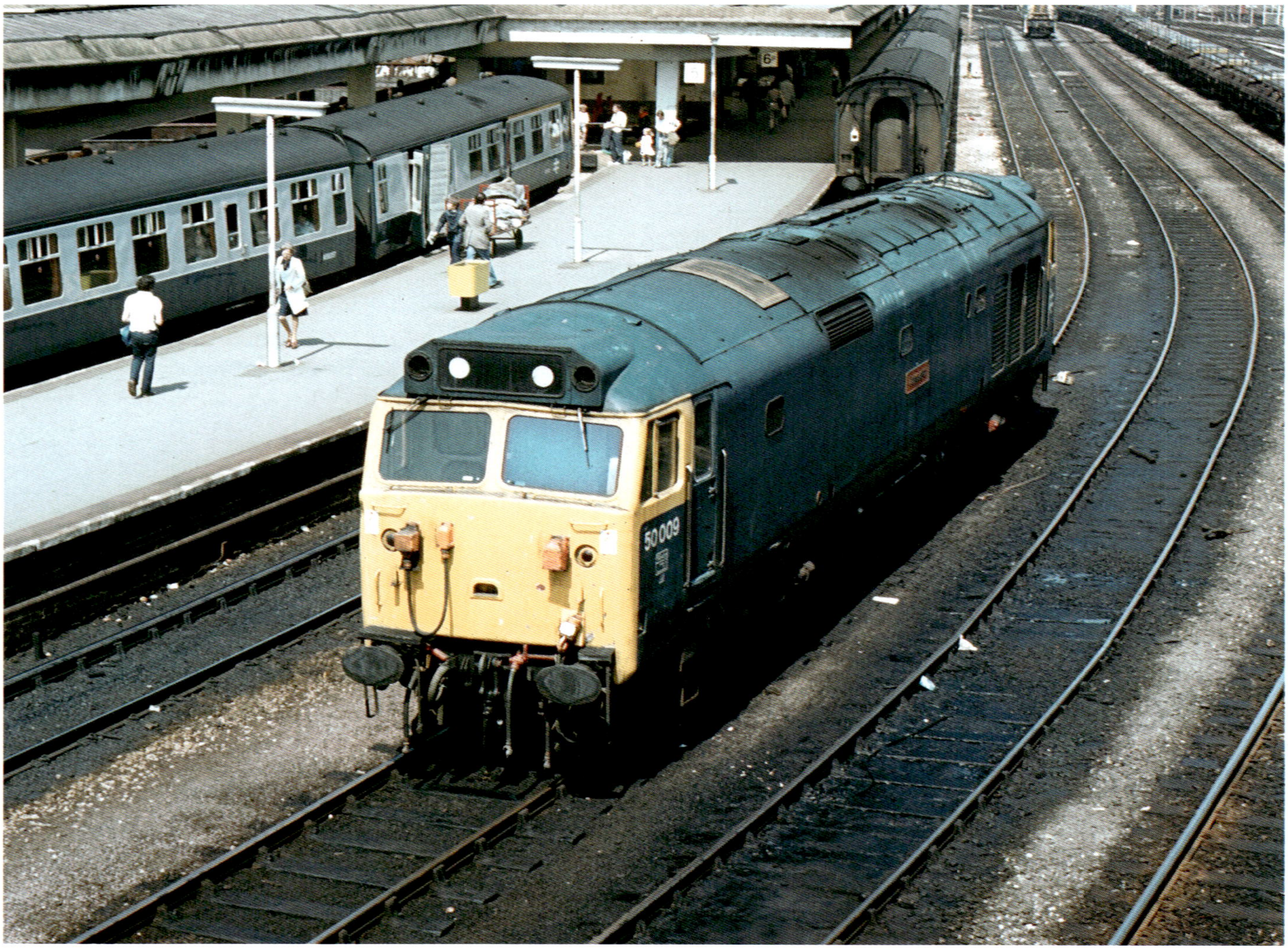

Filling in turns would still take the class back into London Midland territory with 50009 at Derby having arrived from Birmingham in 1978. With transfer of repairs to Doncaster many would work back onto the Western via Derby for many years to follow after works visits. ***Steve Ireland***

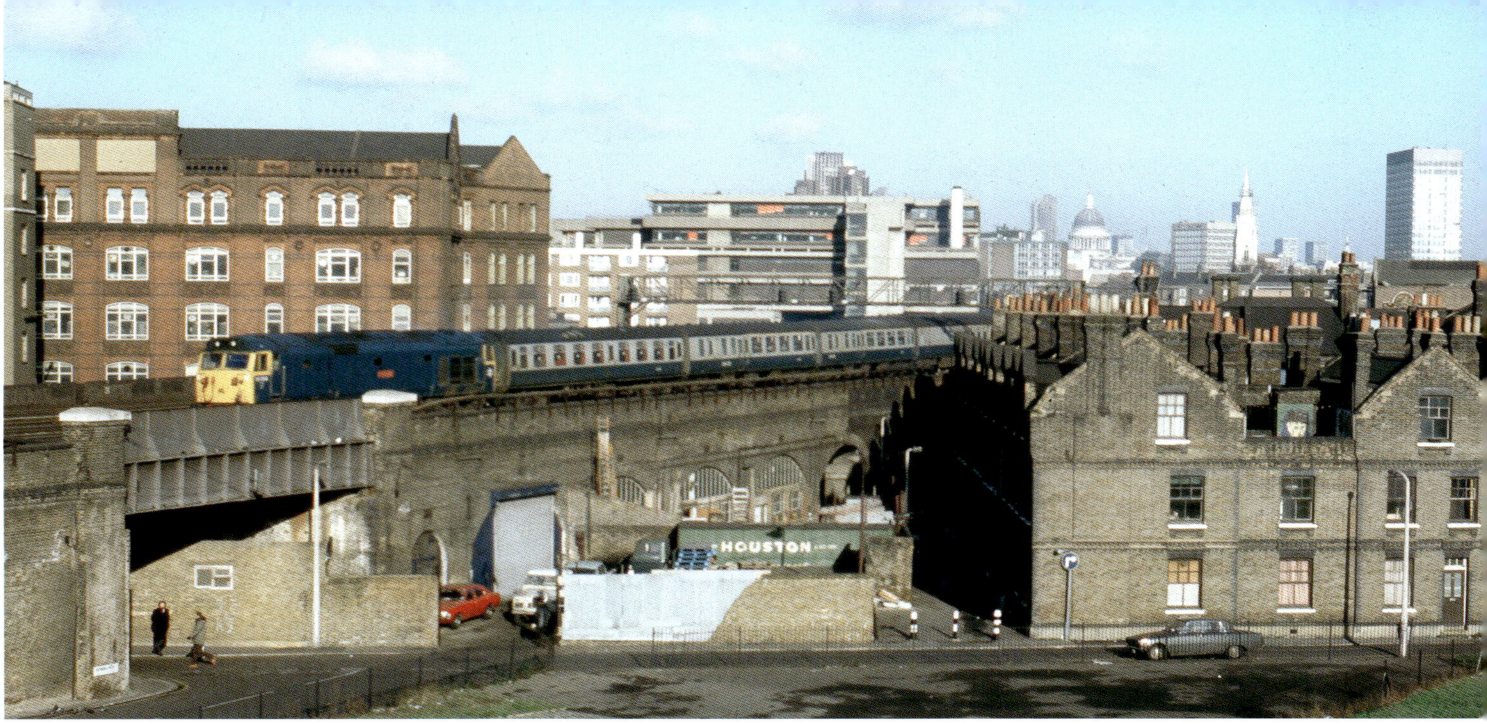

The Class 33s took over from the Class 42 Warships in 1971 and in turn they gave way to the Class 50s which also adopted the names of the Royal Navy's Warships. One such locomotive was 50004 St. Vincent in command of the 13.00 Waterloo to Exeter St.Davids near Nine Elms on Wednesday 16 January 1980. ***Colin Whitbread***

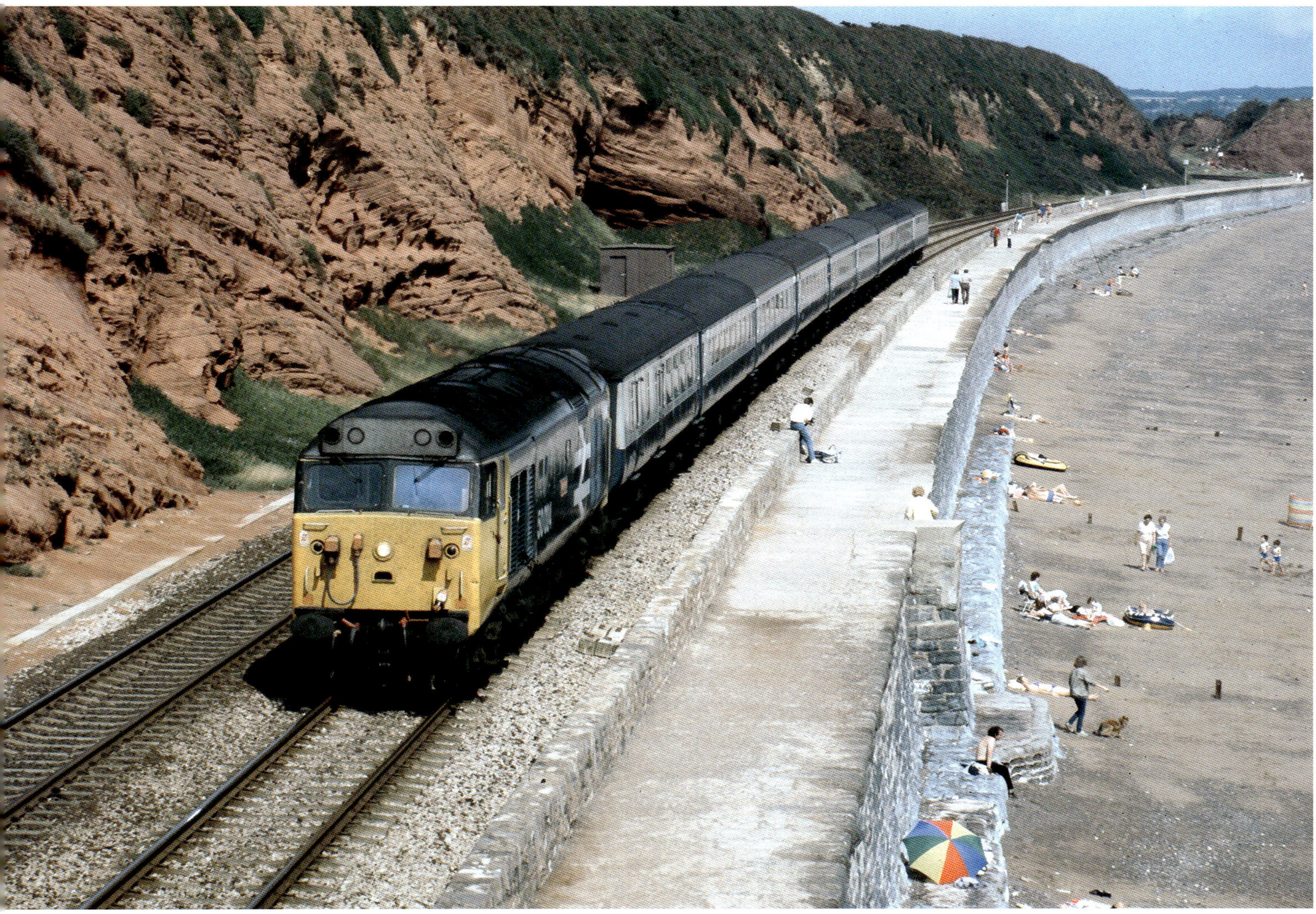

Unfortunately availability was down to 50% of the class on most days by 1978 and a programme of refurbishment was begun to turn things around for the class between 1980 and 1983. Painted into the then fashionable Large Logo livery was 50024 Vanguard running on the level section through Dawlish in 1983. ***Steve Ireland***

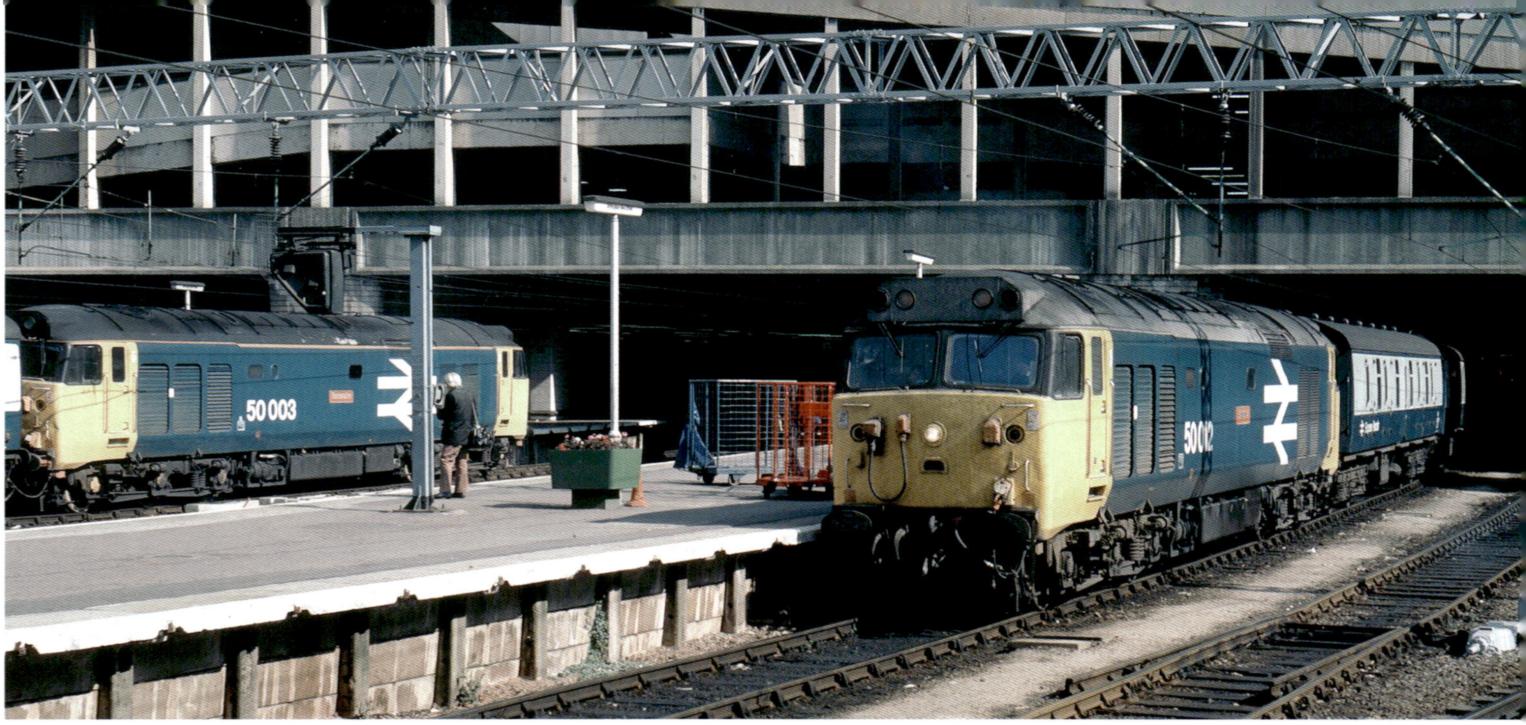

As with any corporate image it seems applied to any class of locomotives, a number of subtle variations began to appear, such as different colour buffer beams, headcode boxes, roofs, warning stripes and so on. This pair at New Street goes some way to showing this with 50003 Temeraire and 50012 Benbow during September 1986. ***David T Williams***

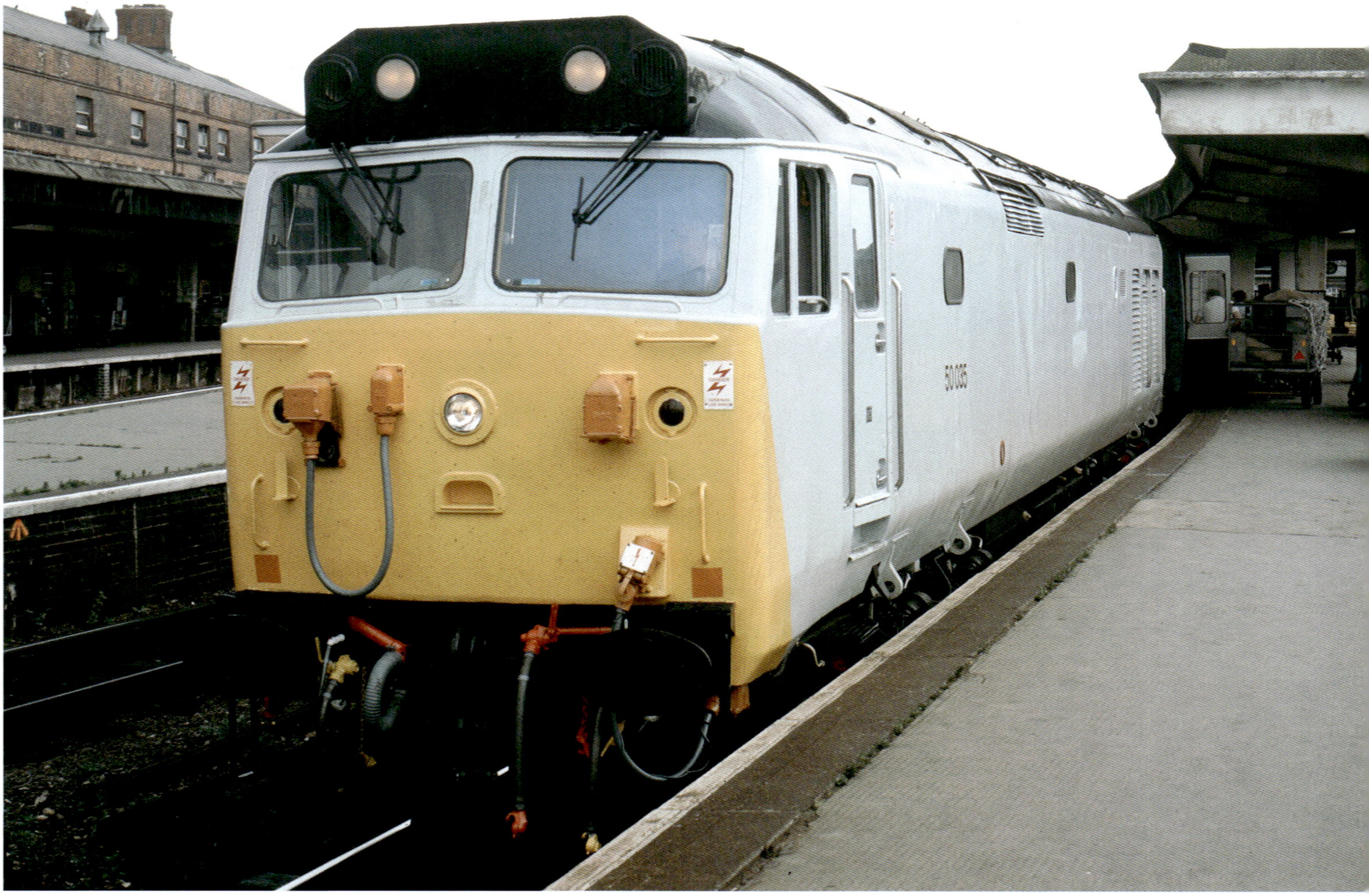

Legendary among fans of the class was the working of 50035 Ark Royal from Doncaster after a works overhaul back onto the Western Region in a grey livery seen here at Derby on 15 July 1986. This was as a result of the Works not having either the paint or the patterns to paint the locomotive into the soon to be launched Network South East livery. After working back to Old Oak Common, it received its smart new livery in the factory there. ***Steve Ireland***

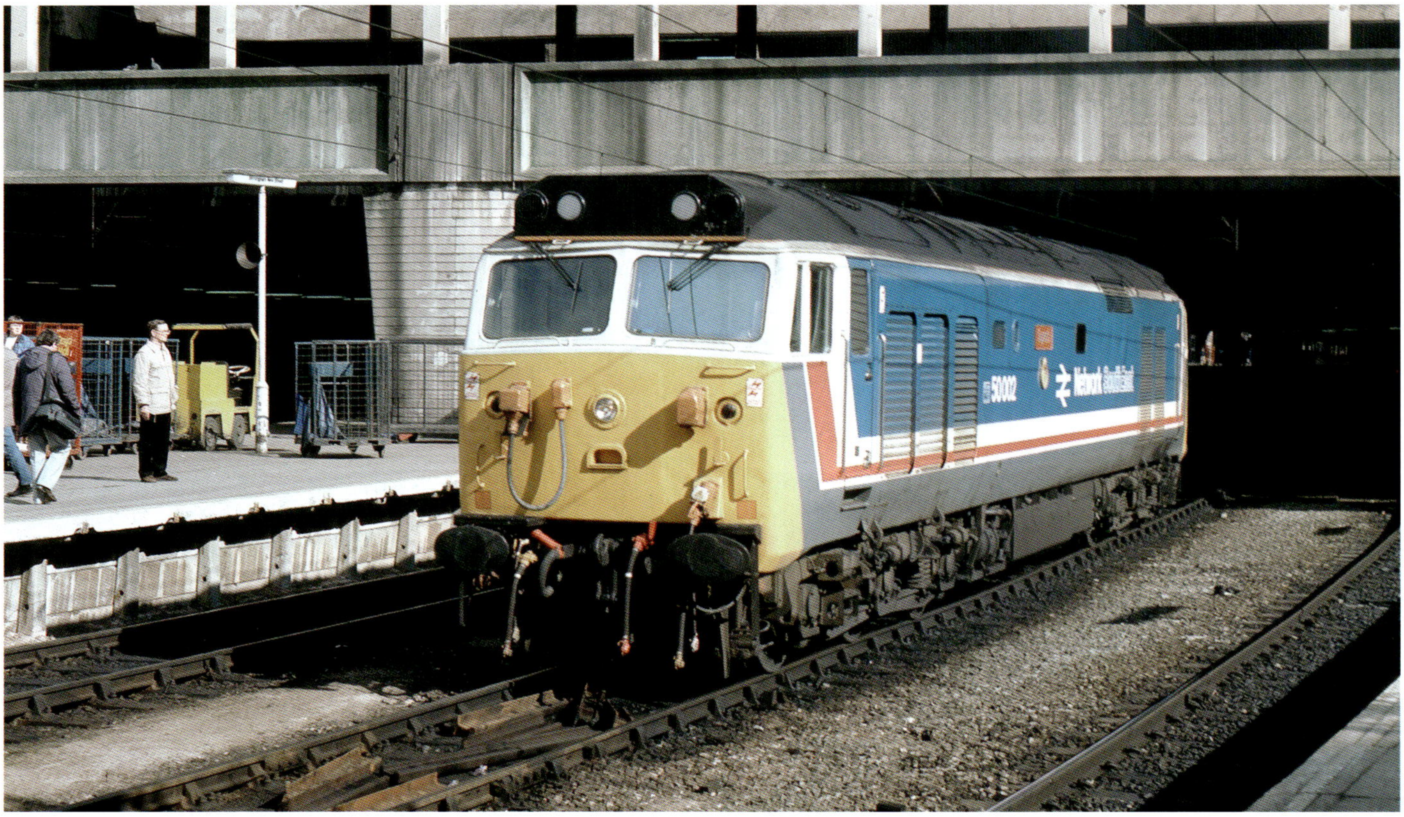

Not always easy to keep clean, but a very pleasing livery for a number of classes including those Class 50s adorned in this scheme, whilst others will no doubt prefer the Large Logo scheme. As the name suggests 50002 Superb brightens up New Street in the March sunshine of 1987. ***David T Williams***

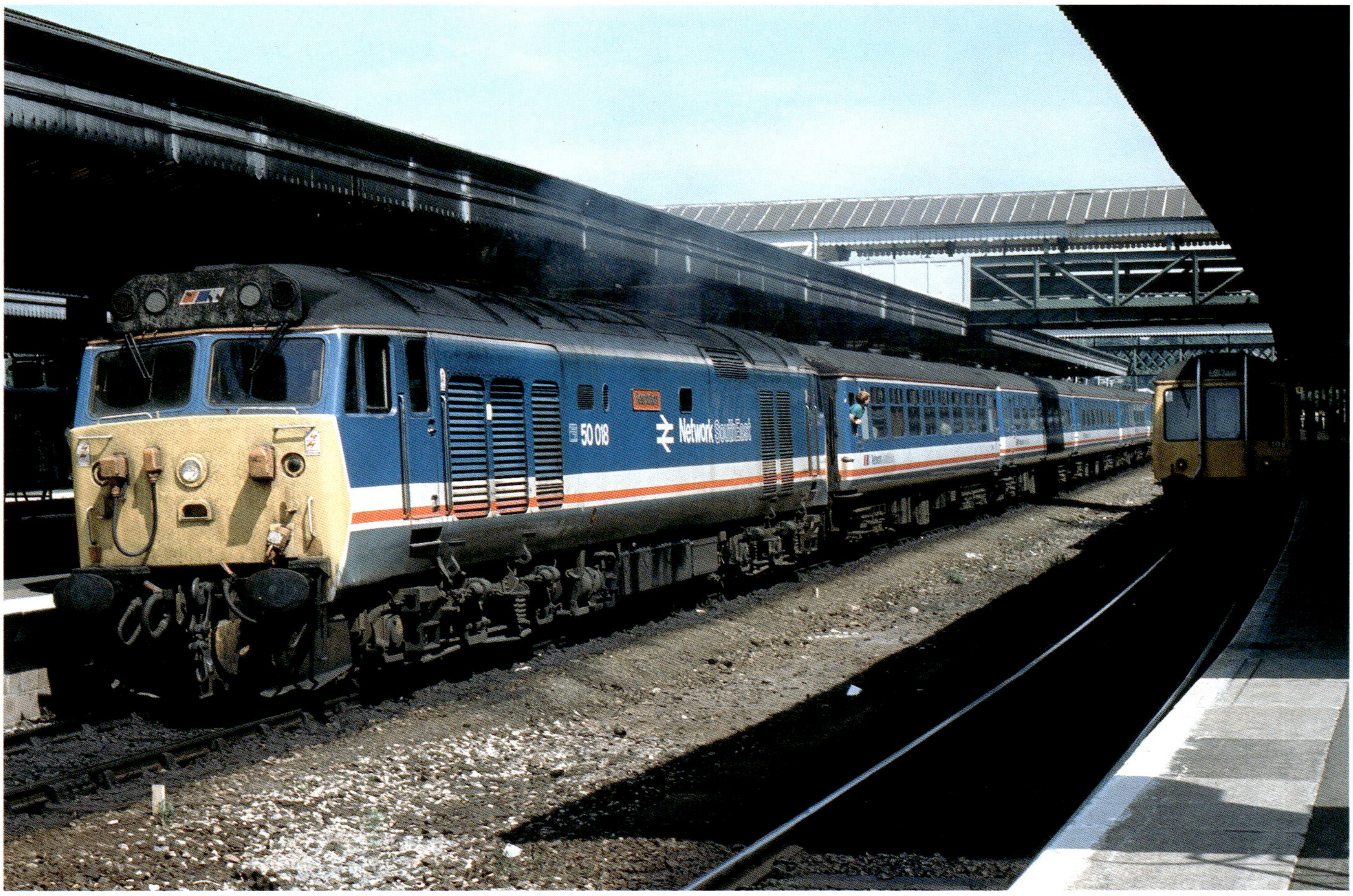

Once again no sooner than many of the class had been repainted, another executive comes up with a fresh version of Network South East livery as worn by 50018 Resolution waiting to leave Exeter St.Davids with the Sundays only Basingstoke to Paignton on 18 June 1989. Both versions required the raising of the nameplates and crests where fitted along the engine's flanks. ***Stuart Broughton***

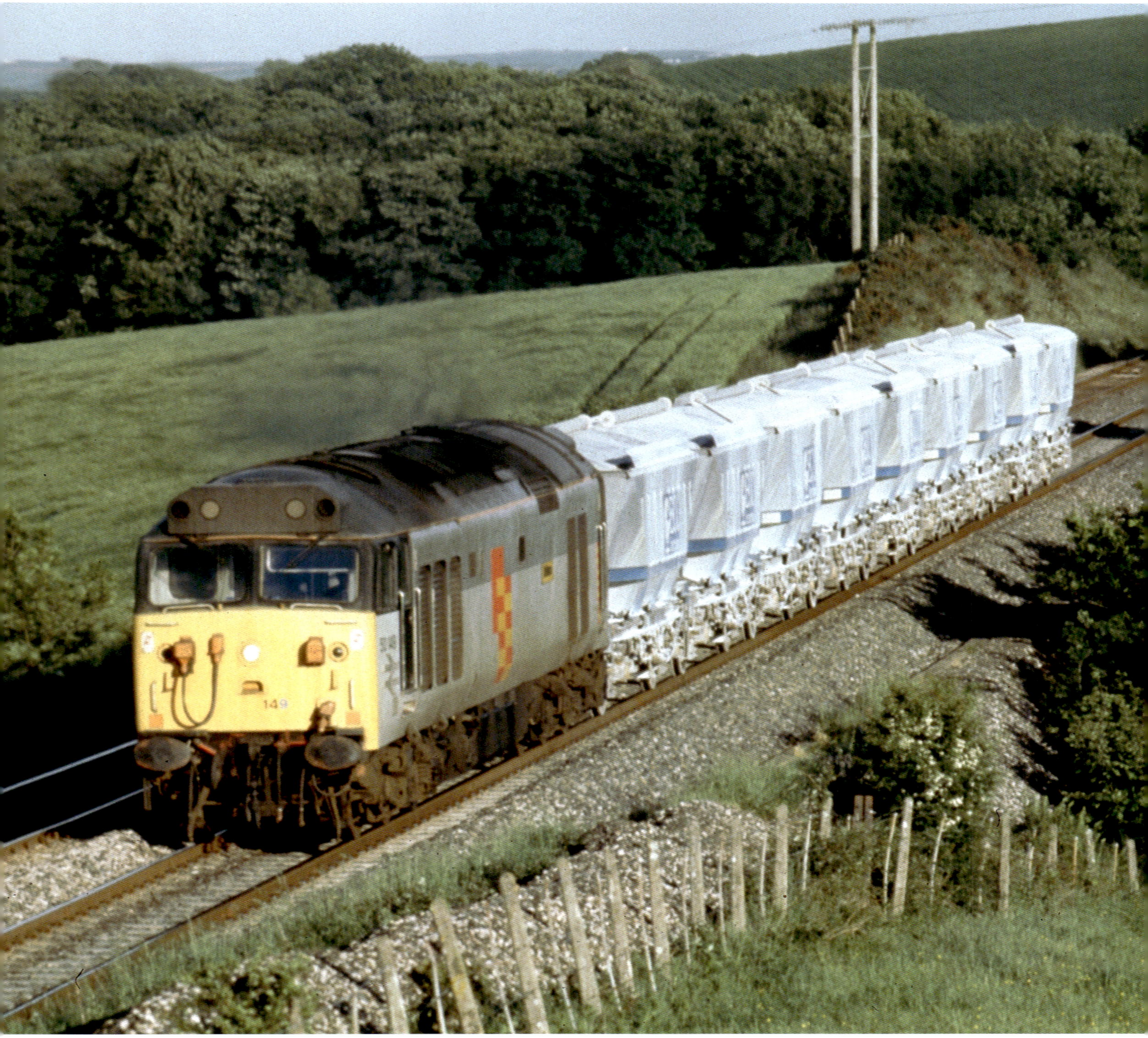

The later years of the eighties brought forward a host of new colour schemes. Among these was Railfreight in various guises, this one applied to 50149 Defiance at Bathany on 2 June 1988 with a Tavis Yard to Lostwithiel working. Before the class arrived on the Western Region the Hoover nick name had been coined by enthusiasts. This would be shortened to Vac when used by fans of the class. After refurbishment had removed the rheostatic braking system and the fans that cooled the resistors (the cause of the vacuum cleaner type sound the locos made when first coming to rests in a station), the Hoover name no longer seemed appropriate. Although the older enthusiasts continued with it, the younger ones started using Dub-dub, derived this time from the engine sound under load. Those enthusiasts who disliked the class might use the derogatory term Log, however to many of us they are just plain Fifties. ***Michael Szlzeblewski***

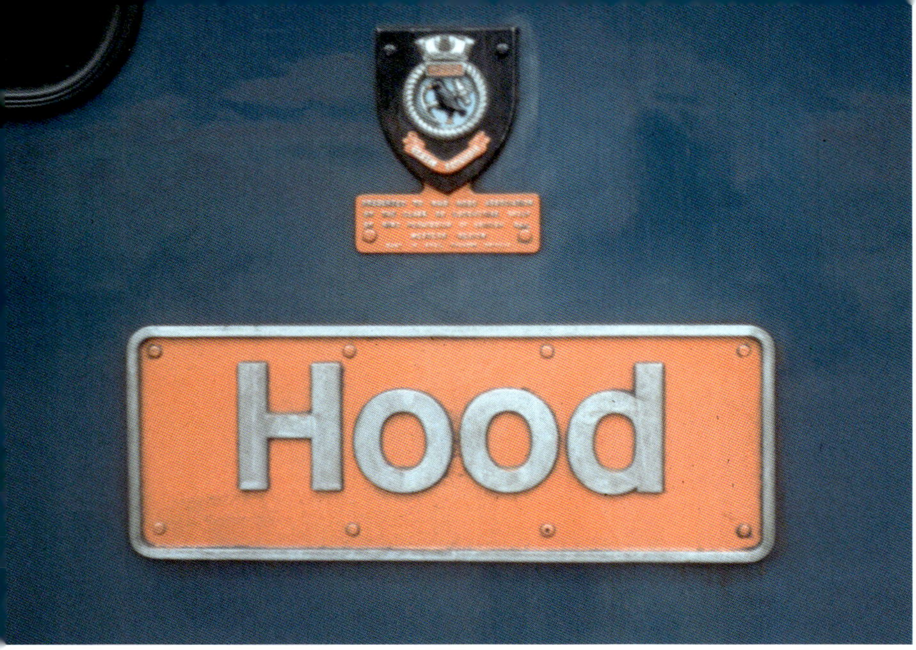

The practice of twining the locomotives with the surviving warships carrying these evocative names resulted in several of the class receiving crests or badges from the ship concerned. One such locomotive was 50031 Hood first named at Laira, on 28 June 1978. Subsequently a crest was added at Old Oak Common, on 22 April 1983. Those special crests presented by the Class 50 Locomotive Group, carried the following inscription "Presented to HMS Hood Association by the Class 50 Locomotive Group by kind permission of British Rail Western Region". They were cast in the BREL Foundry at Swindon. In May 1991, to commemorate the 50th anniversary of the sinking of HMS Hood, 50031 was re-dedicated with the fitting of new crests at a ceremony held at Old Oak Common. ***Ian Beckey***

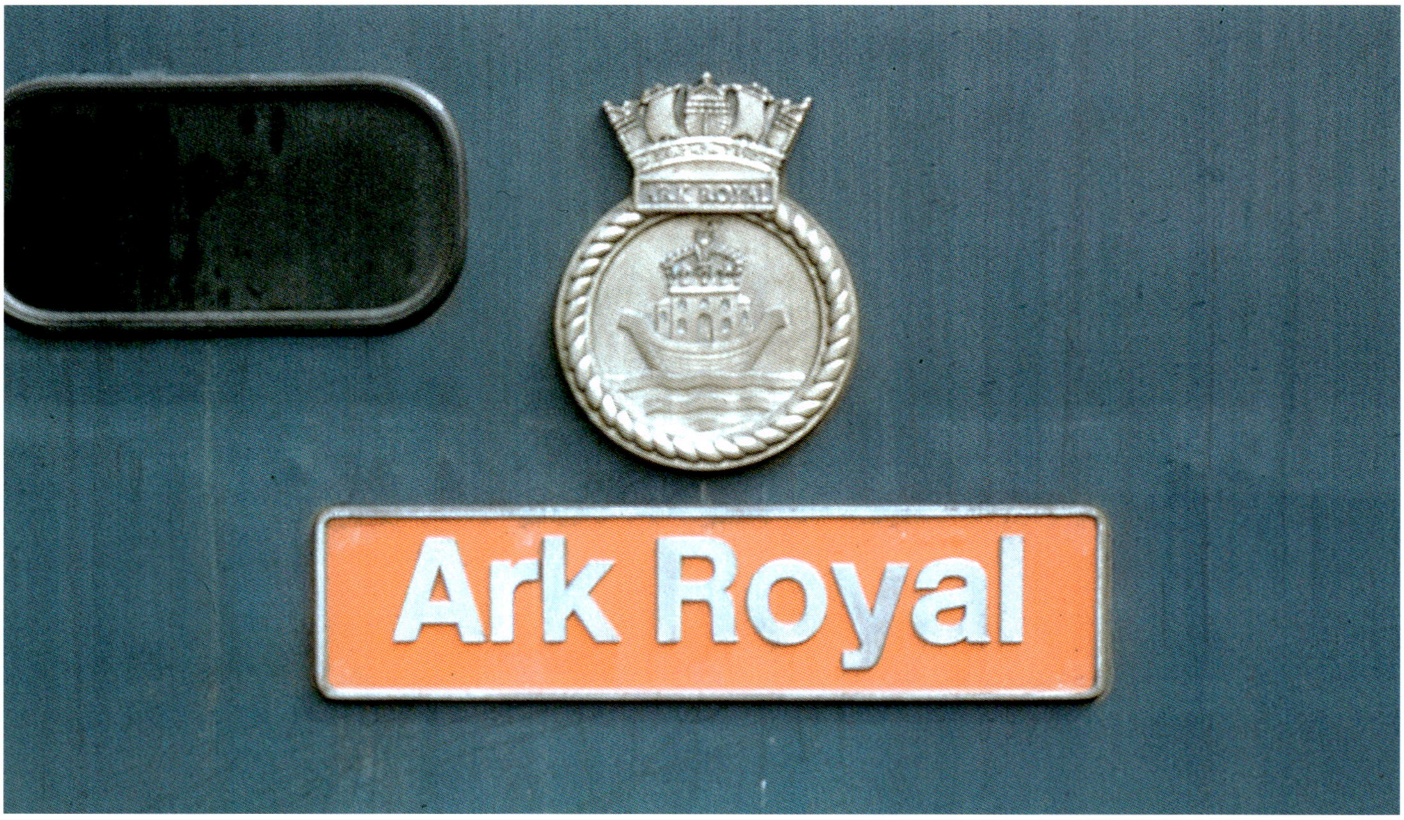

The first Class 50 to be named was 50035 Ark Royal on 17 January 1978 at Plymouth station with the crests being affixed strangely two days later without ceremony at Laira. ***David T Williams***

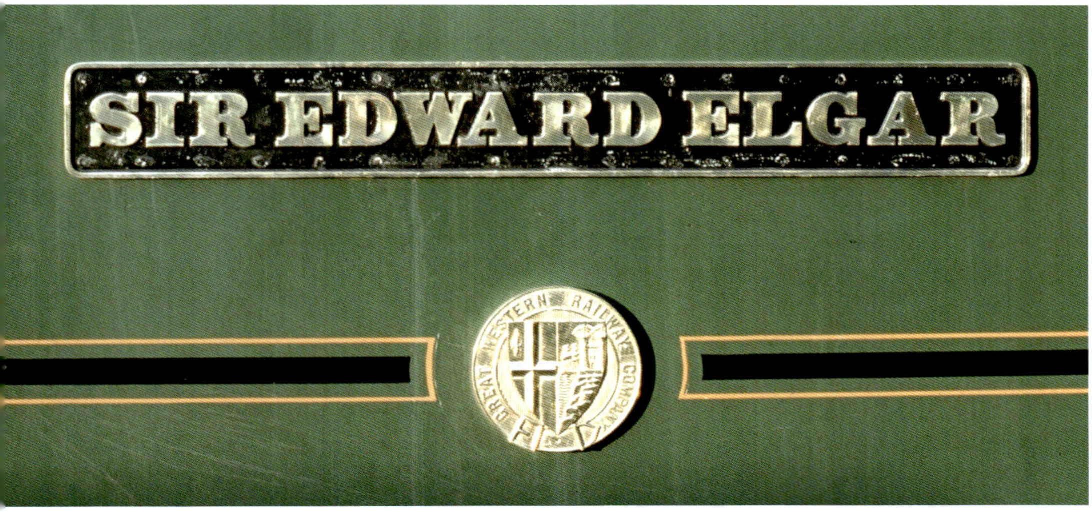

Previously 50007 was named Hercules on 6 April 1978, however as part of the GW150 celebrations and in commemoration of the 50th anniversary of Elgar's death, new name and cast number plates were unveiled at Paddington on 25 February 1984. ***Colin Whitbread***

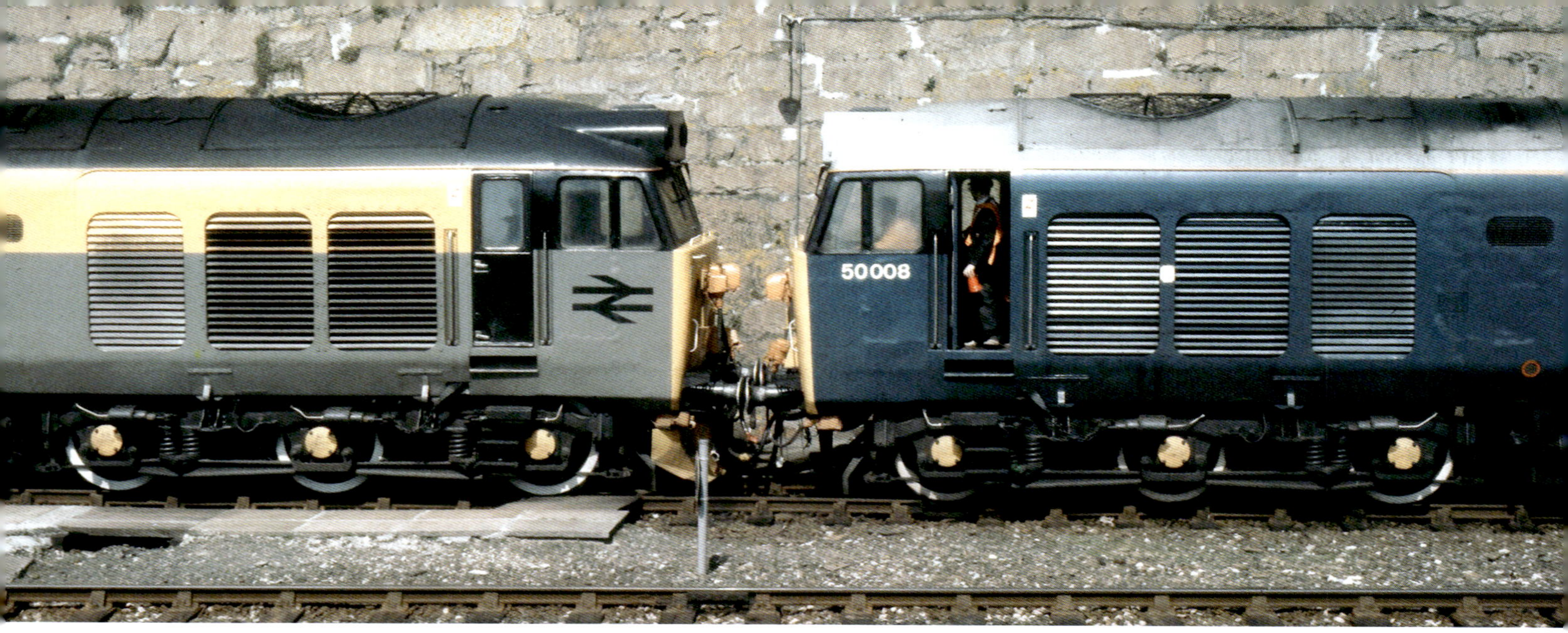

Further livery variants applied to 50015 Valiant and 50008 Thunderer at Penzance to work the Pathfinder Tours Cornish Centurion 2 on 4 May 1991. ***Strathwood Library Collection***

Sweet music indeed to Class 50 devotees as 50007 Sir Edward Elgar nears Exmouth Junction with the 11.15 Waterloo to Exeter St.Davids on 23 June 1989. ***Stuart Broughton***

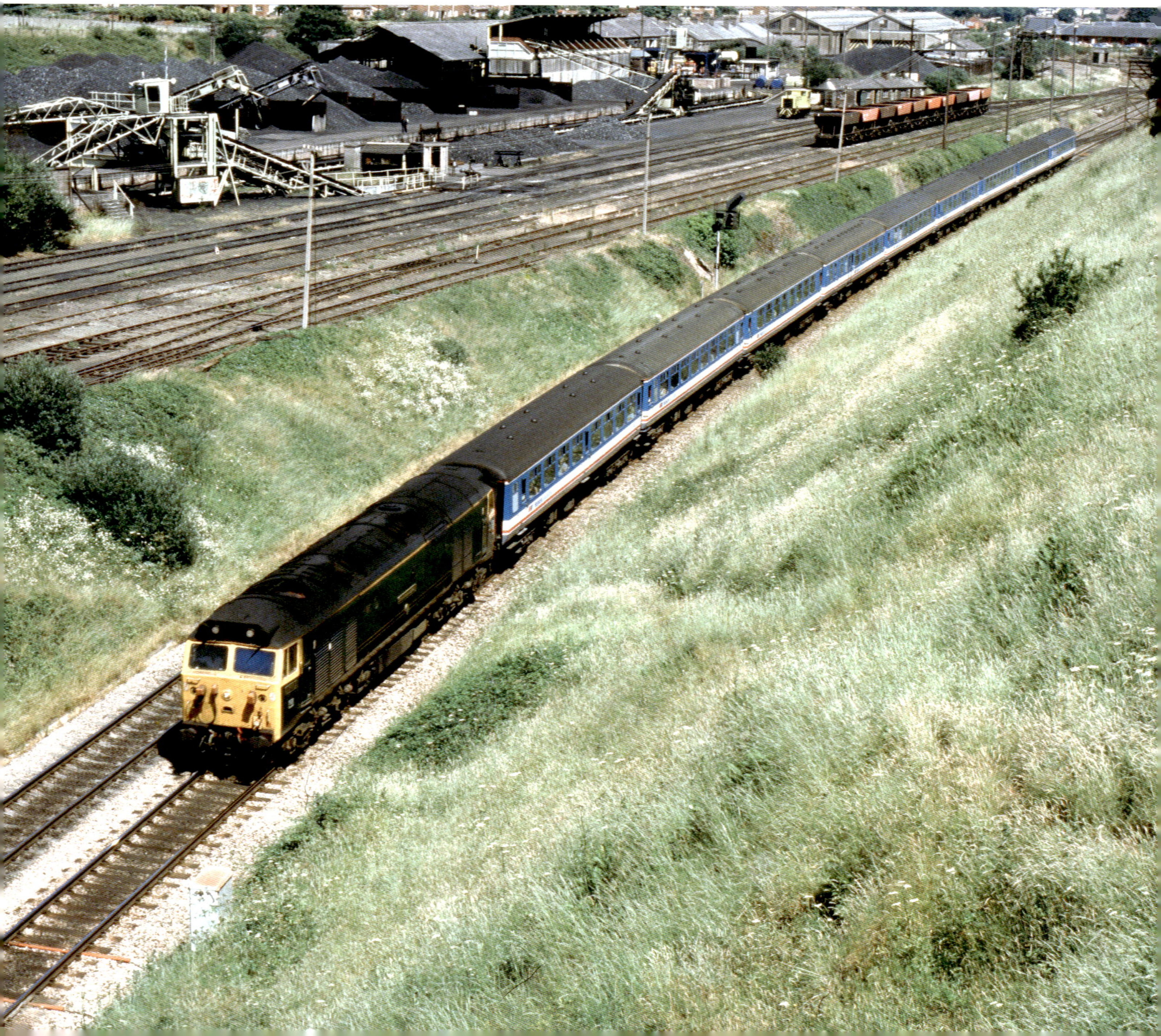

Twenties, Choppers or Dominoes?

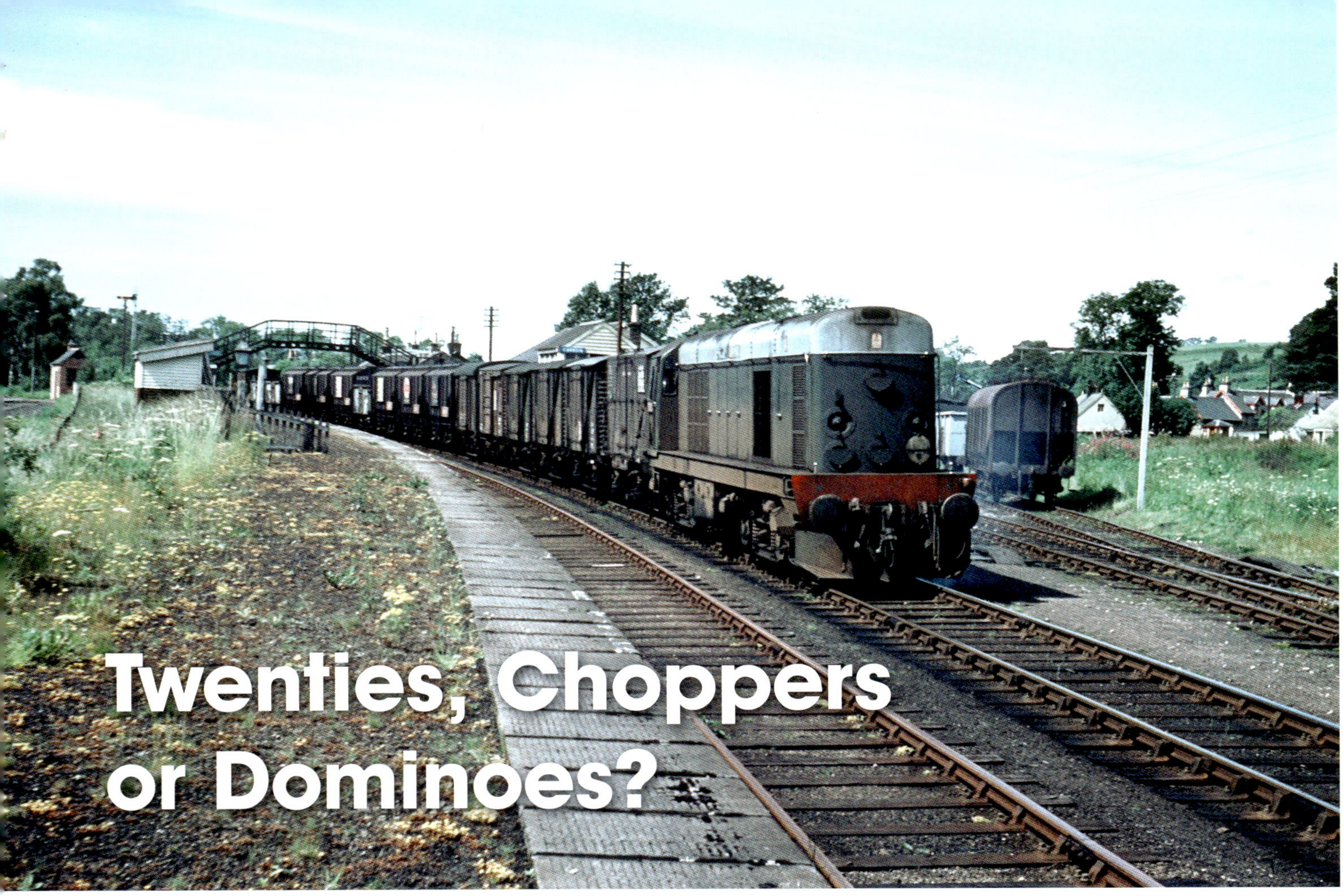

The first six years in service for D8033 would be based at 60A Inverness performing duties such as the 10.10 Aviemore to Craigellachie seen here at Carron on the now closed Speyside lines in 1961. ***Late Roy Hamilton/ Strathspey Railway***

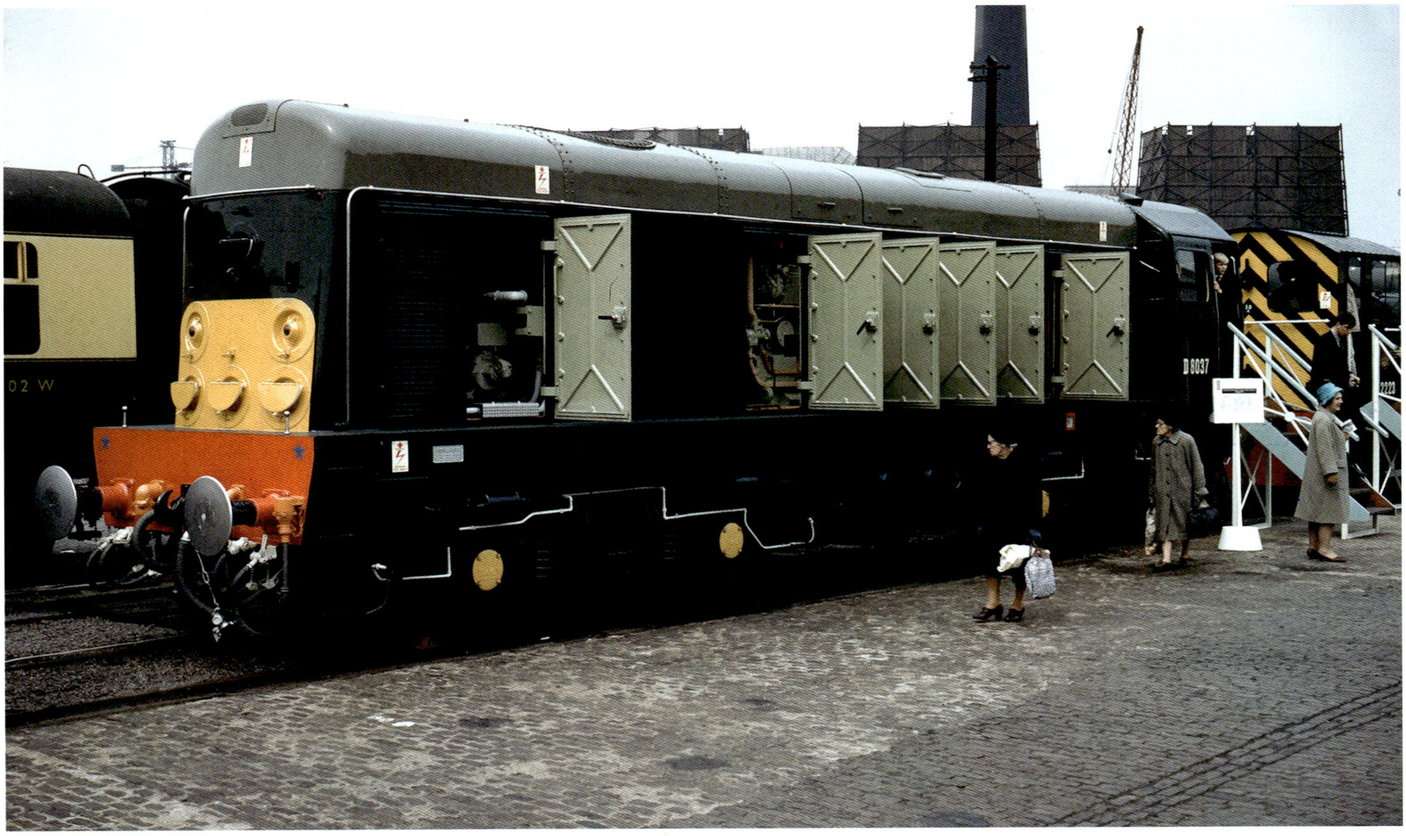

A recently ex works D8037 is open for public inspection and the gaze of the shopping ladies at Marylebone in 1965 with Drewry shunter D2223 behind also on display. ***Bob Treacher/Alton Model Centre***

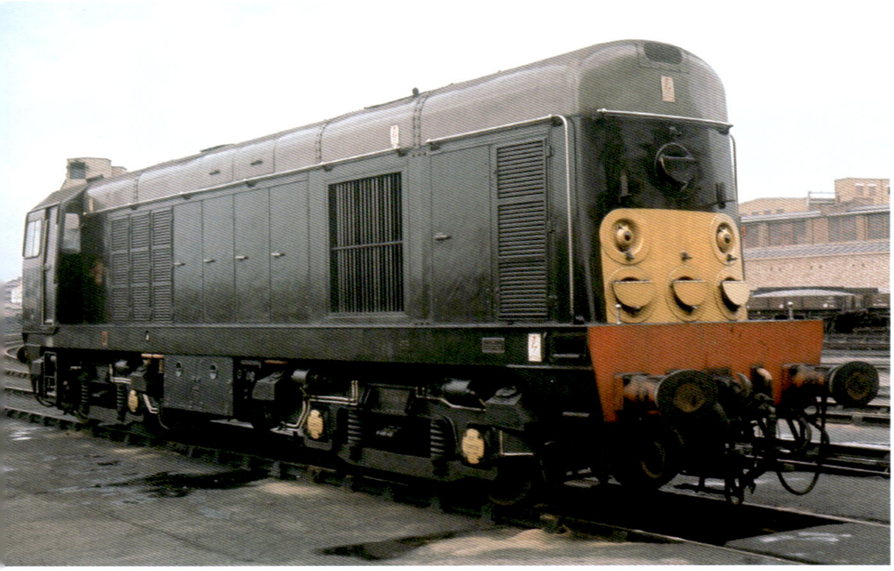

One of the original pilot batch of locomotives D8009 retains oval buffers but has lost the bonnet ladders first fitted due to concern with overhead wires and the engine crews. Further safety measures have seen the introduction of a small yellow warning panel being added to both ends in the view at Devons Road, Bow in May 1963. ***Richard Sinclair Collection***

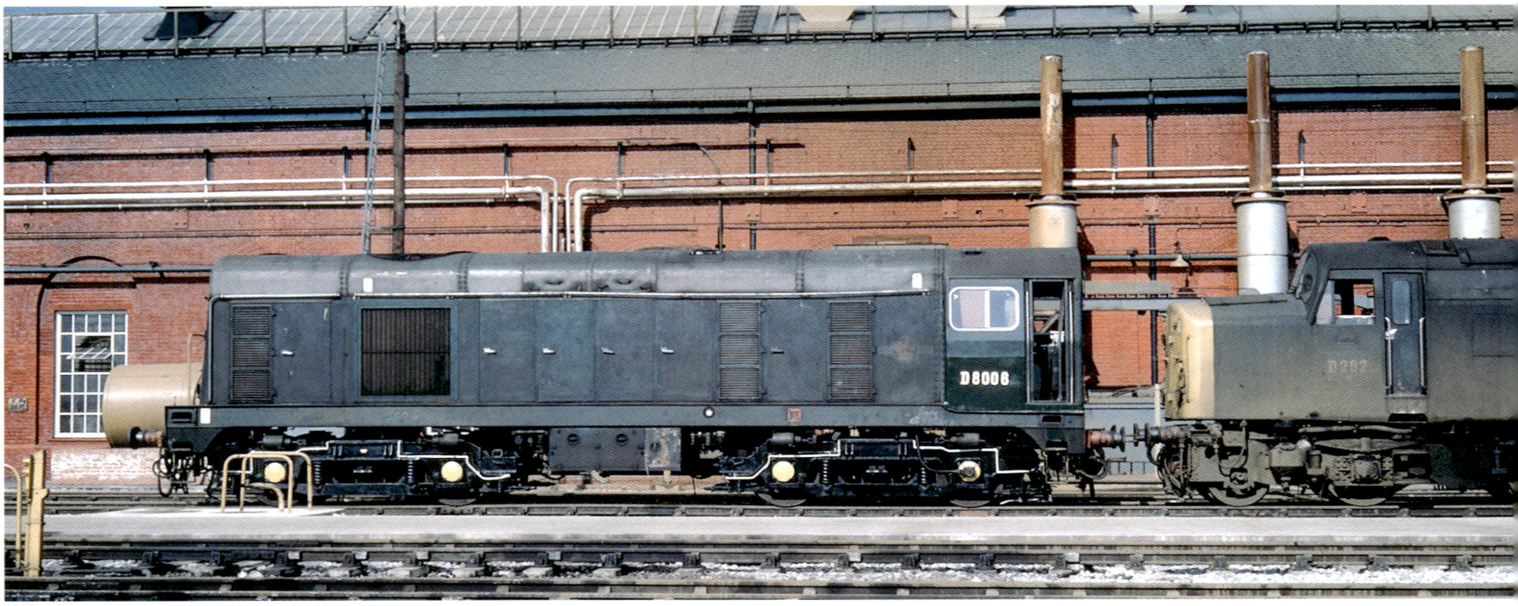

Another of the pilot locomotives D8006 waits near a fellow English Electric product at Crewe Works on 30 March 1969 after attention to its bogies. ***Frank Hornby***

Below: Delivered on Christmas Eve 1966 to Toton, D8181 had most likely yet to be cleaned for the first time since taking delivery when seen here on 5 March 1967. ***Colin Rodgers/Strathwood Library Collection***

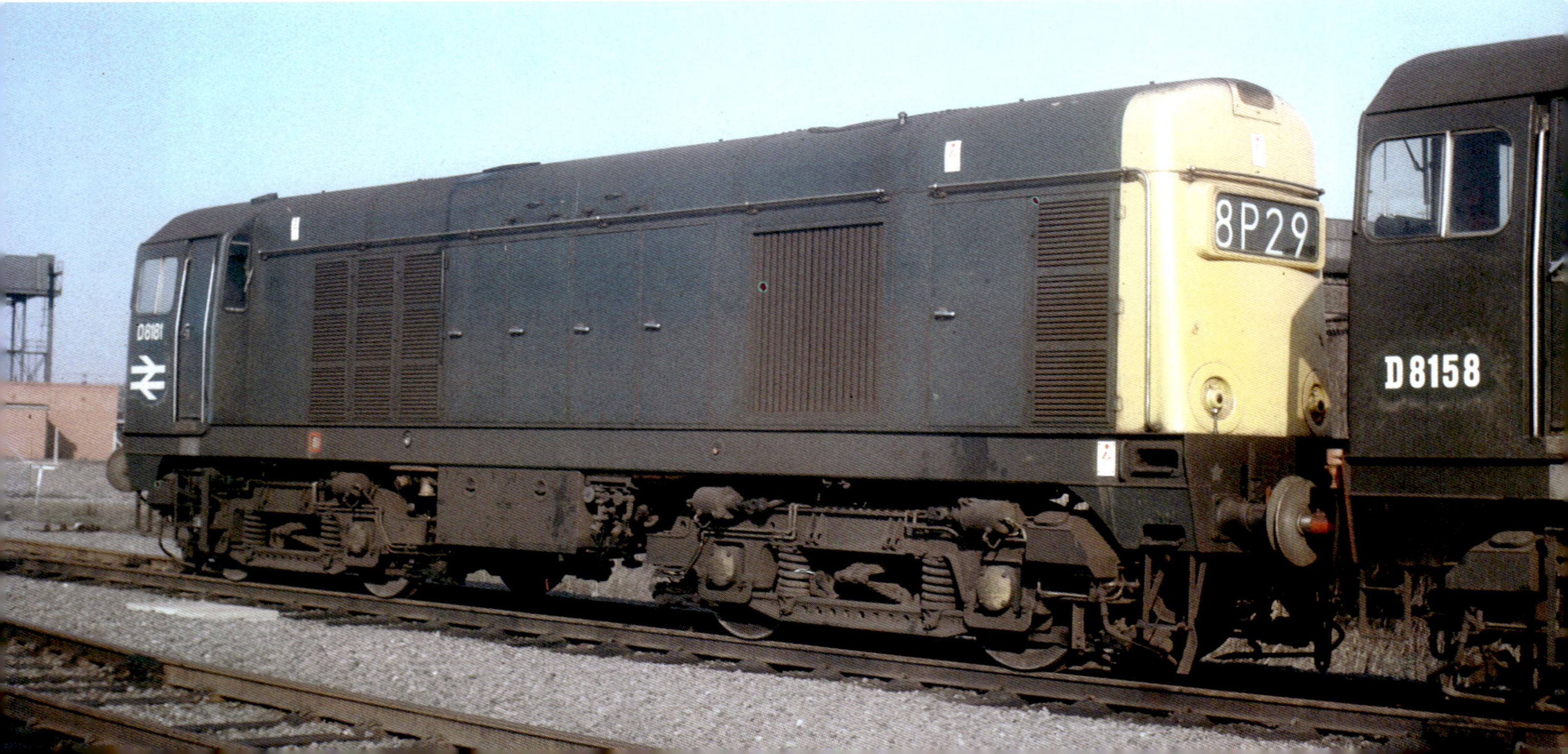

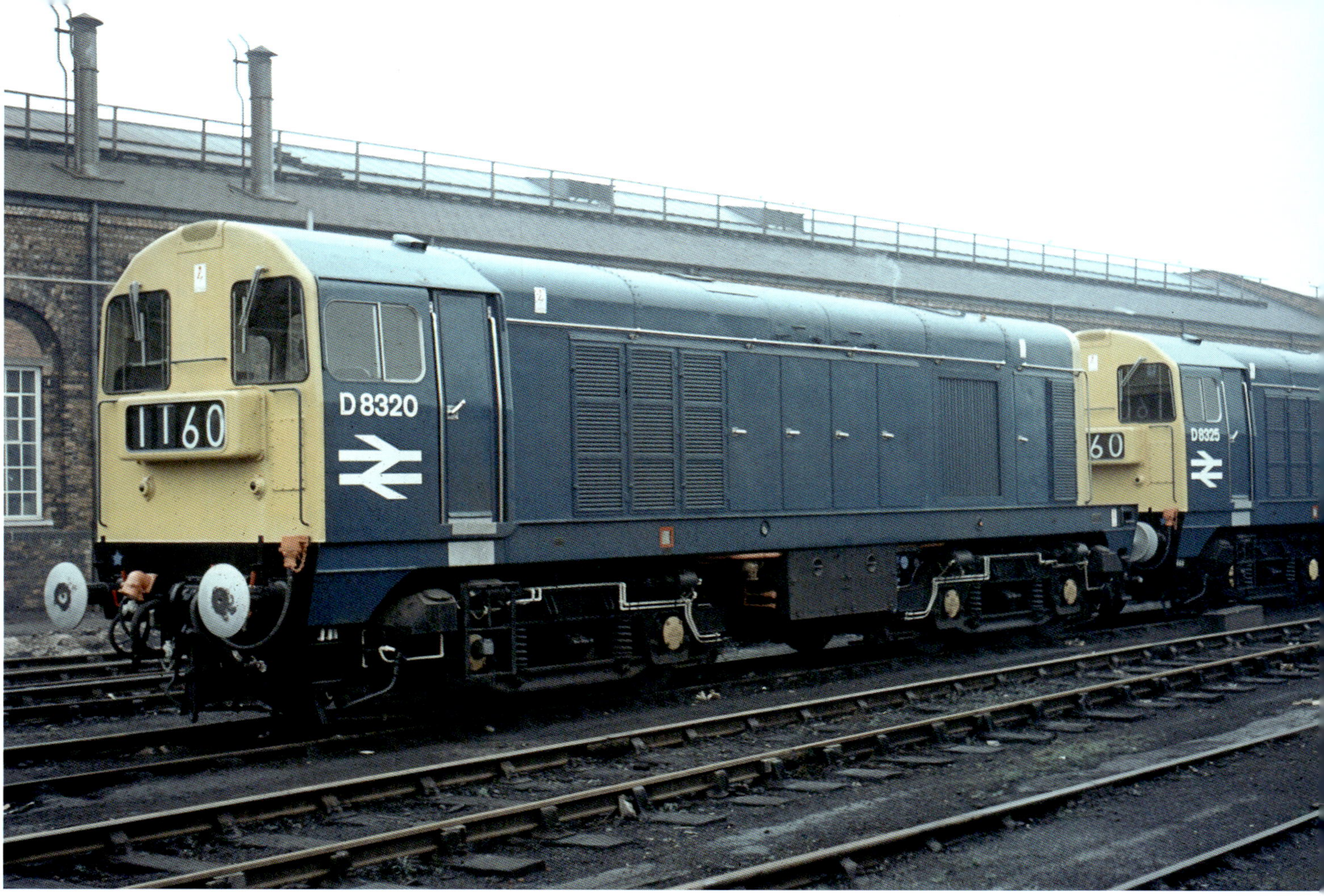

Newly delivered from Vulcan Foundry D8320 at Crewe in November 1967. After acceptance tests this Class 20 would be sent to Scotland to be based firstly at 66A Polmadie. ***Noel Marrison***

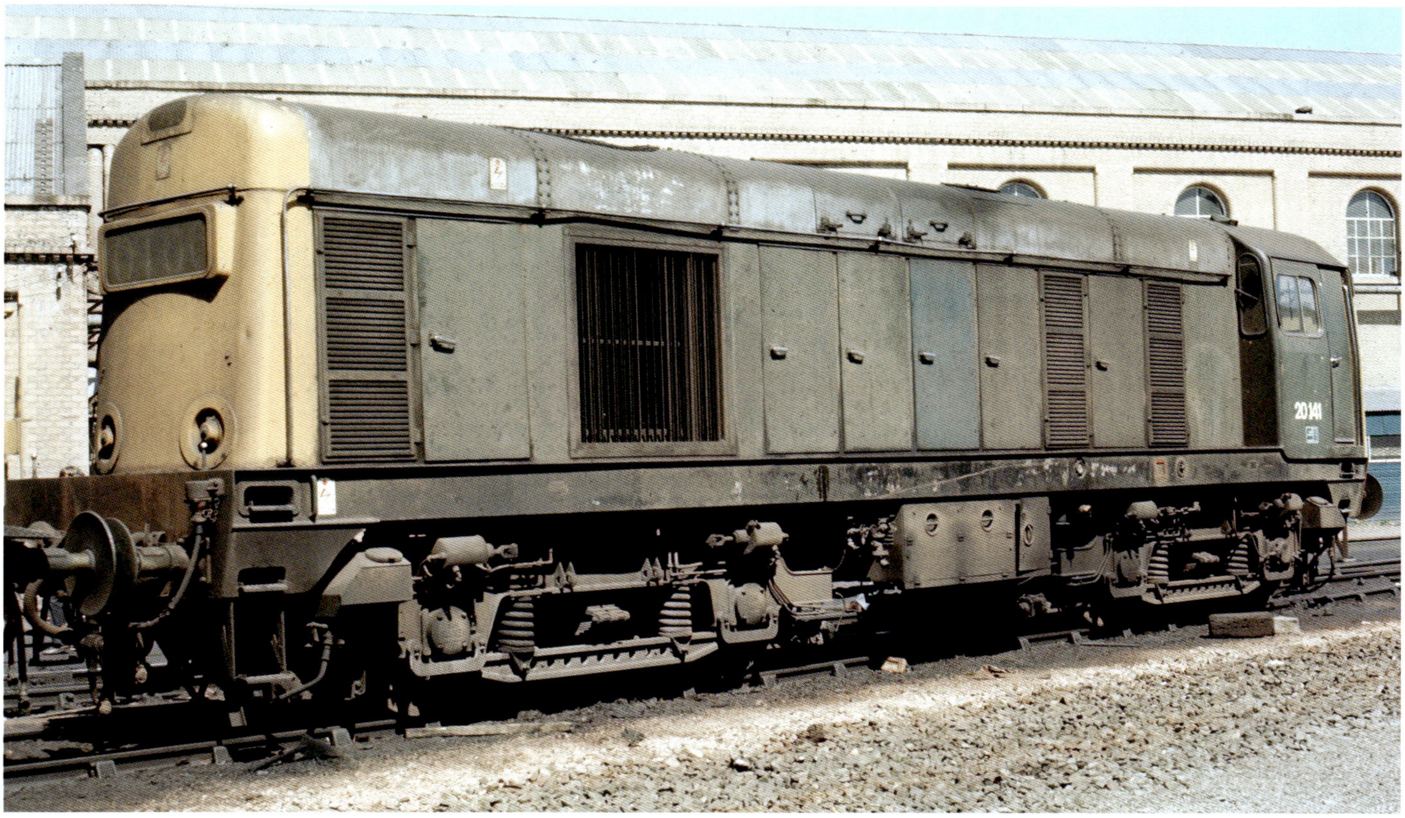

One of the last to survive in green livery was 20141 awaiting entry into Glasgow Works on 17 May 1980. ***Steve Barnes***

Another survivor into the TOPS era in green was 20020 at Polmadie in the late seventies, spending a good while in storage, being withdrawn in December 1982 and then reinstated to traffic in June 1984 finding another six years of use before being sold into preservation. Amazingly forty six of the class remained in their original green livery long enough to pick up TOPS numbers. One each from Immingham and Haymarket, two from Eastfield, eleven from Tinsley's allocation. of course it would be Toton with their huge fleet that would boast the largest number with thirty still to be repainted. Among some of the variations was number 8048 which ran for a while with Inter City arrows reversed as one of the earlier repaints into the blue livery. One or two of the earlier works or depot repaints whilst still in green livery had the British Railways coaching stock roundel applied in place of the tradional style seen here. ***Albert C Greig***

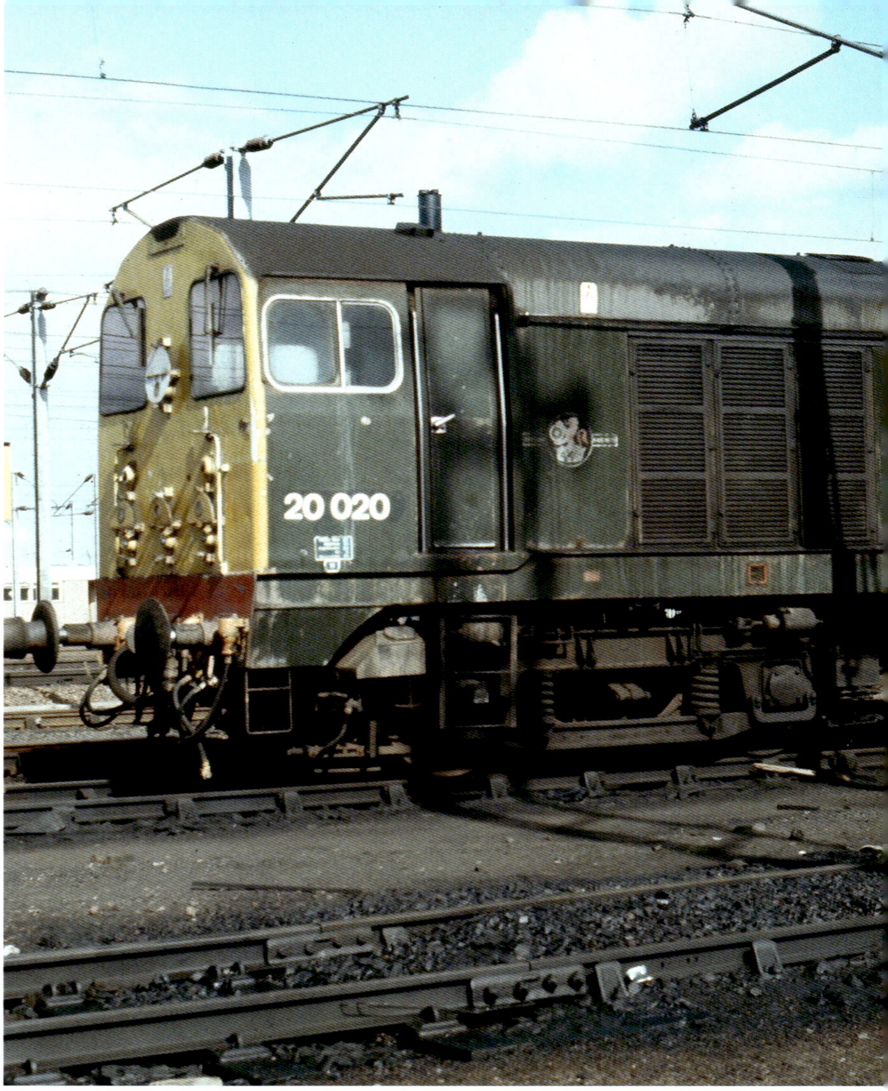

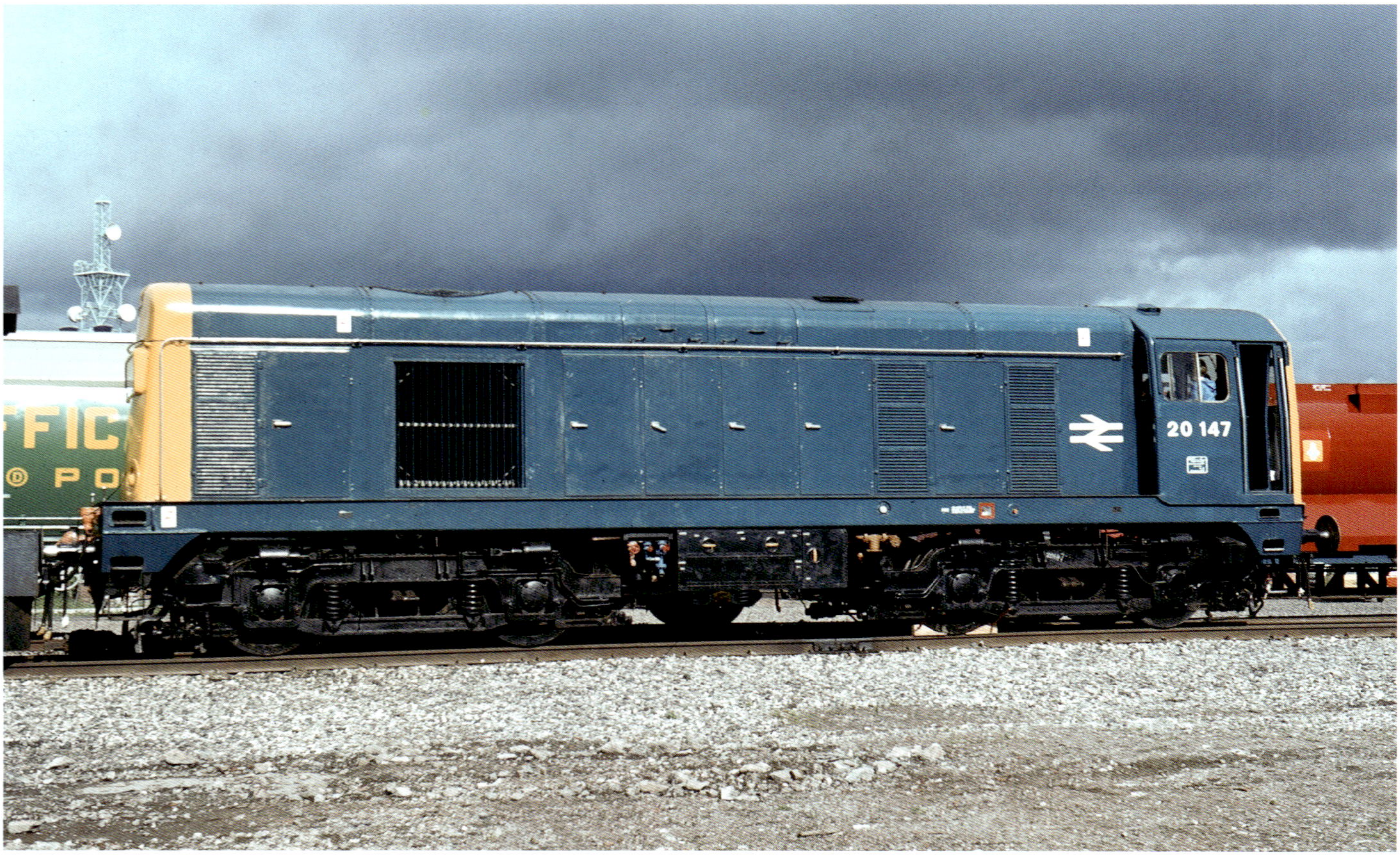

Another longer term green engine was 20147 ex works at Carlisle on 5 July 1980 into blue for the first time and the last of the class to gain this livery, as 20014 was withdrawn in green livery and the second of the class to be scrapped as early as January 1977. For 20147, by May 1989 it was stored out of use and awaiting the final journey to M.C. Metals in Glasgow, joining many of its classmates in being disposed of here. ***Sid Steadman***

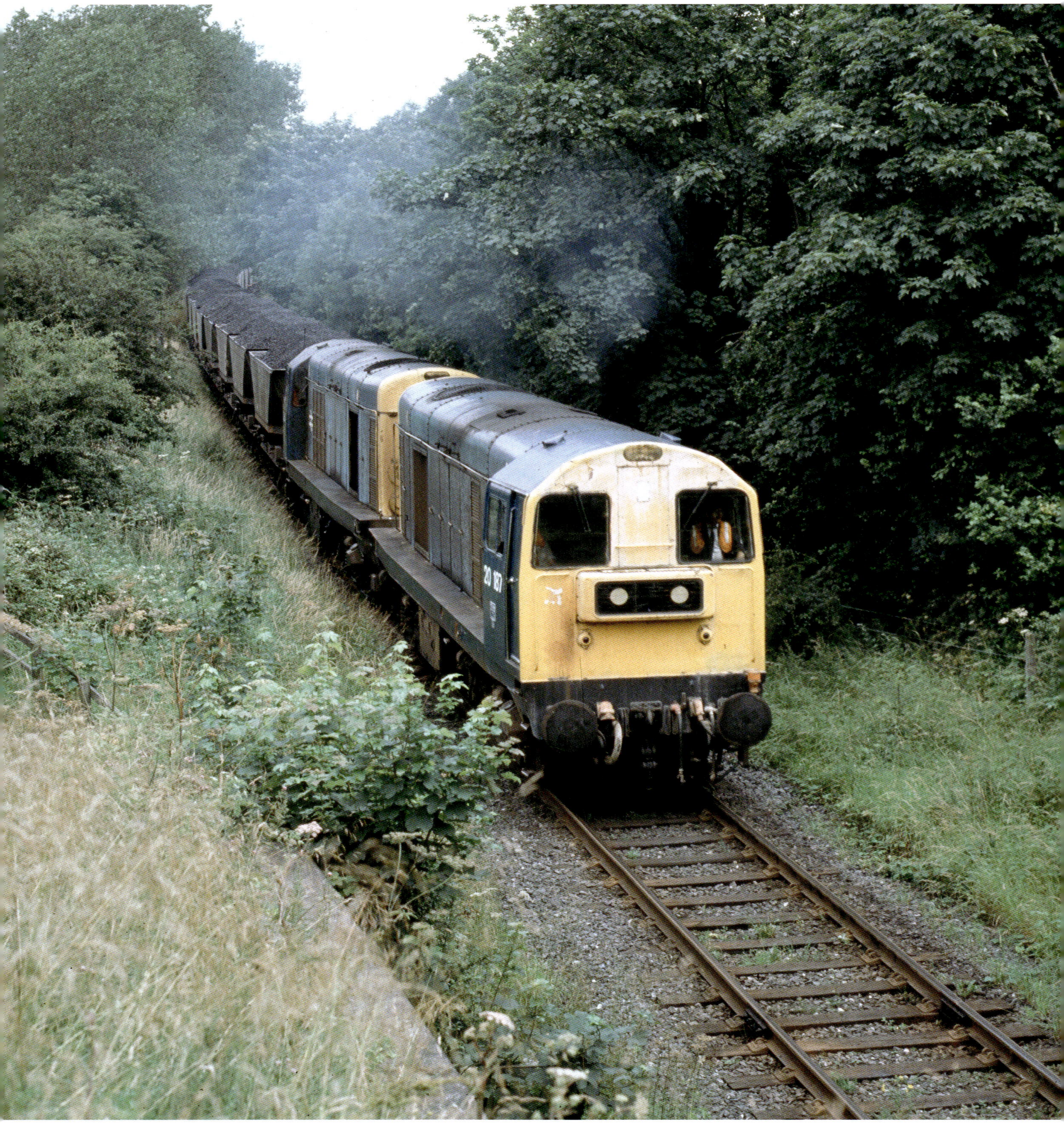

For much of the their careers Class 20s performed useful work on coal and merry go round trains across the Midlands, Yorkshire and Scottish coalfields, such as 20187 and 20040 at Lower Kilburn on another MGR duty on 24 July 1991. ***Stuart Broughton***

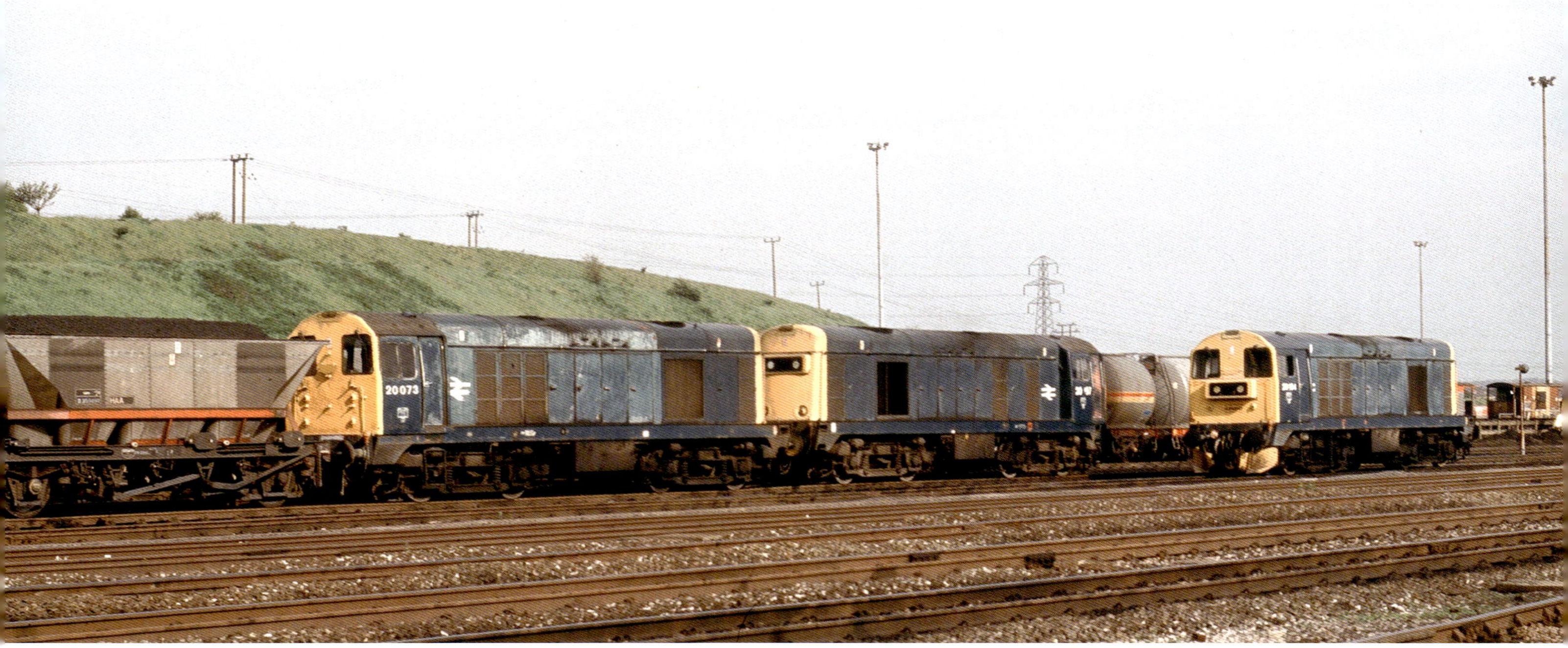

Engaged in similar duties at Toton on 21 May 1991 were 20073, 20197 and 20194 photographed at New Bank Sidings, although the writing was on the wall for the class by this stage. ***Stuart Broughton***

Toton kept many of their extensive fleet working, by robbing spares from various locomotives dumped around the depot at this time such as 20021, 20006 and 20031 set aside for scrap on 22 March 1991. ***Stuart Broughton***

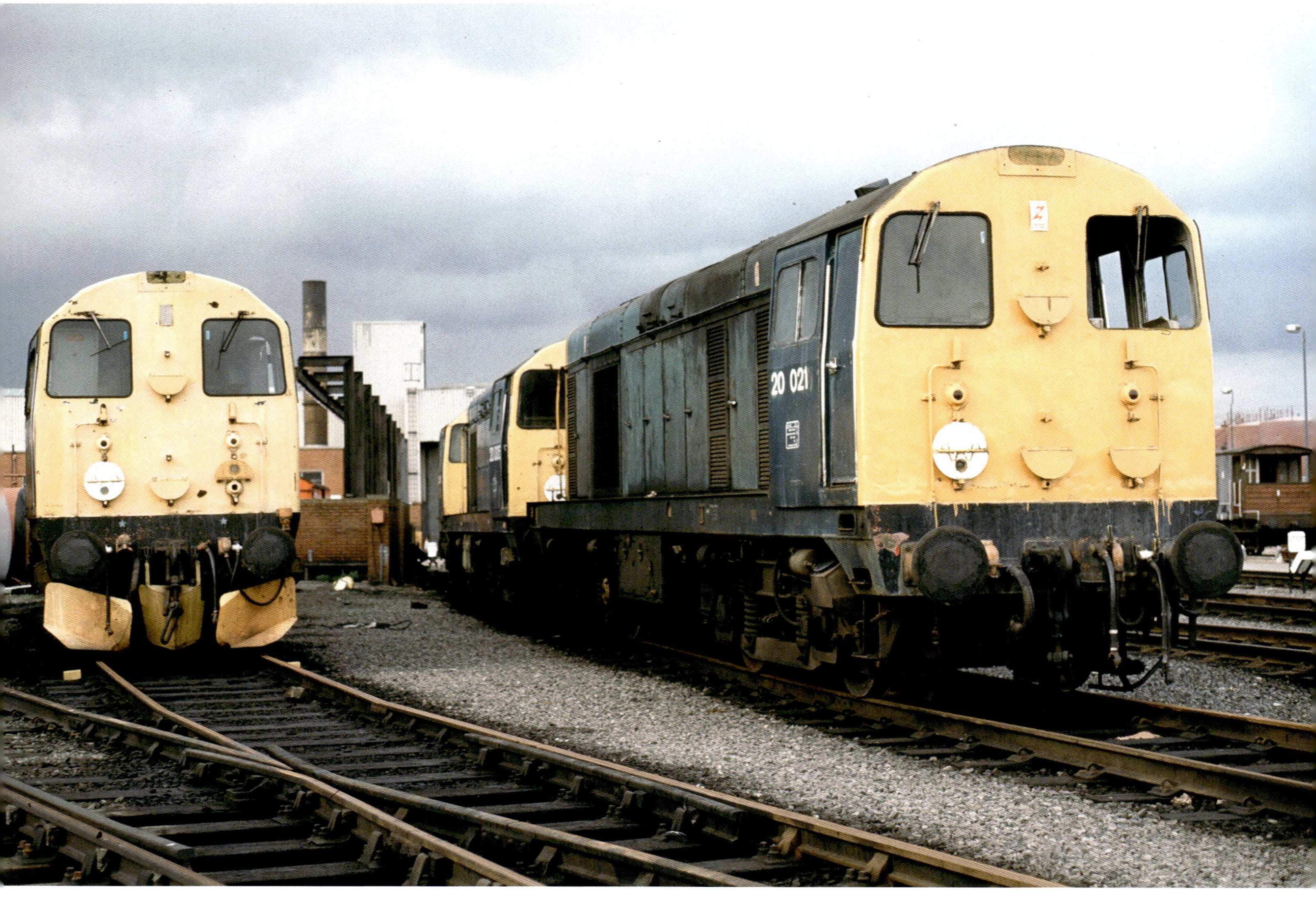

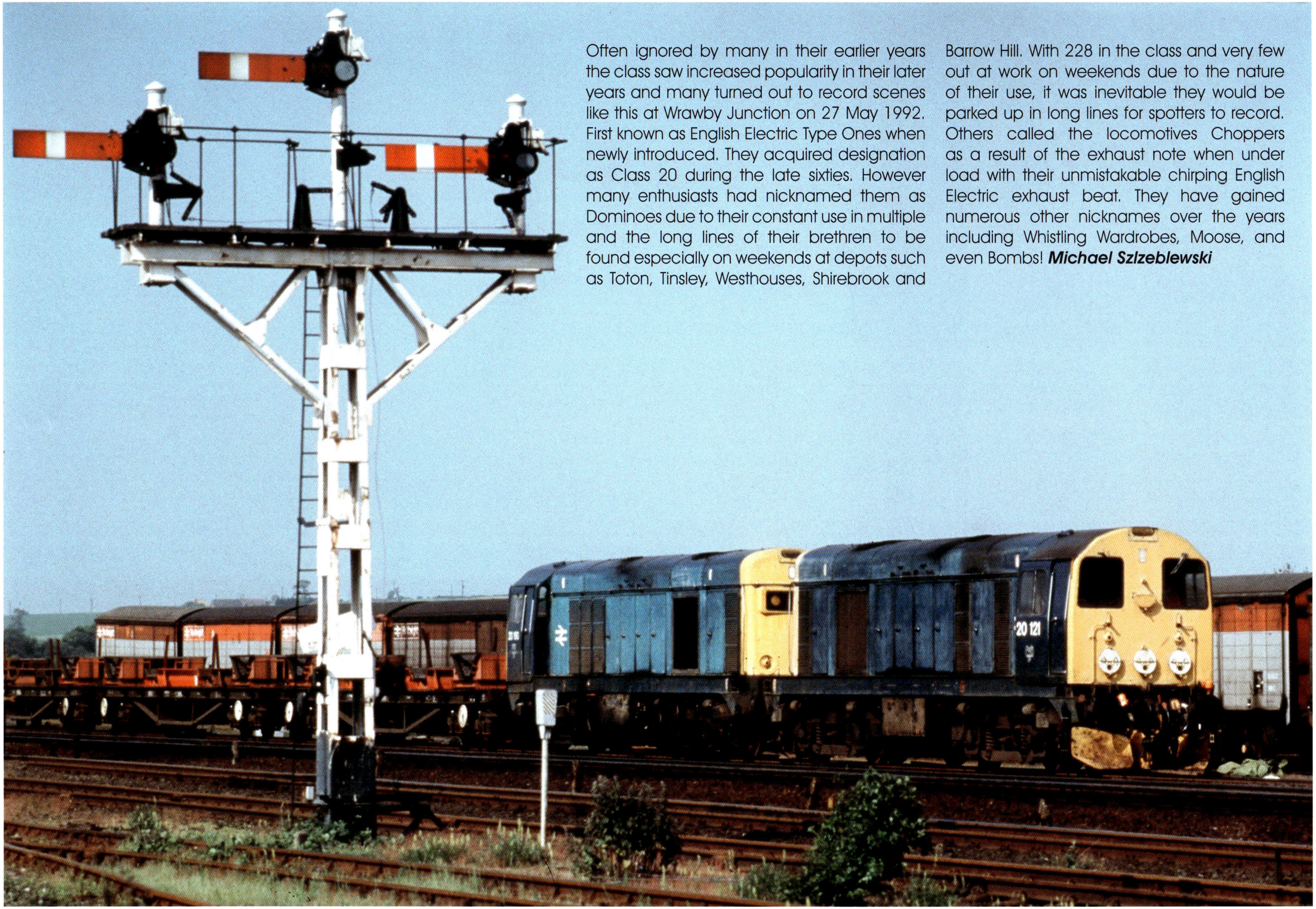

Often ignored by many in their earlier years the class saw increased popularity in their later years and many turned out to record scenes like this at Wrawby Junction on 27 May 1992. First known as English Electric Type Ones when newly introduced. They acquired designation as Class 20 during the late sixties. However many enthusiasts had nicknamed them as Dominoes due to their constant use in multiple and the long lines of their brethren to be found especially on weekends at depots such as Toton, Tinsley, Westhouses, Shirebrook and Barrow Hill. With 228 in the class and very few out at work on weekends due to the nature of their use, it was inevitable they would be parked up in long lines for spotters to record. Others called the locomotives Choppers as a result of the exhaust note when under load with their unmistakable chirping English Electric exhaust beat. They have gained numerous other nicknames over the years including Whistling Wardrobes, Moose, and even Bombs! ***Michael Szlzeblewski***

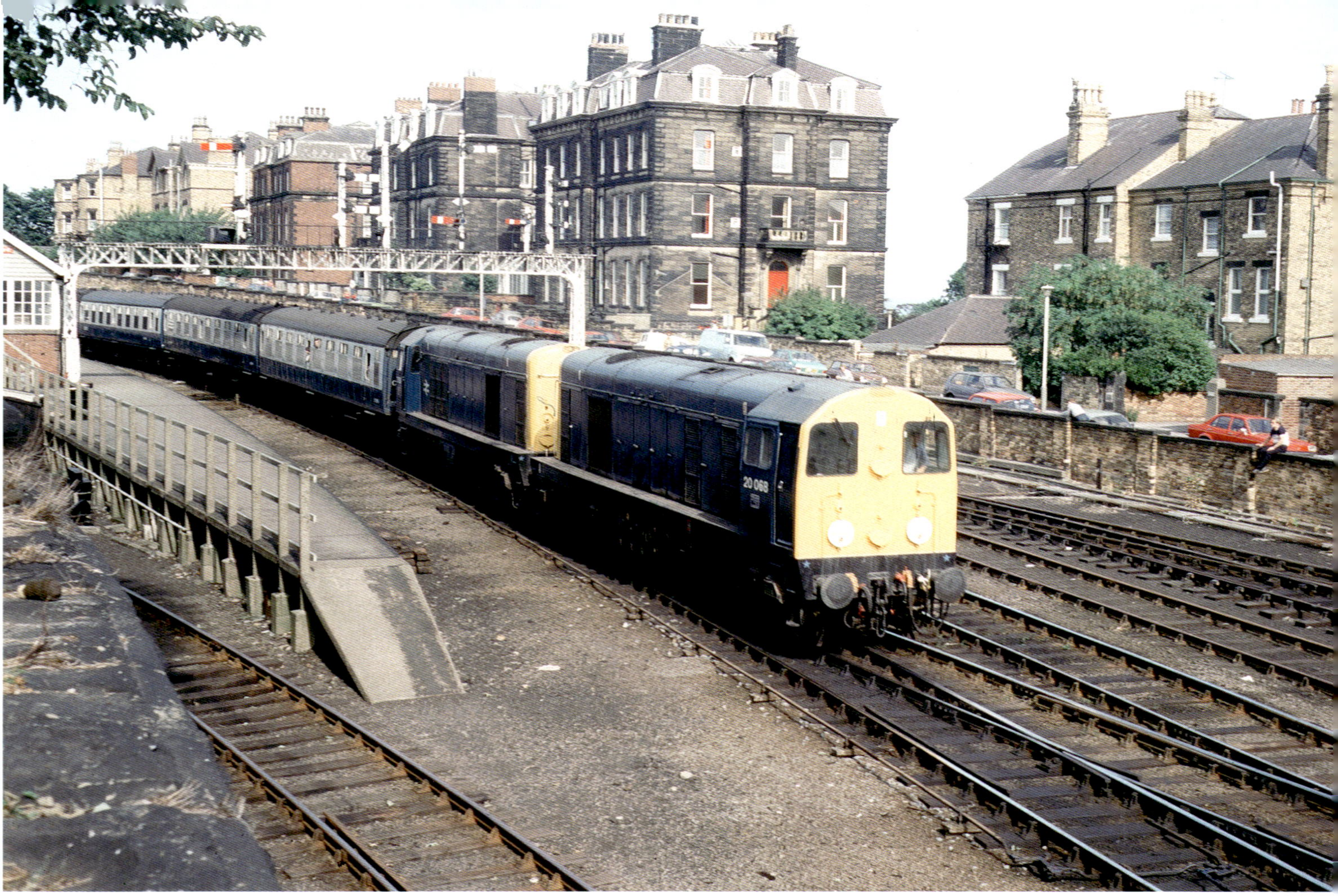

The use of Class 20s on summer holiday trains to seaside resorts with excursion traffic and even regular services was a popular distraction for many enthusiasts in the seventies and eighties. This pairing of 20068 and 20054 will take day trippers back to the Midlands from Scarborough in 1985. ***Strathwood Library Collection***

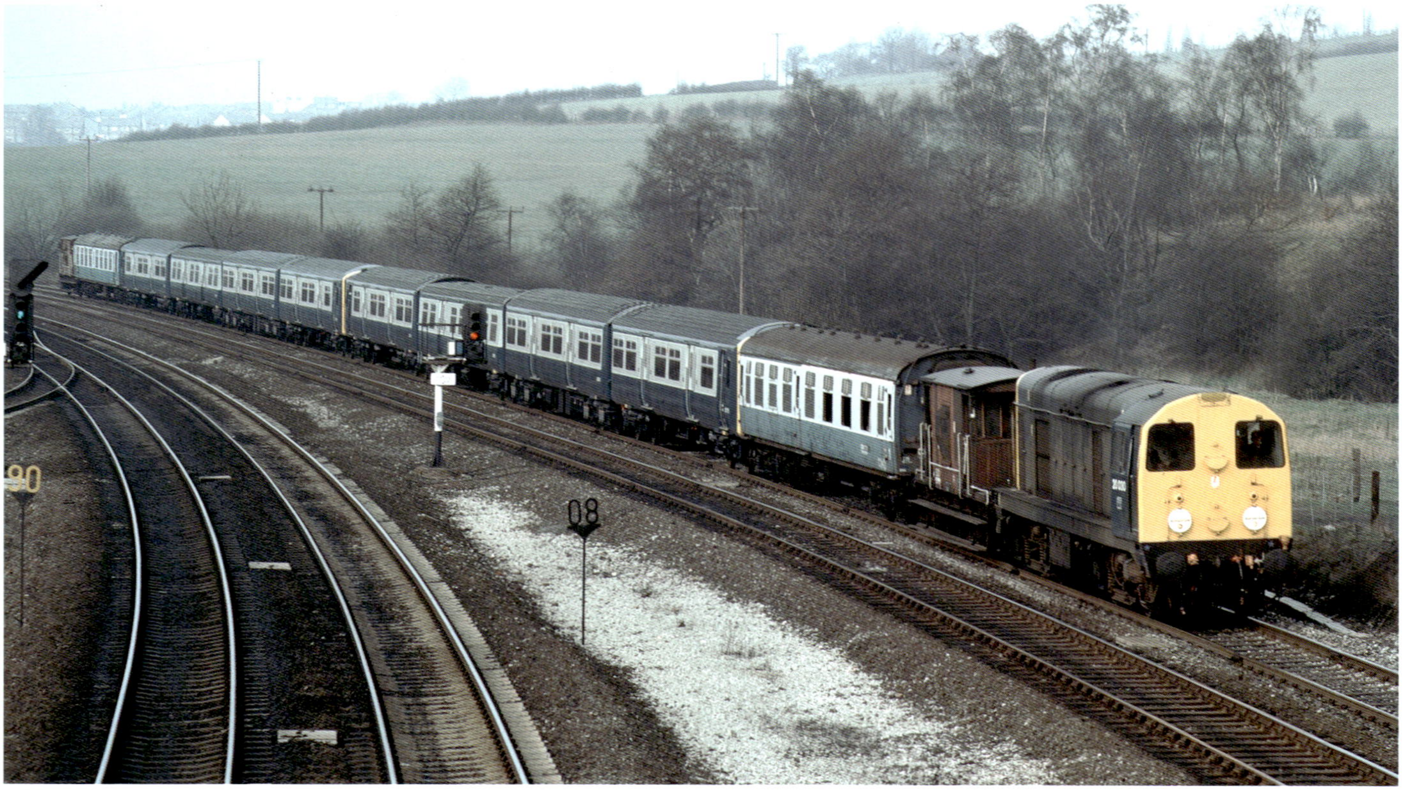

Not a passenger working but the delivery of new rolling stock from BREL at York employs 20030 at Clay Cross Junction in March 1983. Note the use of two brake vans and two barrier coaches from redundant Mark One stock. ***David T Williams***

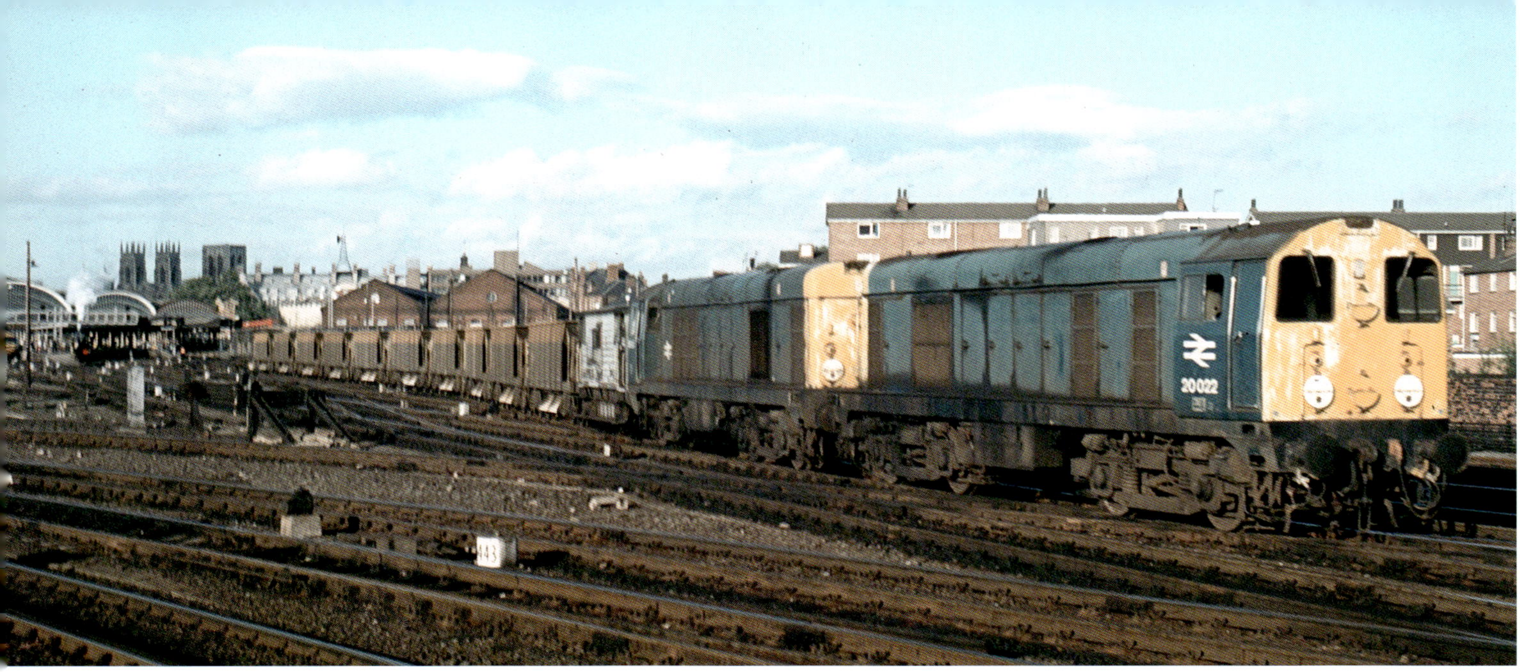

Having run through York station, 20022 leads this pairing with a heavy track ballast train before the overhead wires went up and this once popular photographic location became out of bounds in the modern world. ***Phil Nunn***

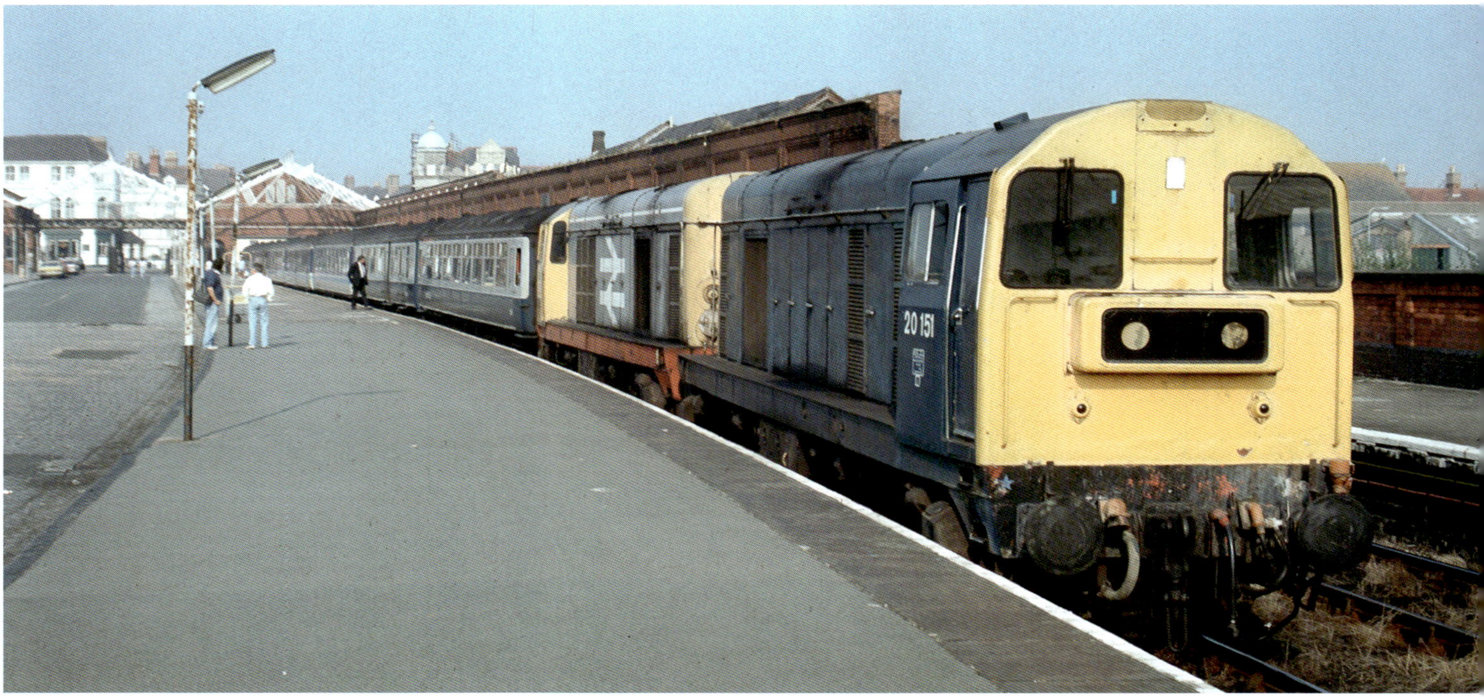

Another working to the seaside brings 20151 and 20059 at Llandudno with the 16.44 to Derby on 4 August 1991. ***Alister Betts***

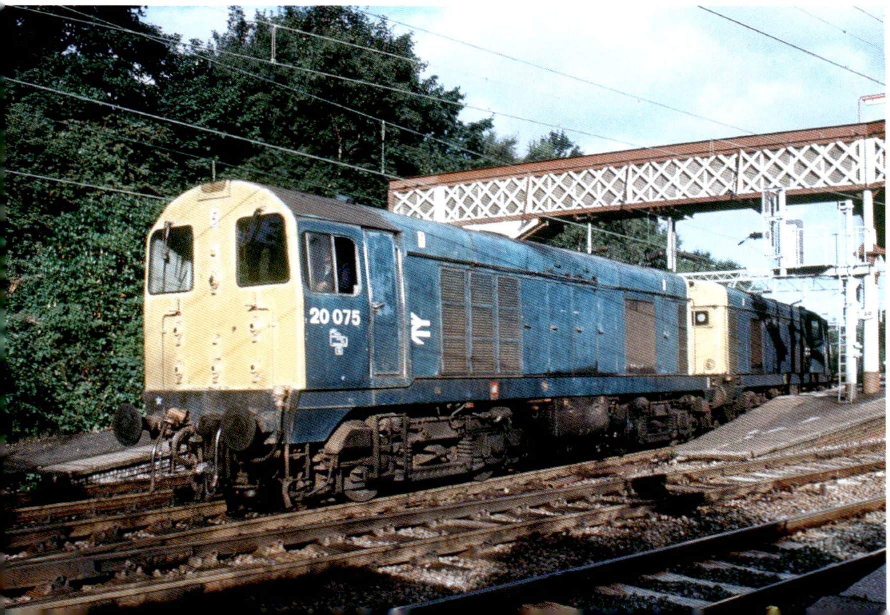

Making that once familiar sound of a Class 20 pairing at Kidsgrove on 31 August 1989 are 20075 and 20169 as they accelerate away with their working. ***Alister Betts***

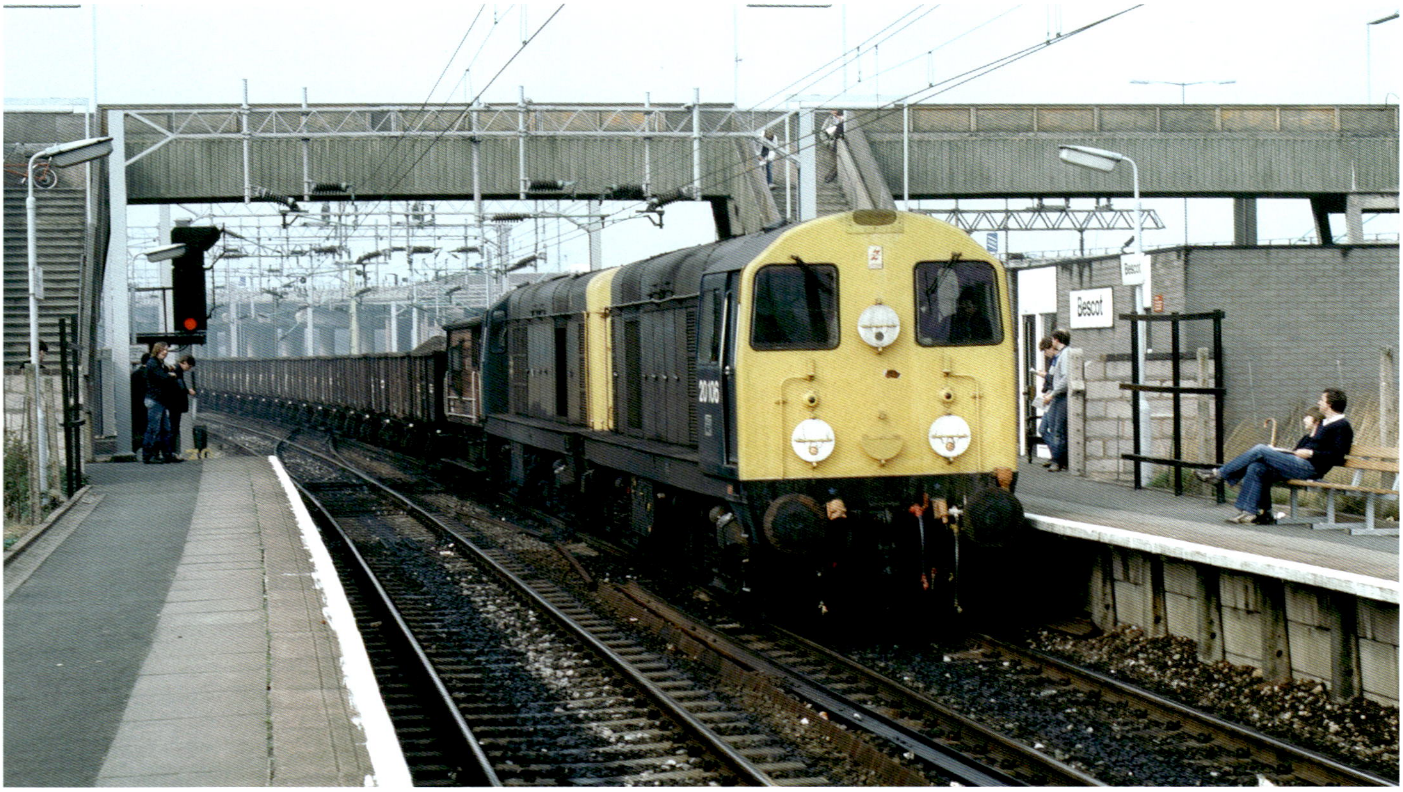

Further Class 20 action at Bescot in October 1985 for 20106 and 20130 with a long rake of sixteen ton mineral wagons in tow. ***David T Williams***

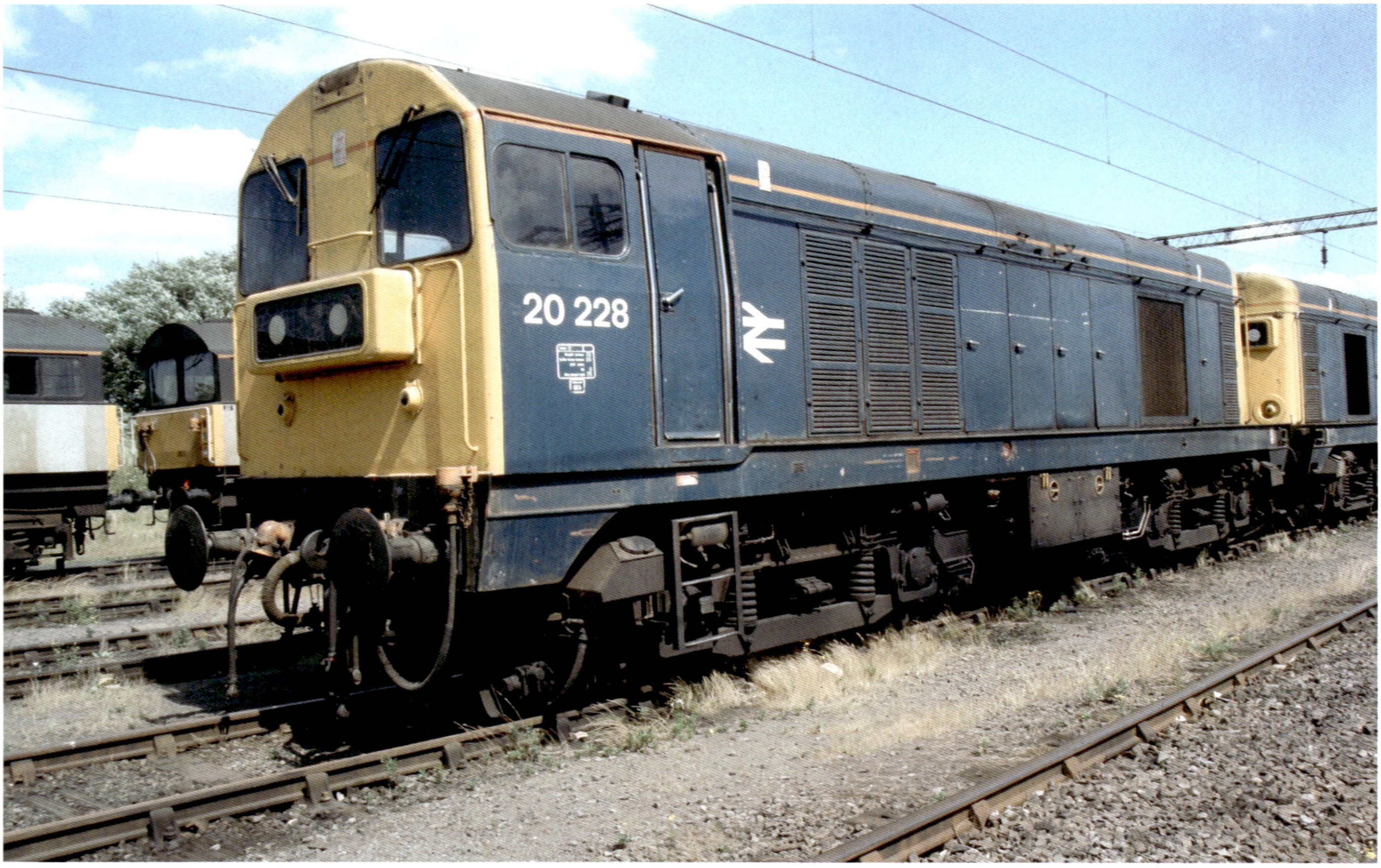

As will be seen, a number of detail differences existed between the 228 strong class. This example was in fact not the last of the class to be delivered but was the first of the second series being originally D8128 when new in January 1966. This number change came about as D8000 took the number 20050, and D8050 became 20128 as the TOPS scheme would not allow a number 20000. Seen at Bescot 20228 in July 1989 we can see the first of the later batch all delivered with headcode boxes. The bogies at this time are of the original flat equalising beam type fitted to the first twenty locomotives only when new, most likely a result of Toton robbing spares to keep this class member in service. ***Strathwood Library Collection***

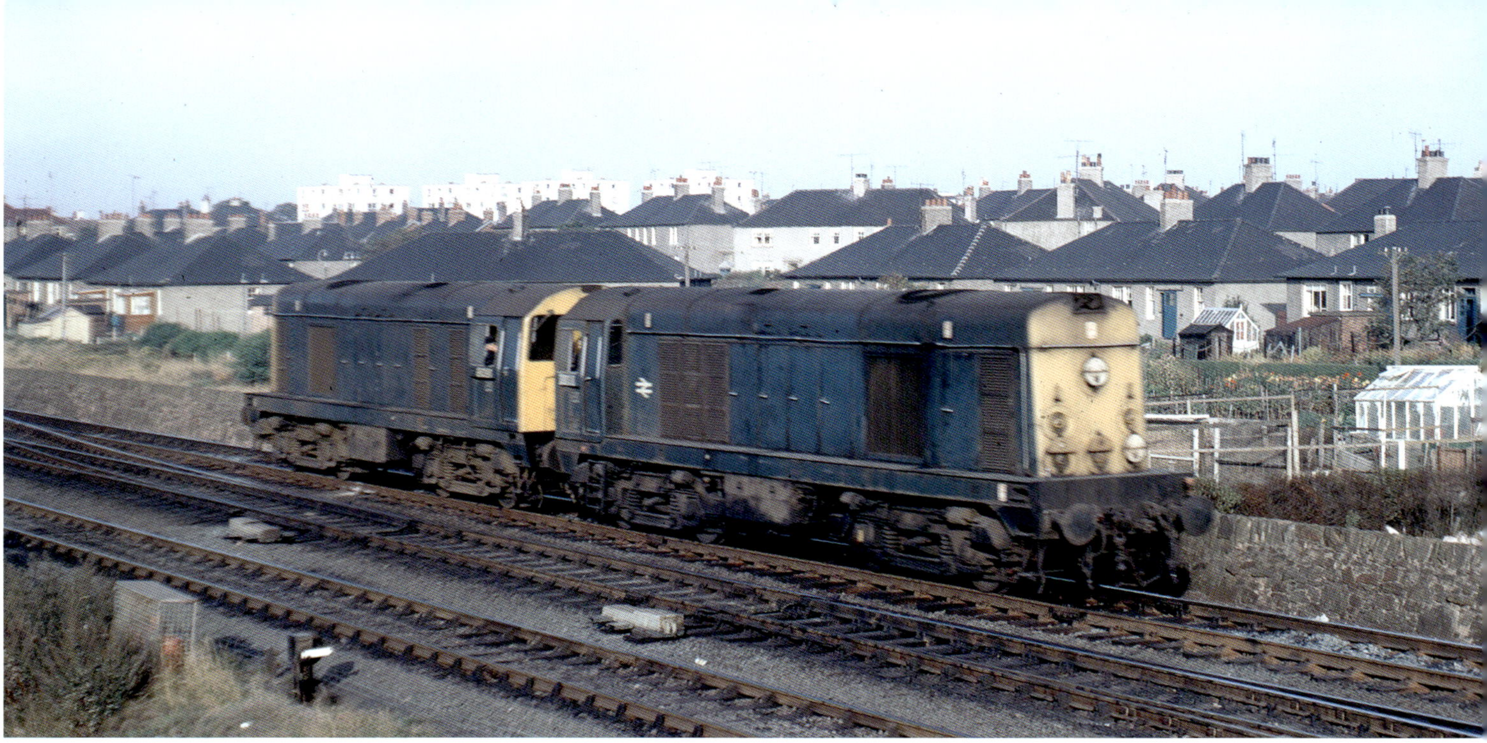

An unusual pairing of 8091 and 8116 near Prestwick in October 1972 running cab to cab for once. ***Arthur Wilson***

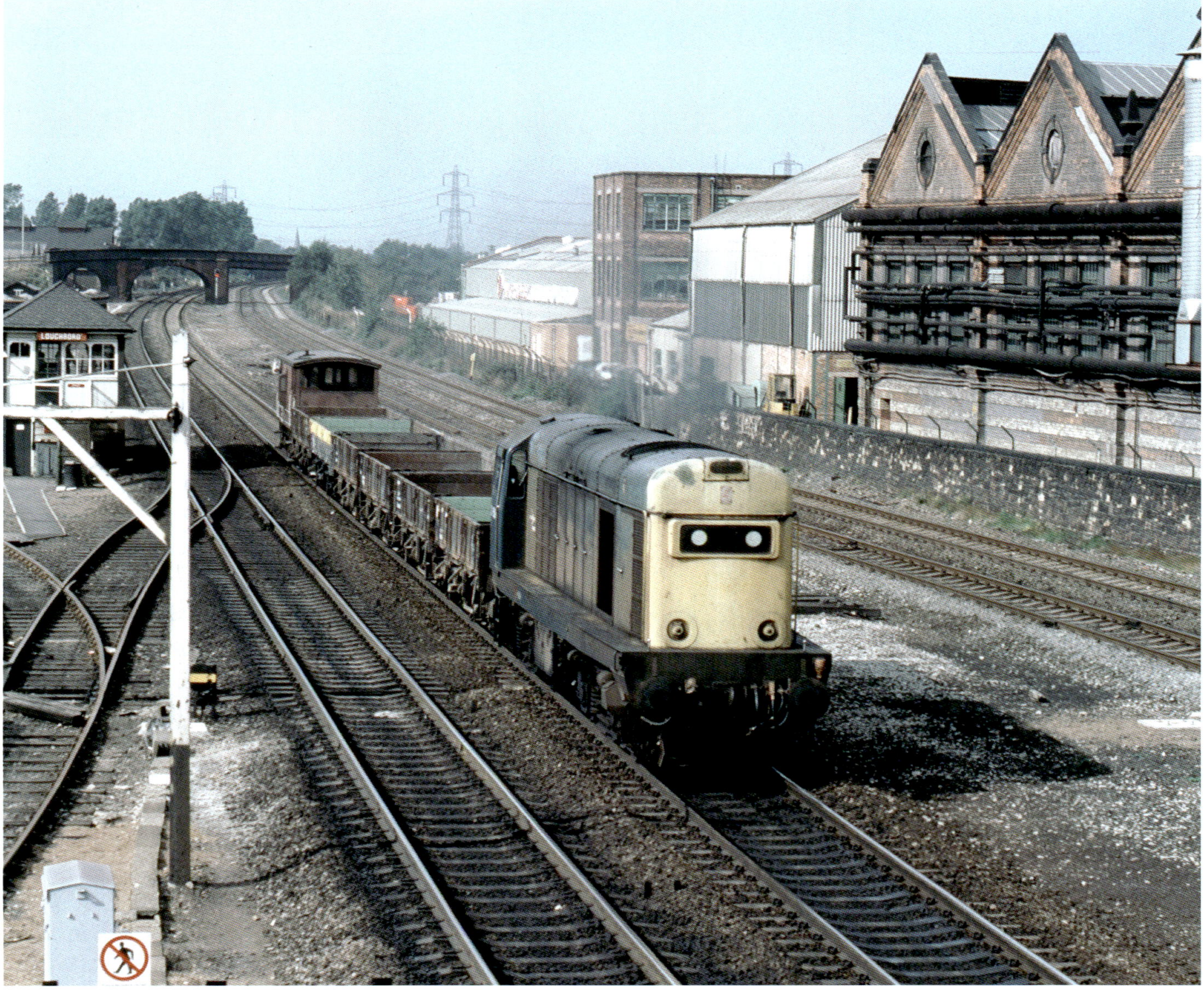

Singular use of locomotives was rarer in their latter years but would often result in at least part of the working requiring bonnet first running as here at Loughborough with 20159 in October 1985, passing the works of the enemy Brush who favoured Sulzer power for their locomotives after a bad experience with Mirlees engines. More of this later. ***David T Williams***

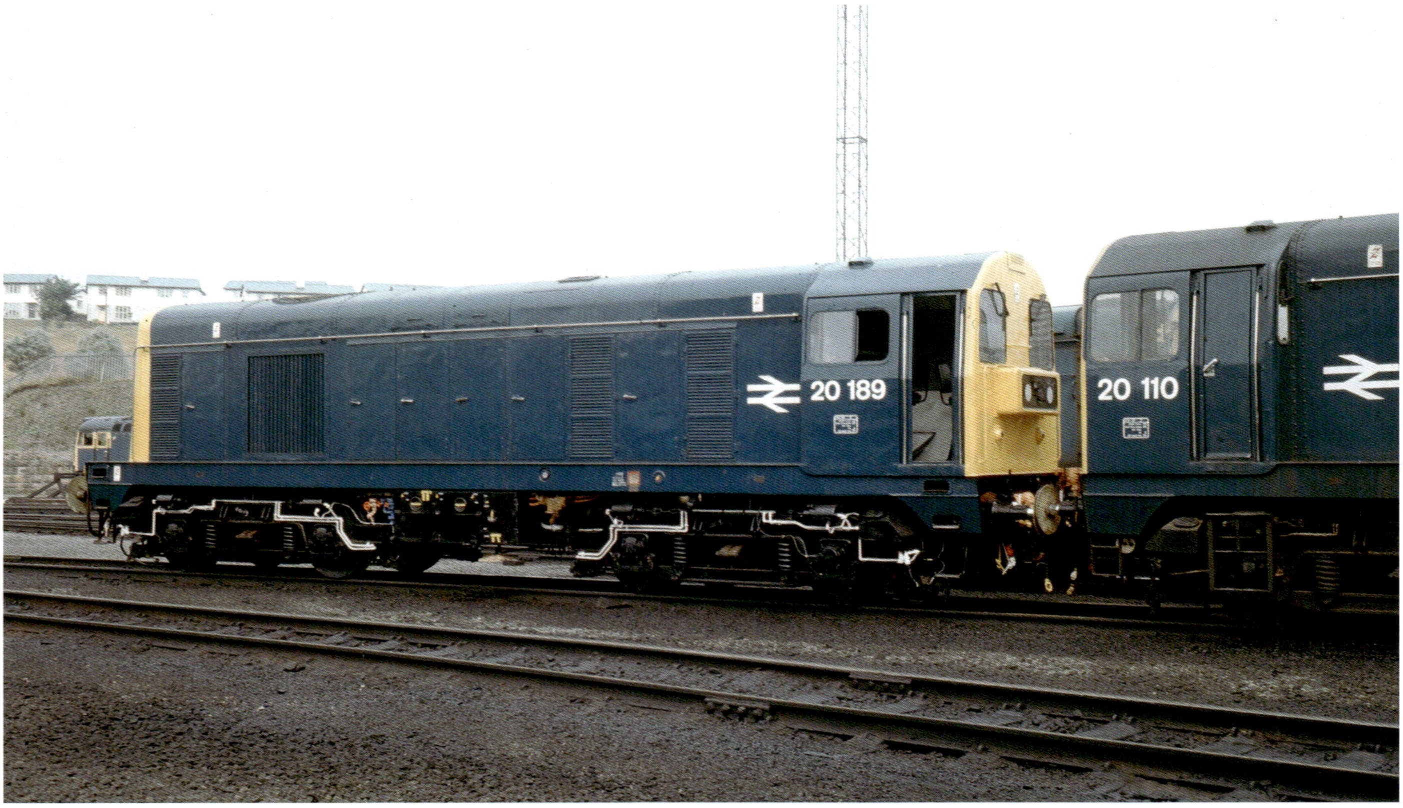

The two types of cab side window can be seen at Eastfield in 1984 with these two class members from different batches. Numbers D8070 to D8127 were built for the Scottish depots with deeper windows to allow drivers to pick up single line tokens easier. This batch having the recesses for the equipment later plated over during works visits in the seventies. ***Strathwood Library Collection***

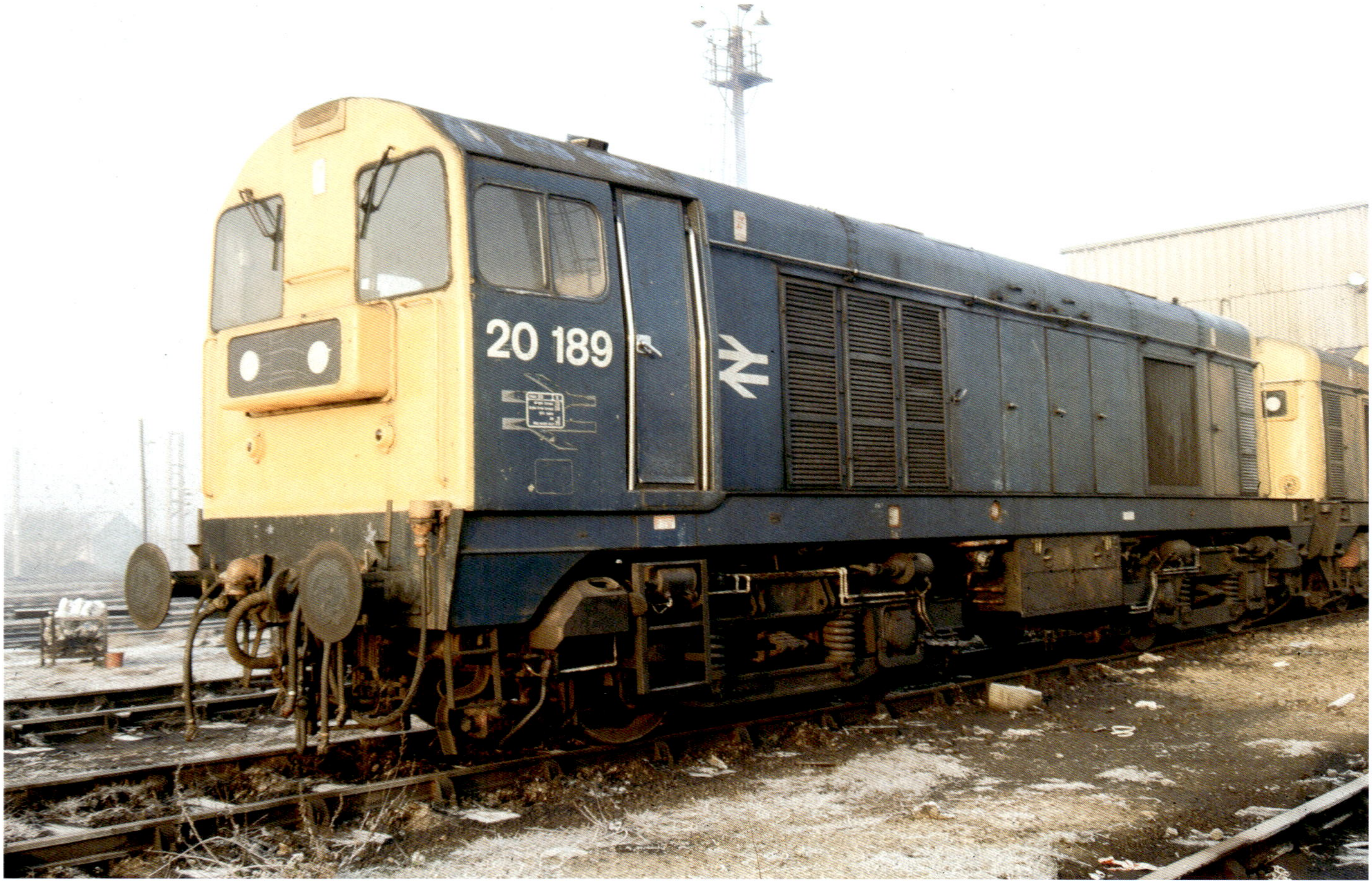

The same Class 20, 20189 again at Bescot this time in November 1988. Note the side frames of the bogies from differing batches evidence of further of Toton's handiwork perhaps? ***Strathwood Library Collection***

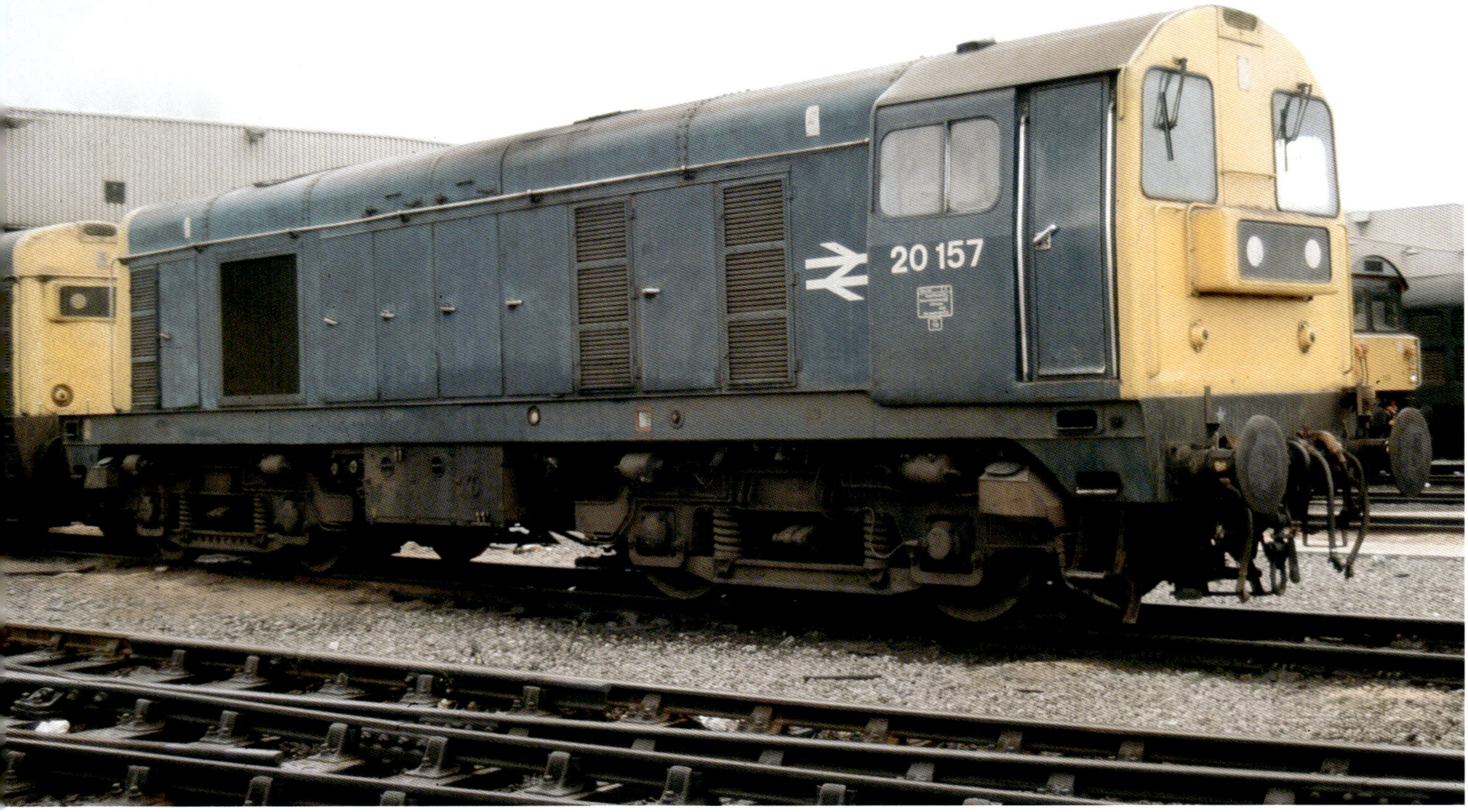

Slightly smaller 6" numbers are used on 20157 at Toton seen during December 1988 as opposed to the 8" numbers favoured by St. Rollox. Again the bogies are an odd pairing with both types of fluted variety to be seen. Those with the holes drilled through the equalising beams were to save weight, although as the class were prone to slipping this may not have helped. The sandboxes were modified during the life of the class to try and assist the drivers with this problem. ***Strathwood Library Collection***

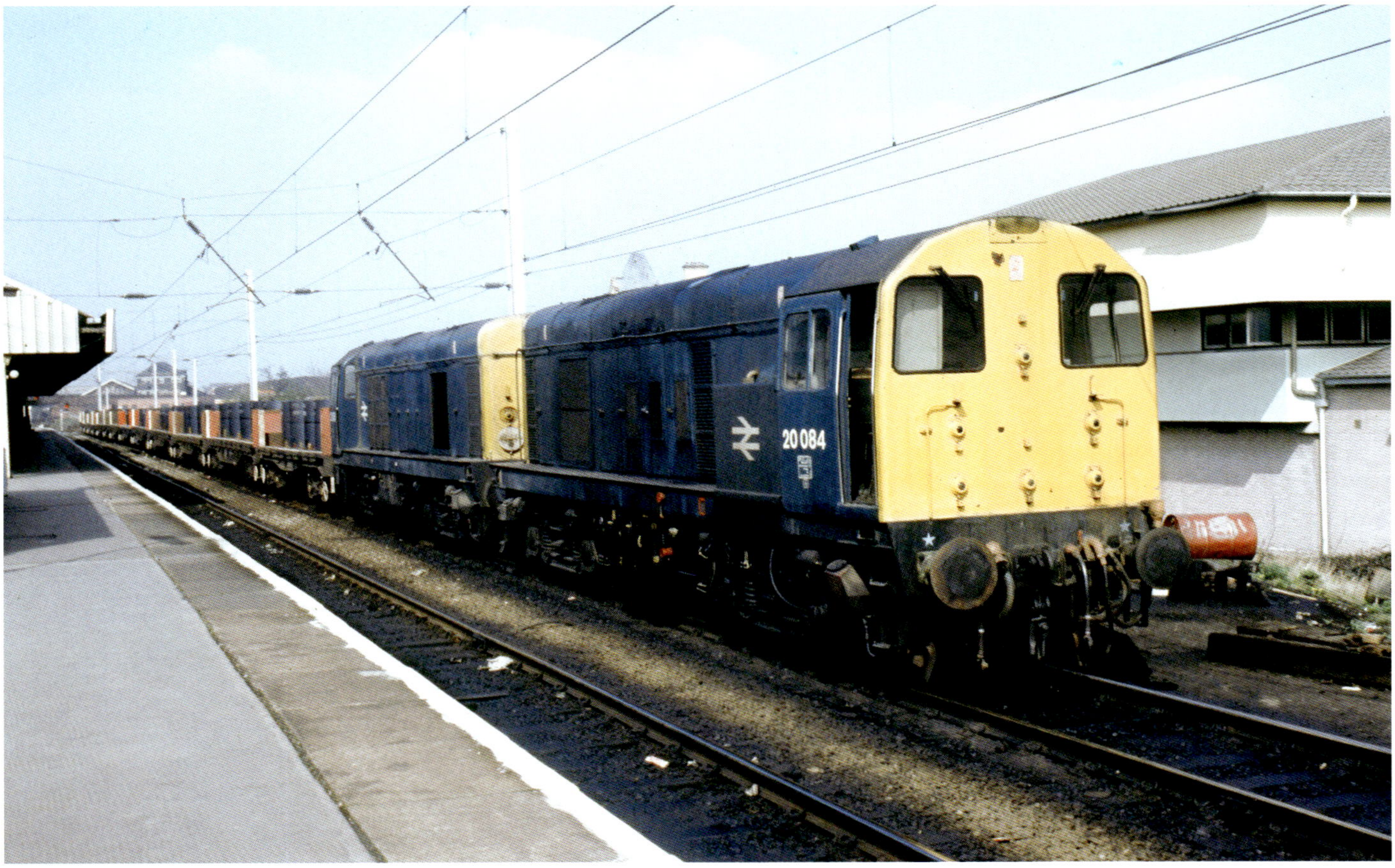

A number of the earlier batch with disc head codes which were now of course redundant, lost their discs during works visits. Another modification was to provide extended fuel tanks as on 20084 at Warrington in April 1988. ***Strathwood Library Collection***

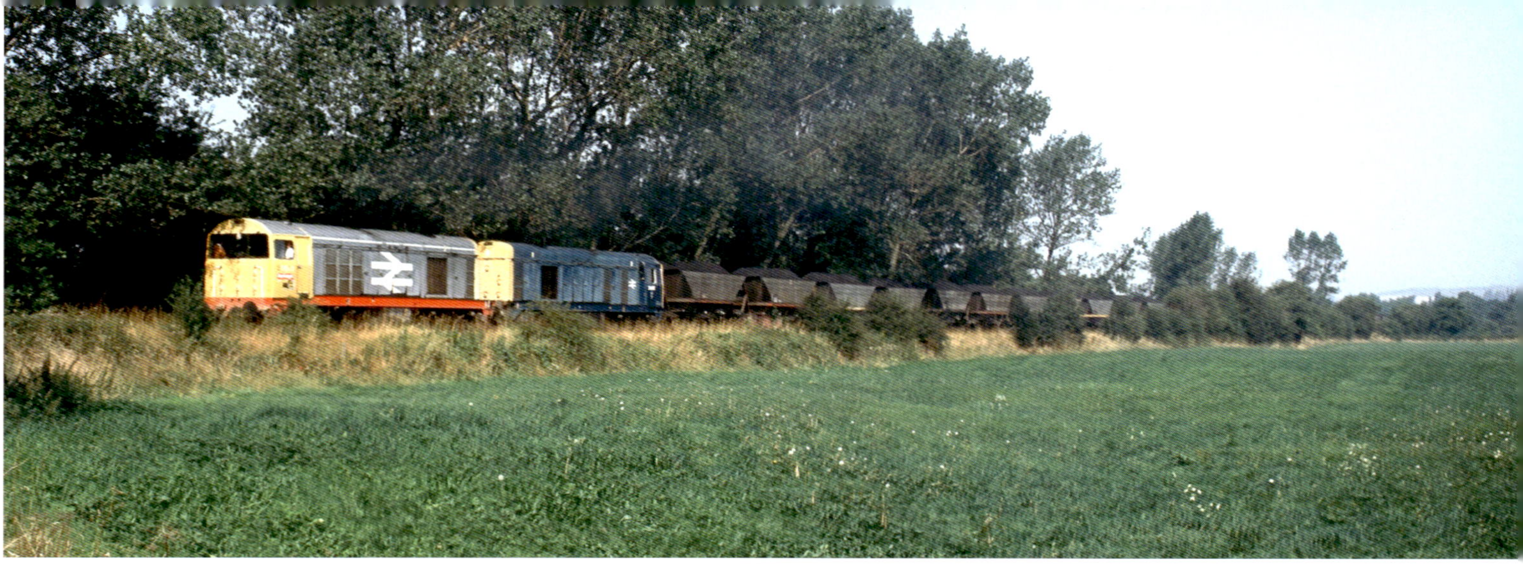

Odd livery combinations were a common enough feature of Class 20 workings from 1966 as new locomotives came into traffic in blue and were sometimes paired with earlier green locomotives. This continued beyond the blue era as some of the class gained later livery styles as here with 20010 and 20082 on a loaded MGR working at Lower Kilburn on 3 September 1991. ***Stuart Broughton***

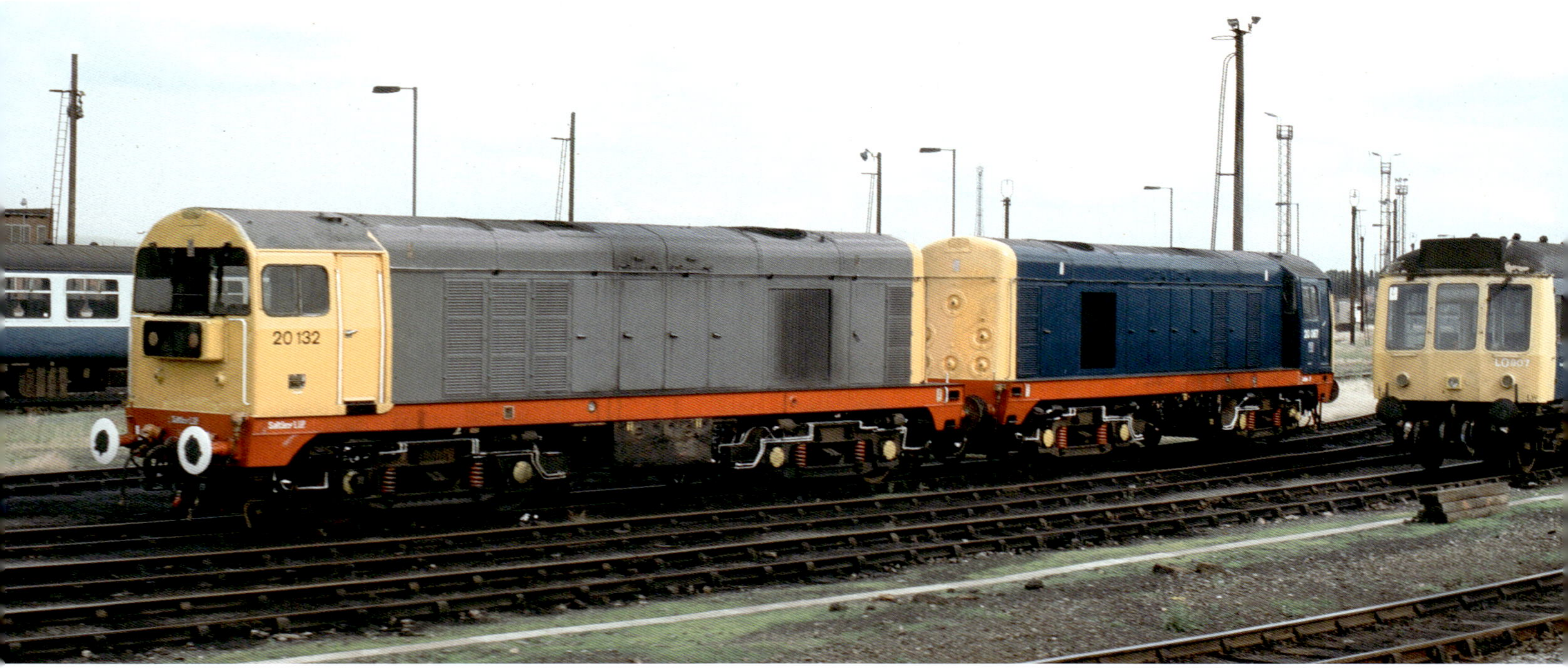

Another odd couple pairing this time at Derby on 24 August 1993 with 20132 and 20087. ***Phil Nunn***

Several of the class gained names during the last few years of their service careers. Among these was 20227 named Traction after the magazine of the same name at Doncaster Works on 10 July 1994. ***Steve Scott***

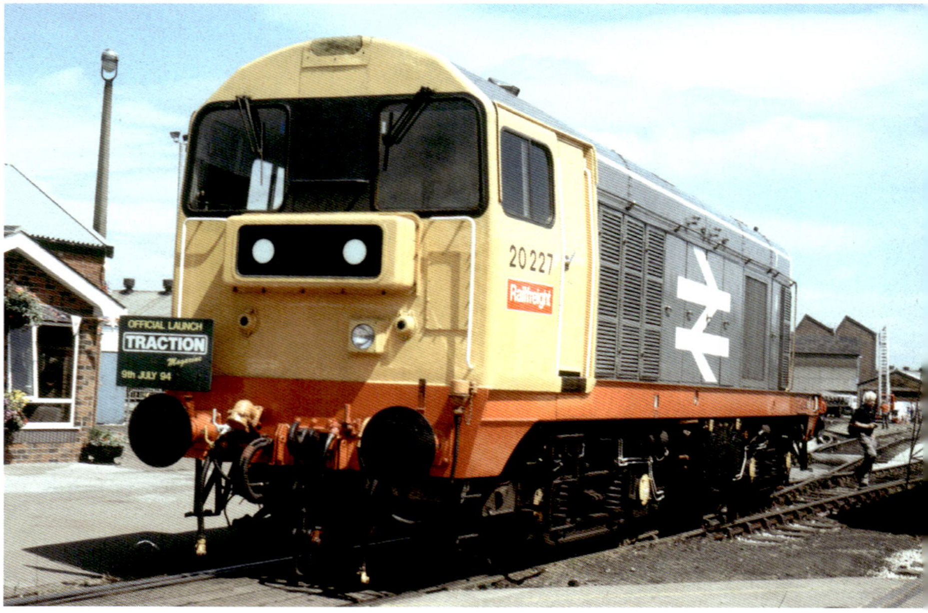

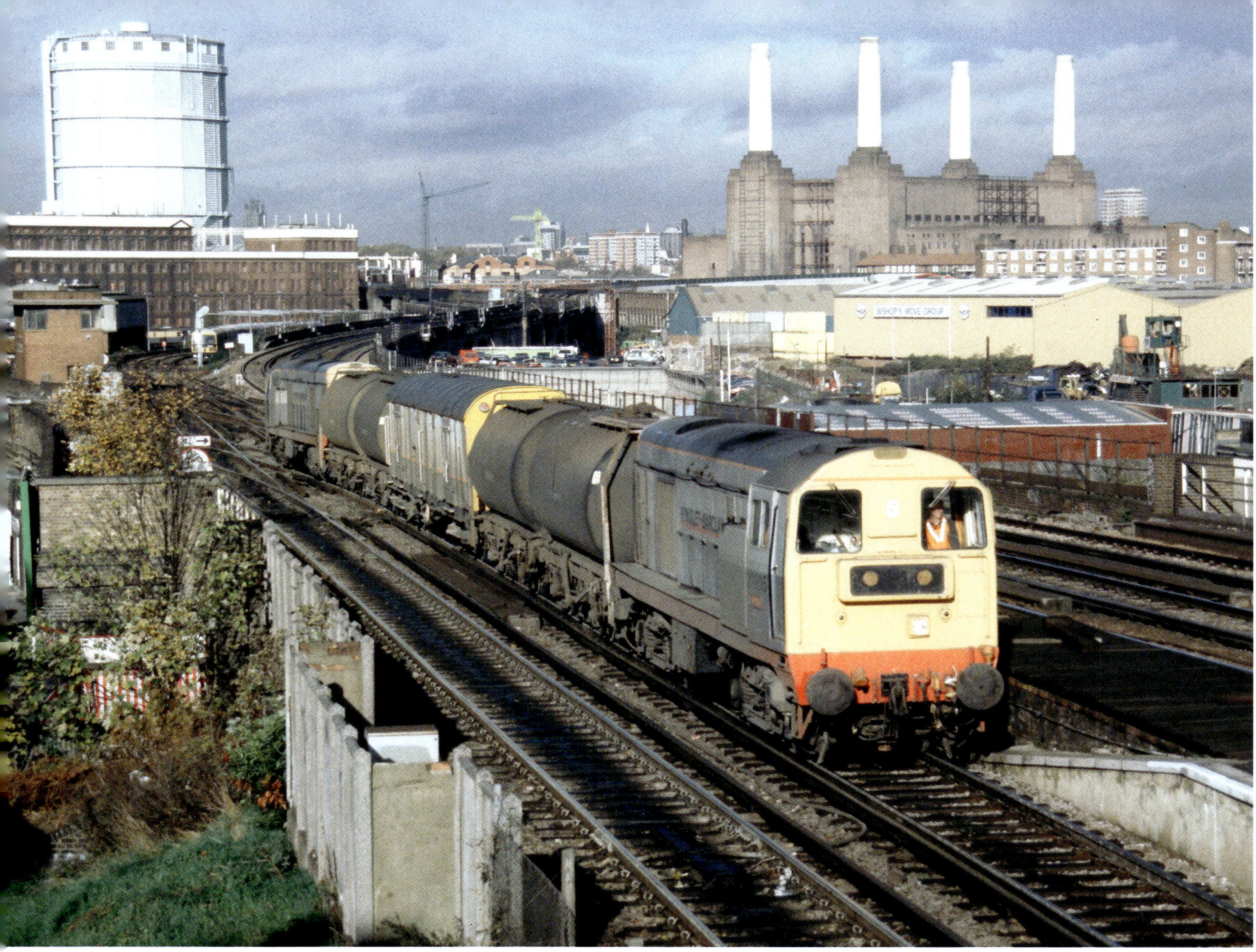

Killer Twenties 20905 and 20902 bring their short but foliage deadly train through Wandsworth Road on 15 November 1995. ***Frank Hornby***

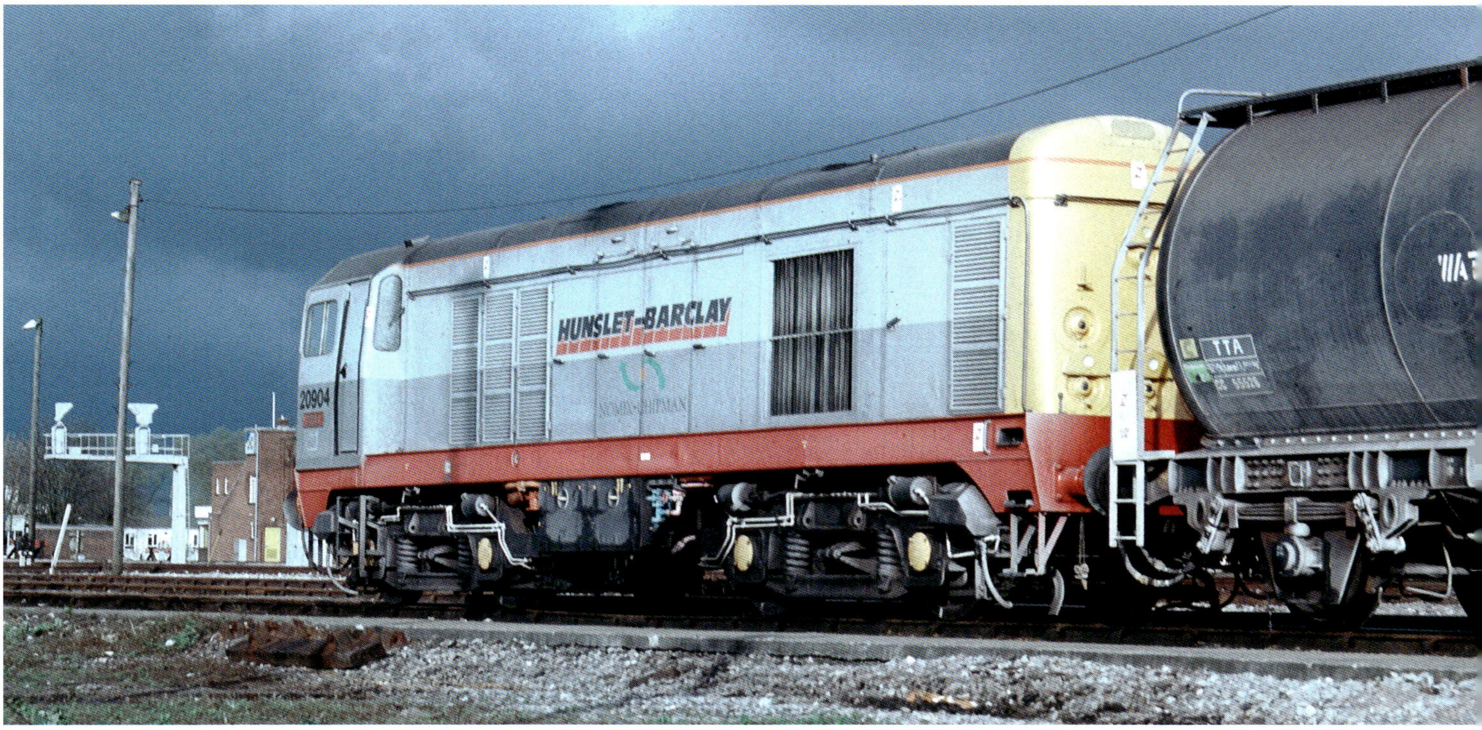

The erstwhile D8101 now as 20904 stands ready for duty under a stormy sky at Westbury on 12 April 1992. ***Alister Betts***

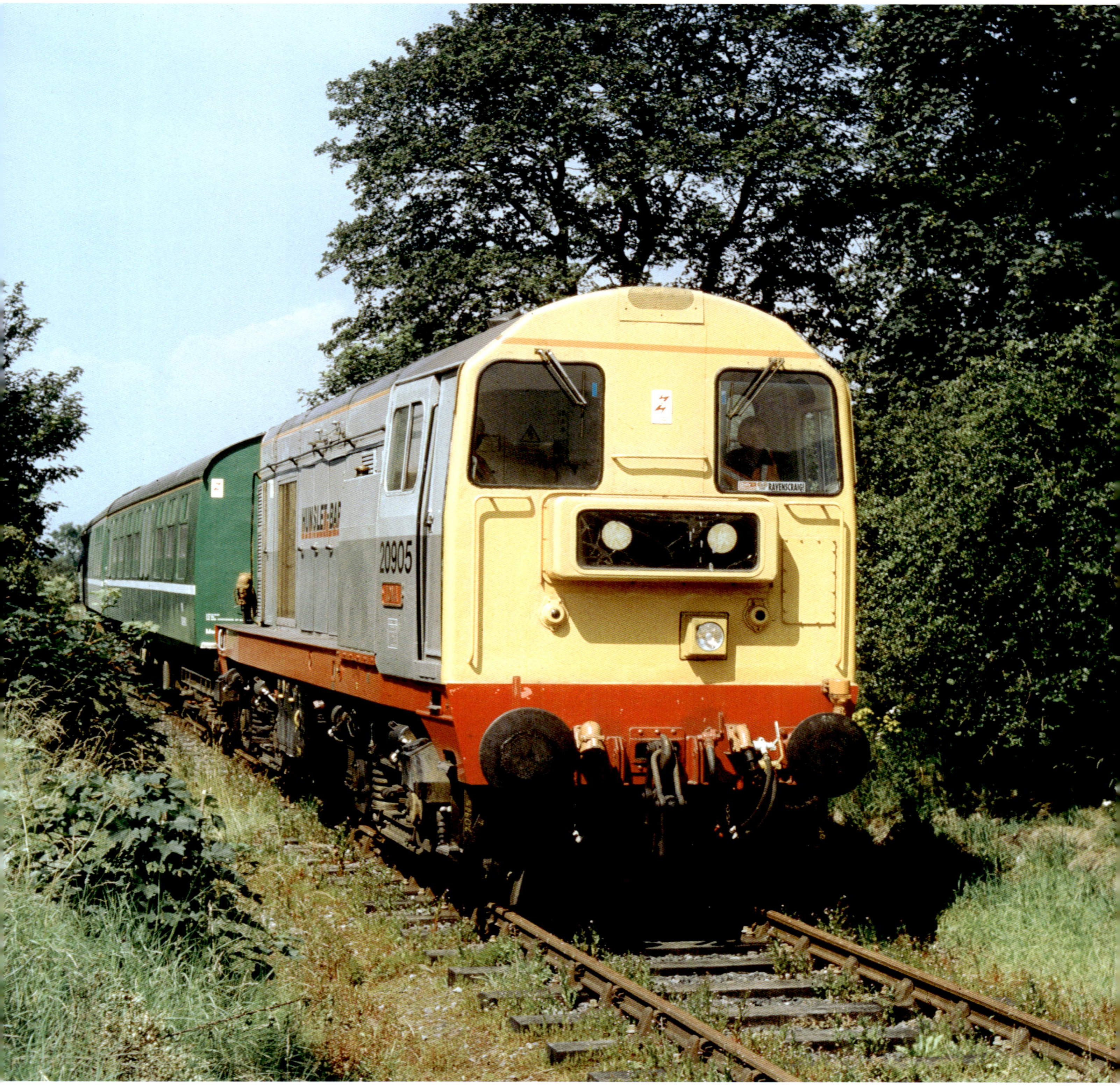

The conversion of seven locomotives was to be undertaken by Hunslet Barclay at their Kilmarnock Works during 1988 with new train wiring to allow them to work in multiple at differing ends of the train. In the event 20209 was not converted, leaving six to be renumbered into this new series. The headlights fitted to the locomotives would help with operations both on and off the trains. In this combination 20905 leads near Warcop during July 1990. ***Late Pete Walton/Sid Steadman***

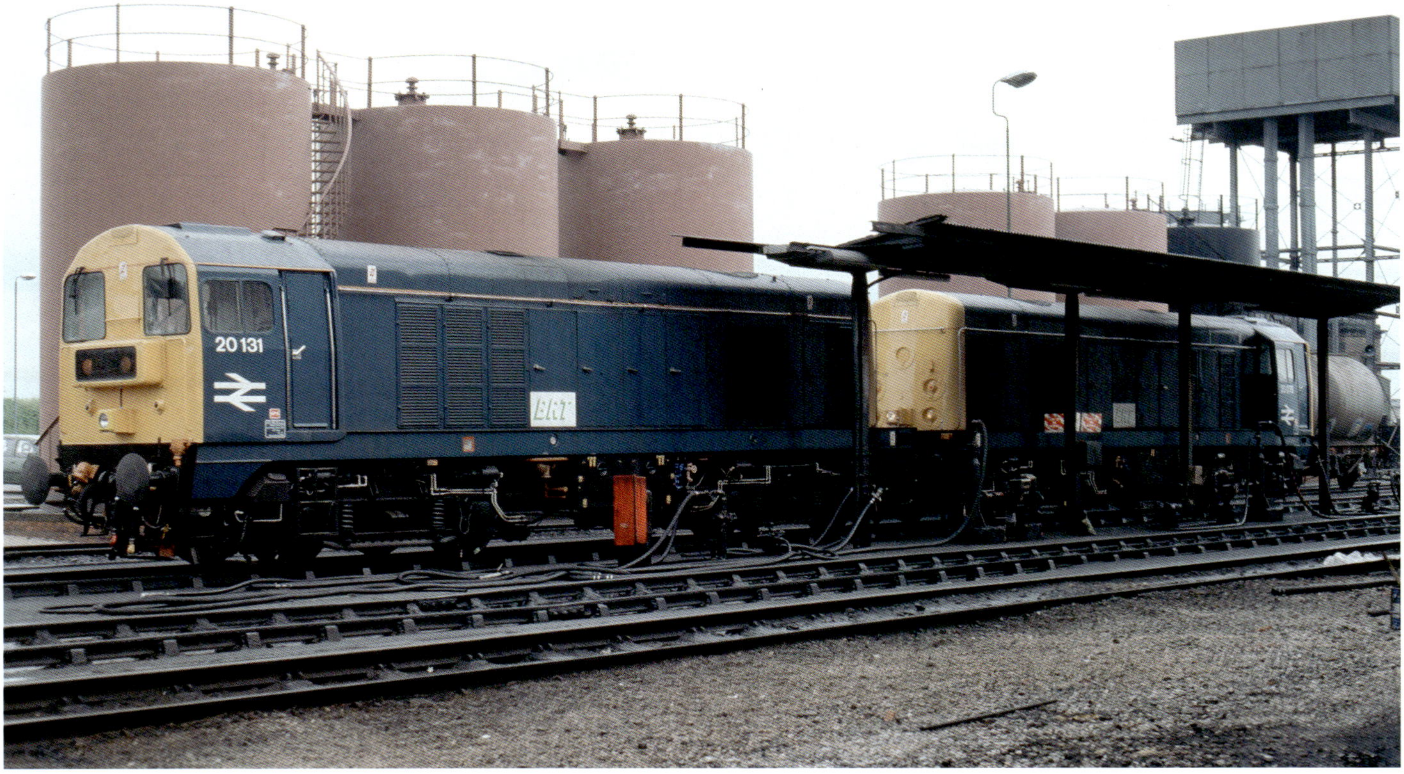

This smart duo at Toton of 20131 and 20075 on 9 July 1993 have gained the BRT branding. ***Stuart Broughton***

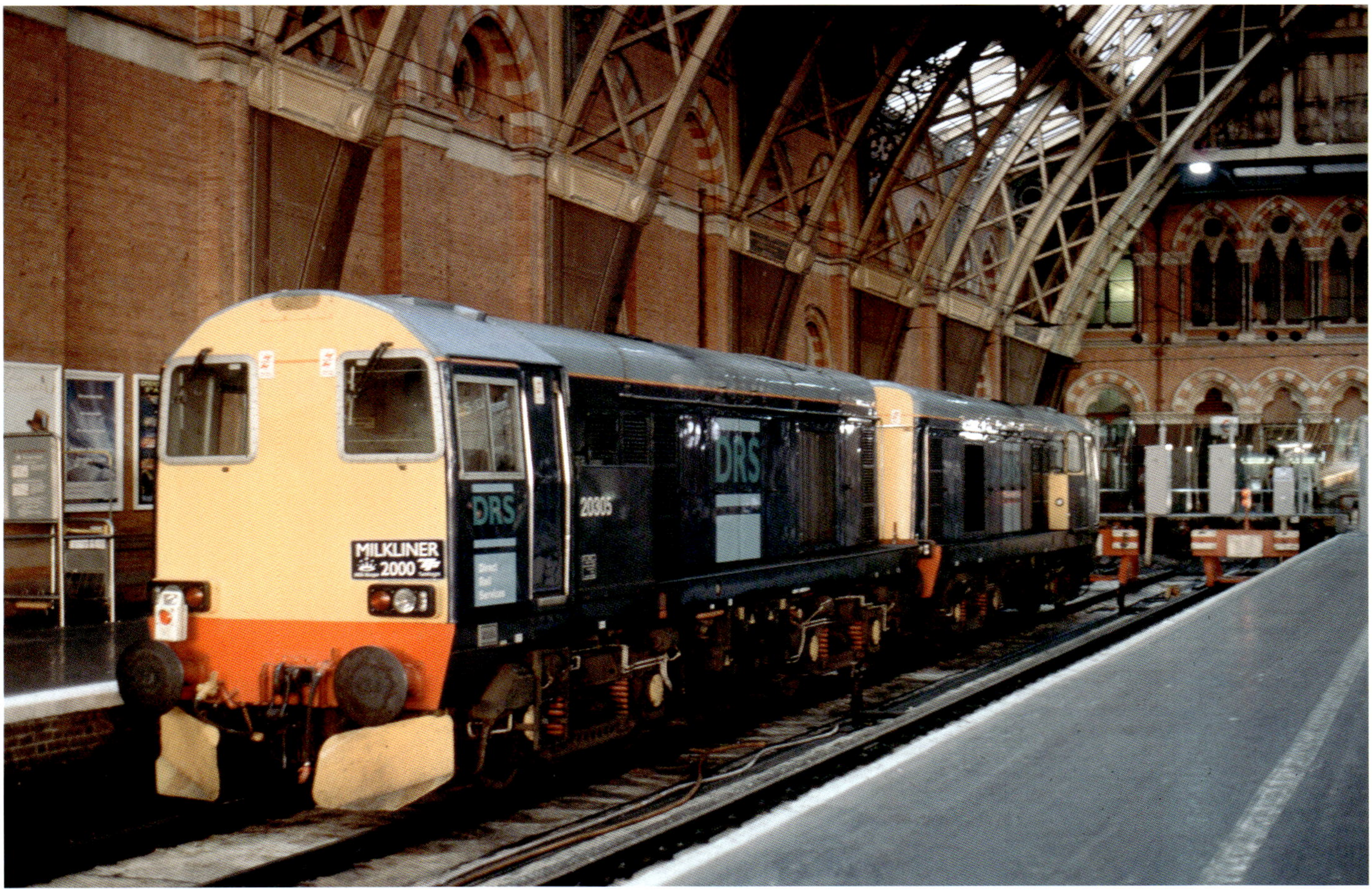

While 20305 and 20304 at St.Pancras on 16 July 1997 gained a much more extensive makeover to include a cleaning up of the fronts of the locomotives, installation of new Wipac style high intensity lamps and just in case, a full set of snow ploughs. Internally new multiple wiring systems were fitted along with extra fuel capacity being added on the foot plating along the sides. ***Phil Nunn***

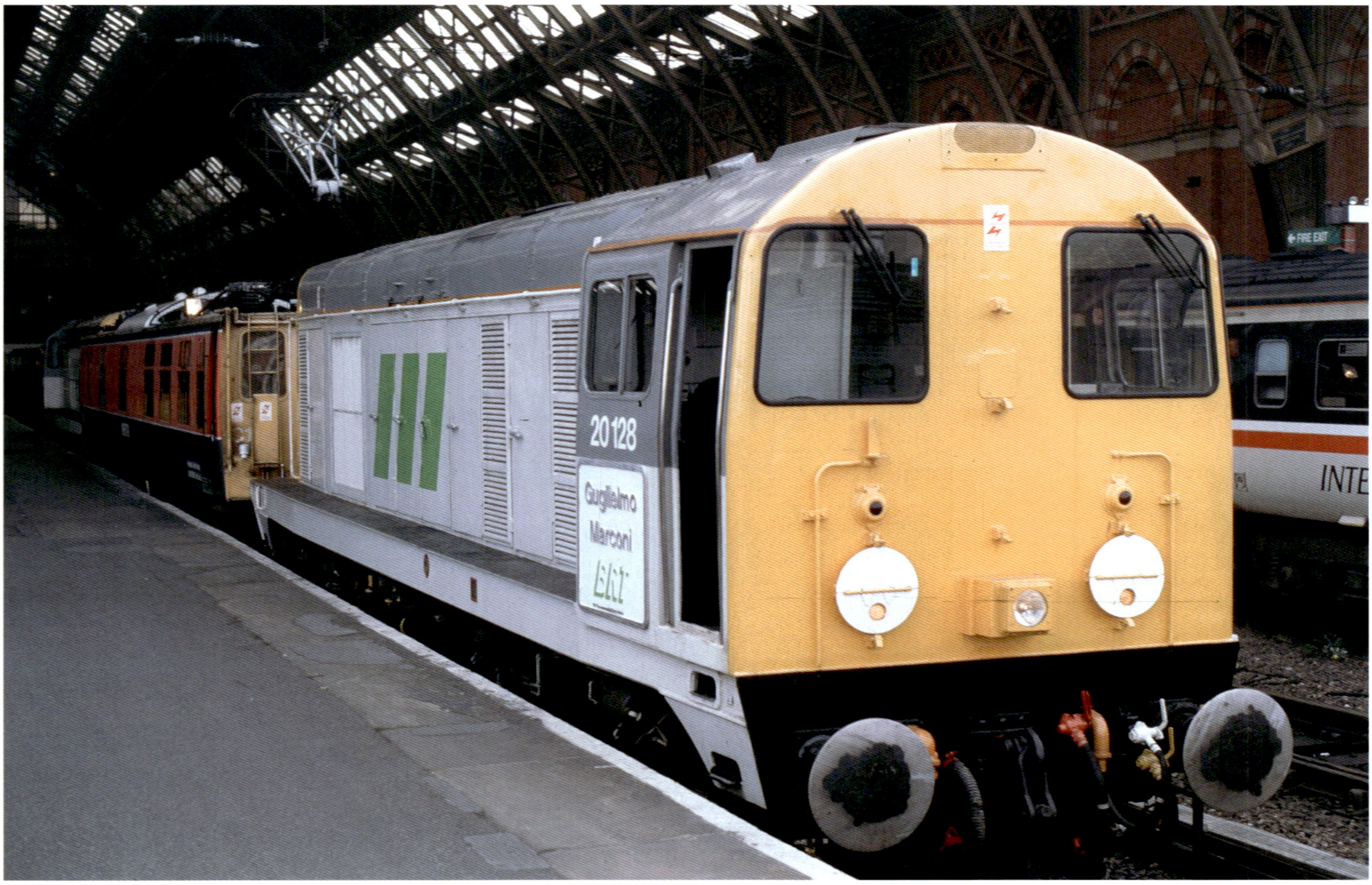

Although BRT acquired thirteen Class 20s they only overhauled four locomotives. Among the fortunate examples was 20128 now in the companies new livery at St. Pancras on 22 May 1995. ***Phil Nunn***

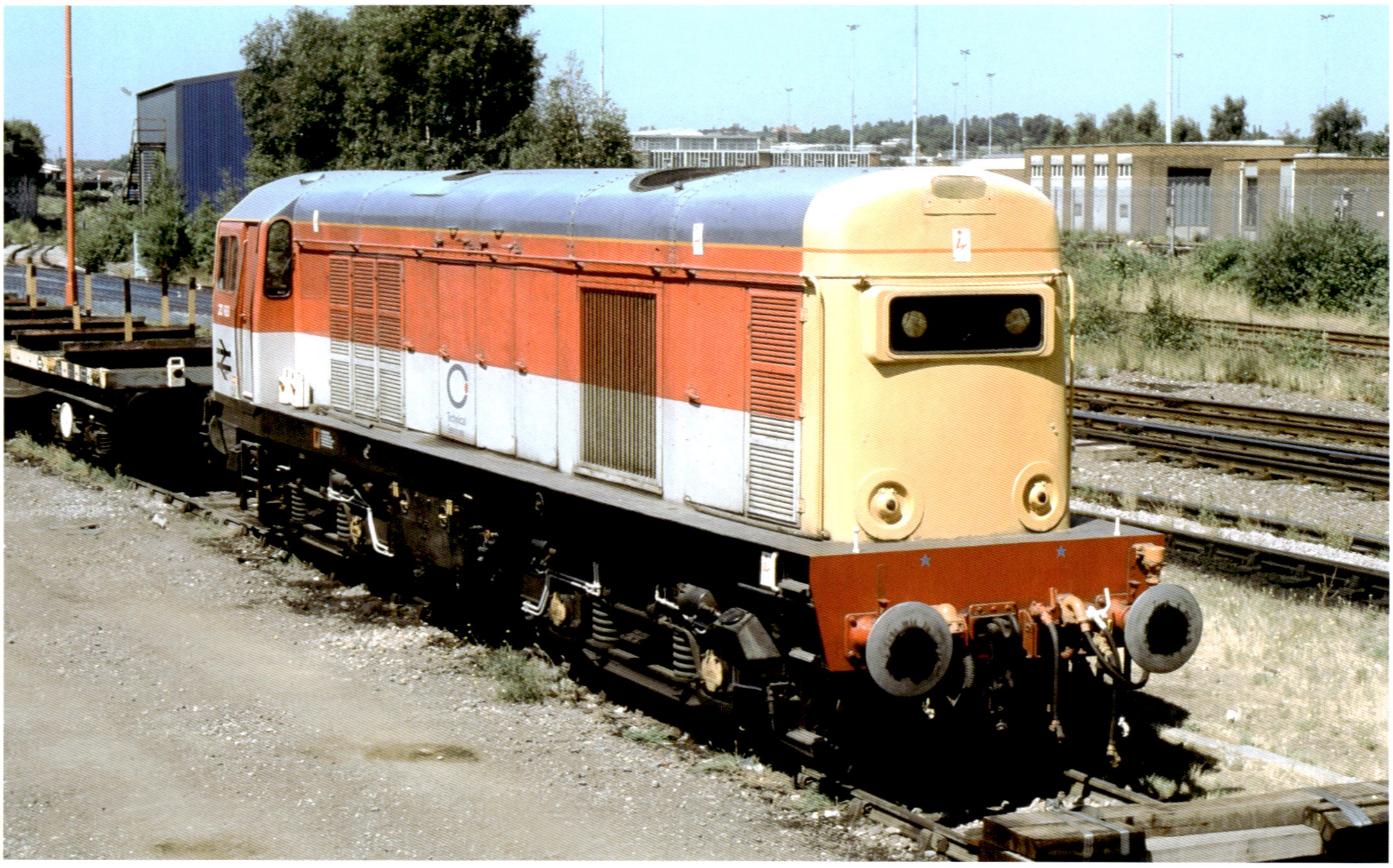

Central Services saw a bargain and picked up two locomotives 20092 and 20169 seen here at Neasden in August 1995, although their use for test train working was short lived. ***Strathwood Library Collection***

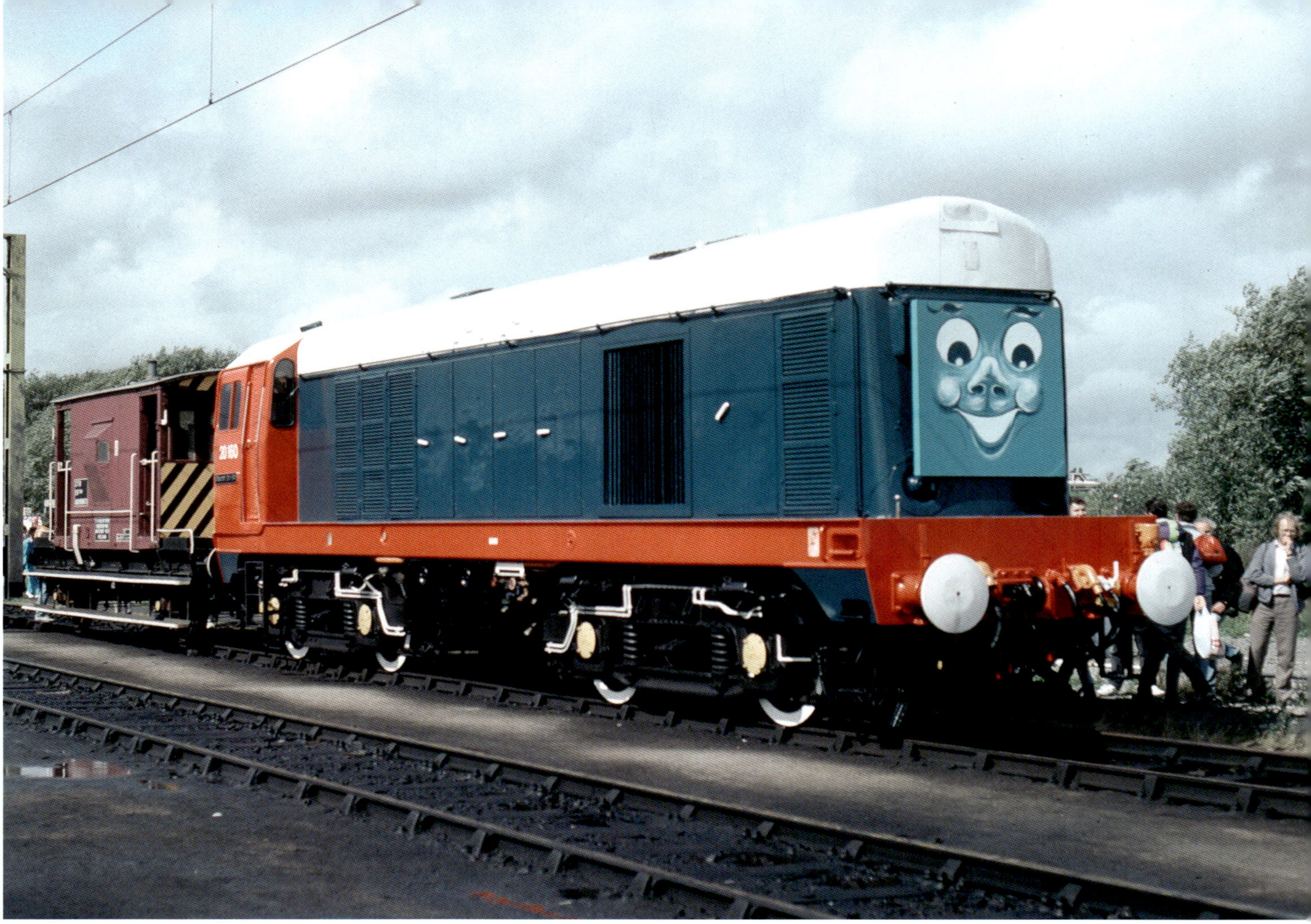

Although other livery variants and differences are beyond the scope of this volume we had to include 20160 at Bescot on their Open Day on 30 August 1992. ***David T Williams***

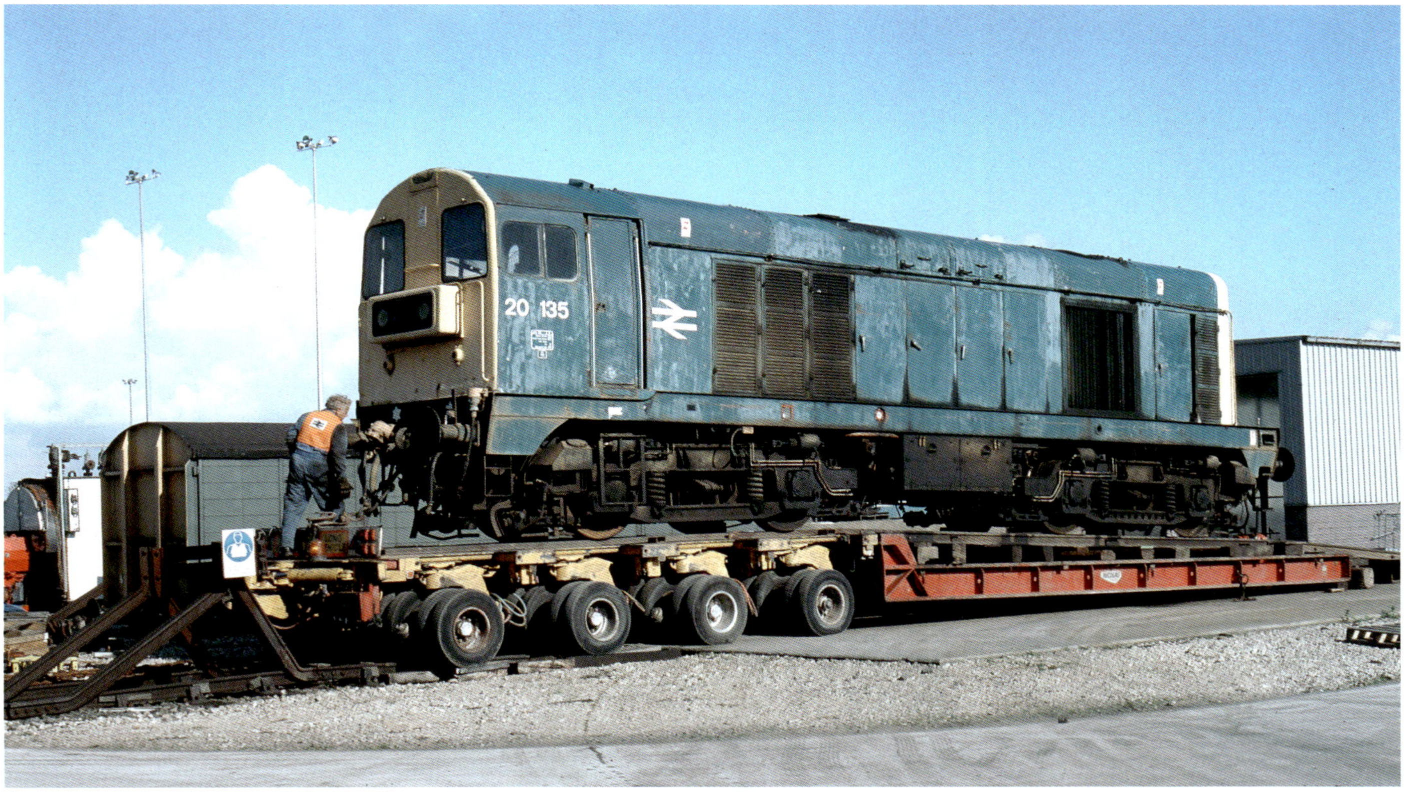

Prospects were considered to be bright for 20135 at Toton being loaded onto a low loader for a journey to the Great Central Railway at Ruddington in June 1994. However twelve years later things did not work out and the locomotive was dismantled at the MoD premises at Caerwent in July 2004. ***Stuart Broughton***

Growlers Galore

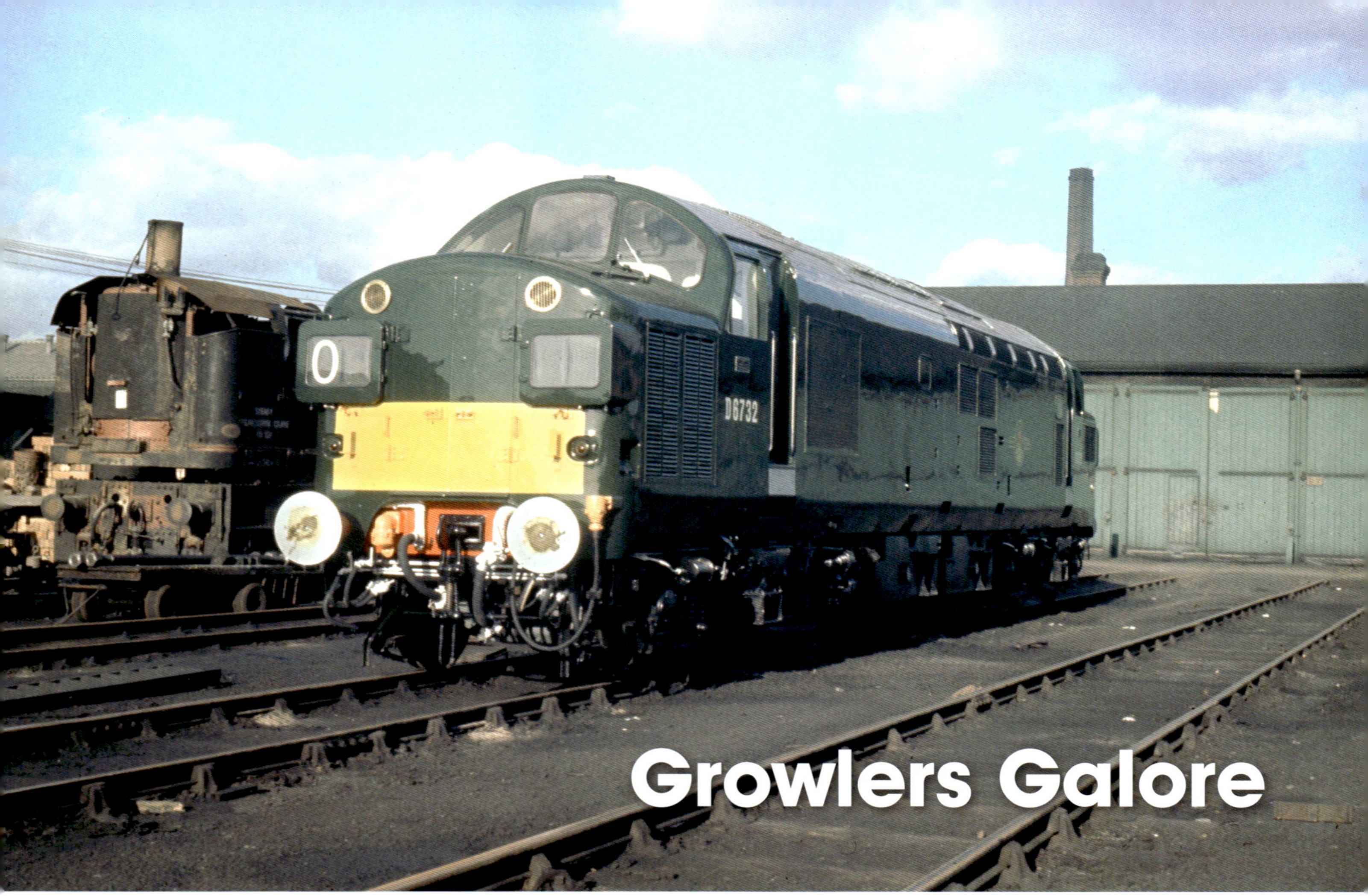

Fresh from the Vulcan Foundry at Newton le Willows was Type 3 Co-Co D6732 at Doncaster in February 1962. On 9 March 1962 it would be allocated to 50B Hull Dairycoates to begin work from the mouth of the Humber. ***Strathwood Library Collection***

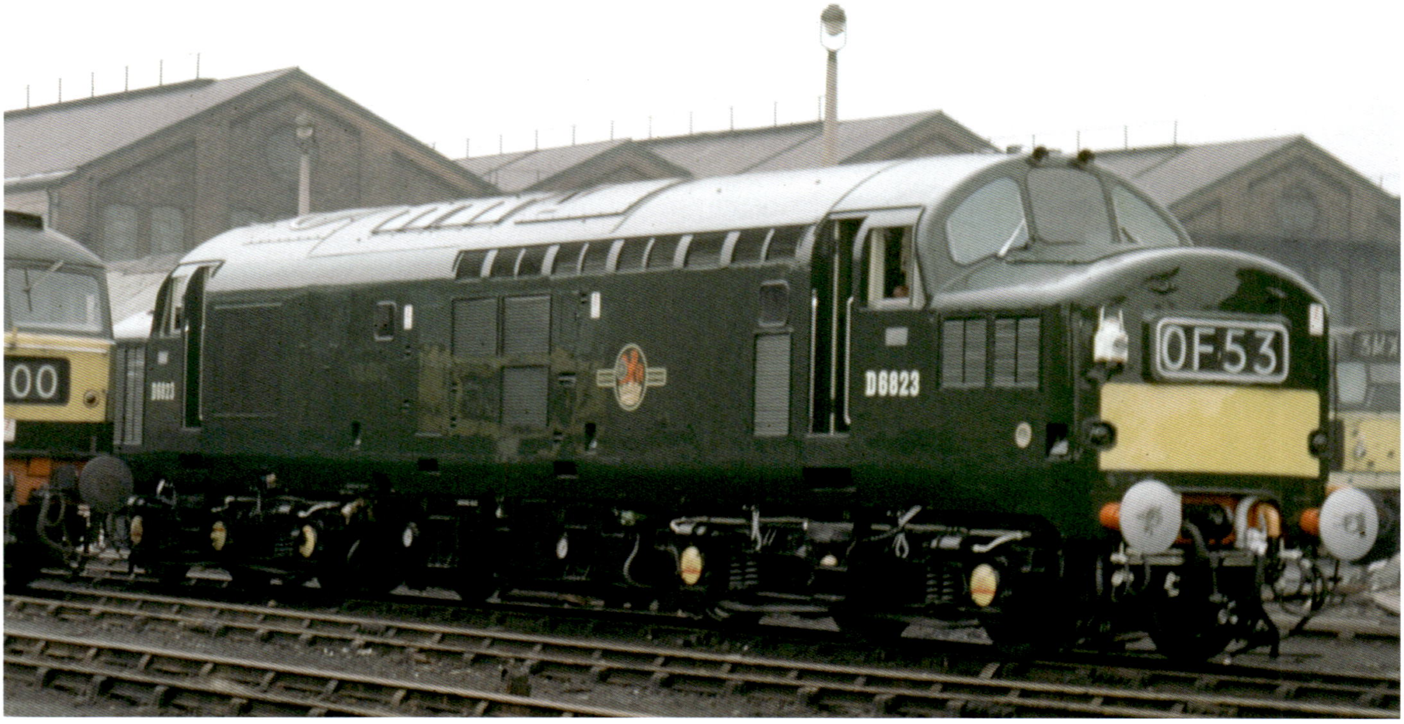

Deliveries would take until January 1966, therefore the early sixties would see many opportunities for scenes such as the arrival of D6823 at Doncaster Works. This example was one of several batches built at the English Electric plant at Darlington, formally the premises of Robert Stephenson & Hawthorn. This engine would be sent on from Doncaster in April 1963 to take up duties from 88A as it was then, Cardiff Canton. ***Frank Hornby***

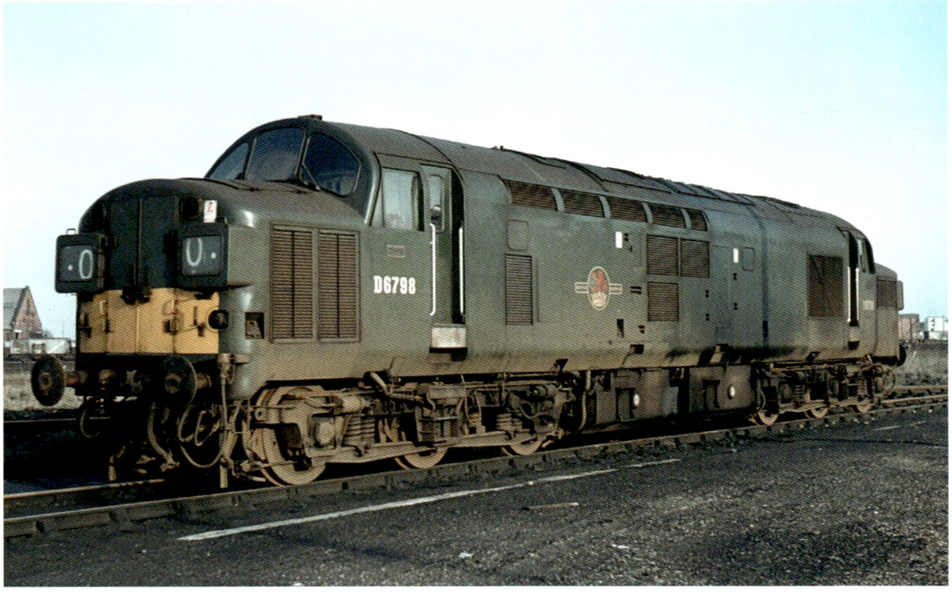

Three years into its service career was D6798 stabled at March on 24 January 1965. ***Eric Sawford/ Stewart Blencowe Collection***

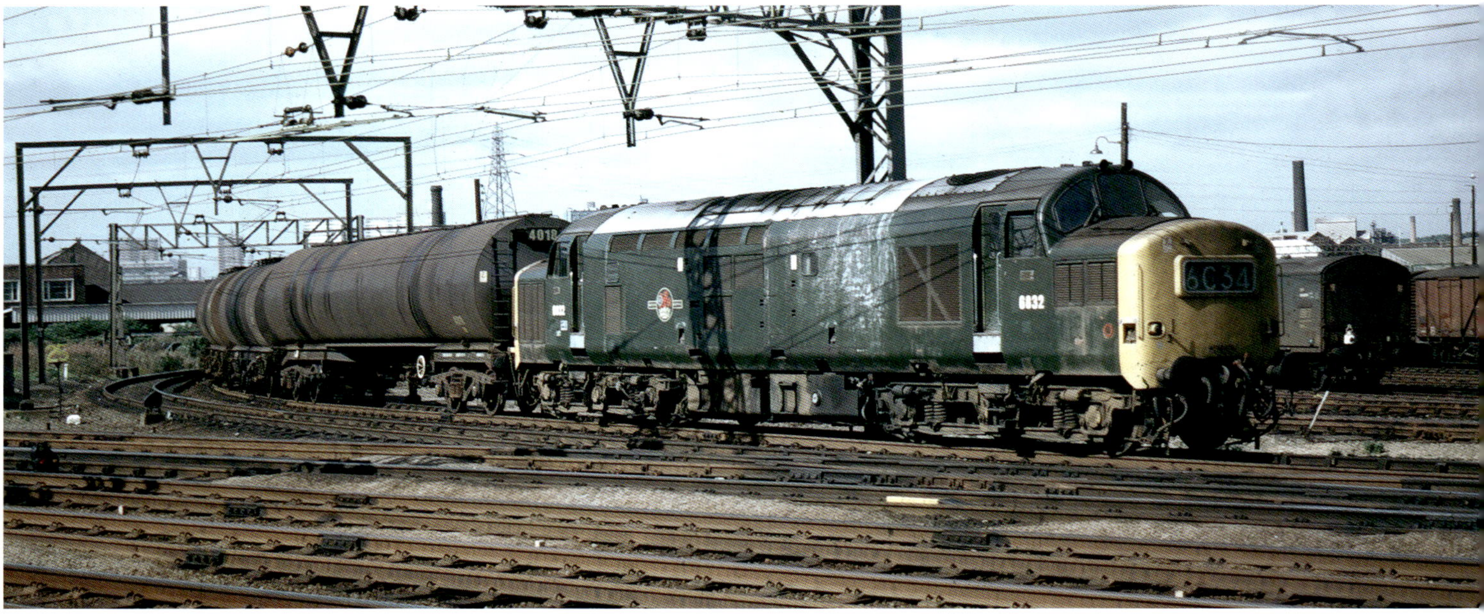

Many of the class would gain full yellow fronts before being repainted into blue. One such example was D6832 at Stratford on 28 August 1971, albeit creating a very shabby image to the general public. ***Frank Hornby***

Much smarter in appearance was D6800 at Wath on 24 August two years previously in 1969. ***Frank Hornby***

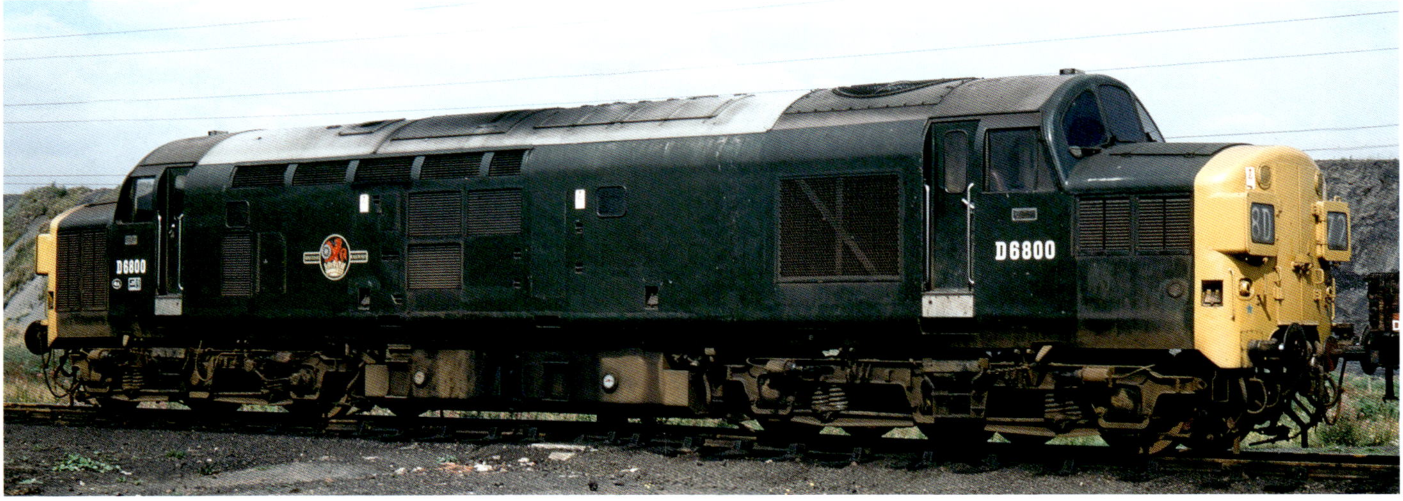

All except D6983 which was destroyed when just seven months old in a smash with D1671 Thor, itself almost new in 1965 at Bridgend, the entire class would succumb to blue at some point. Among these was 6987 running light at West Ealing on 29 August 1973. ***Frank Hornby***

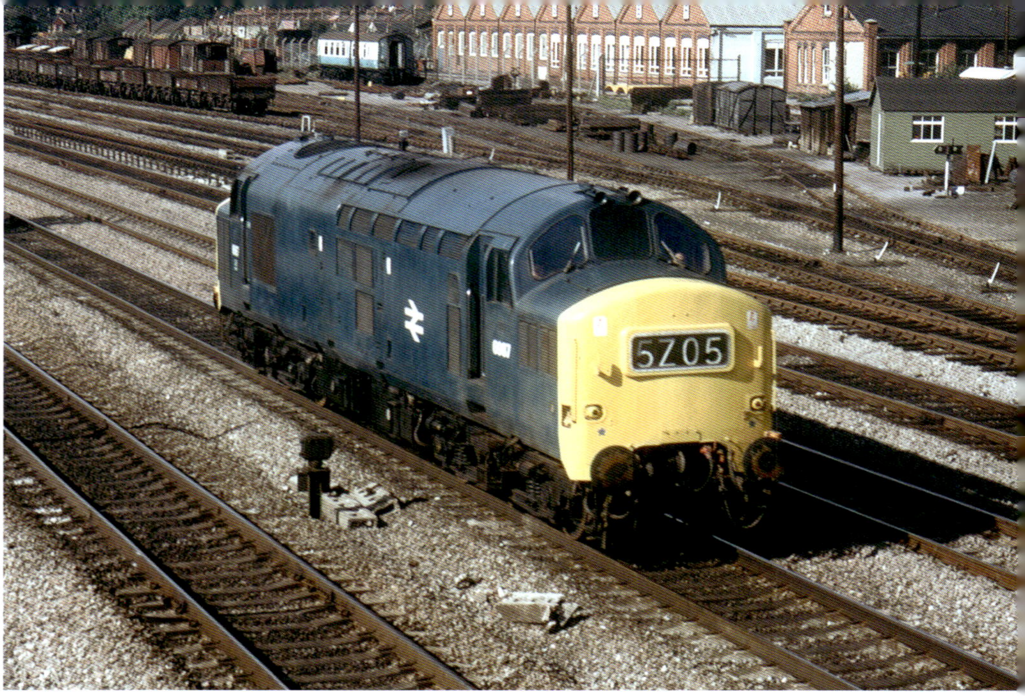

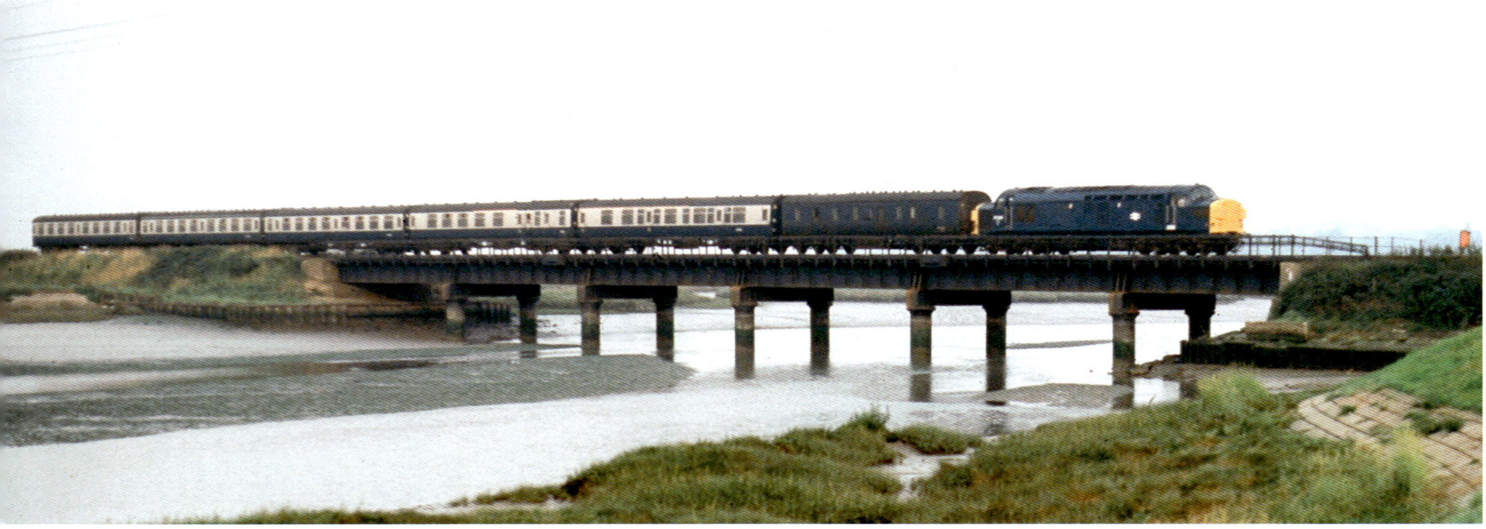

The corporate Inter City scheme is personified by 37036 at Manningtree with the 16.42 Peterborough to Harwich and Parkeston Quay on 4 August 1981. ***Colin Whitbread***

The draughts through the defunct connecting doors would not be pleasant on days such as this on board 37109 at Ipswich. ***Martyn R Hunt***

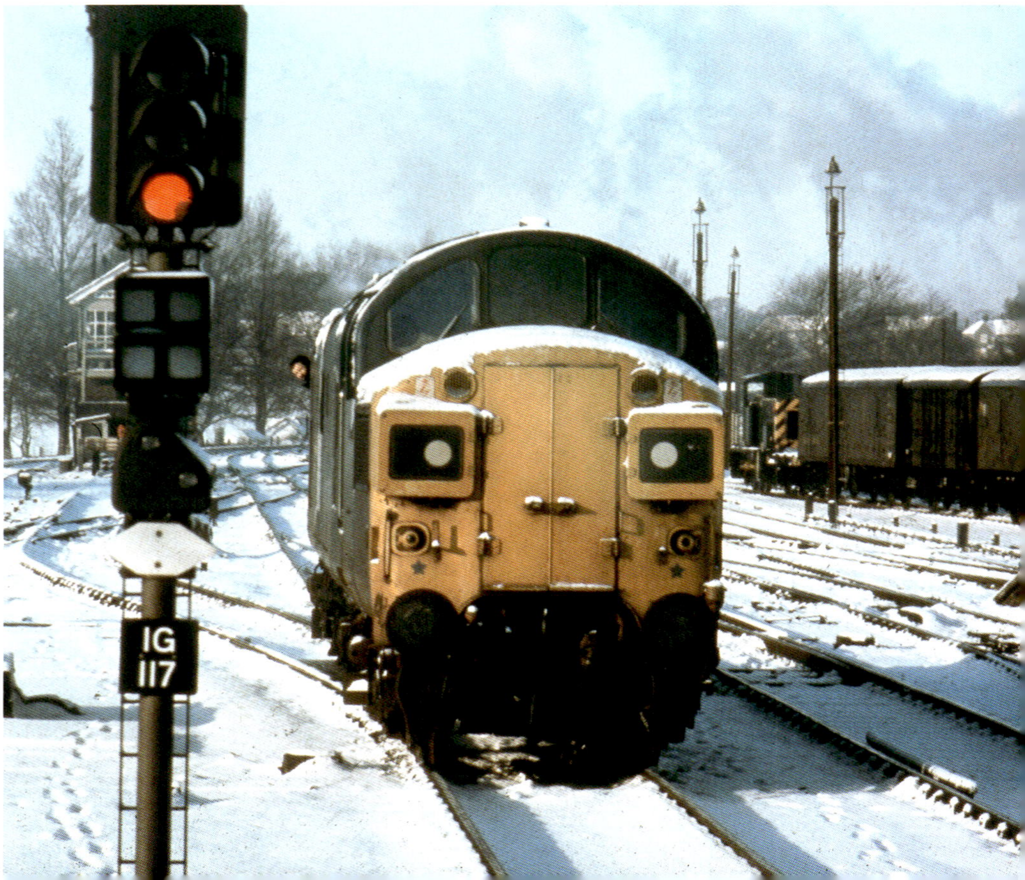

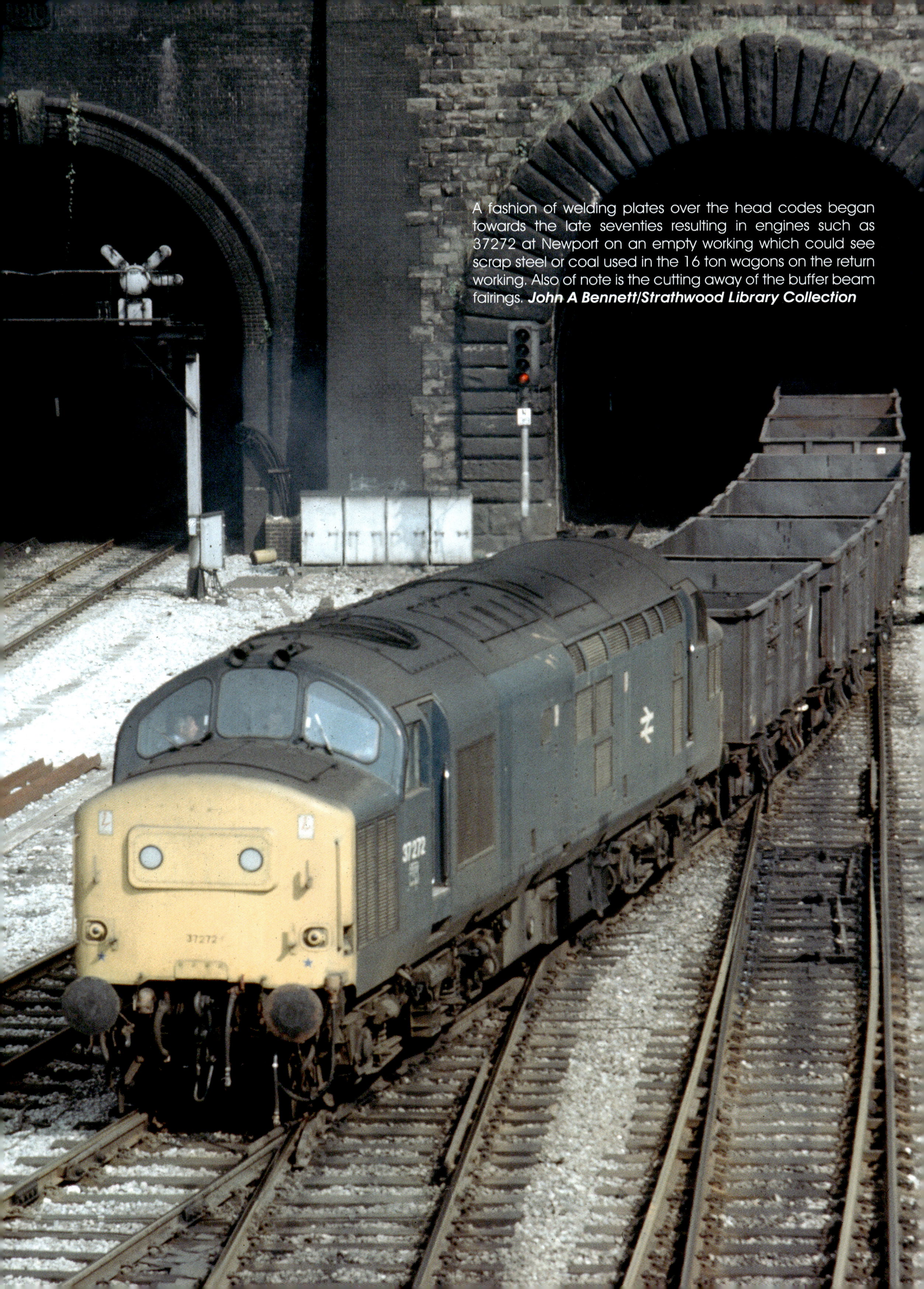

A fashion of welding plates over the head codes began towards the late seventies resulting in engines such as 37272 at Newport on an empty working which could see scrap steel or coal used in the 16 ton wagons on the return working. Also of note is the cutting away of the buffer beam fairings. ***John A Bennett/Strathwood Library Collection***

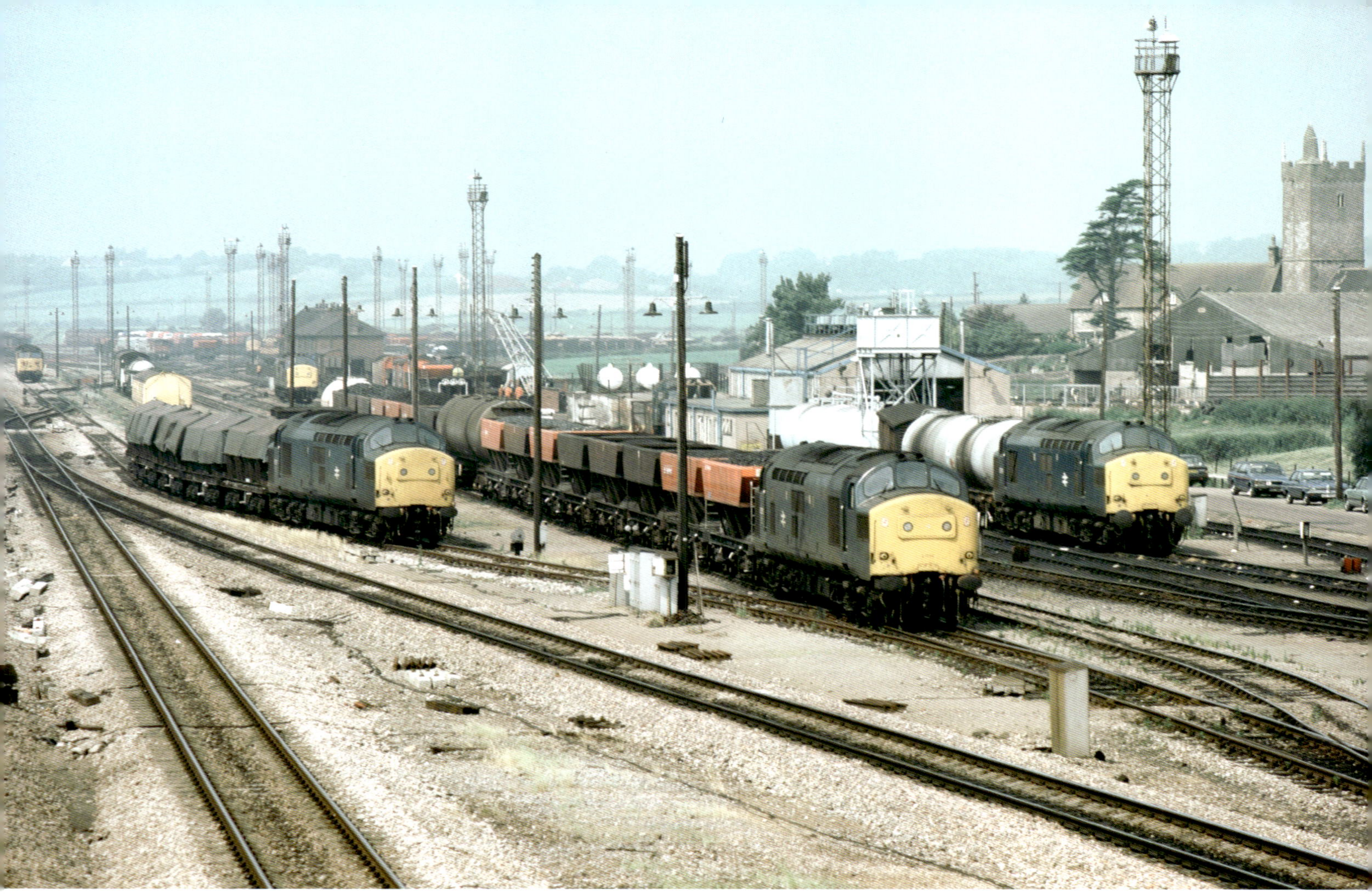

Among a gaggle of Growlers at Severn Tunnel Junction in July 1986, 37205 would be the first to get away with a Speed Freight working, in July 1986. ***David T Williams***

Below: Double heading is the order of the day for this duty at Greenholme for 37102 and 37266 most likely to keep to time on the inclines, and so as not to hold up the faster electric services on 25 June 1985. ***Sid Steadman***

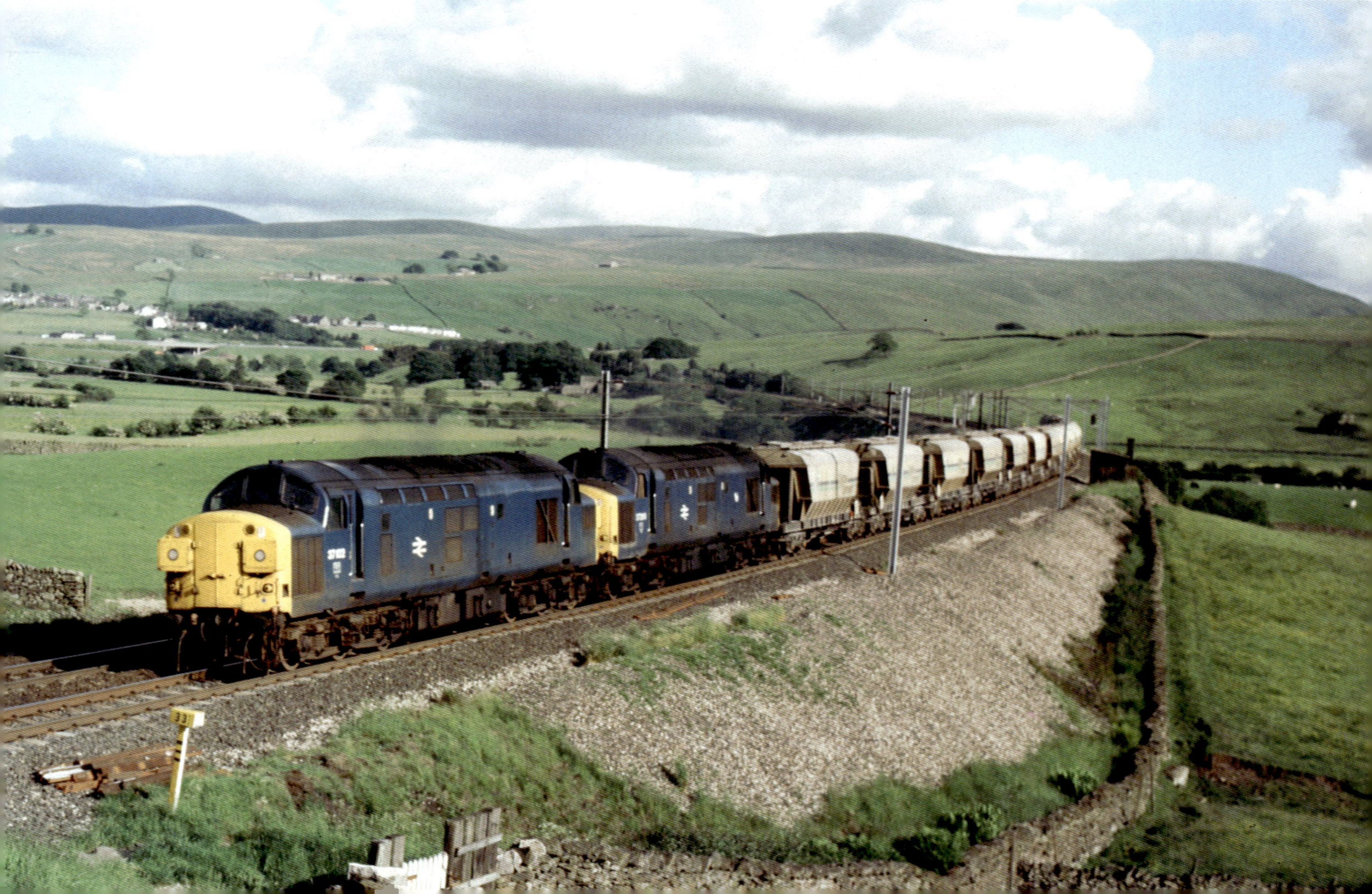

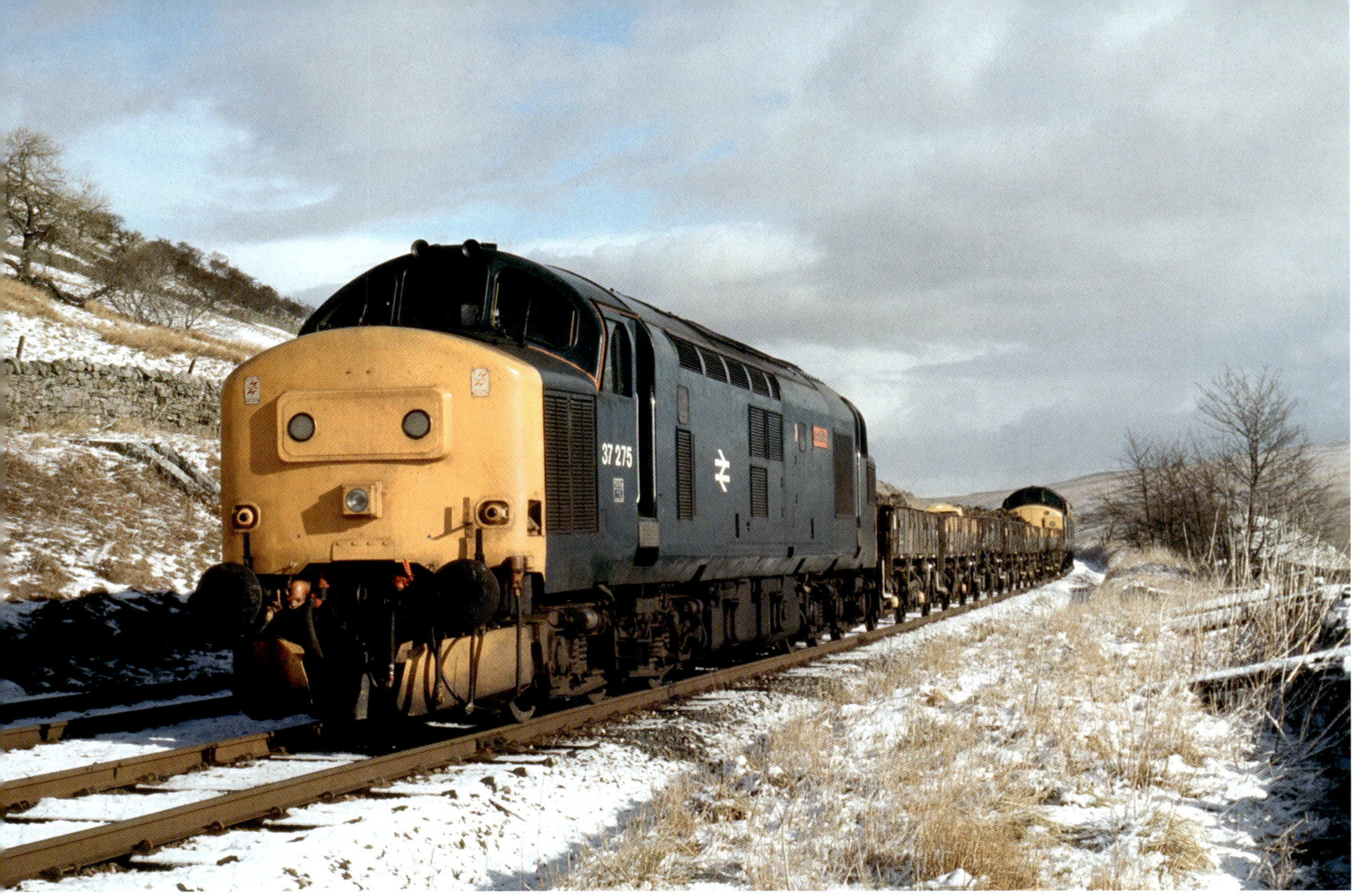

Armed with a high intensity headlamp now 37275 waits near Kirkby Stephen with a special ballast working after a landslip at Mallerstang in 1994 with another classmate top and tailing. ***Late Pete Walton/Sid Steadman***

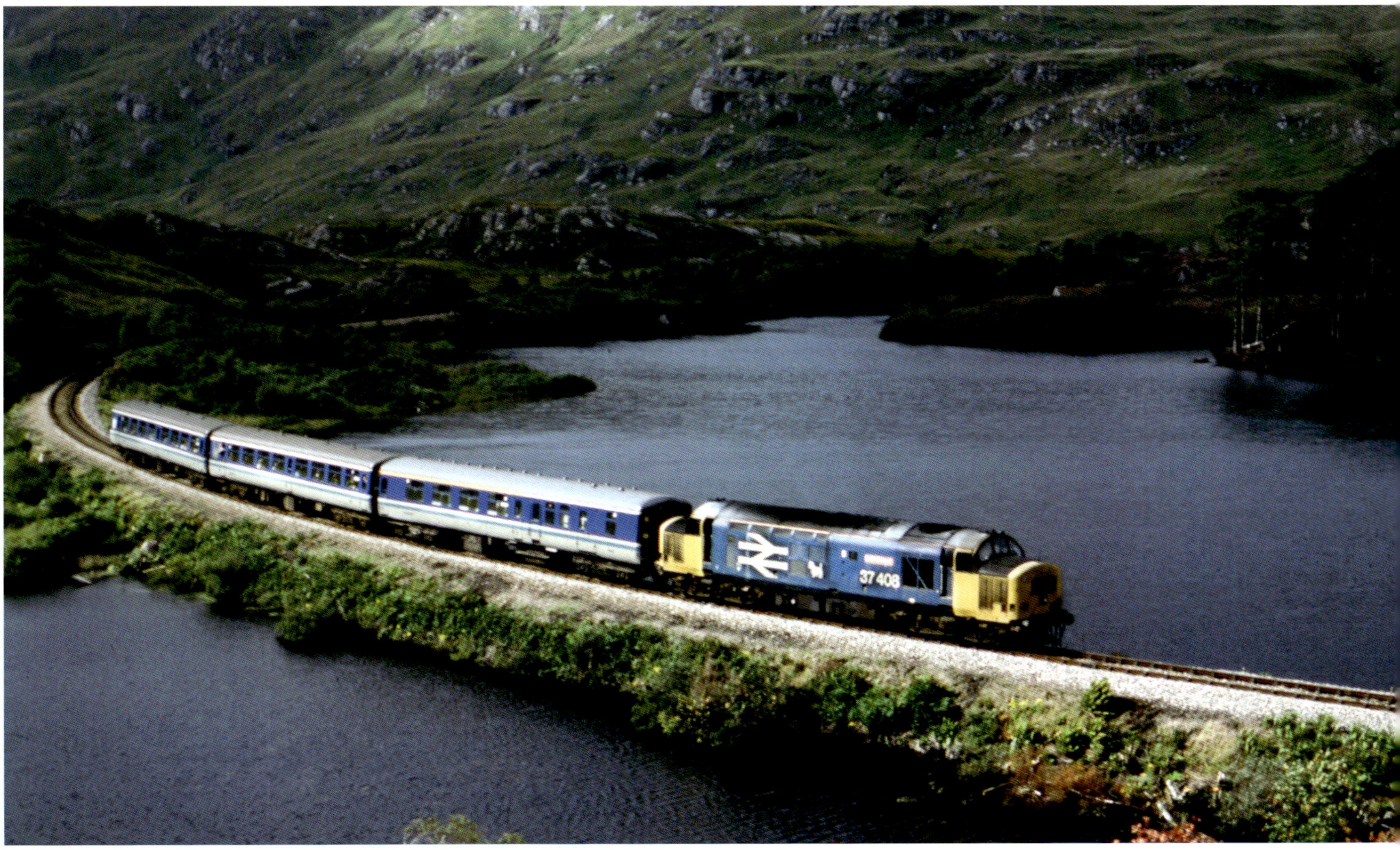

The scenery and the sounds of Class 37s working through the Scottish Glens would attract many enthusiasts after the class had displaced the Class 26s and 27s. Dressed with a Scottie Dog motif, 37408 eases past Loch Eilt with a Mallaig to Fort William working on 25 August during 1992. ***Michael Szlzeblewski***

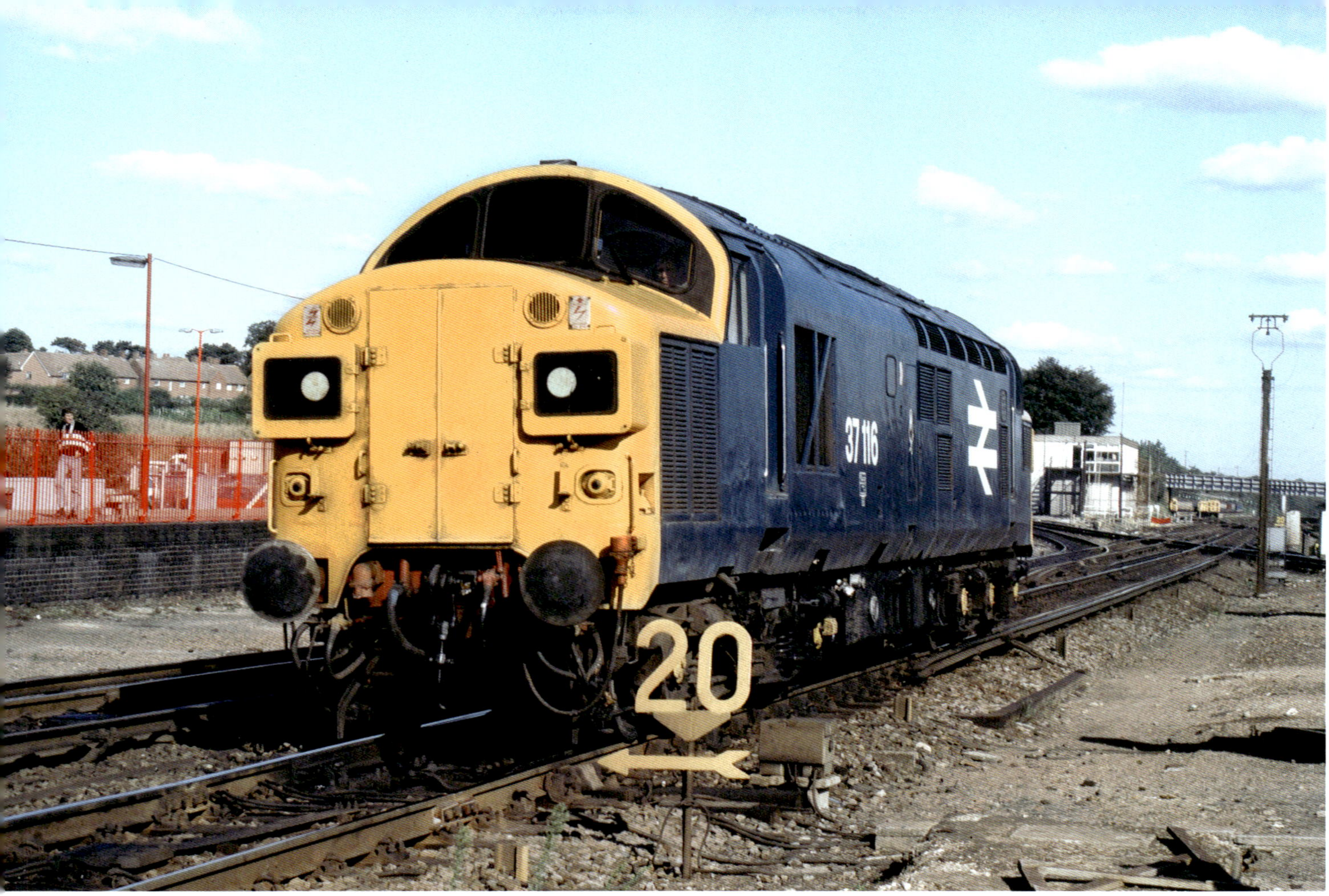

The painting of some of the yellow scheme on the top the front bonnet of 37116 at Basingstoke on 26 September 1987 would be short-lived due to perceived sun reflection problems for engine crews. ***Ian Hampton***

Exhibited at Crewe during an Open Day in 1987 was 37068 almost ready for a return to traffic in RailFreight livery, now with connecting doors welded shut, headcode boxes sealed and the cowlings around the buffer beams cut away as part of the refurbishment programme of the time. ***David T Williams***

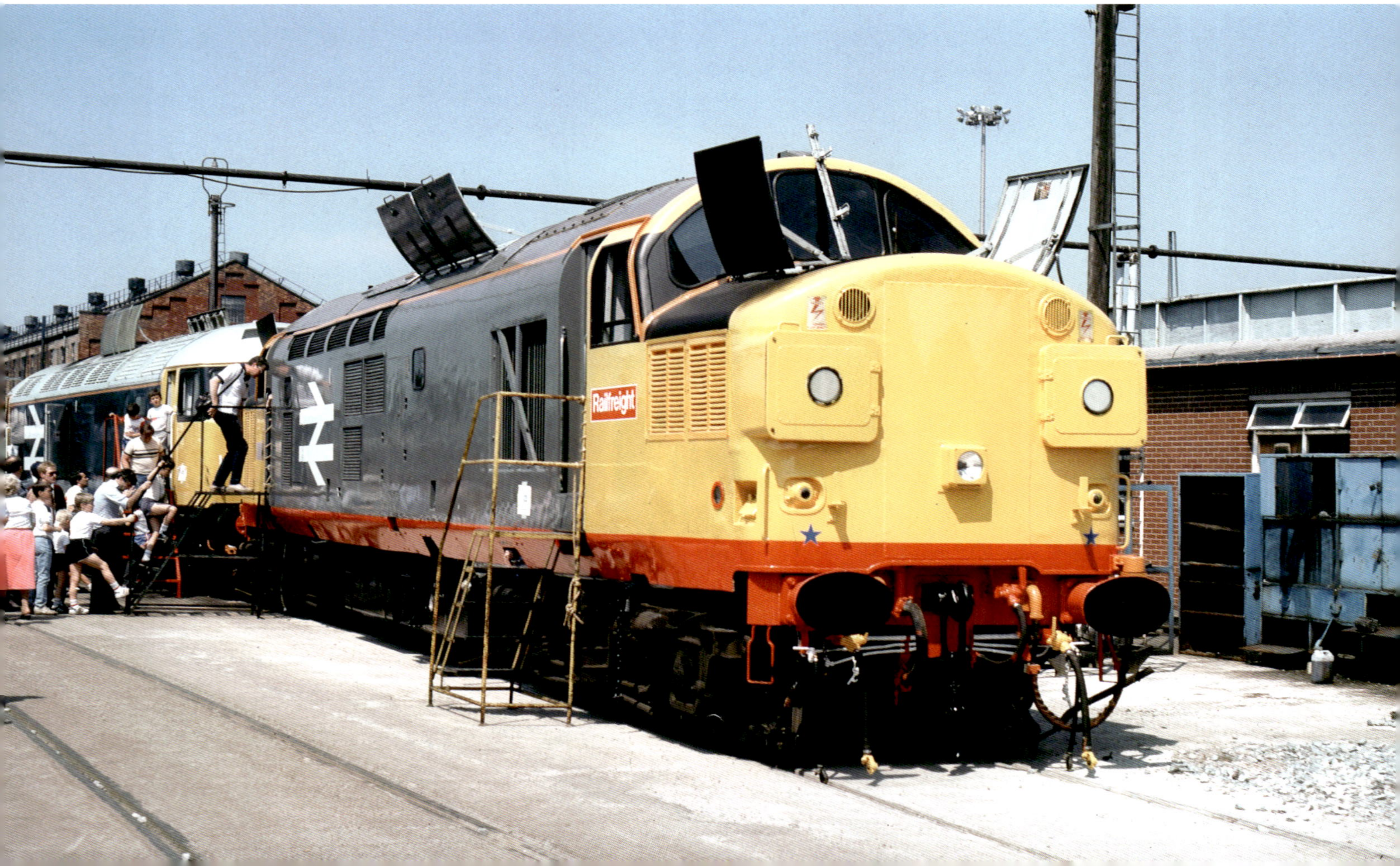

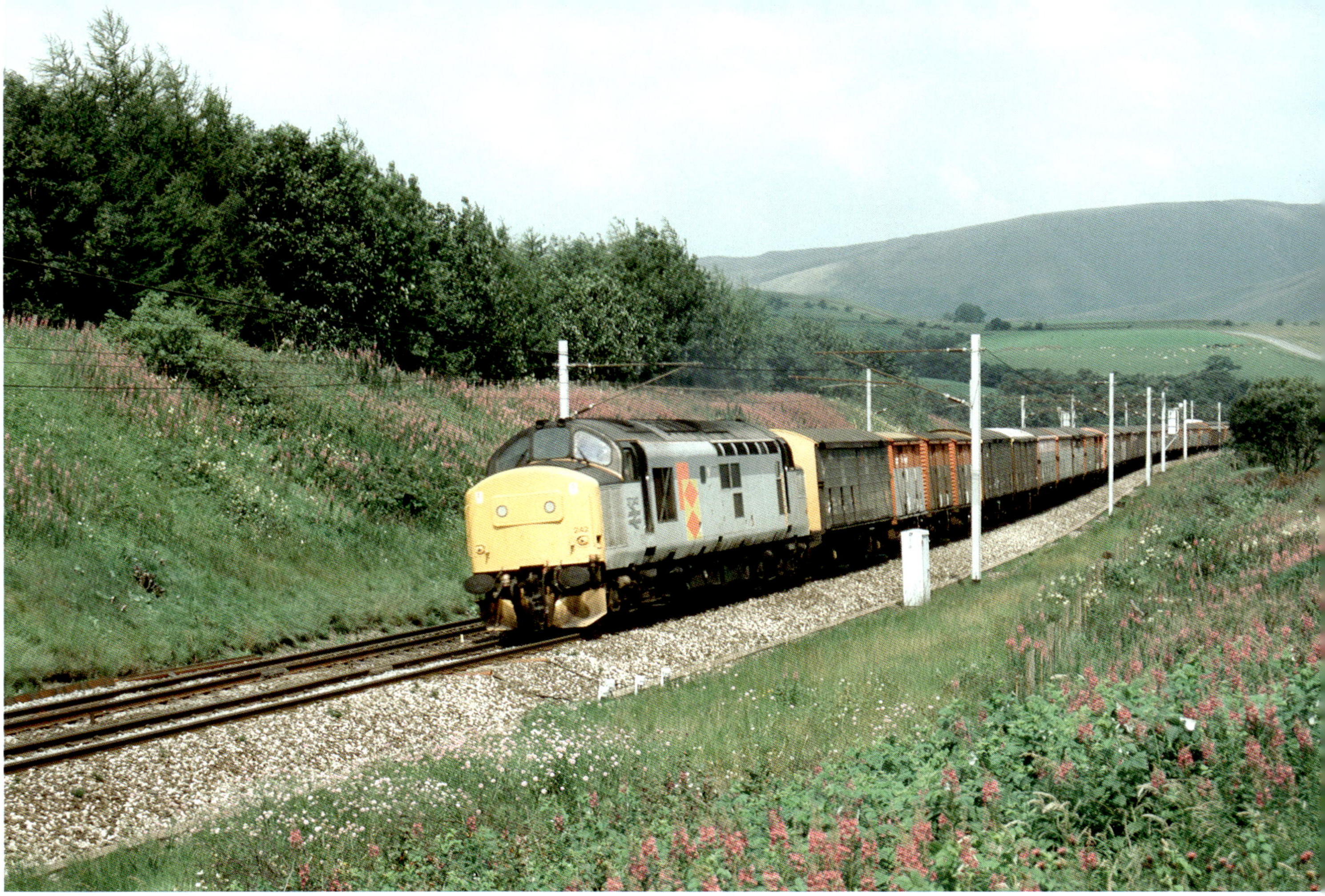

Again with such a large class of locomotives, livery variations and modifications were considerable. Sectorisation would increase the variations still further such as 37242 at Beckfoot on a Mossend to Warrington Speedlink on 29 July 1991. ***Peter Robinson***

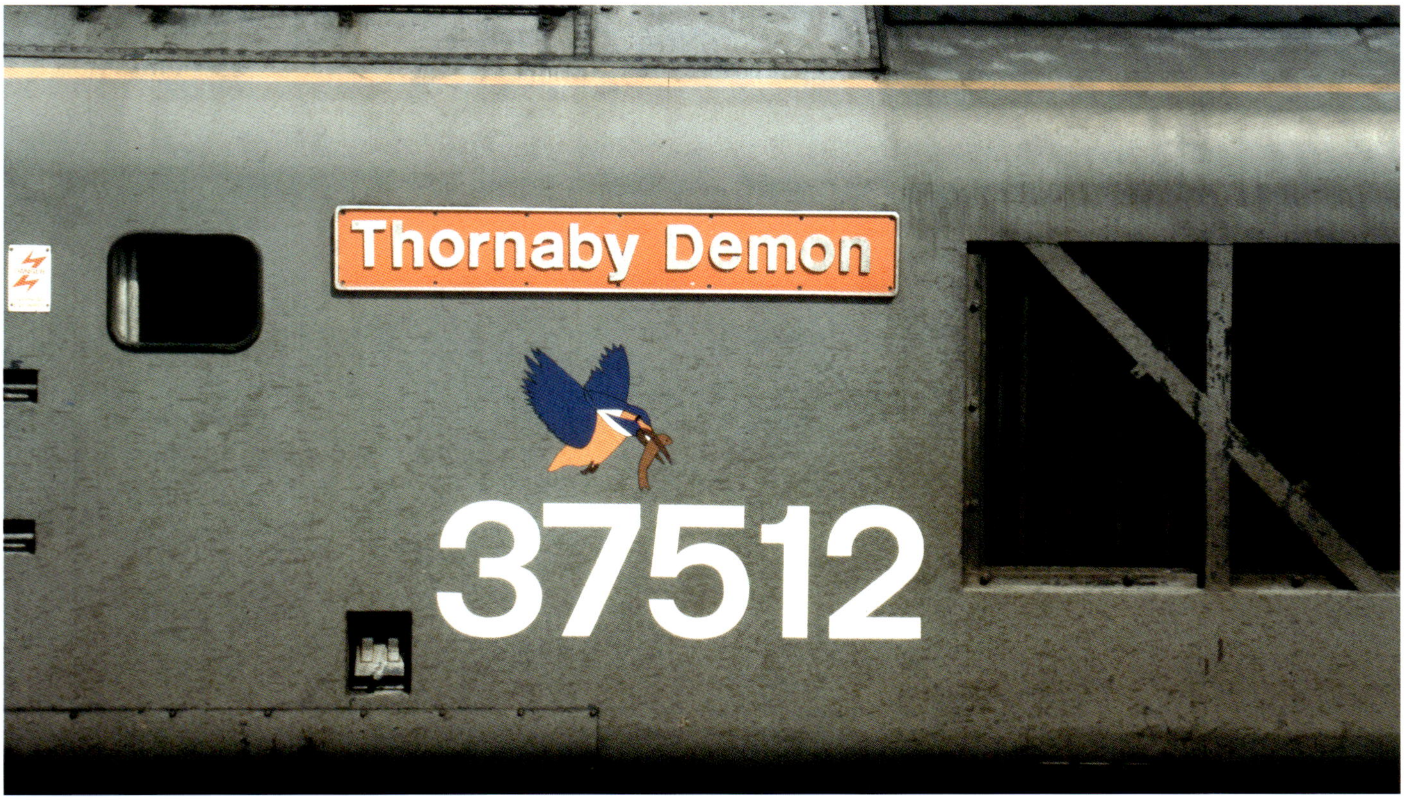

Many depots during the eighties personalised their own fleets of locomotives, one was Thornaby adopting a pleasing design of motif of a Kingfisher from the higher reaches of the Tees. It certainly went some way to dressing up the sides of 37512 on 21 April 1989, one of a sub group of twenty one locomotives in the first batch of Class 37/5. ***N P Cannon***

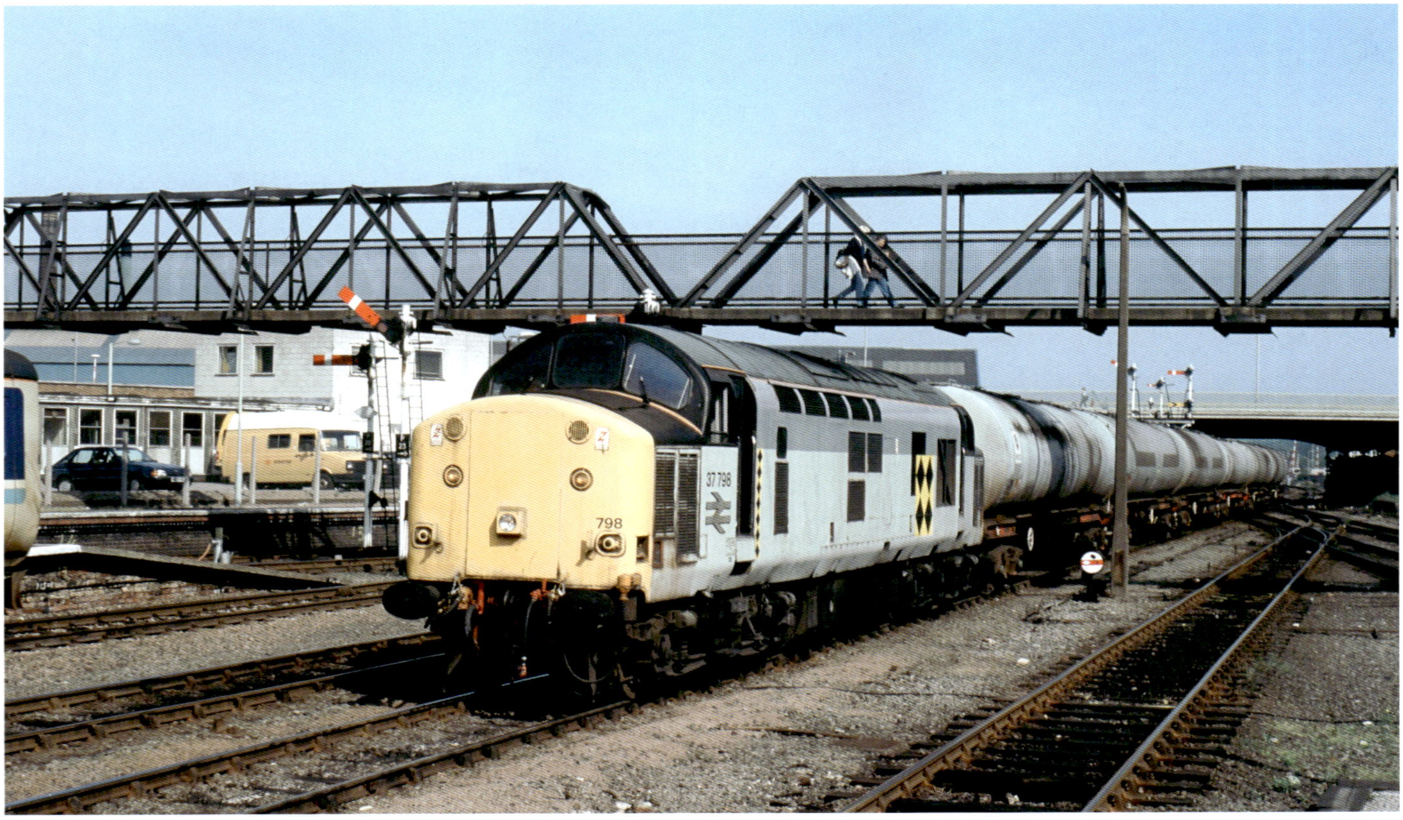

Another freight only sub group was created as Class 37/7 with additional ballast weight added to improve adhesion. Brush traction motors were fitted to the majority of locomotives except 37796 to 37803 which were equipped with GEC traction motors for comparison. Among these was 37798 at Lincoln on 24 May 1993. ***Michael Hill/Strathwood Library Collection***

Among the external modifications was the removal of headcode boxes from the locomotives, resulting in a cleaner appearance, although the ventilation grills were retained. Once again at Lincoln we find Transrail liveried 37701 on 27 August 1997. ***Michael Hill/Strathwood Library Collection***

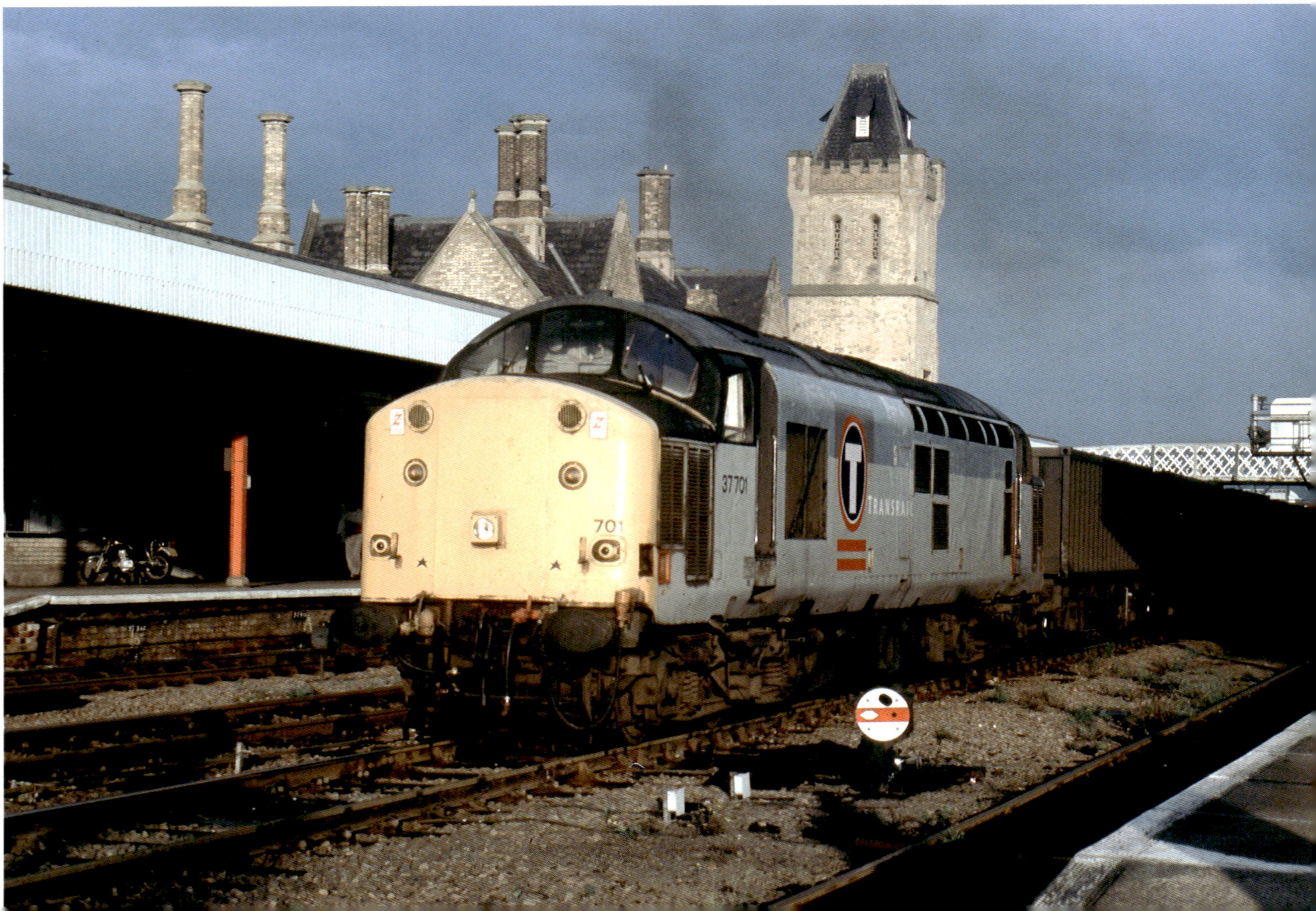

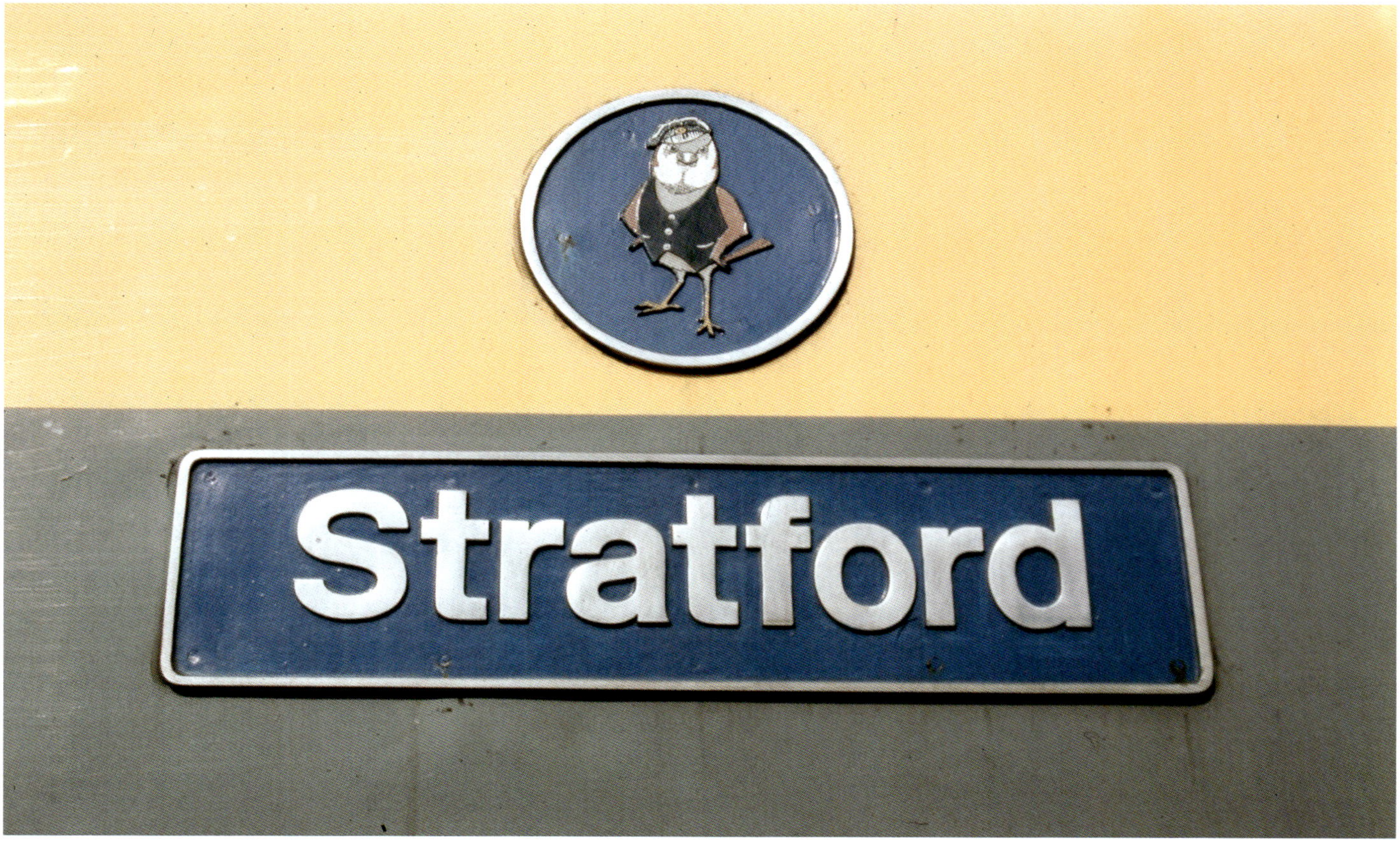

Rather than just paint the cheeky Cockney Sparrow motif on 37023, separate plates were cast to show off the design, seen here in October 1992. ***Strathwood Library Collection***

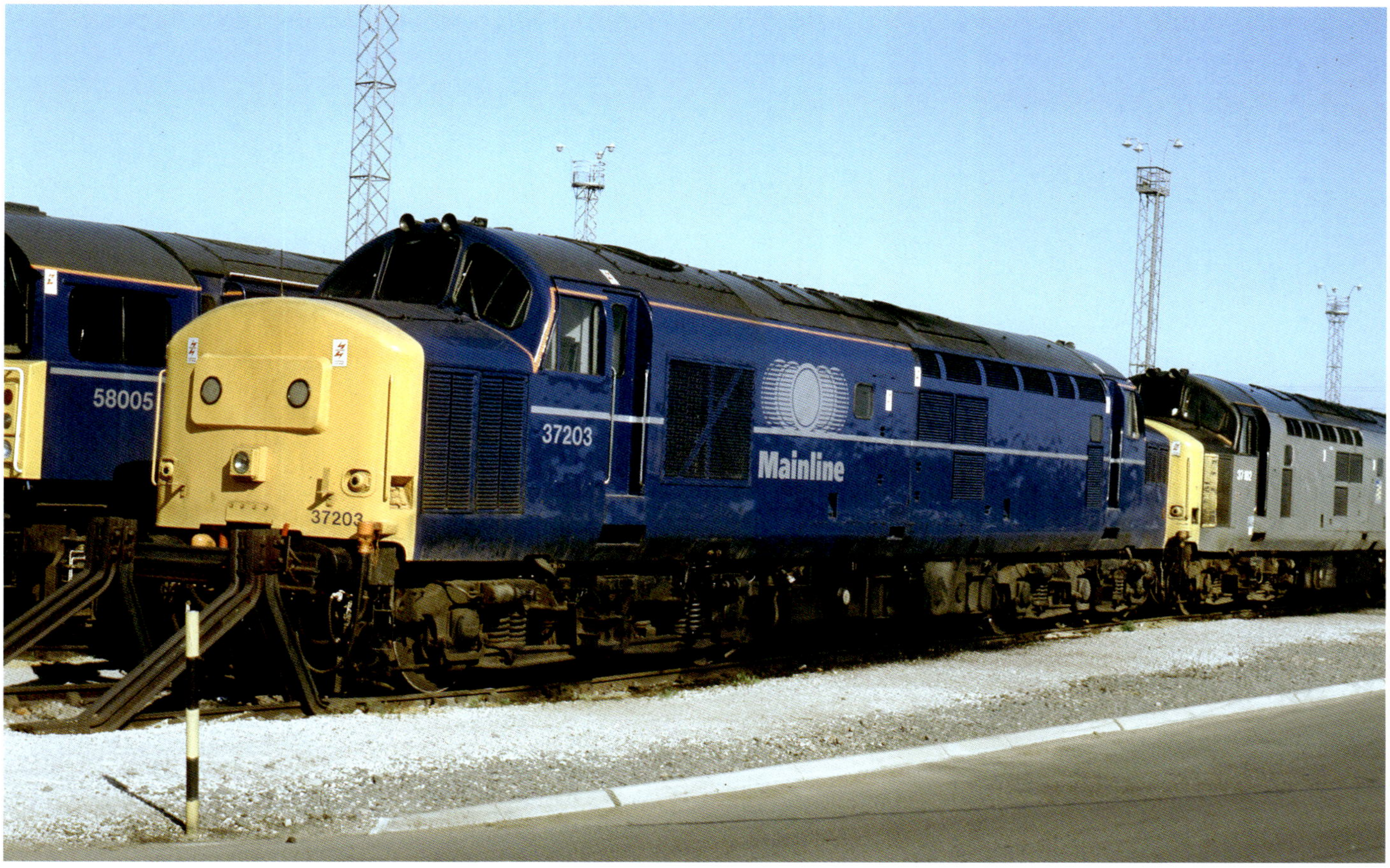

Mainline chose a royal blue scheme for their locomotives as here on 37203 at Toton on 5 May 1996. However not all of their fleet gained this scheme, some were merely rebranded with Mainline logos onto the two tone grey livery already carried. ***Michael Hill/Strathwood Library Collection***

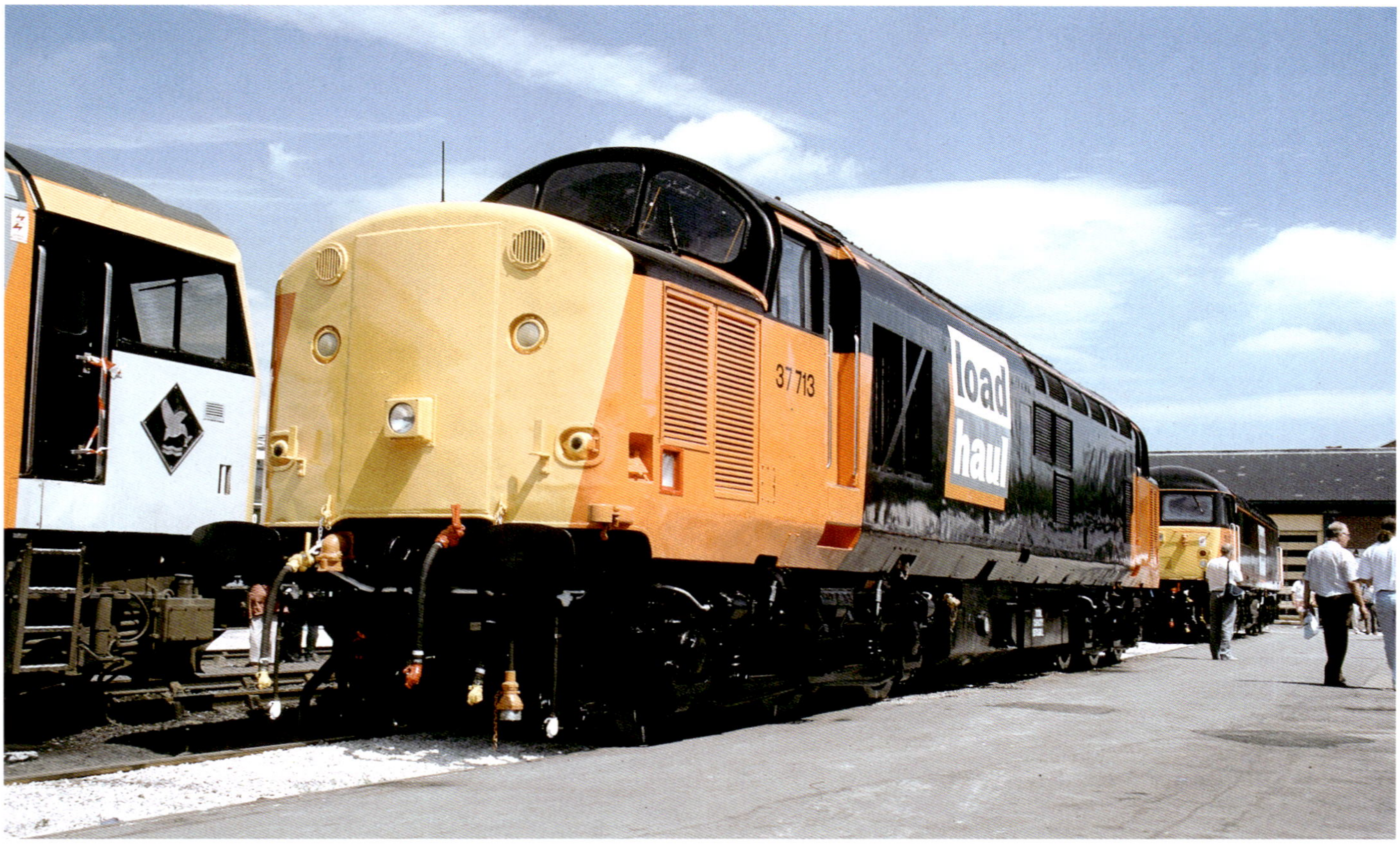

A much more dramatic design was applied by Loadhaul to their locomotives during 1994 to 1996. Among the repaints was 37713 at Doncaster Open Day. This engine had the identity of D6752 when first introduced in September 1962 at 41A Tinsley. ***Phil Quantock***

The sub class of 37/4 locomotives were well travelled seeing much use in both Scotland and Wales, as here at Llandudno Junction on 21 July 1991 with 37418 in Regional Railways guise. ***Late Pete Walton/Sid Steadman***

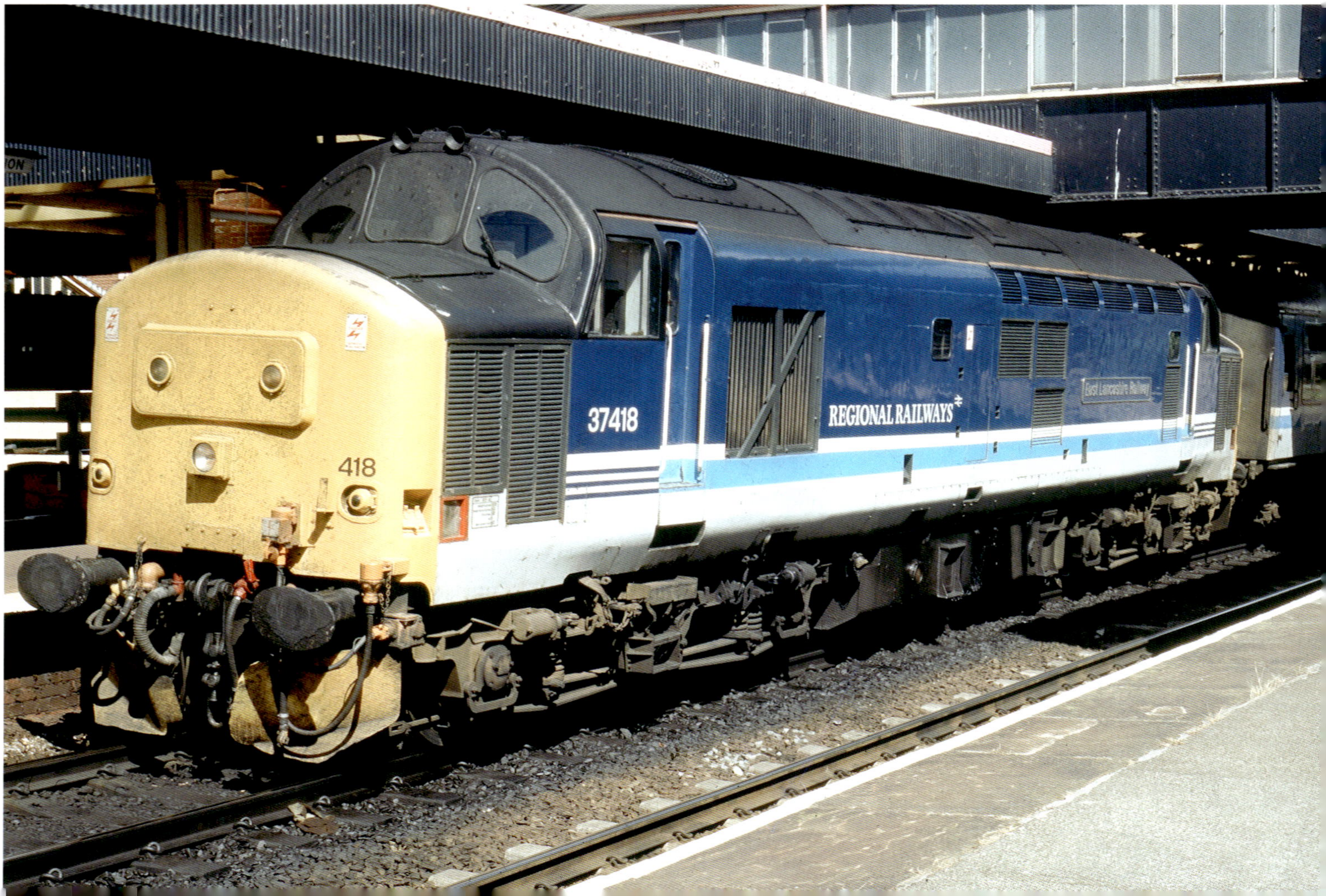

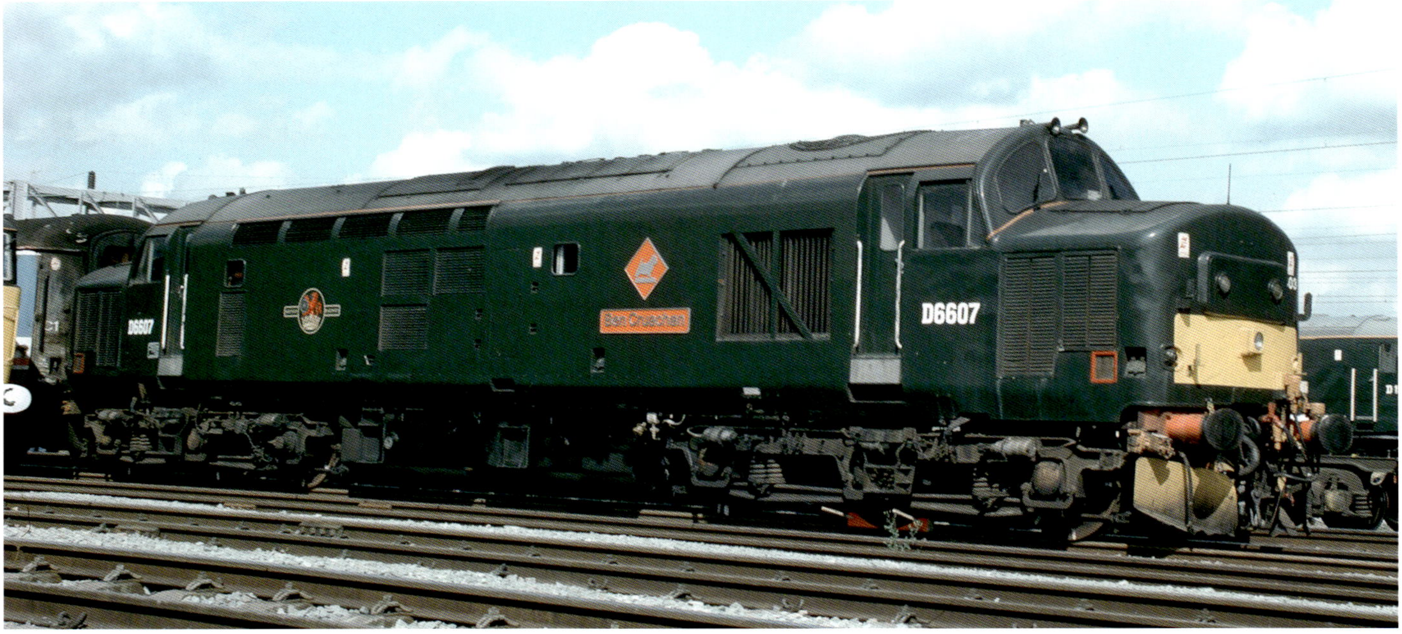

A fondness for heritage liveries saw 37403 at Crewe Basford Hall open Day on 21 August 1994 recalling past glories. ***Phil Quantock***

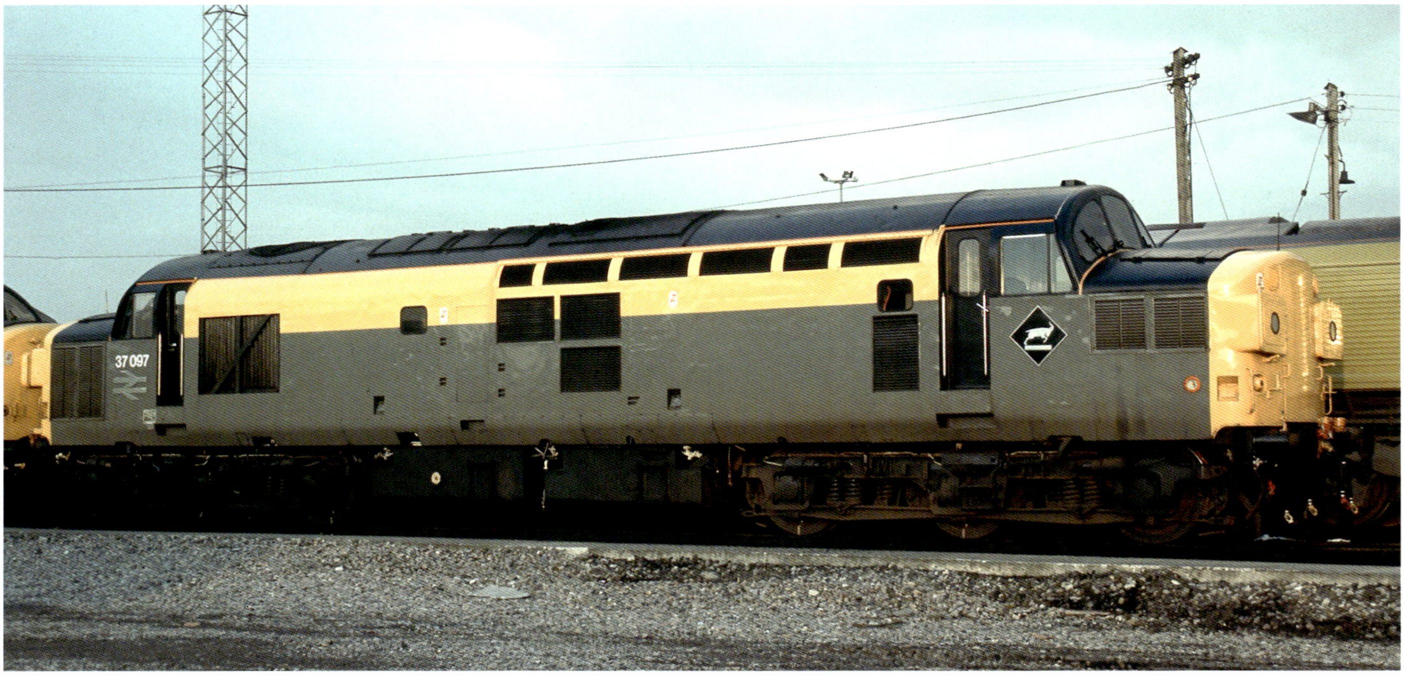

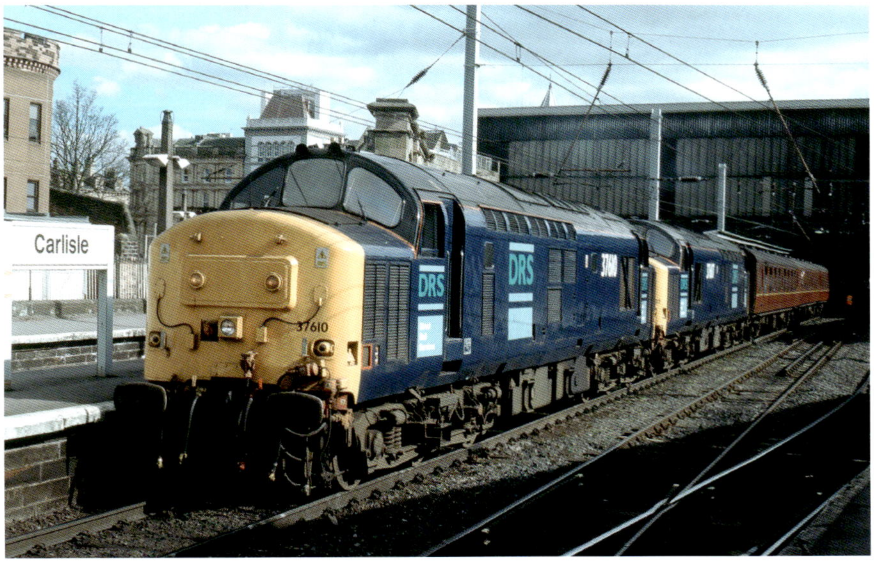

Not quite the dullest livery, but certainly getting there was Dutch dressed 37097 at Westbury on 16 June 1991. ***Michael Hill/ Strathwood Library Collection***

In contrast Direct Rail Services Class 37/6s 37610 and 37607 at Carlisle on 27 September 1998 look much more the part. ***Late Pete Walton/Sid Steadman***

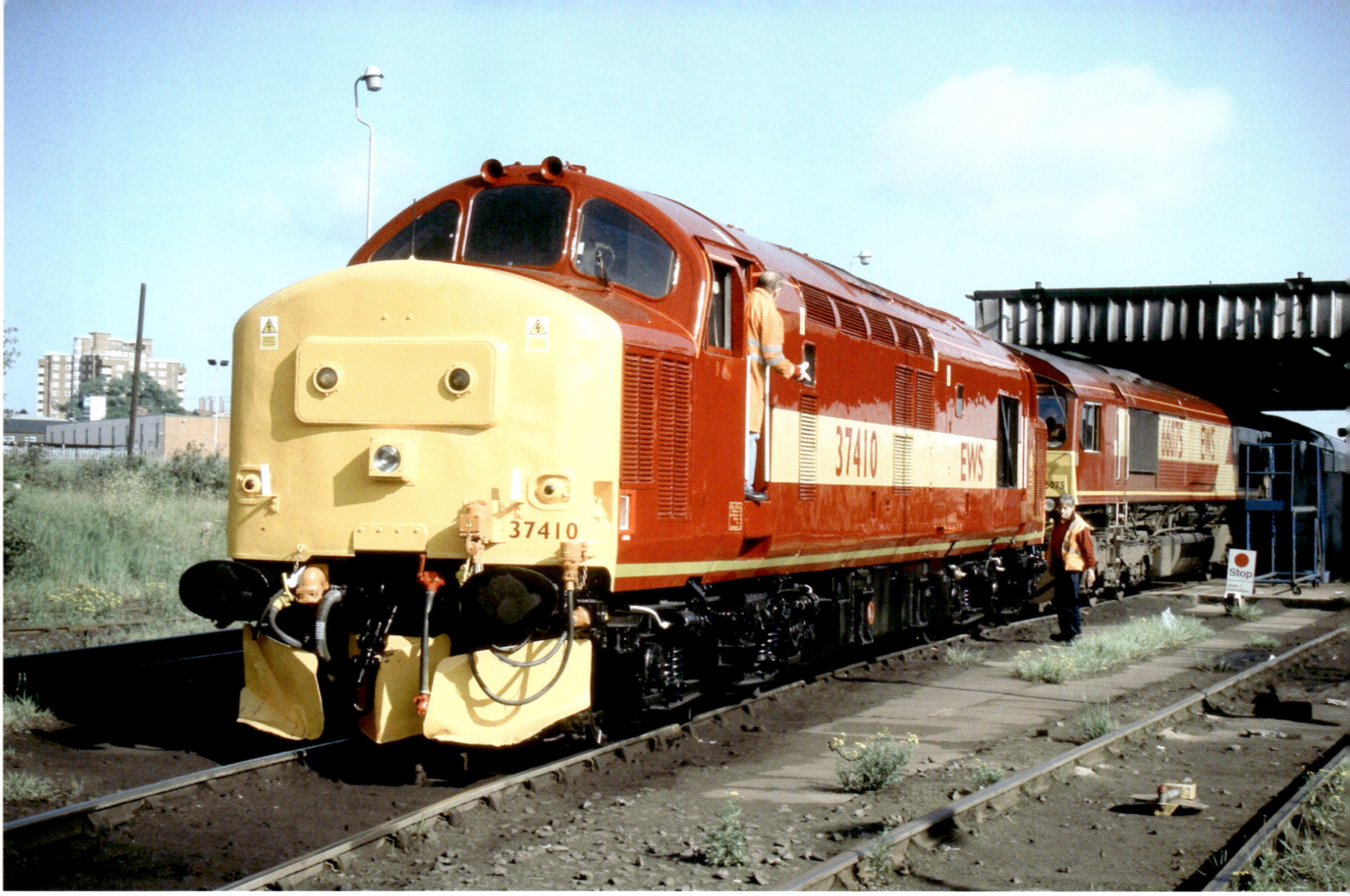

There is no denying the EWS colours look good when clean and shiny, but carry less favour once weathered. Spick and span is 37410 in company with 66075 at Saltley on 11 June 2003. ***Jason Hickling***

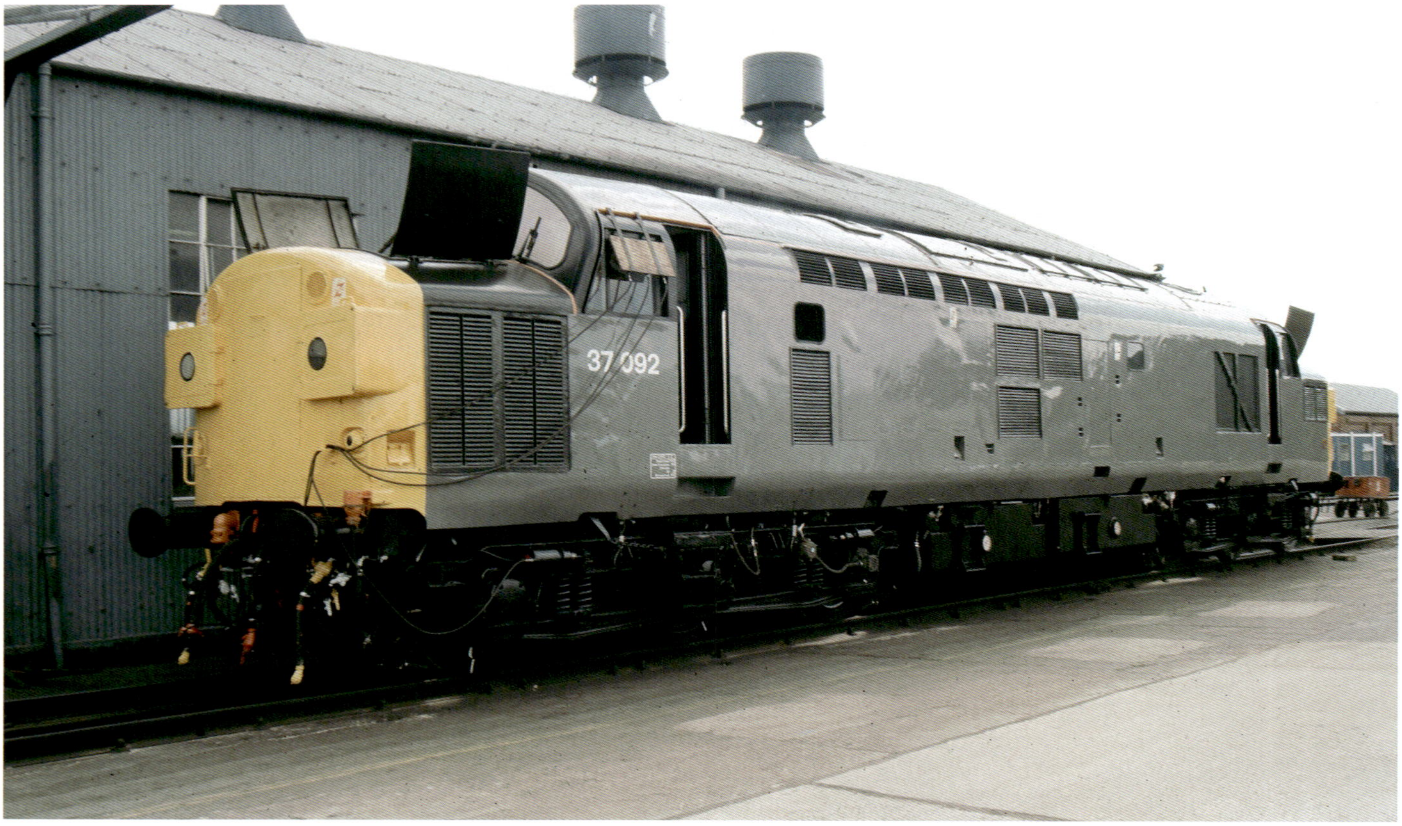

Just how drab can you go? Well look no further than 37092 at Doncaster in September 1990 undergoing testing before a return to service outside the Plant. ***Strathwood Library Collection***

Mainline and Shunting Genesis

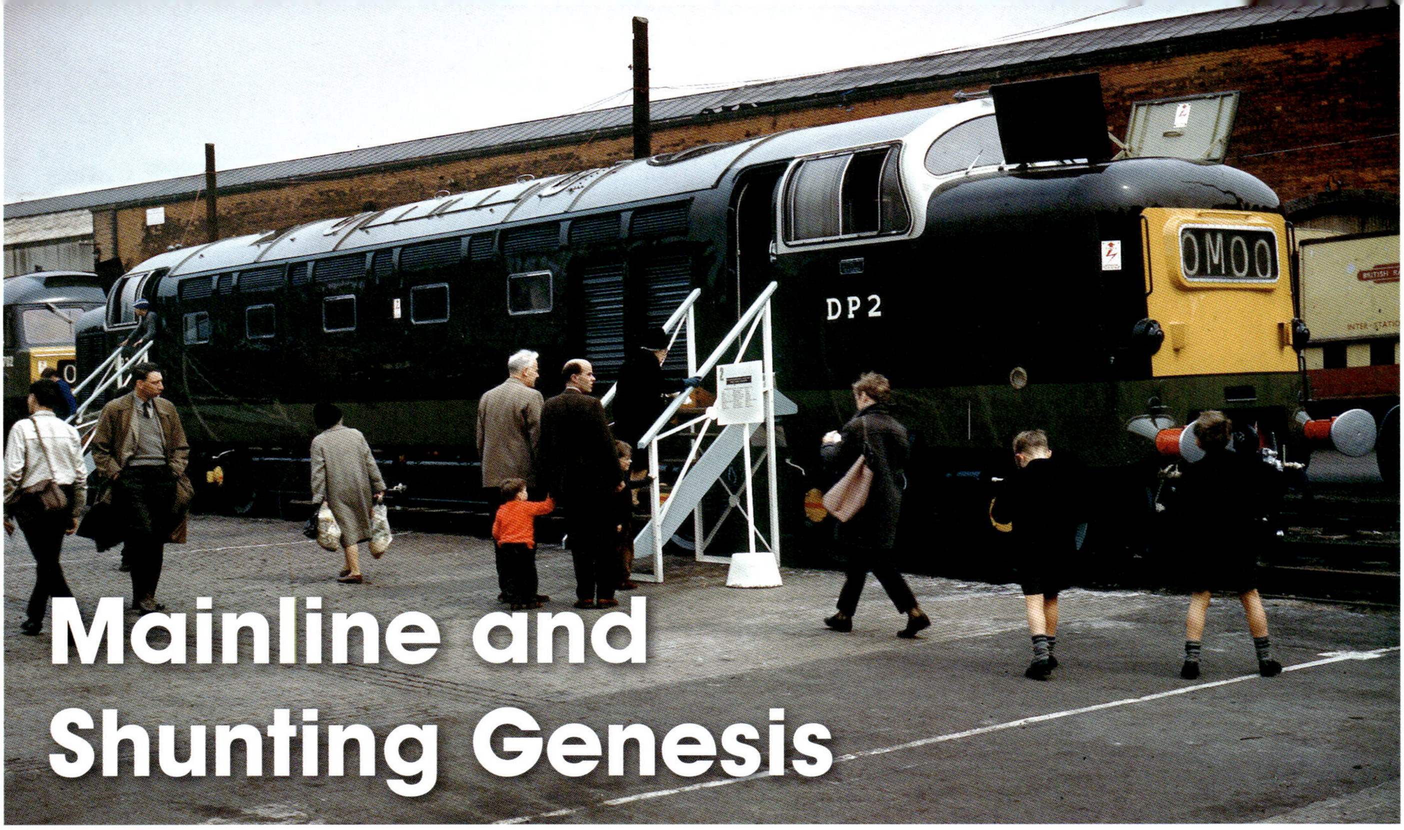

Excitement for two schoolboys but just another diesel to the old lady with the hat at Marylebone in 1965 with DP2 on display. ***Bob Treacher/Alton Model Centre***

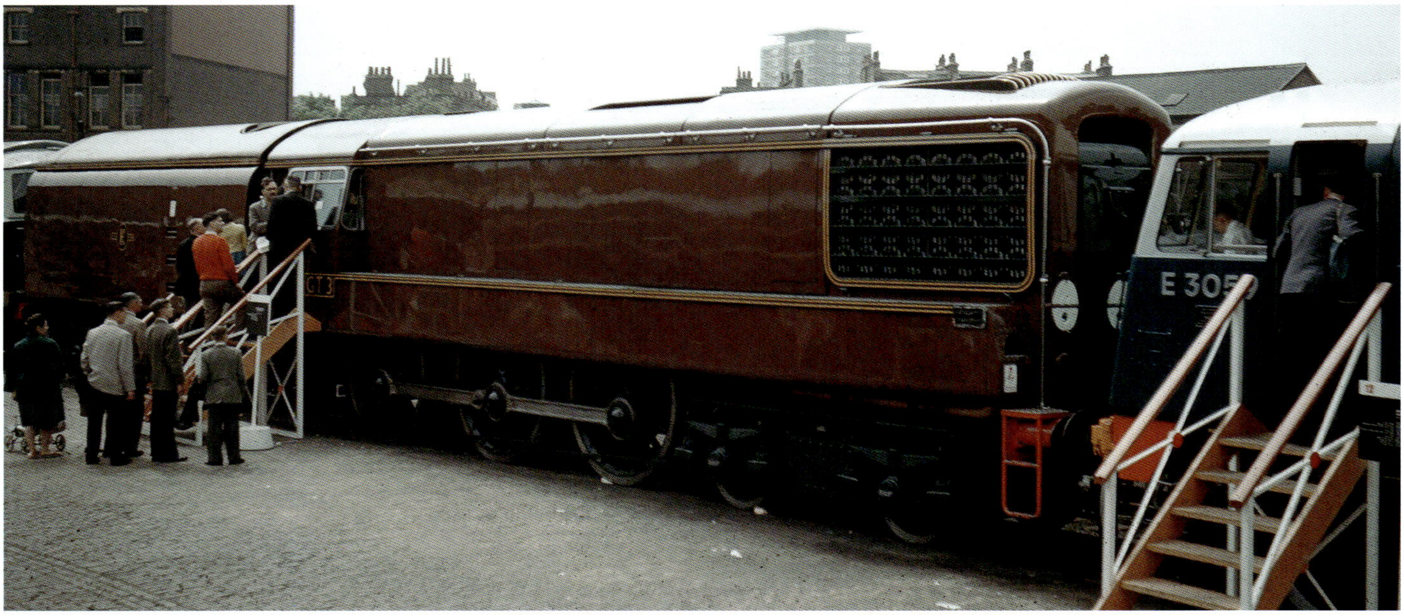

Much more radical was the English Electric gas turbine prototype GT3 also on display at Marylebone Parcels Depot on 14 May 1961. ***Stewart Blencowe Collection***

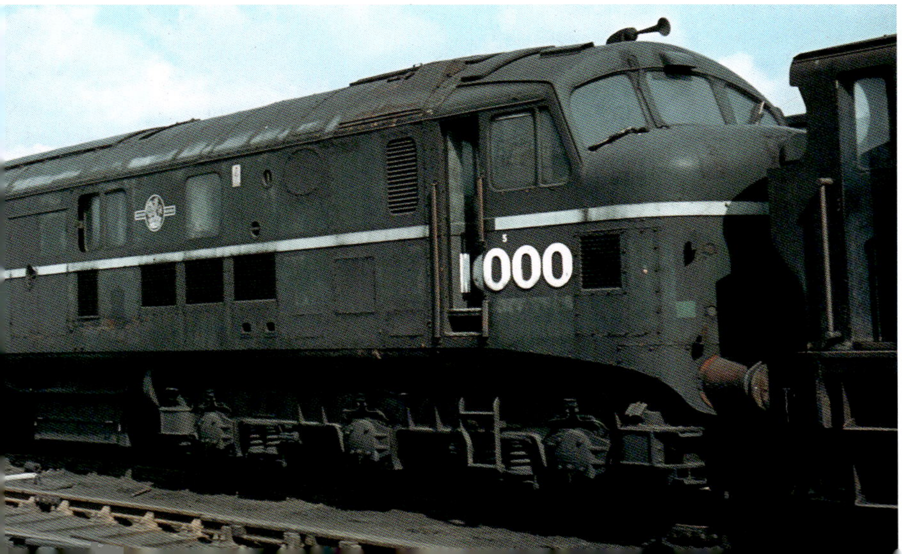

The success of the company must be pinned to 10000 now cast aside at Derby where it remained from late 1962 until early 1968. ***Richard Sinclair Collection***

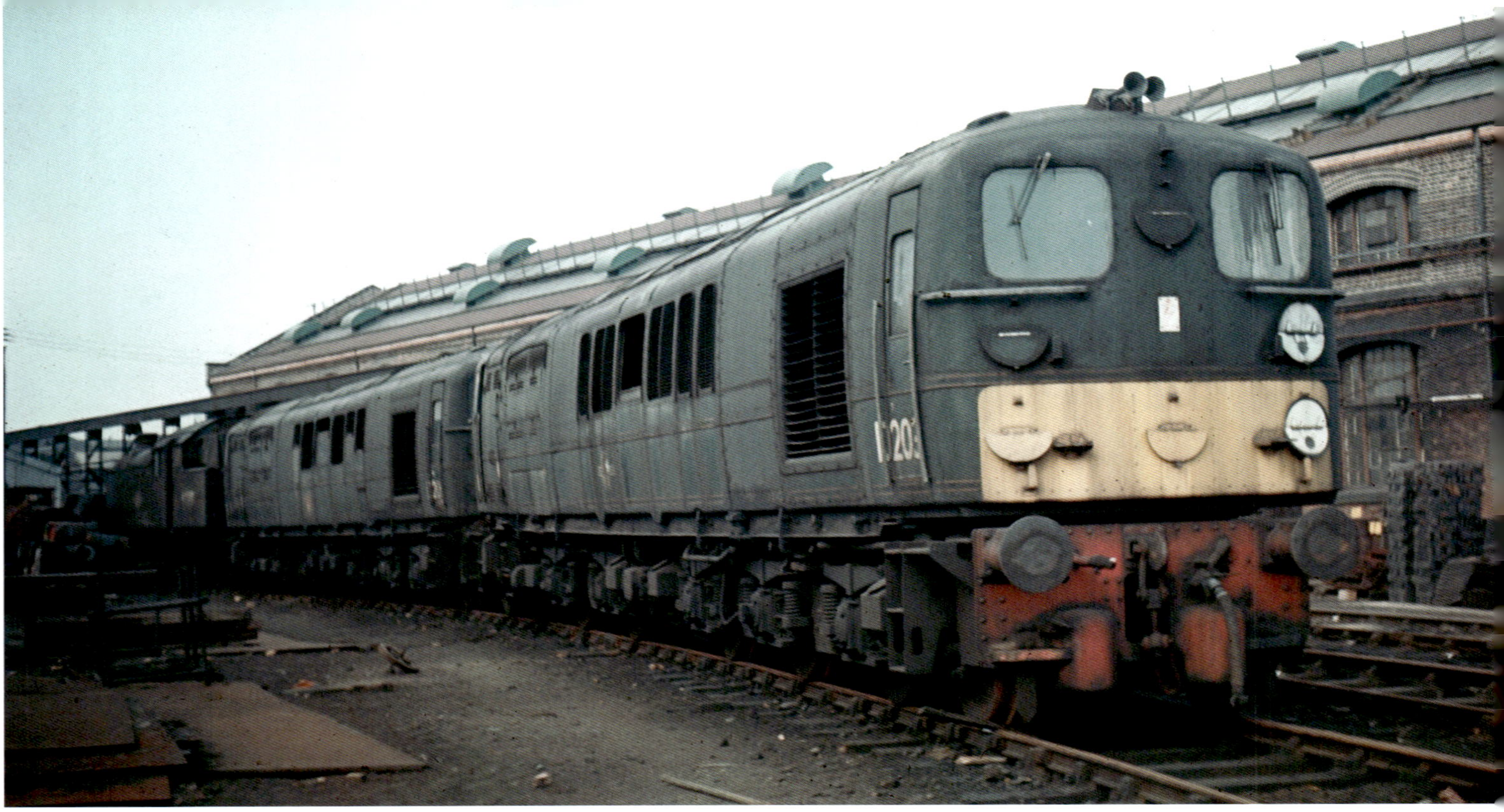

Also dumped at Derby were the prototypes built at Ashford and Brighton for the Southern. The last of the three built was 10203 in early 1954 taken into store here in October 1962, sharing the same fate as 10000. ***Len Smith***

Fortune kept DELTIC safe from destruction via the Science Museum in London for many years. Here we can recall days on the ECML near Newark around 1960. ***Strathwood Library Collection***

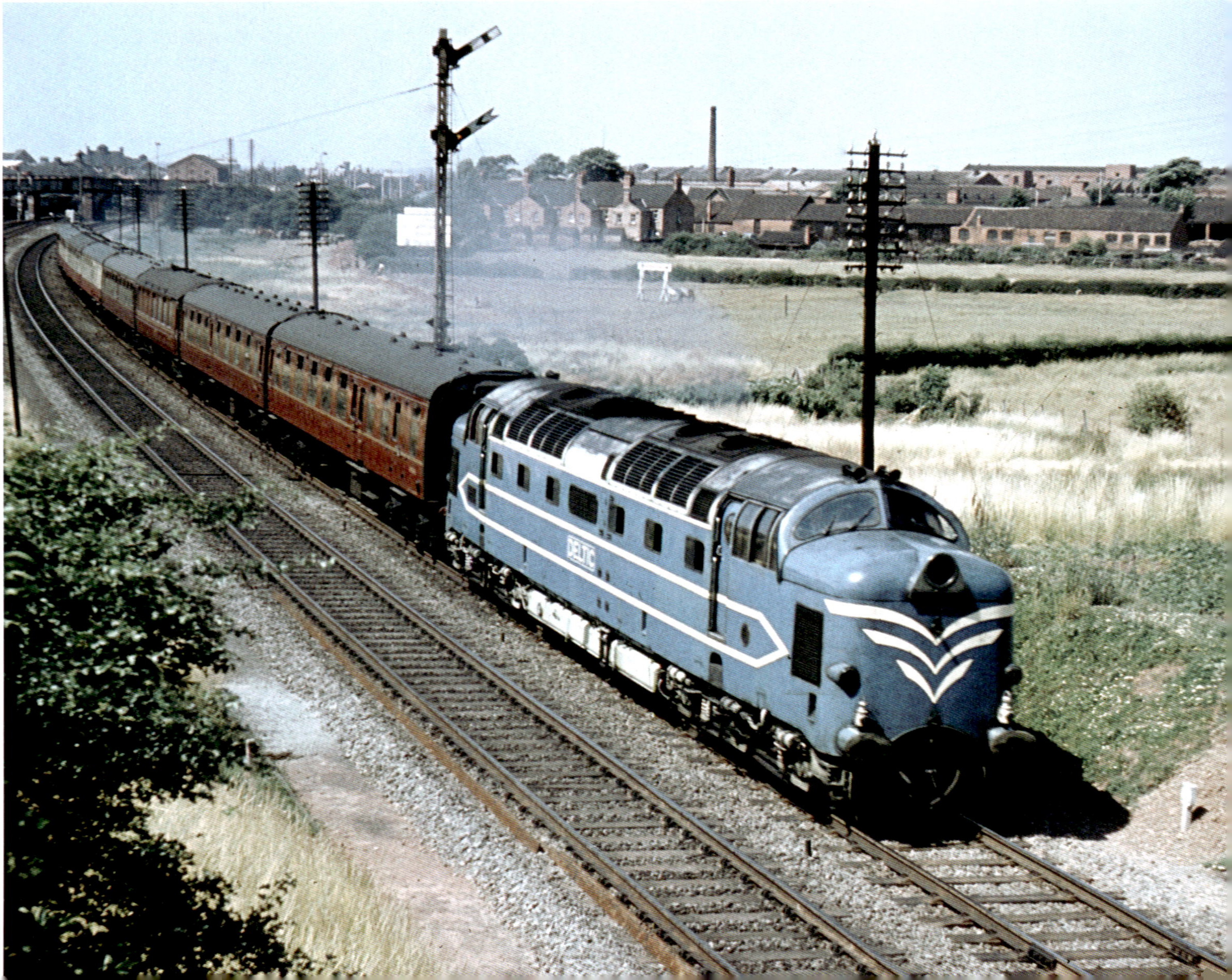

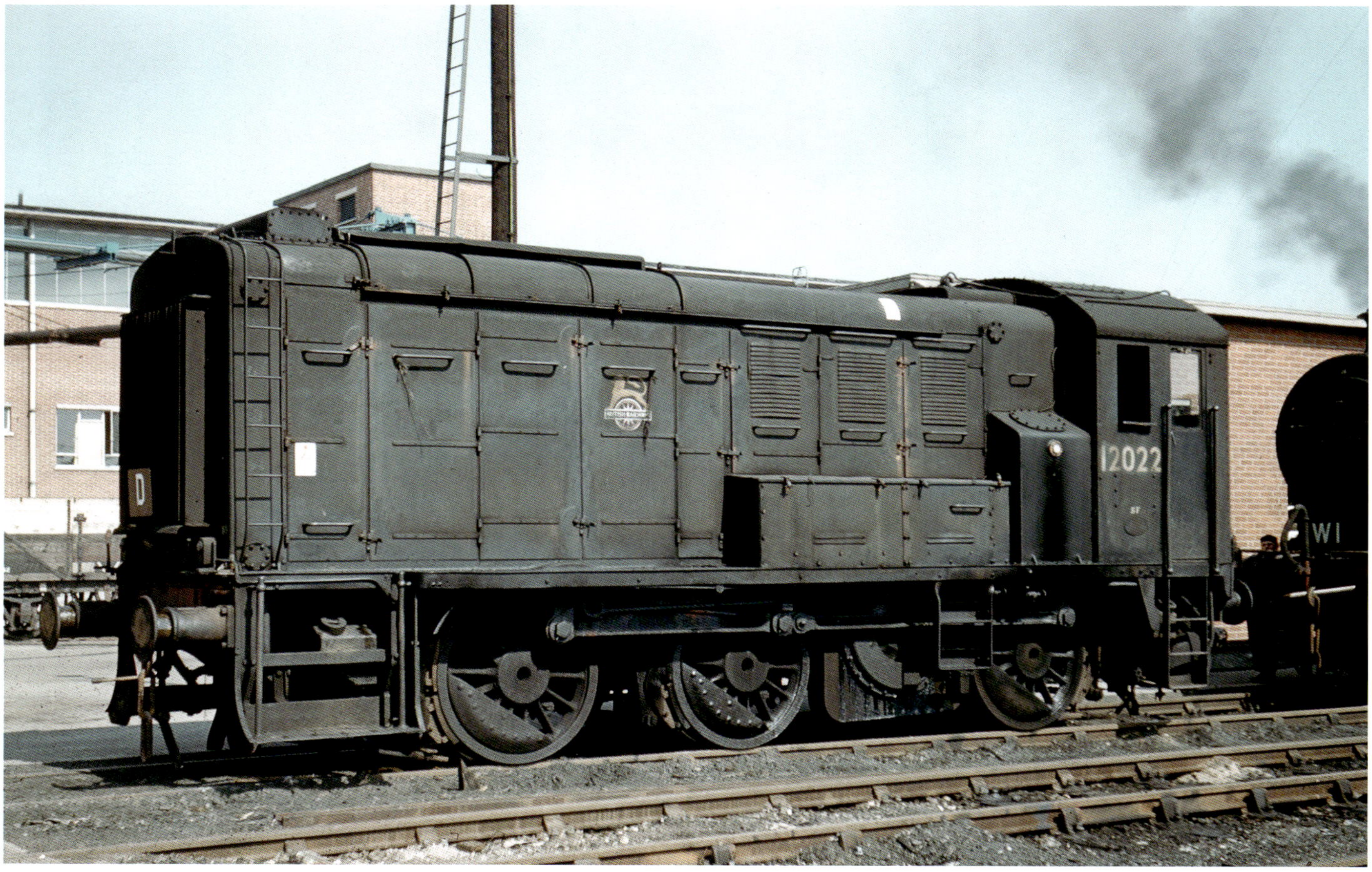

It was during the dark days of 1940 just before the Battle of Britain that 12022 came into traffic, numbered 7099 by the LMS. Further service will be made of this engine within the works at Crewe on 16 April 1961. In 1964 it went to Horwich Works who put it into storage until it was sent back to Crewe in 1966 for another year before going for scrap, the jackshaft drive variants of shunter were all gone by 1968. ***Stewart Blencowe Collection***

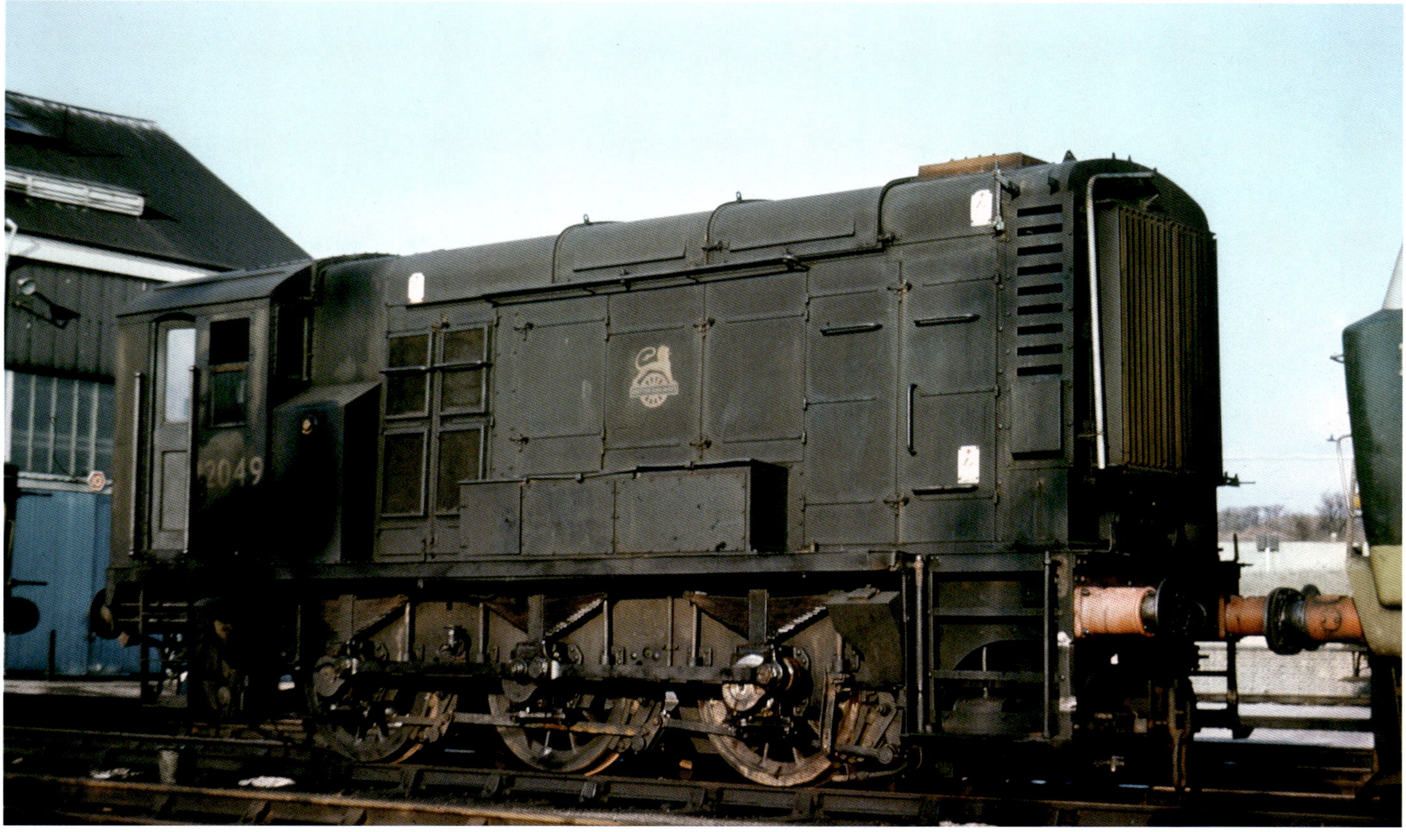

More successful were the Class 11 design built at both Derby and Darlington Works. Here taking refuge at Old Oak Common is Willesden allocated 12049 on 8 January 1967. ***Frank Hornby***

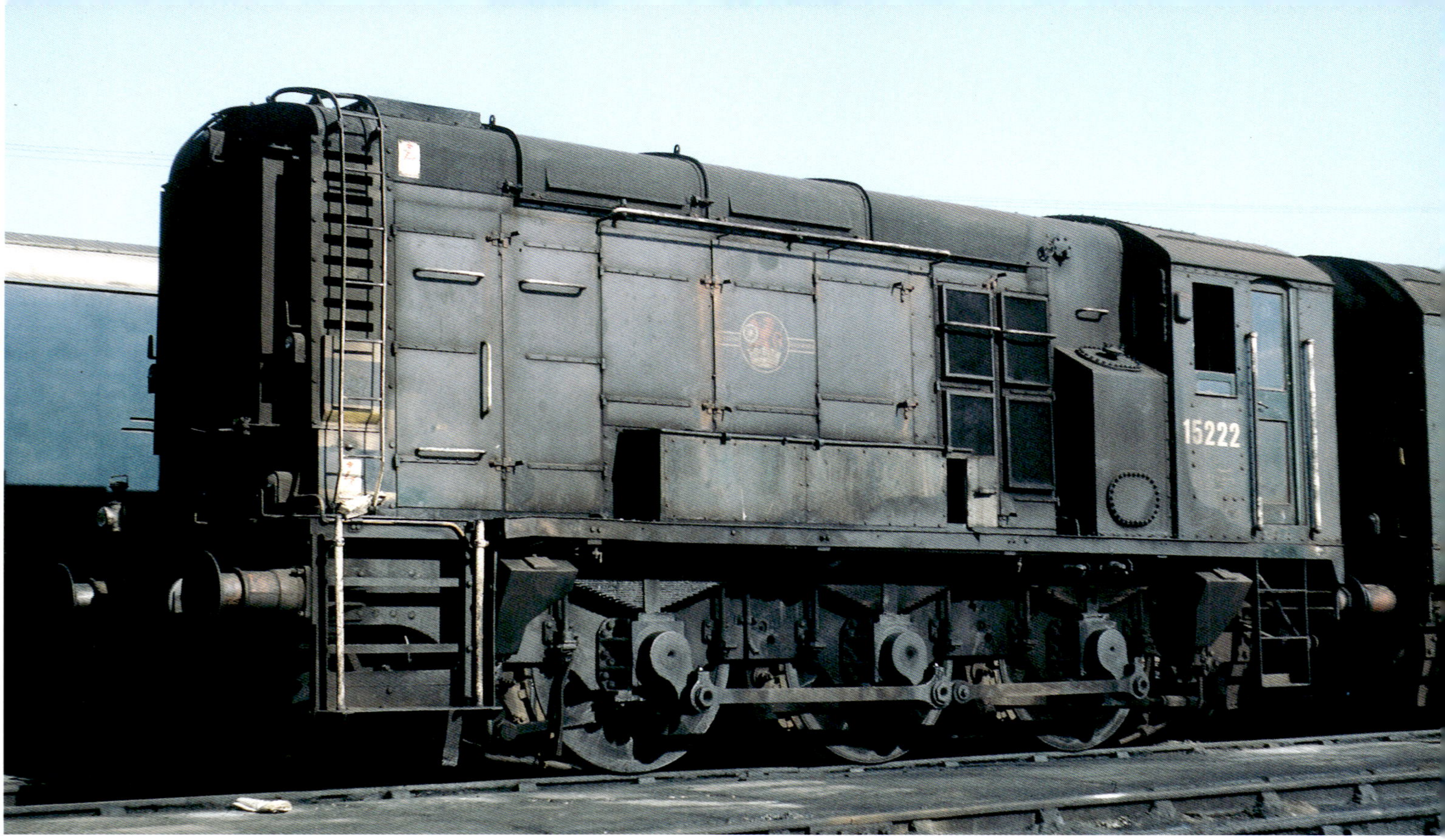

English Electric power was also chosen for later designated Class 12 shunters built for the Southern Region at Ashford between 1949 and 1952. It is just possible to discern the Bulleid style of wheels fitted to the class on 15222 at Hither Green on 5 April 1969. ***Colin Rodgers/Strathwood Library Collection***

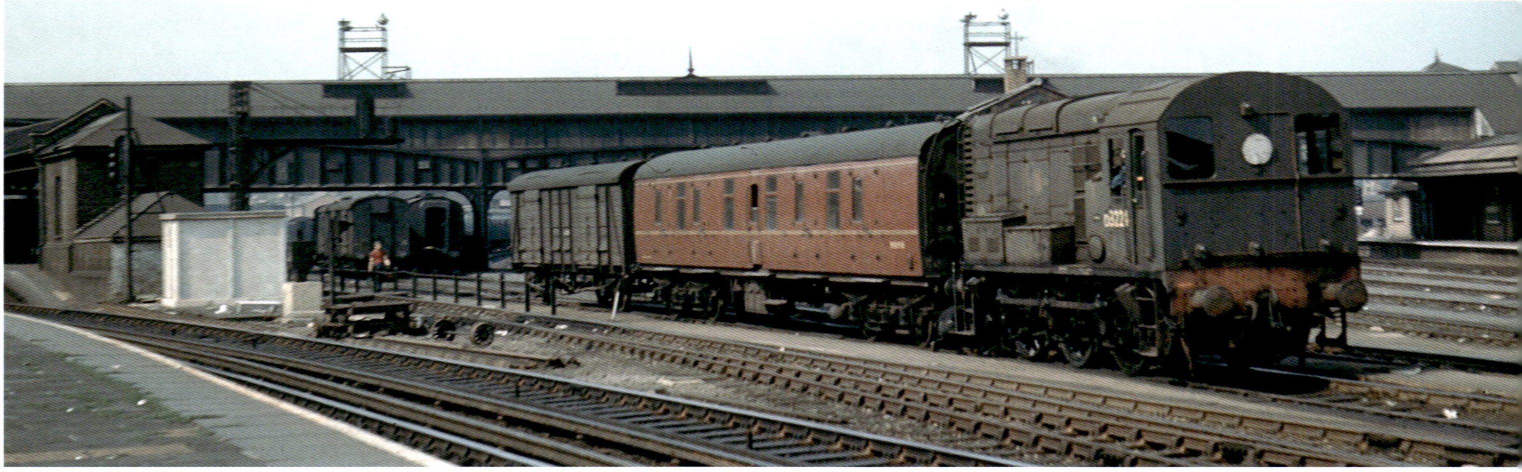

The bulk of the British Railways fleet of shunters would be fitted with English Electric engines. Among them was D3224 at Clapham Junction on 8 August 1959. ***Frank Hornby***

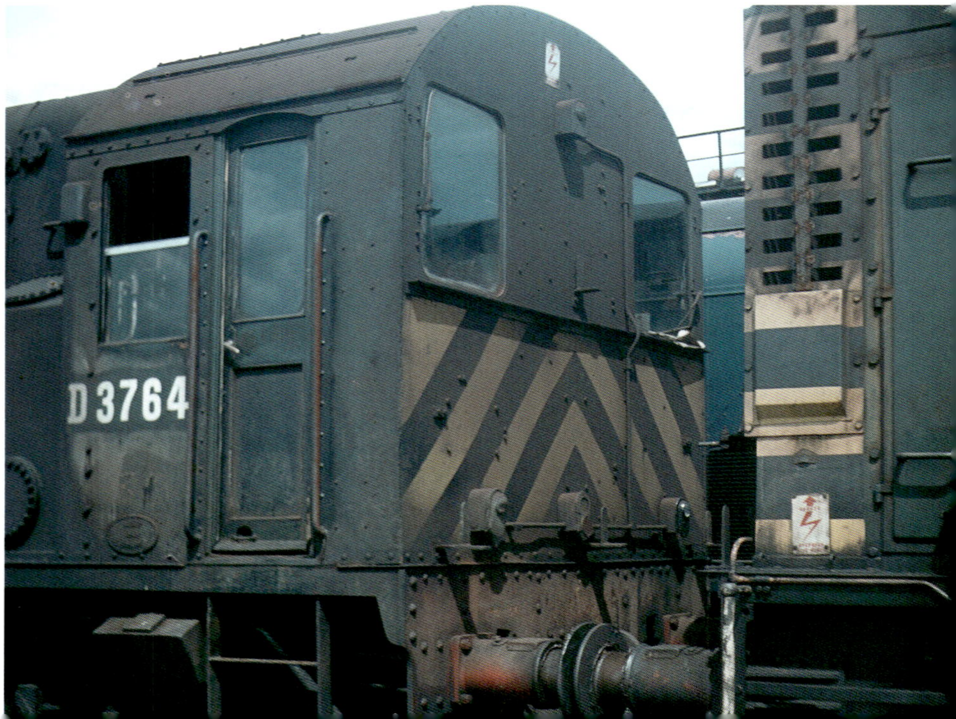

This one D3764 at Crewe in 1969 shows an interesting arrangement of stripes. ***Neil Snuggs***

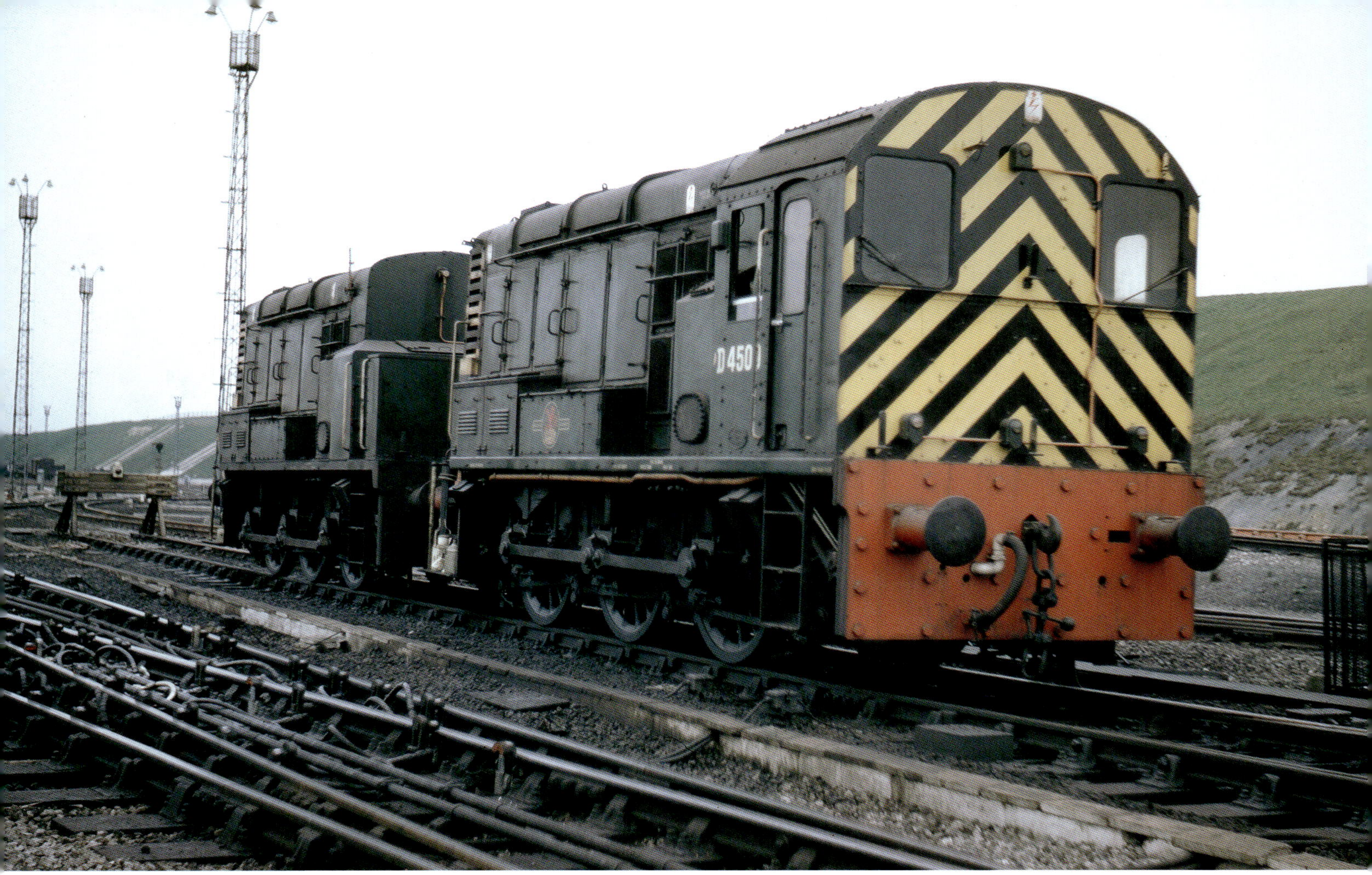

Three super shunters were created to work as master and slave units for Tinsley's once busy hump yards. The beefed up buffer beam stands out on D4500 between duties on 22 April 1967. ***Stewart Blencowe Collection***

Trip working was also the forte of the Class 08s such as 08765 at Tame Bridge Parkway in February 1998 before a storm. The Southern Region chose to re-gear some of their engines to run a little faster on this type of work due to the increased line occupation such workings would otherwise take. ***David T Williams***

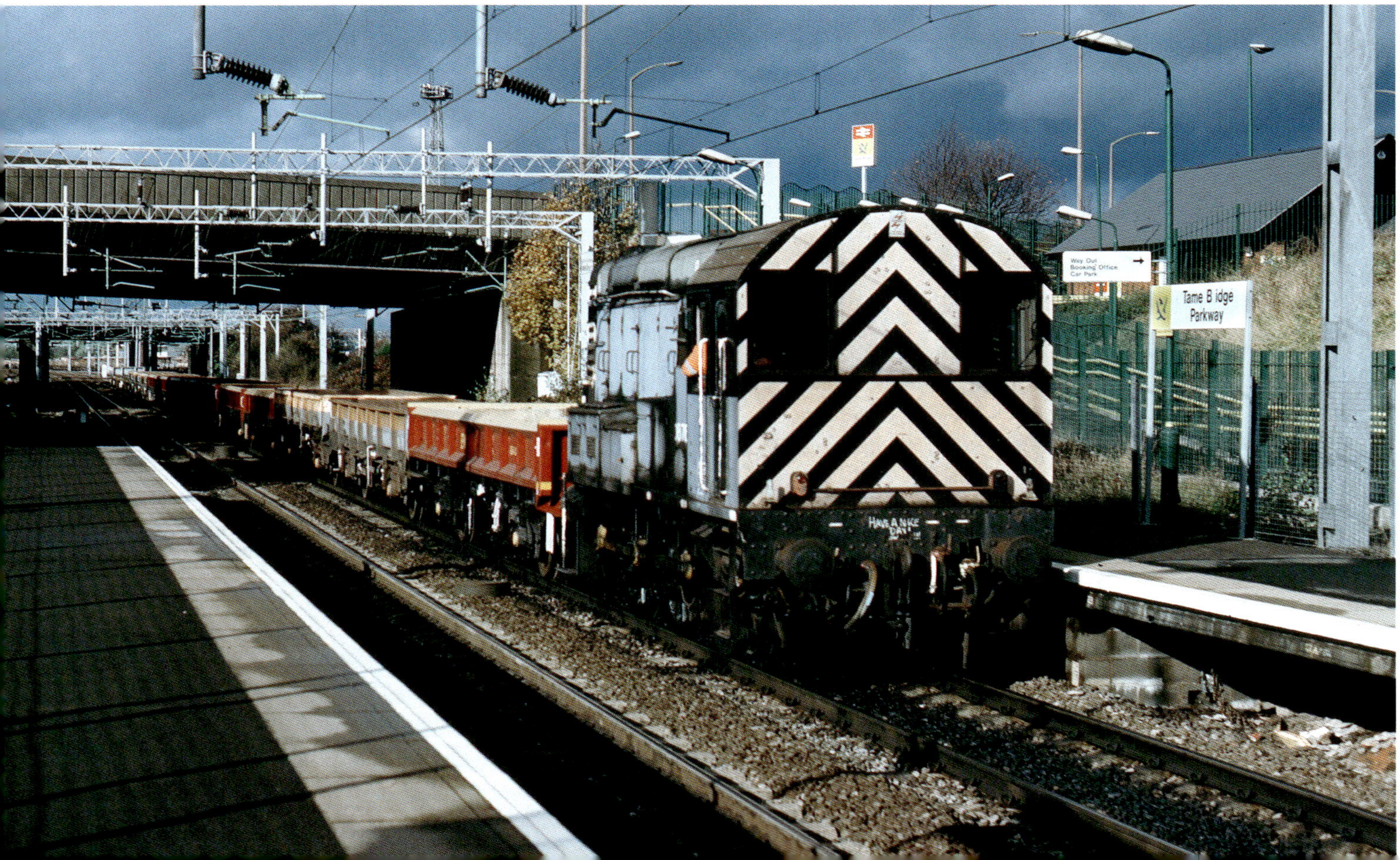

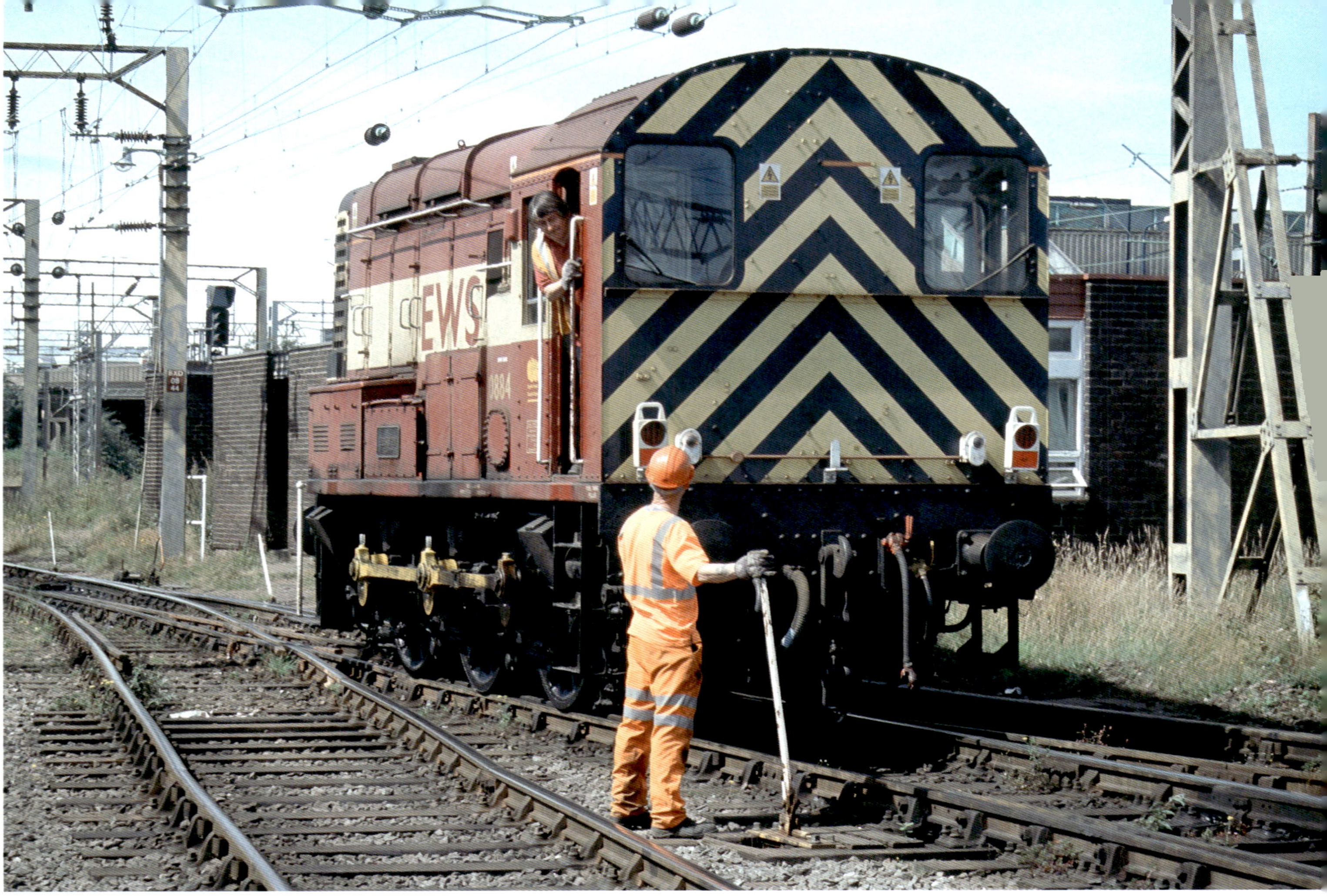

A plethora of liveries have been given to the shunter fleet over the years, but EWS stamped their mark on 08844 at Bescot at work on the North End on 10 August 2007. ***Jason Hickling***

Several were chopped down for working through the limited clearances on the Burry Port & Gwendreath Valley route. They were also given large cast number plates affixed to the cab sides as seen here in March 1995. ***Strathwood Library Collection***

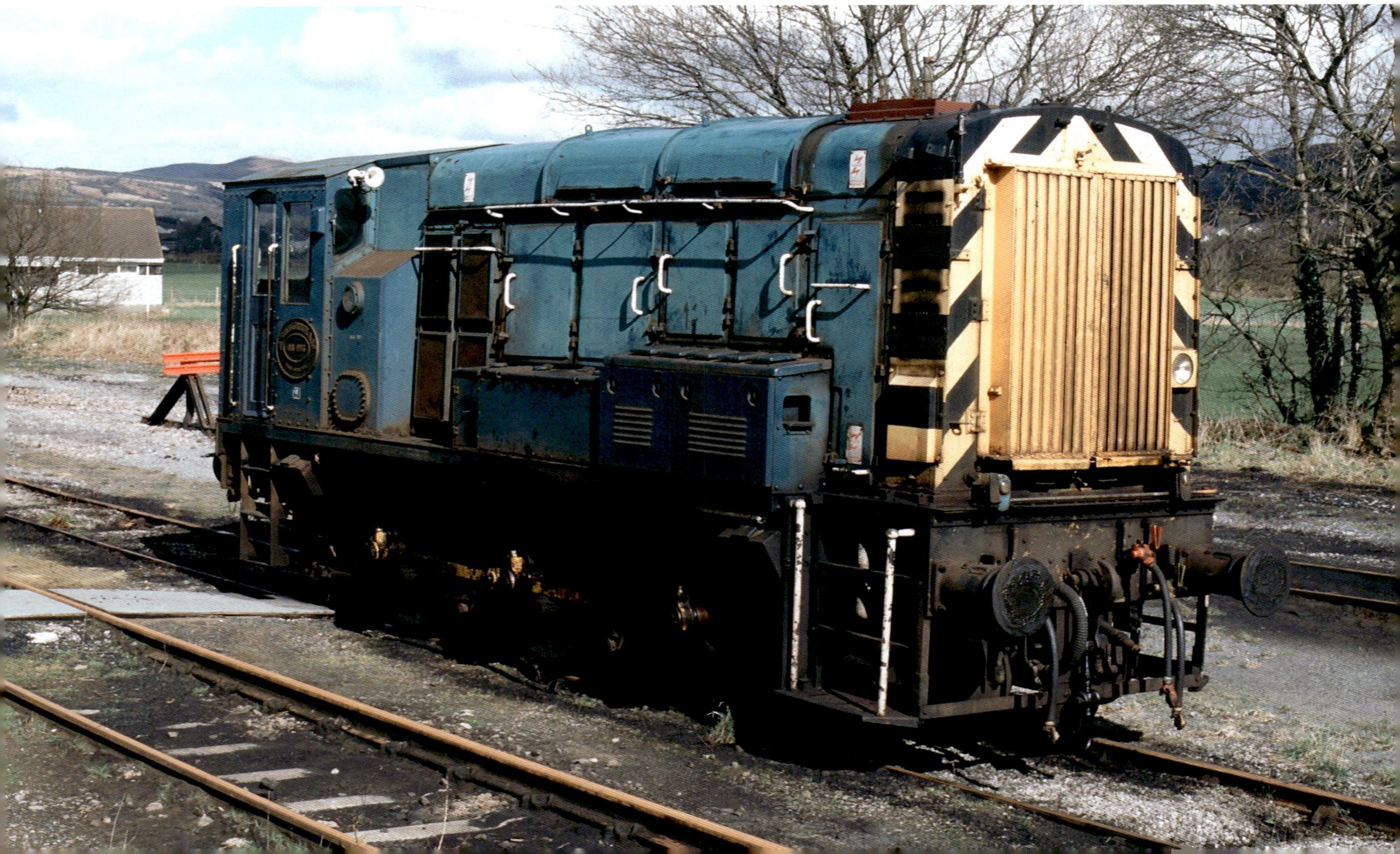

New For Old

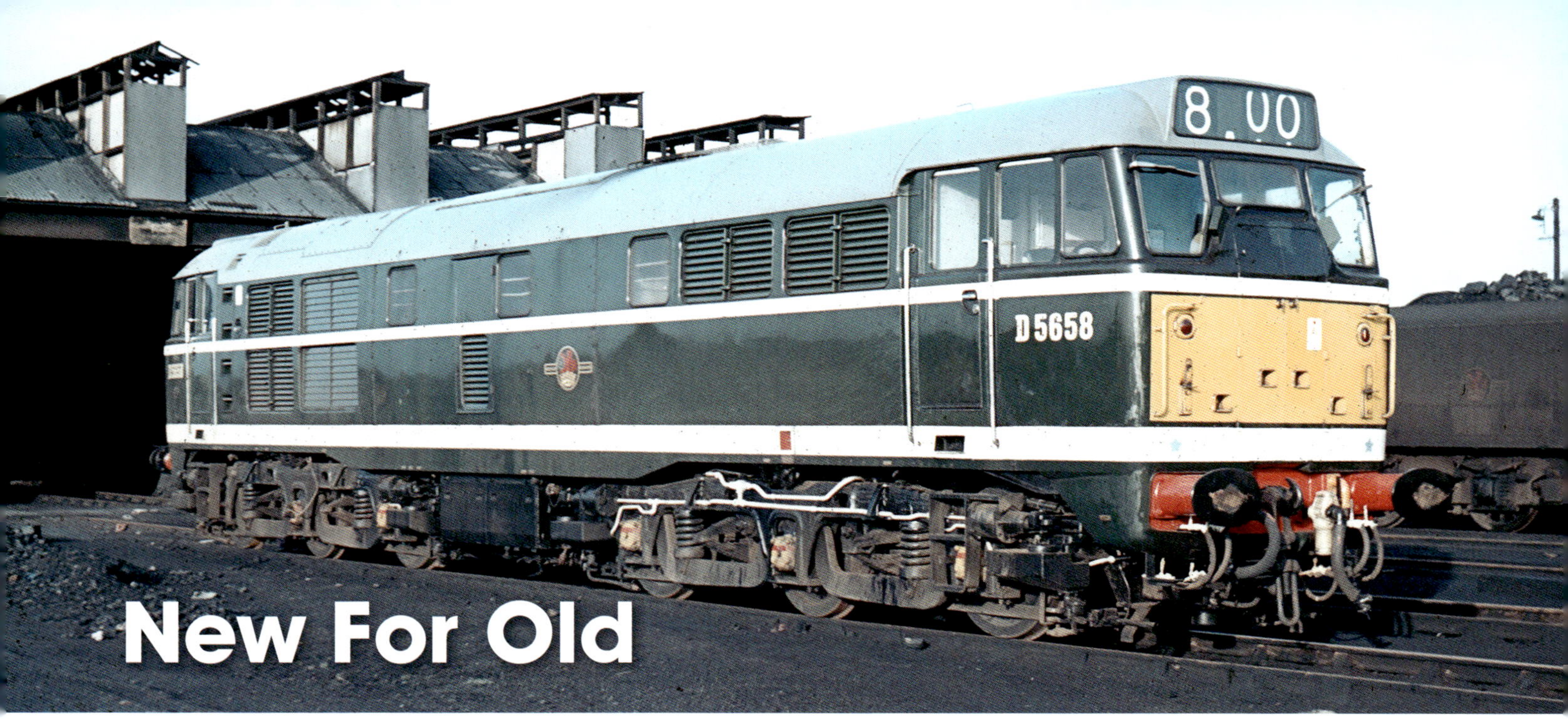

Originally fitted with a Mirlees engine when new, were all of the Brush Type Two design such as D5658 seen at March on 24 January 1965. ***Stewart Blencowe Collection***

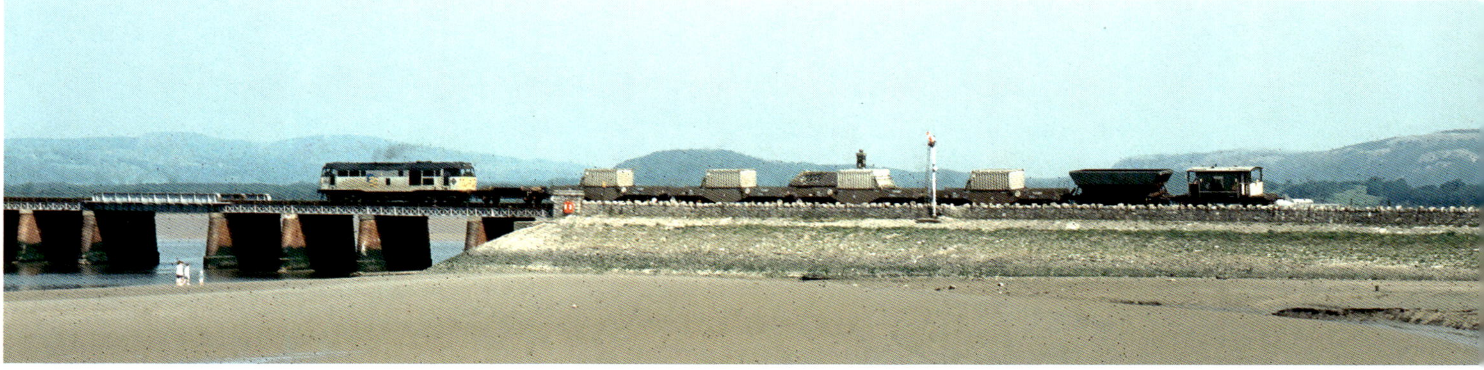

The exhaust and sound of the English Electric 12SVT engine subsequently fitted to 31199 reverberates across Arnside on 6 June 1992. ***Late Pete Walton/Sid Steadman***

Below: The programme of fitting new engines to these A1A-A1A locomotives brought about a long service life for many including 31108 at Bescot on 30 August 1992. ***Michael Hill/Strathwood Library Collection***

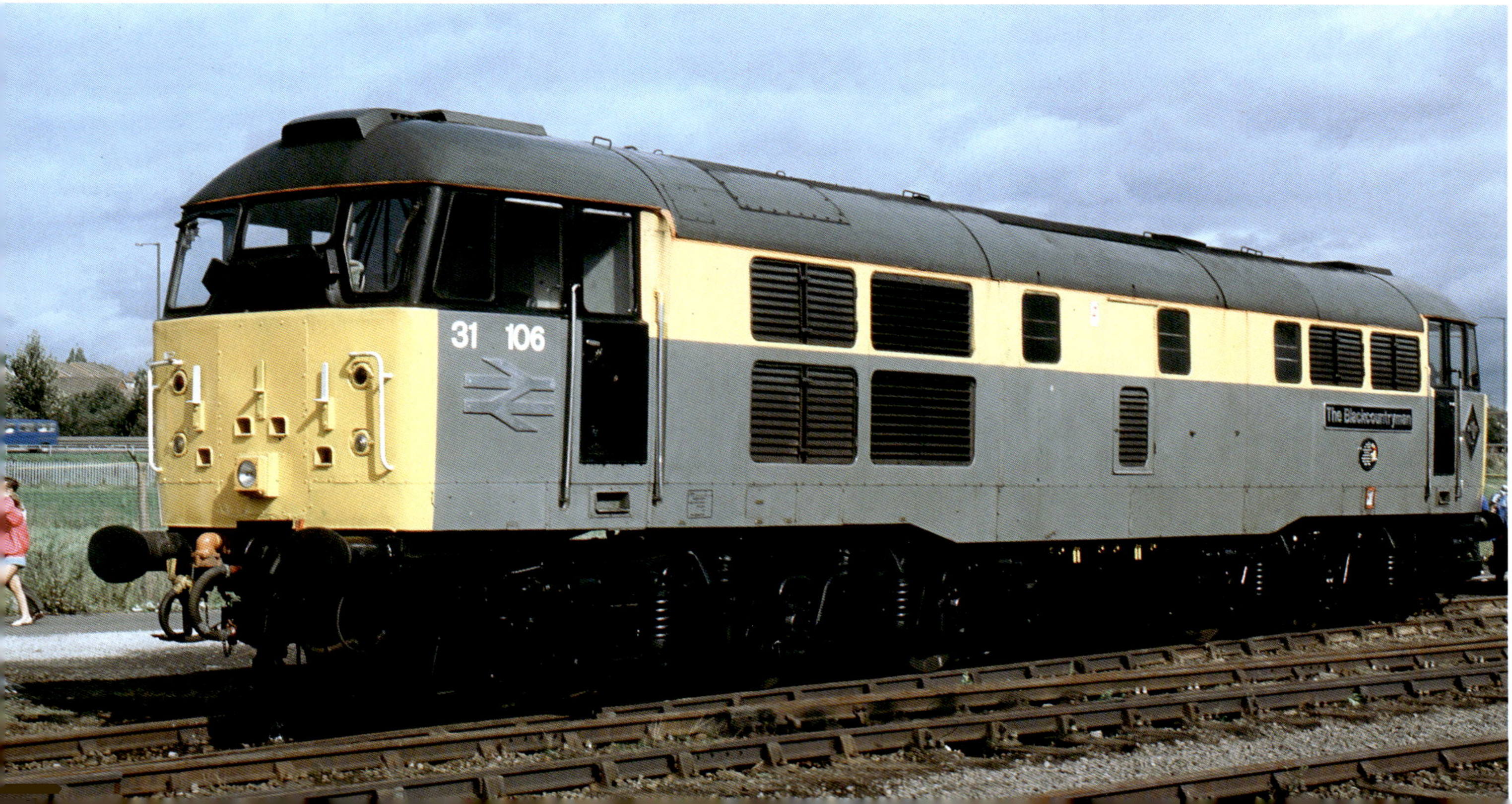

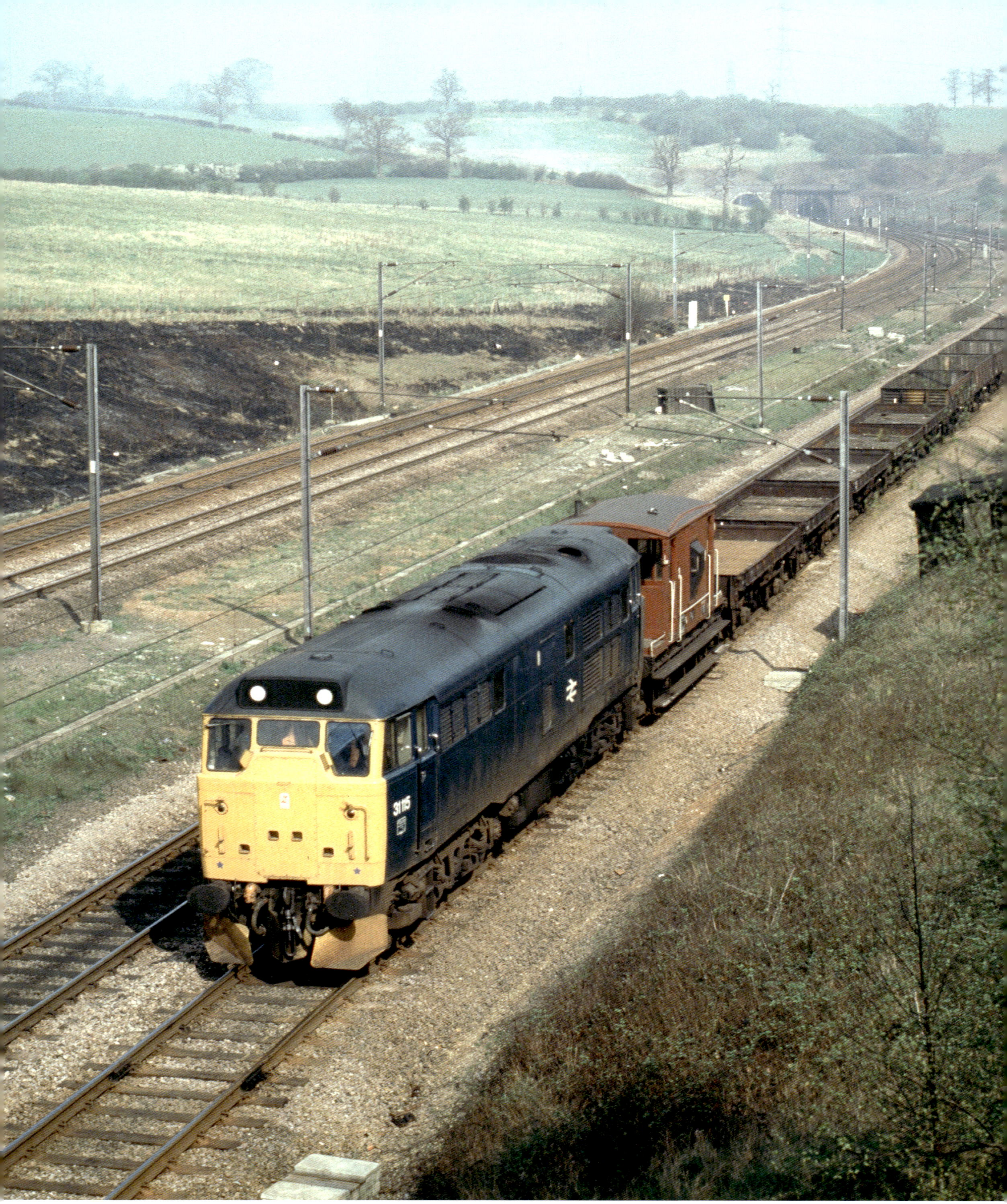

Familiar to the Eastern Region, the Class 31s lived in the shadow of much more illustrious English Electric power, they once were an everyday sight such as 31115 here at Hadley Wood on 10 April 1981. ***Colin Whitbread***

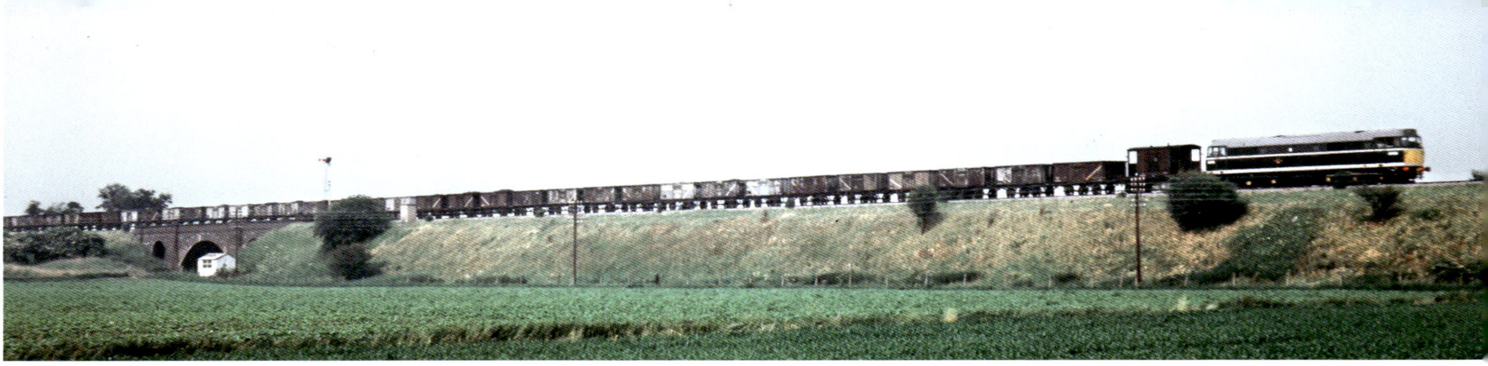

Slow steady progress of another Class 31 on the ECML near Grantham in June 1966. It was this kind of performance that brought about nicknames such as Brian (from the Magic Roundabout's snail character) or Peds (pedestrian). ***Michael Beaton***

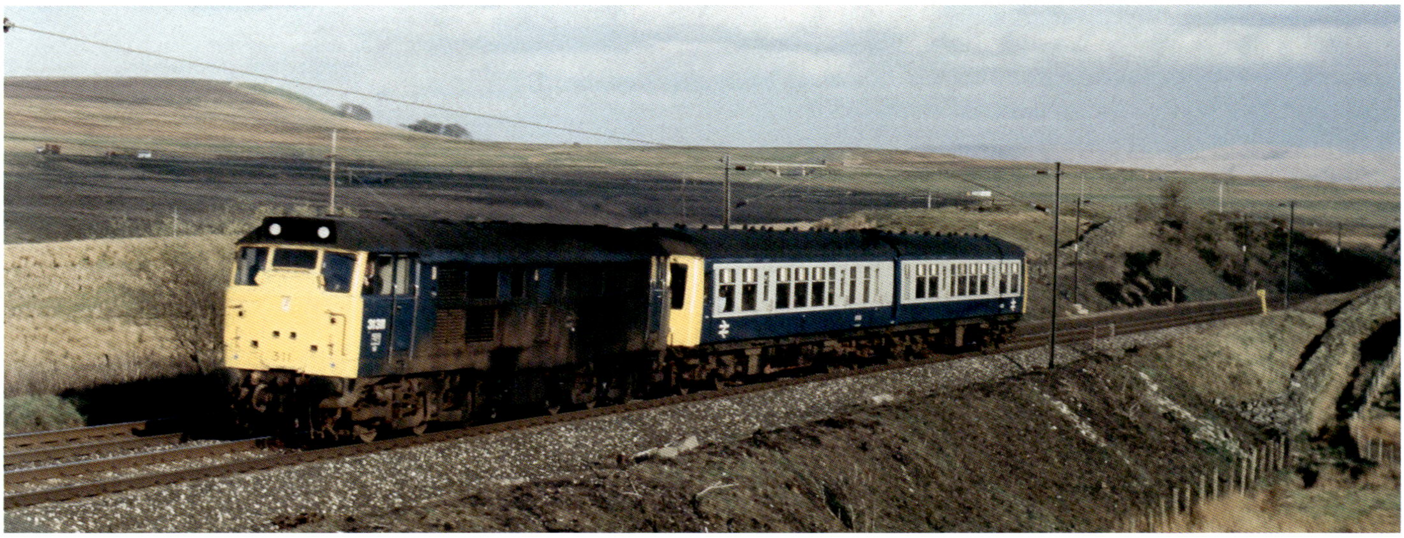

Showing better reliability than the failed DMU it was sent out to rescue is 31311 at Salterworth on 25 April 1985. ***Sid Steadman***

No mistaking the bright yellow paint scheme of the Infrastructure branded 31116 at Exeter Rail Fair on May Day 1994. ***Strathwood Library Collection***

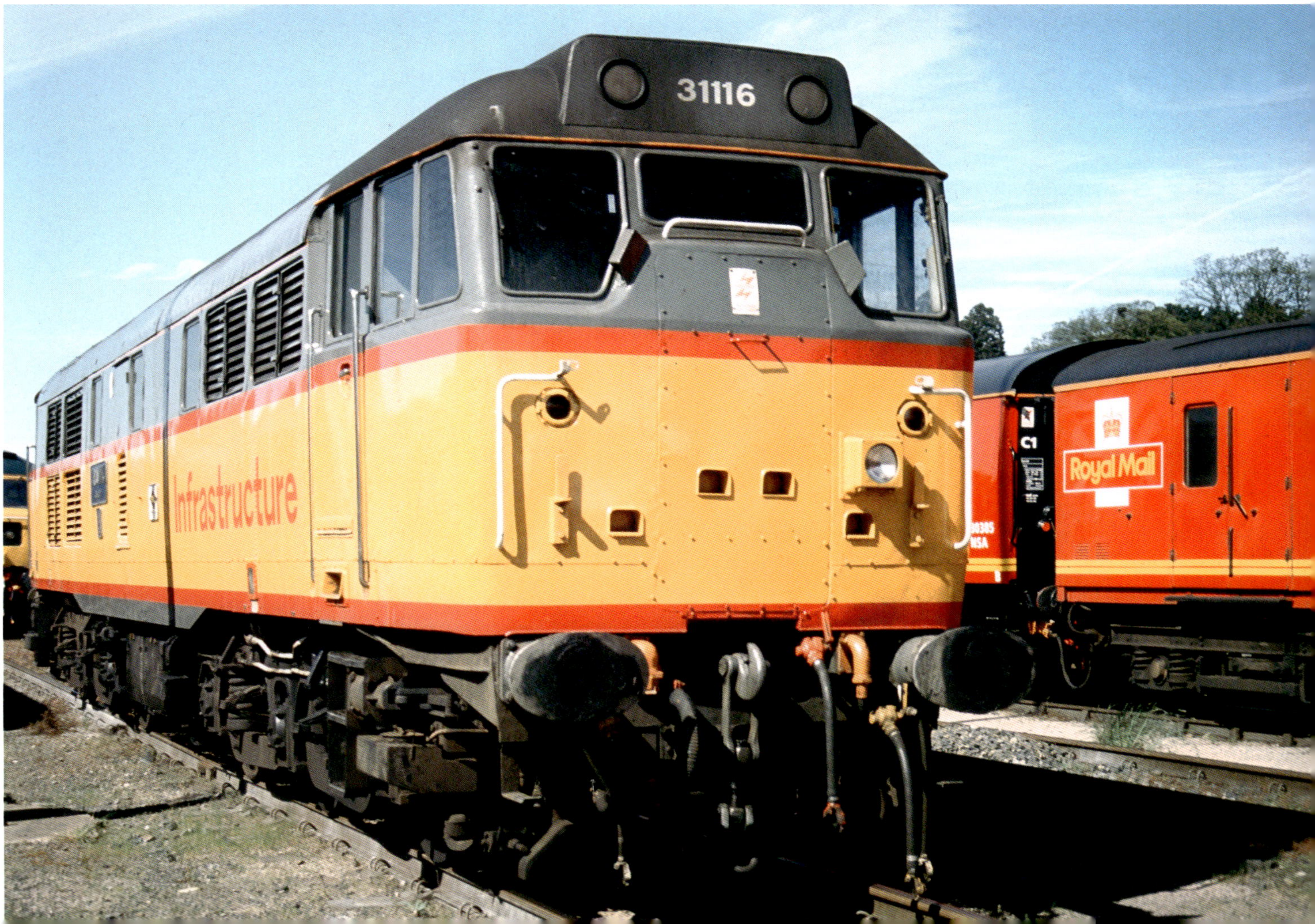

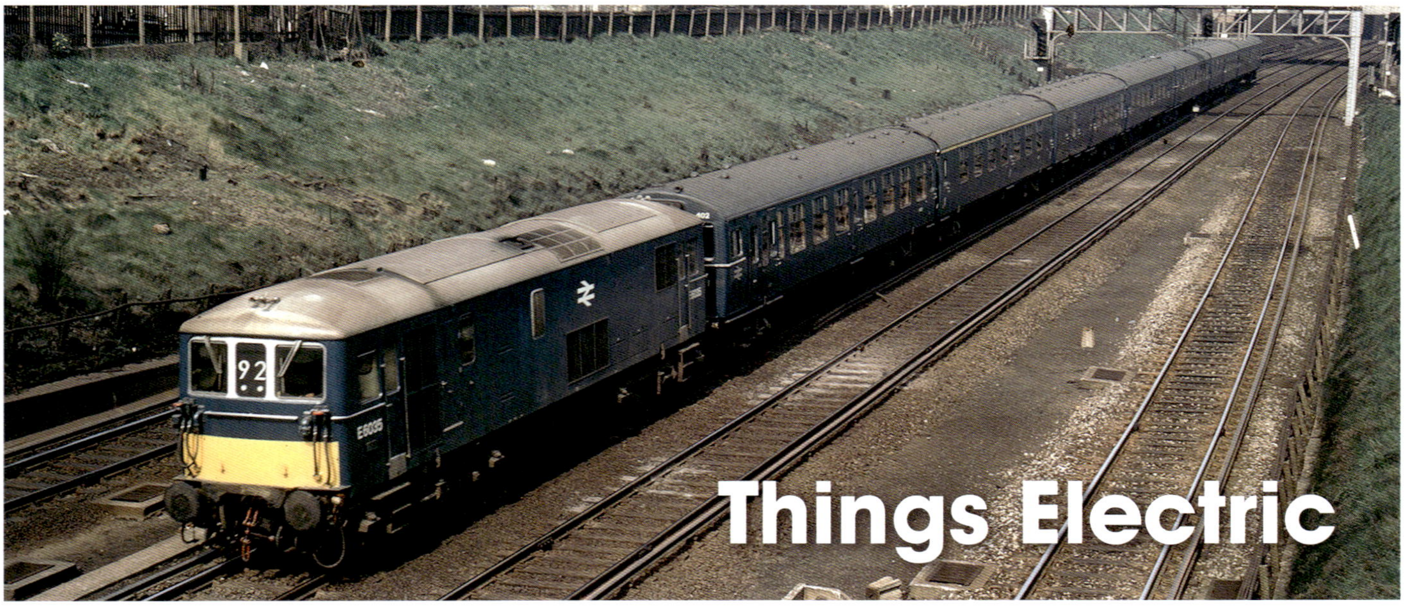

Things Electric

Less than a year old is Vulcan Foundry built E6035 near Clapham Junction on a Bournemouth train on 15 April 1967. ***Frank Hornby***

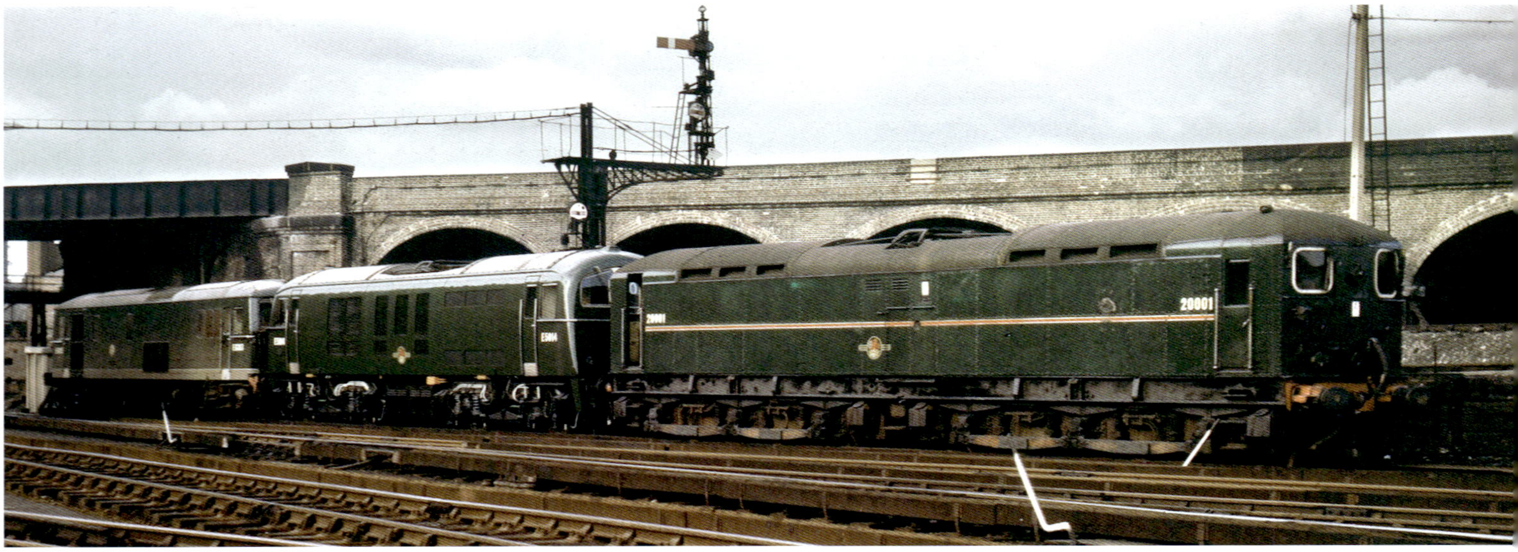

All three designs 20001, E5014 and E6003 at Stewarts Lane in 1963 would rely on English Electric power. ***Late Vincent Heckford/Strathwood Library Collection***

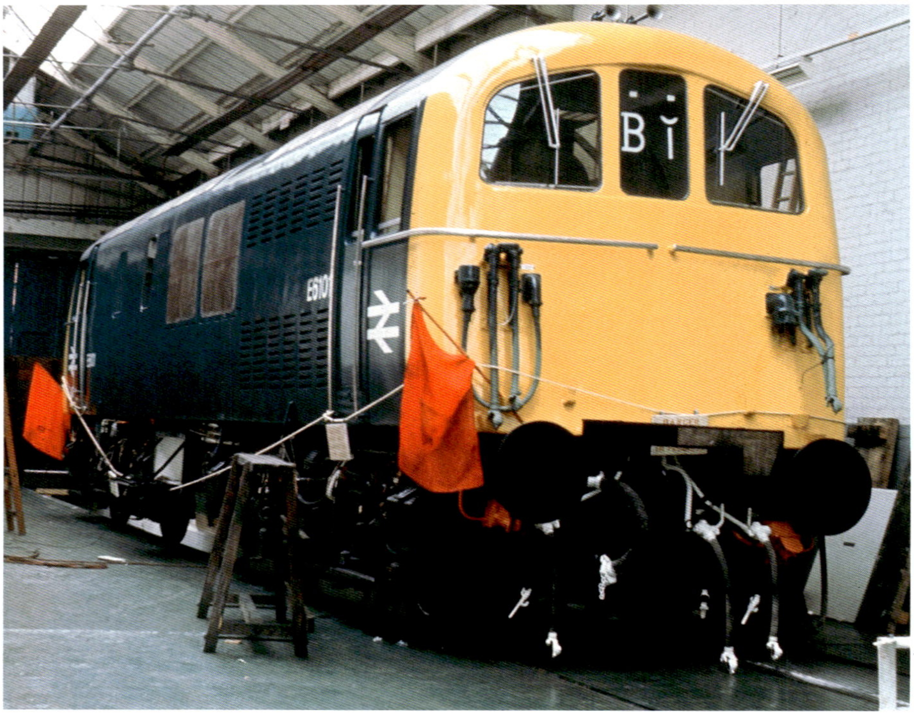

Diesel powered now with a Paxman engine, the English Electric booster sets were to remain in all ten of the Class 74 conversions, such as E6101 at Crewe Works on 10 September 1967. ***Paul Barber***

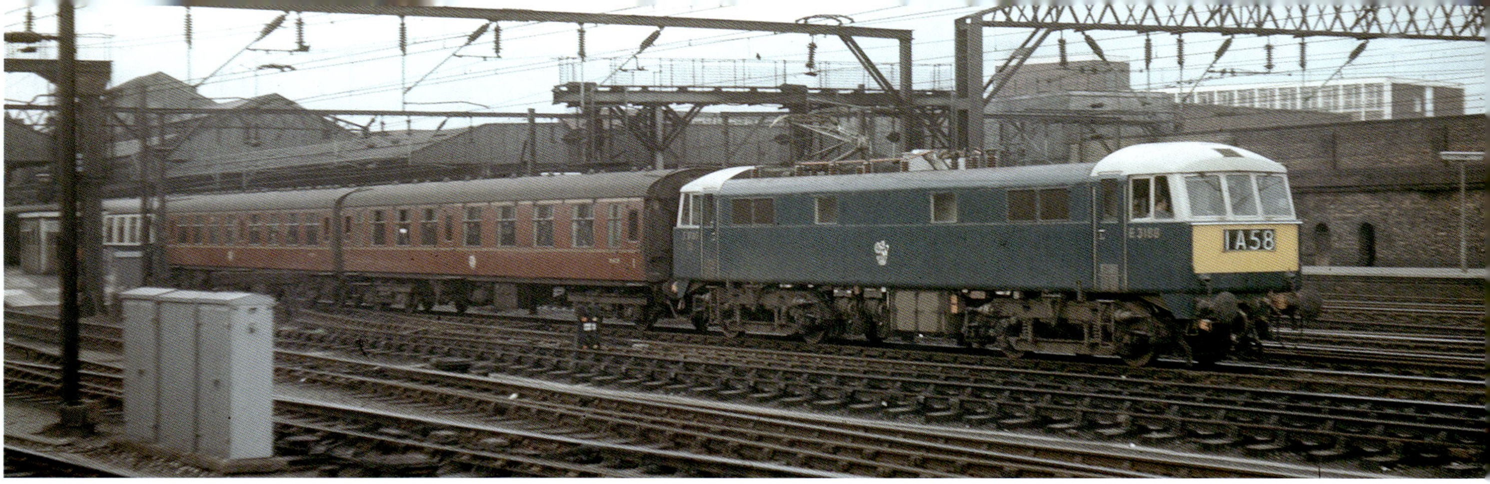

The standard electric design adopted for the WCML was designated AL6 first of all, later becoming Class 86. They were built by both British Railways at Doncaster Works and by English Electric at their Newton le Willows works. Entering service at the end of October 1965 was E3188 seen a few years later departing Crewe for the south. ***Michael Beaton***

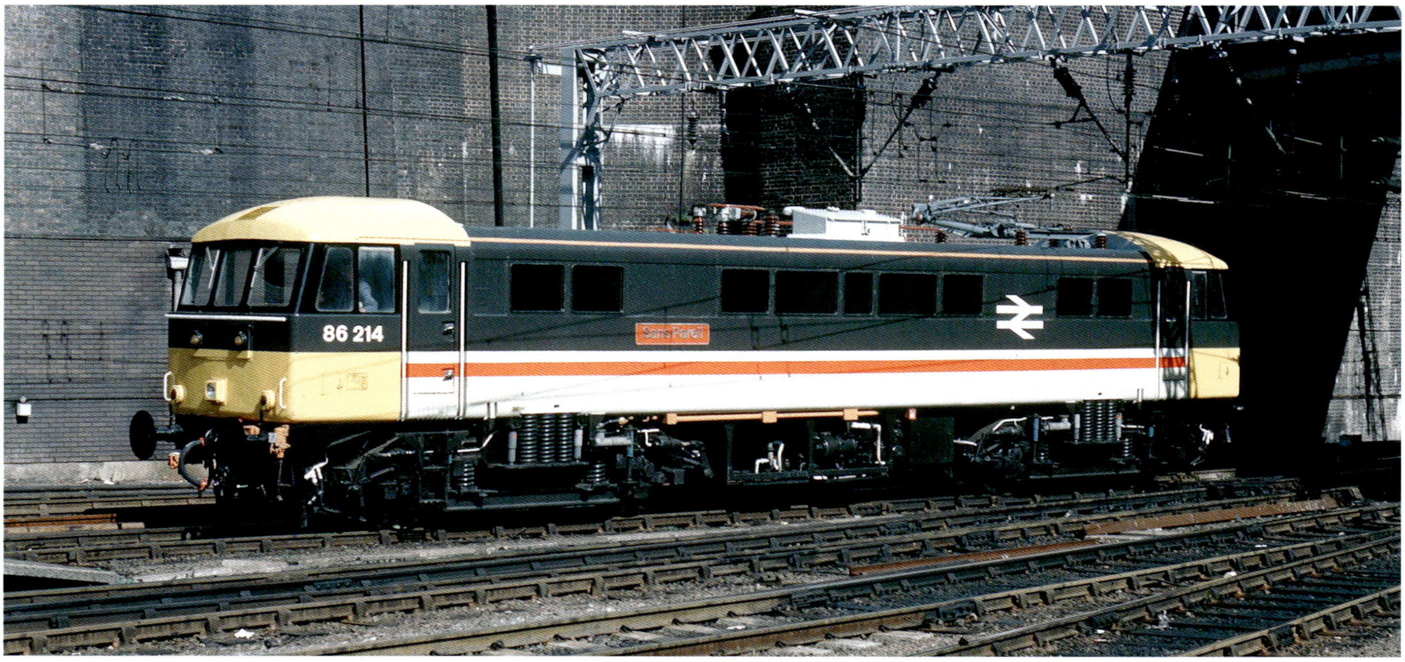

Later rebuilt with flexi coil suspension and recently ex works, is 86214 Sans Pareil at New Street in September 1986. ***David T Williams***

Ready to return to traffic at Crewe Works on 30 March 1969 is E3164 having just gained a full yellow front and cast Inter City arrows affixed to its sides. ***Frank Hornby***

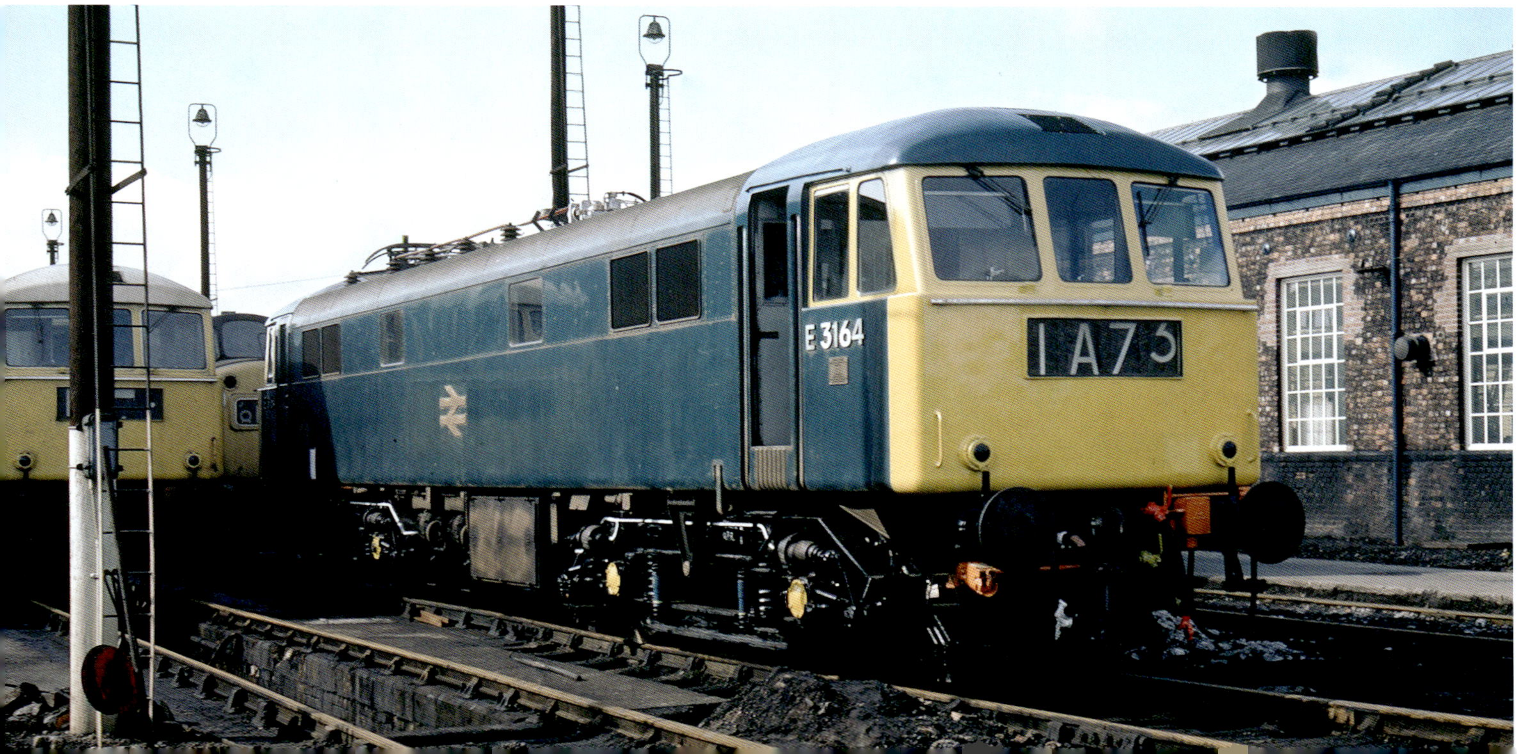

Scrappers

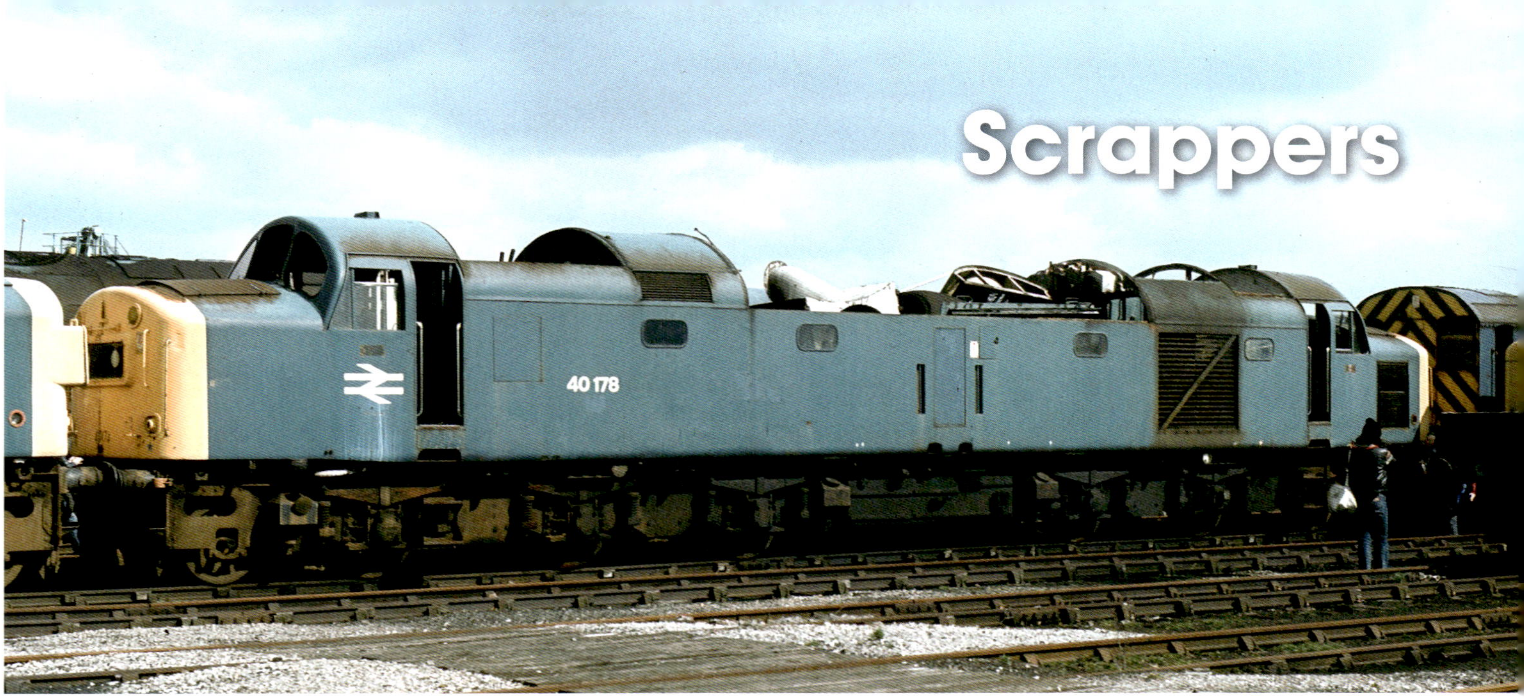

Looking more like a Bucket than ever before is the hulk of 40178 at Swindon Works in April 1983. ***Steve Ireland***

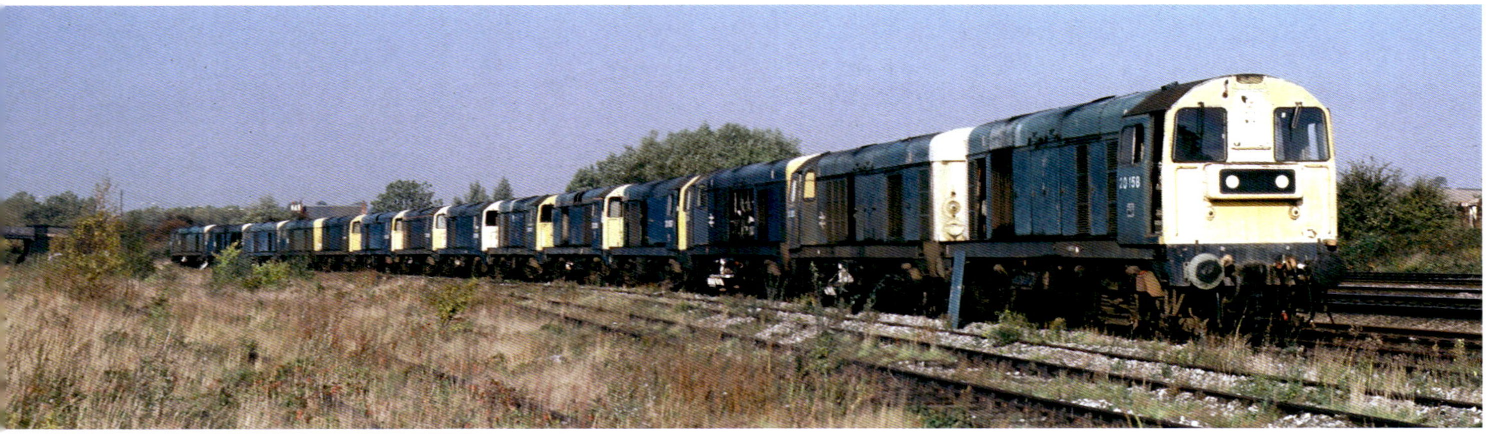

Leading the long line of fourteen classmates at Stanton Gate is 20158 as they await their fate on 17 October 1989. ***Stuart Broughton***

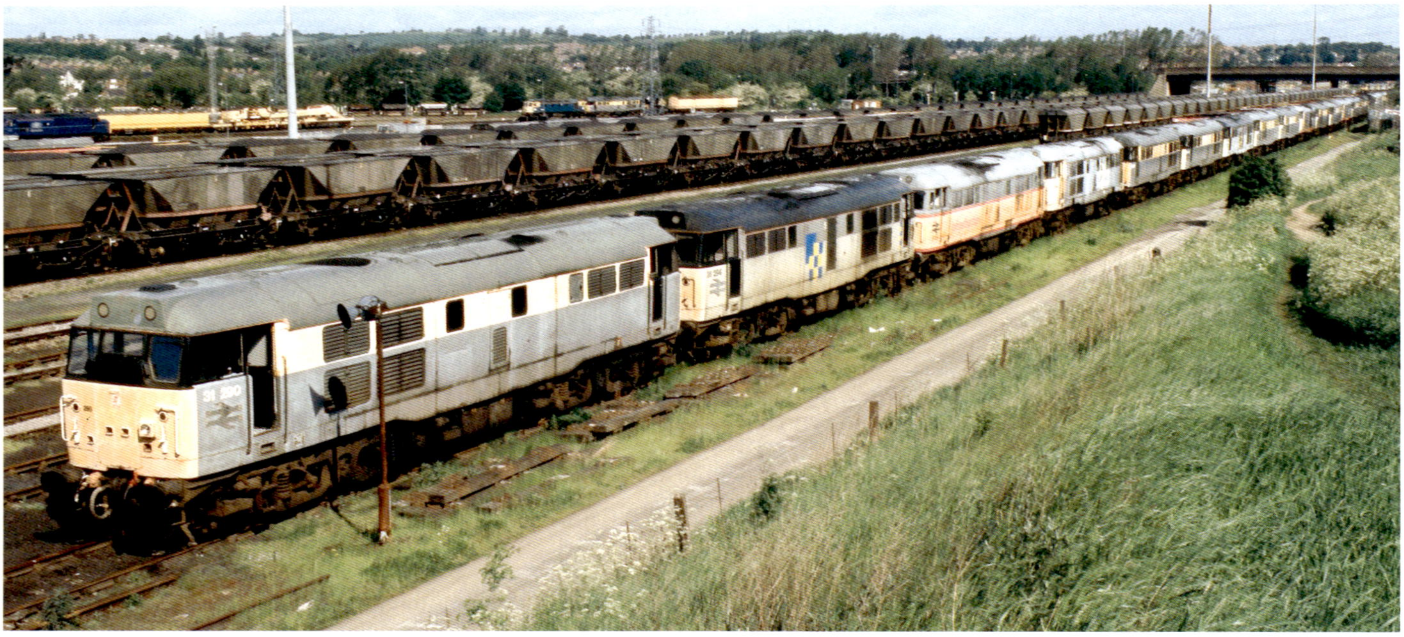

An even longer line of twenty two withdrawn Class 31s is headed up by 31290 on 1 June 1996 at Toton. ***Steve Ireland***

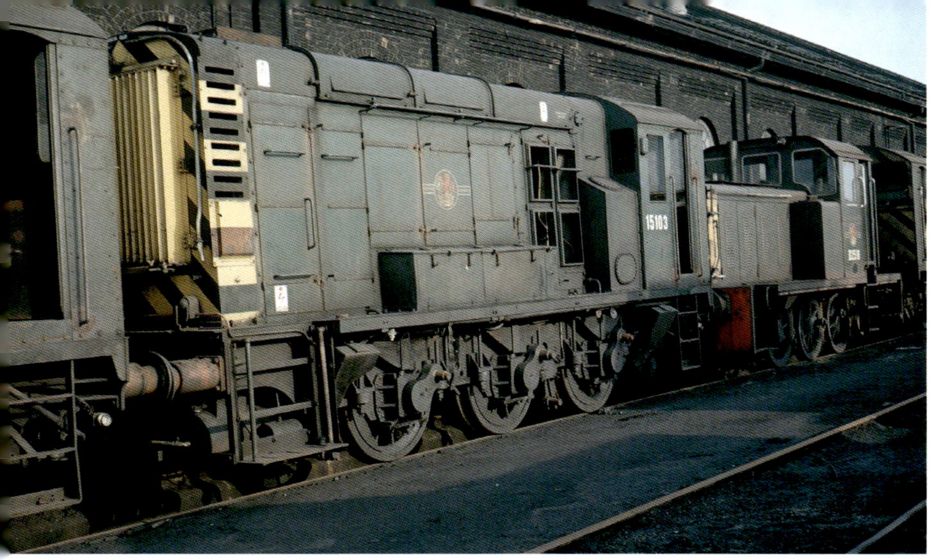

A more modest line of withdrawn locomotives outside Derby Works in February 1968 includes English Electric powered 15103 built at Swindon by British Railways to complete an order made by the GWR just before Nationalisation. ***Late Norman Browne/Strathwood Library Collection***

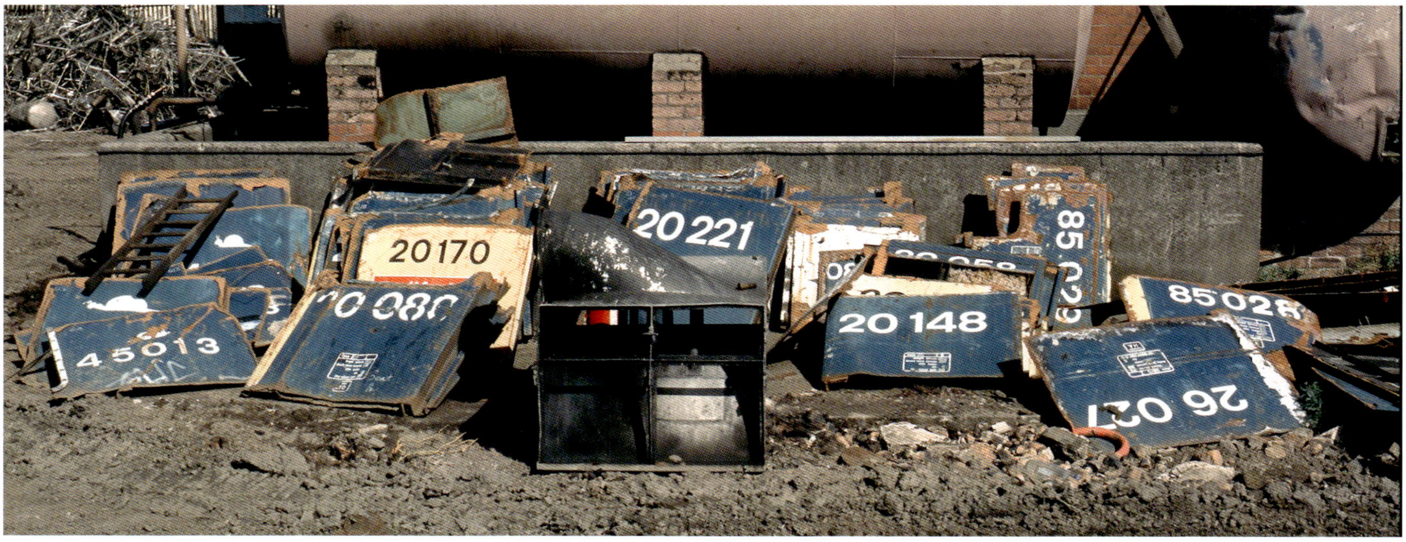

The desire for collectors of flame cut number panels can be assessed from this collection awaiting sales MC Metals on 15 April 1995. ***Michael Hill/Strathwood Library Collection***

Below: It looks like some giant has trodden on 31227 as the cutters of Vic Berry's yard at Leicester have paused in their work a while during in 1989. ***Strathwood Library Collection***

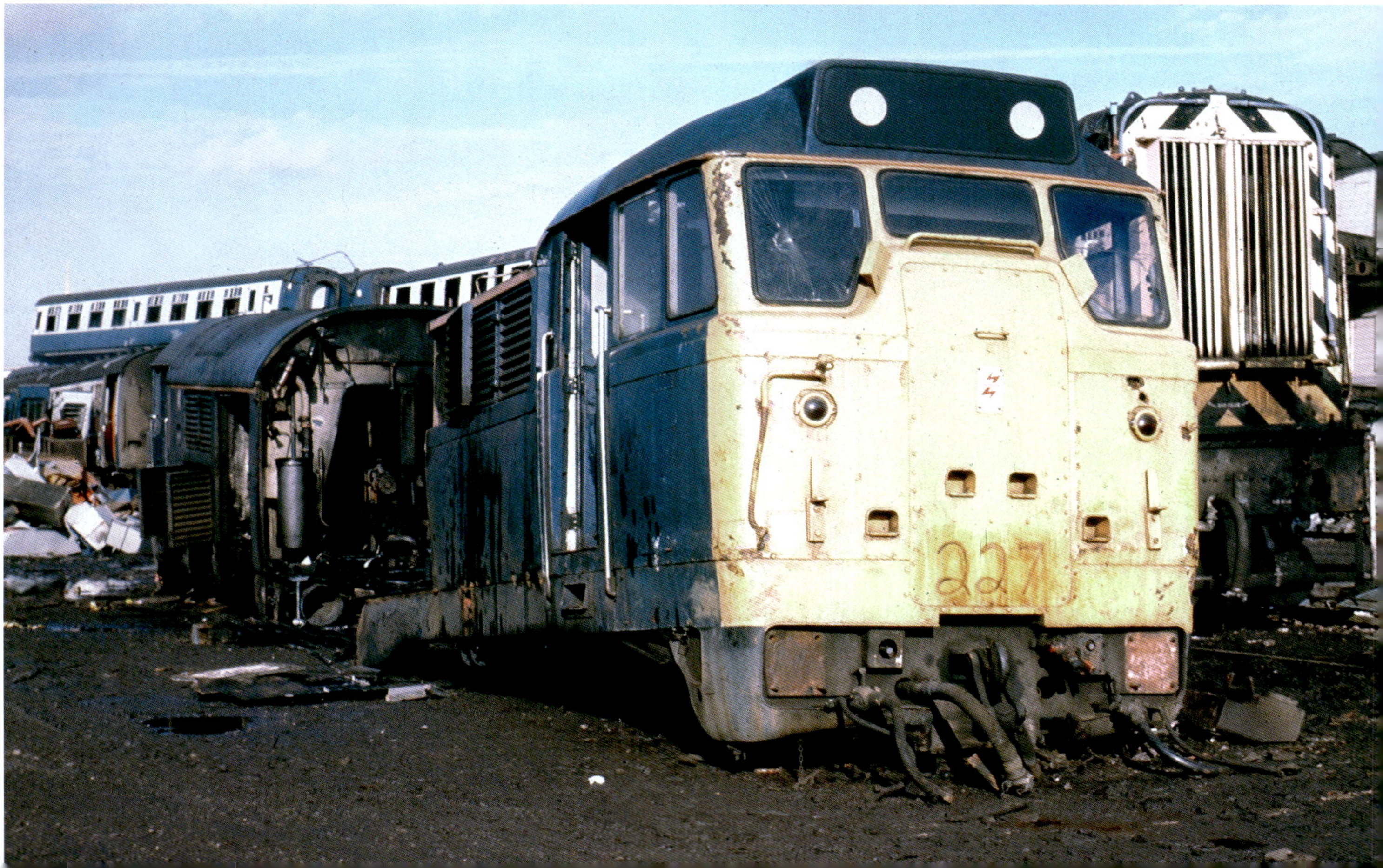

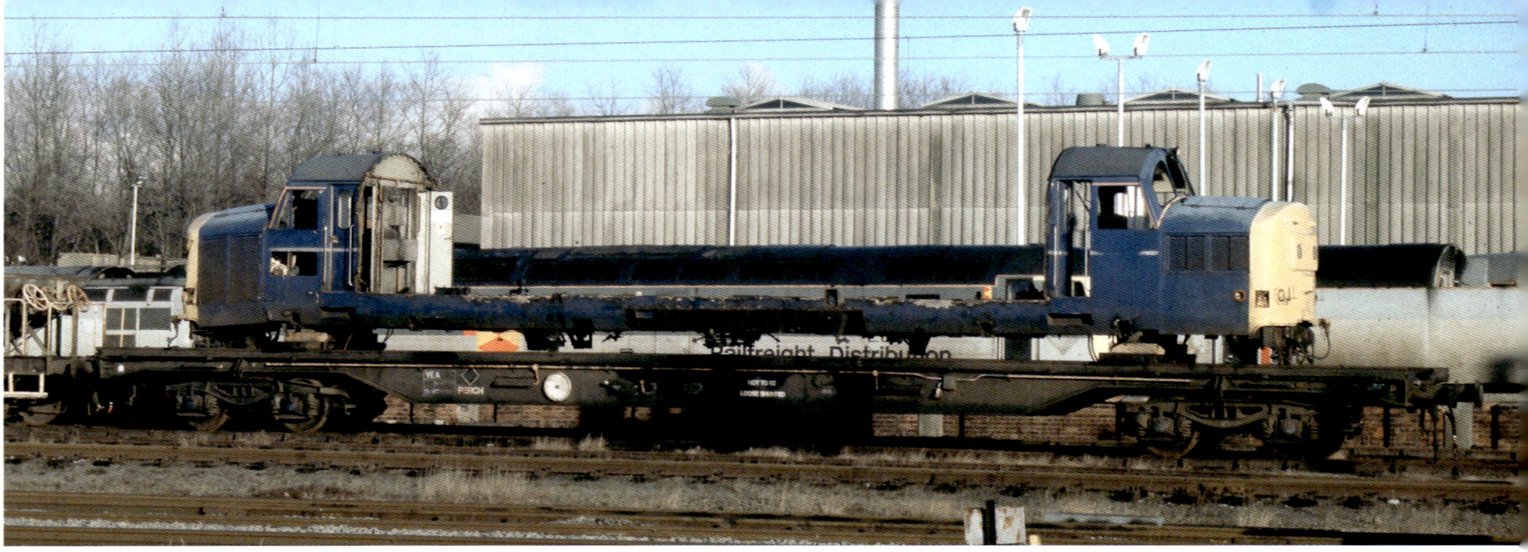

Even more radical is the destruction of 37371 at Wigan CRC on 29 December 1999. ***Stephen Fort***

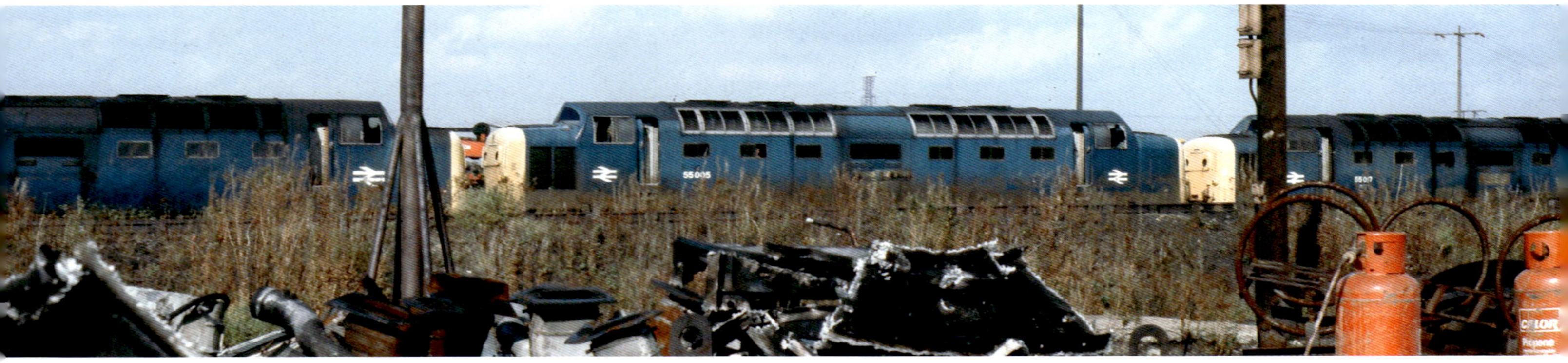

The line up of Deltics such as 55005 at Doncaster was desperate. This example stood on death row for two years before finally being shunted within range of those sinister gas cylinders. ***Strathwood Library Collection***

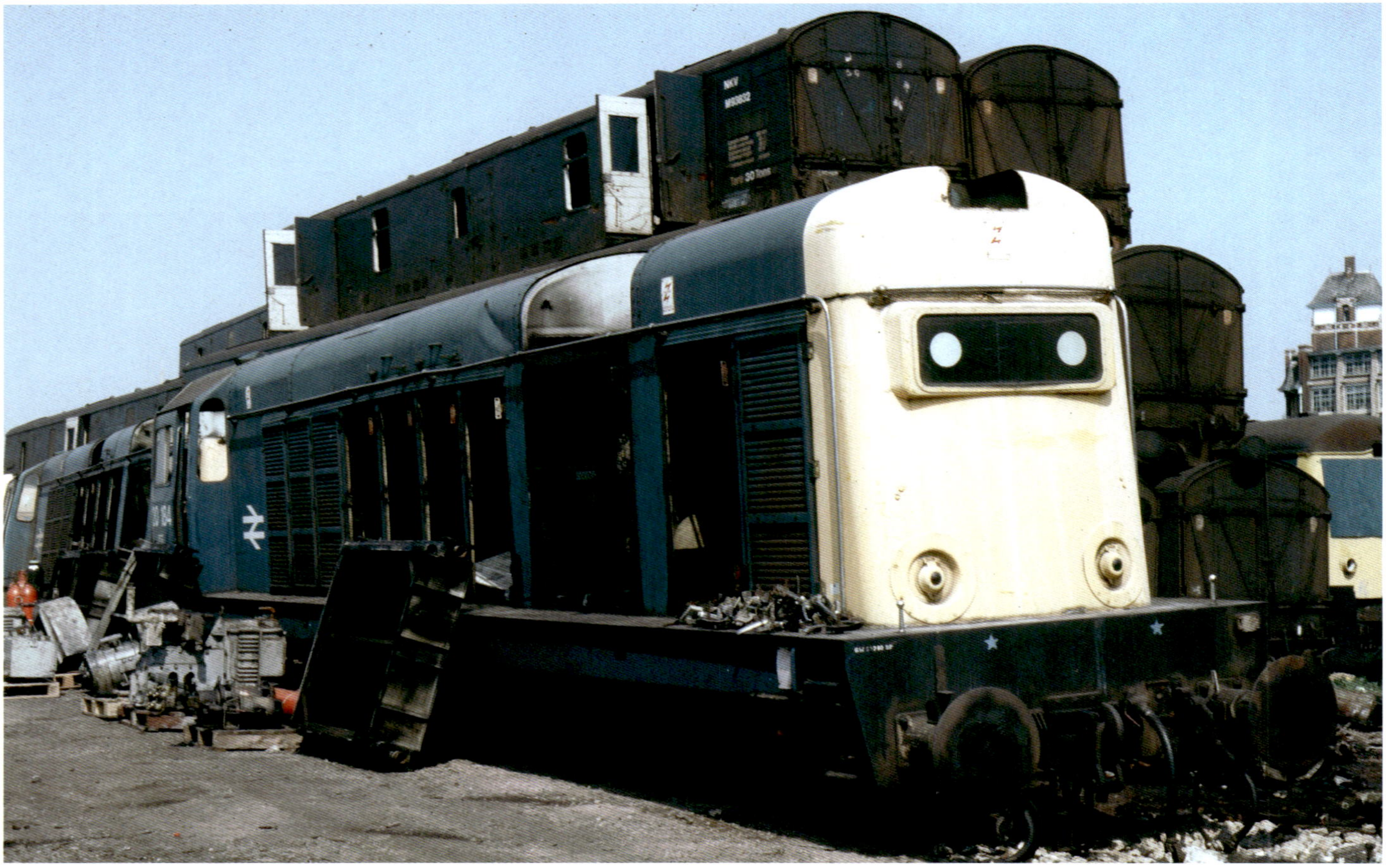

Health and Safety freaks and spotters eat your hearts out at the sight of 20184 within the piled high clutter that was Vic Berry's scrap yard in May of 1988. ***Steve Ireland***

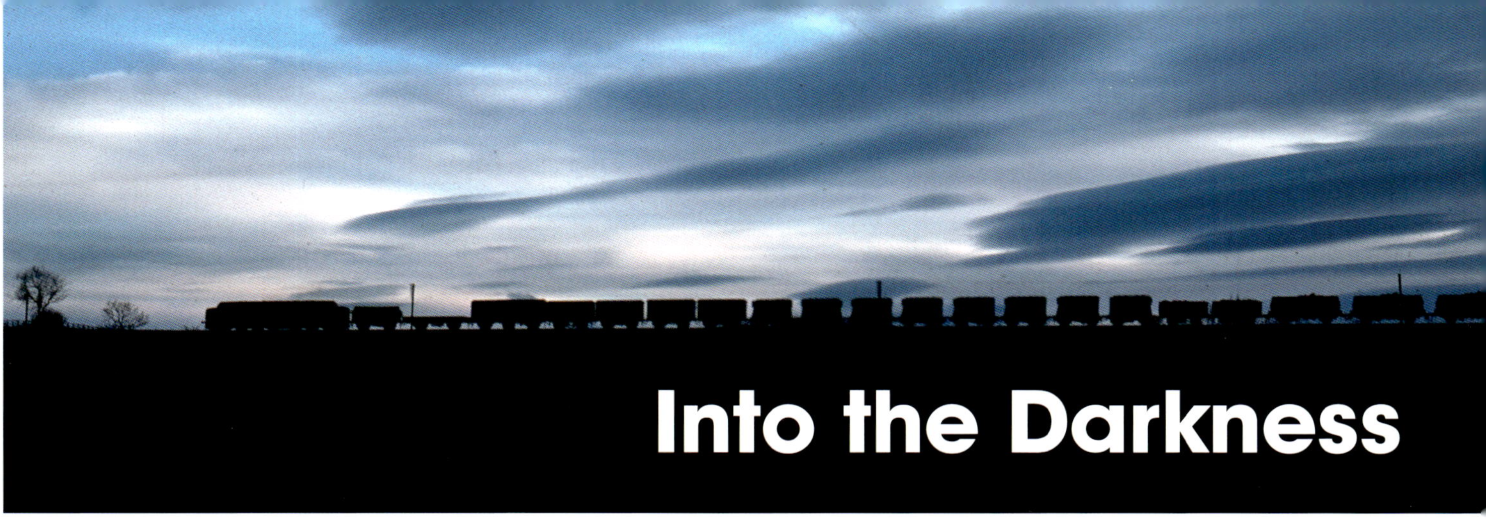

Into the Darkness

An unknown Class 40 whistles into the night at Ormside on 17 April 1980. ***Late Pete Walton/Sid Steadman***

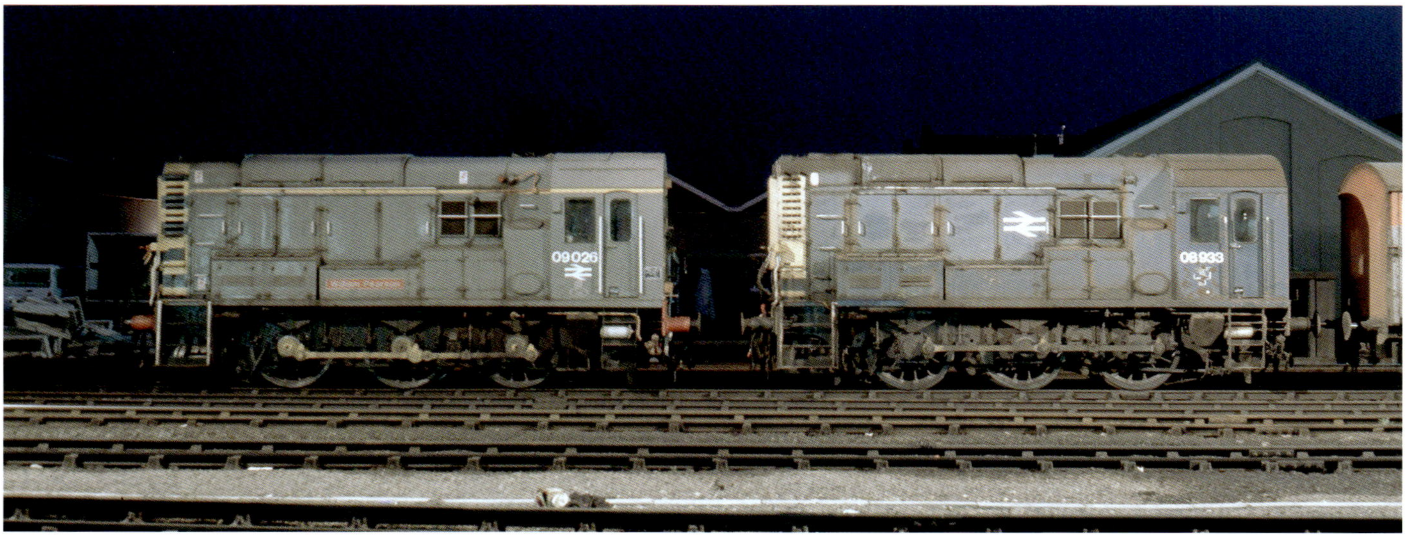

The bright yard lights at Eastleigh pick out 09026 and 08933 on the early evening of 27 March 1990. ***Strathwood Library Collection***

Below: Even more vivid is the effect of the time exposure and the steam heating and exhaust above the roof of 40118 at Appleby on freezing 5 January 1985. ***Late Pete Walton/Sid Steadman***

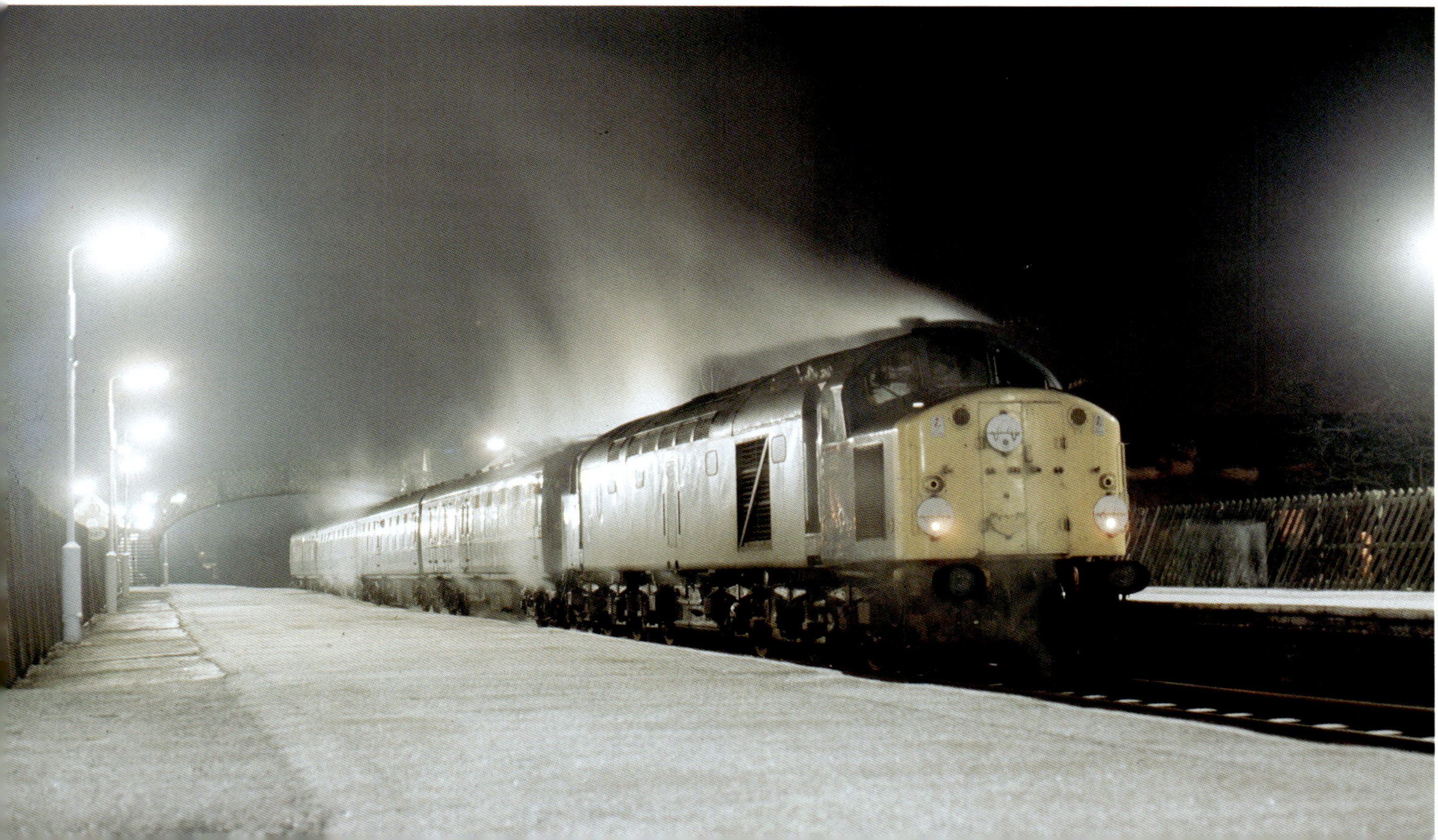

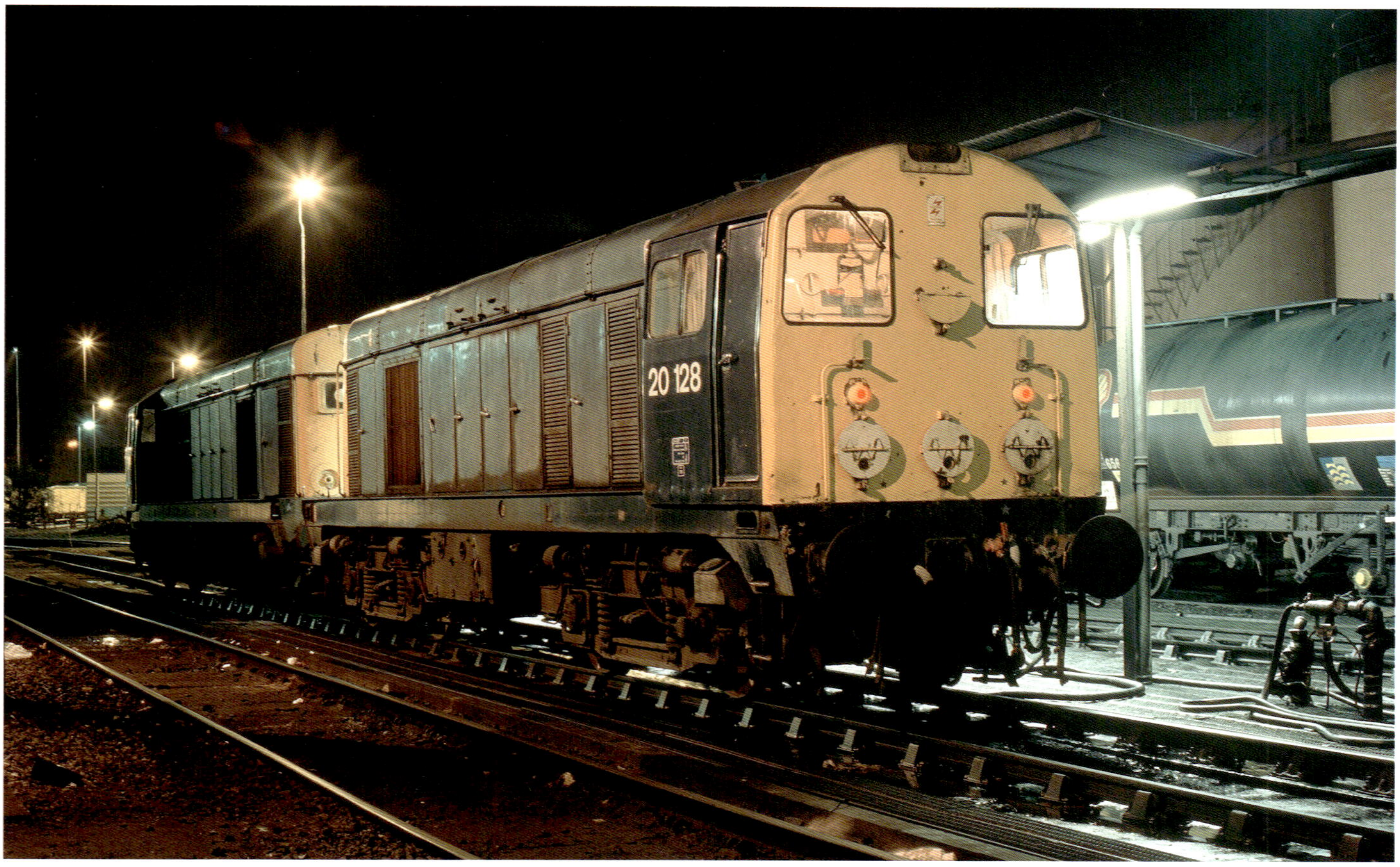

An irresistible chance to capture 20128 and 20168 on Toton's fuel line on 16 March 1992 rewards our lens man with this fine study. ***Stuart Broughton***

Night shots work very well after rain has fallen, bringing attractive reflections of light to the composition, again enhanced by the cab lights of 37047 leading 37252 at Carlisle on 29 March 1985. ***Late Pete Walton/Sid Steadman***

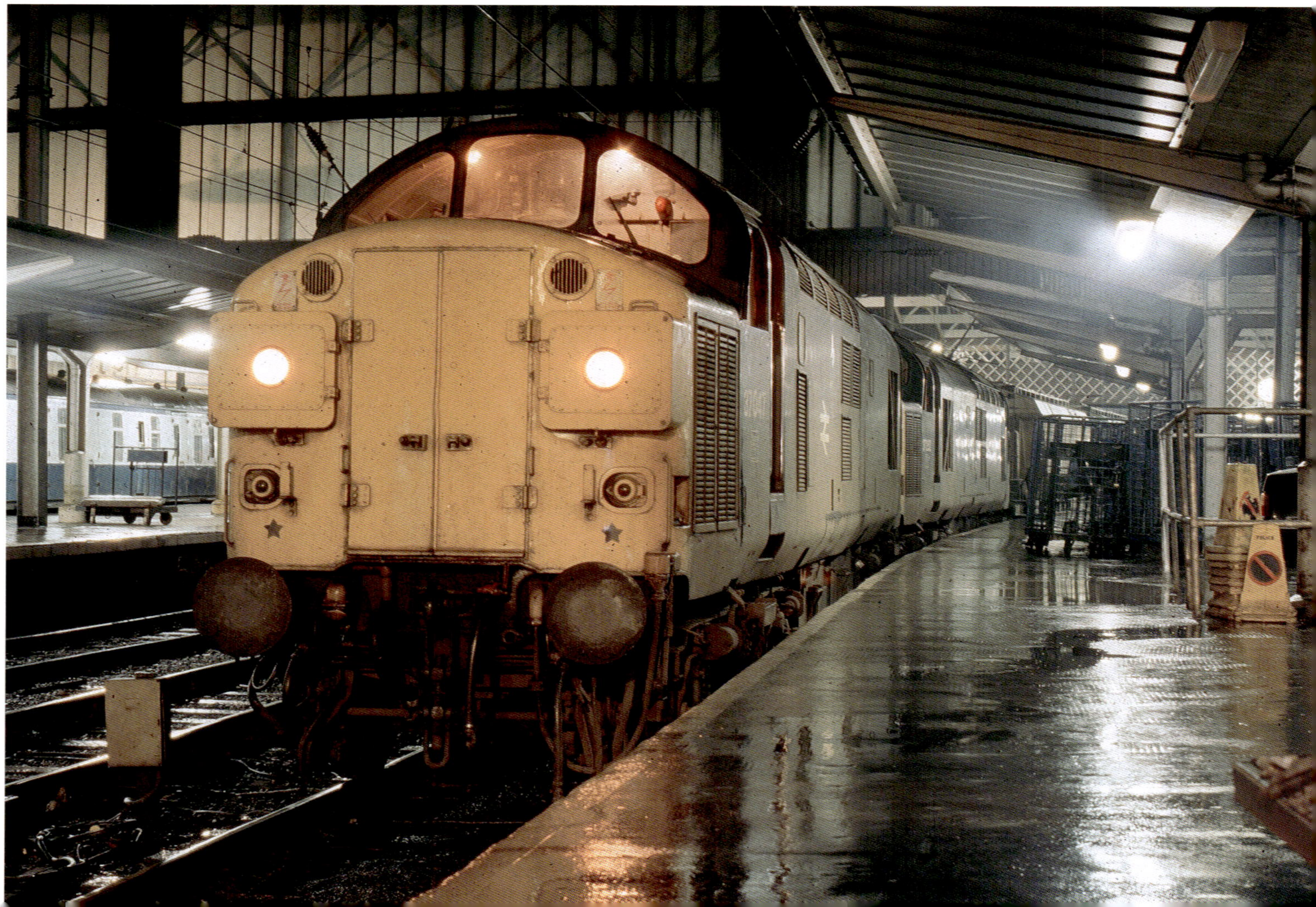

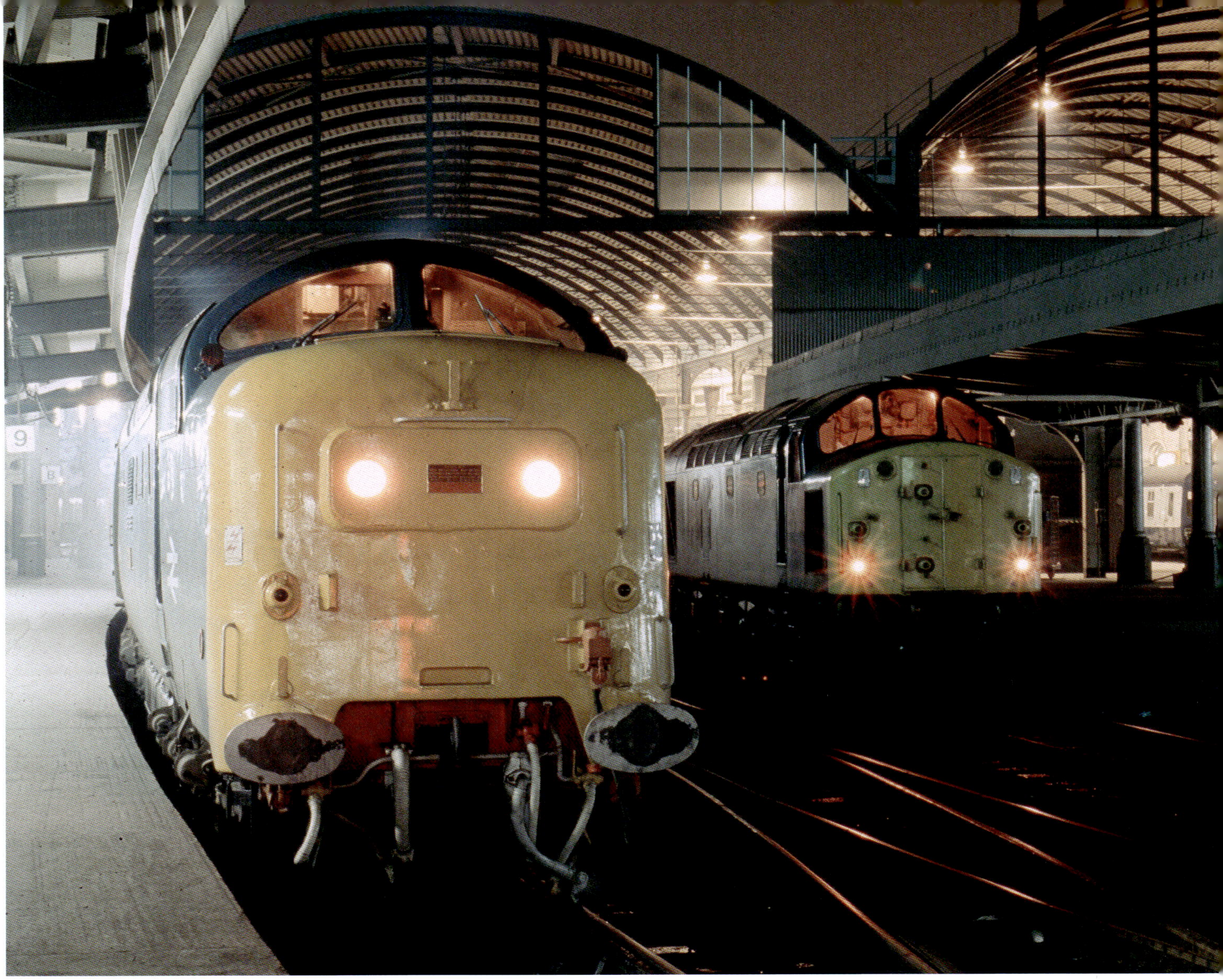

Reflections from the track work at Newcastle during the brief stop for 55015 Tulyar working the 20.15 Kings Cross to Edinburgh Waverley, while 40085 waits alongside on Friday 20 November 1981. ***Colin Whitbread***

Fingers crossed, the figures on the platform keep still while recording 50036 at Exeter St.Davids with the 20.41 to Basingstoke on 2 December 1990. ***Alister Betts***

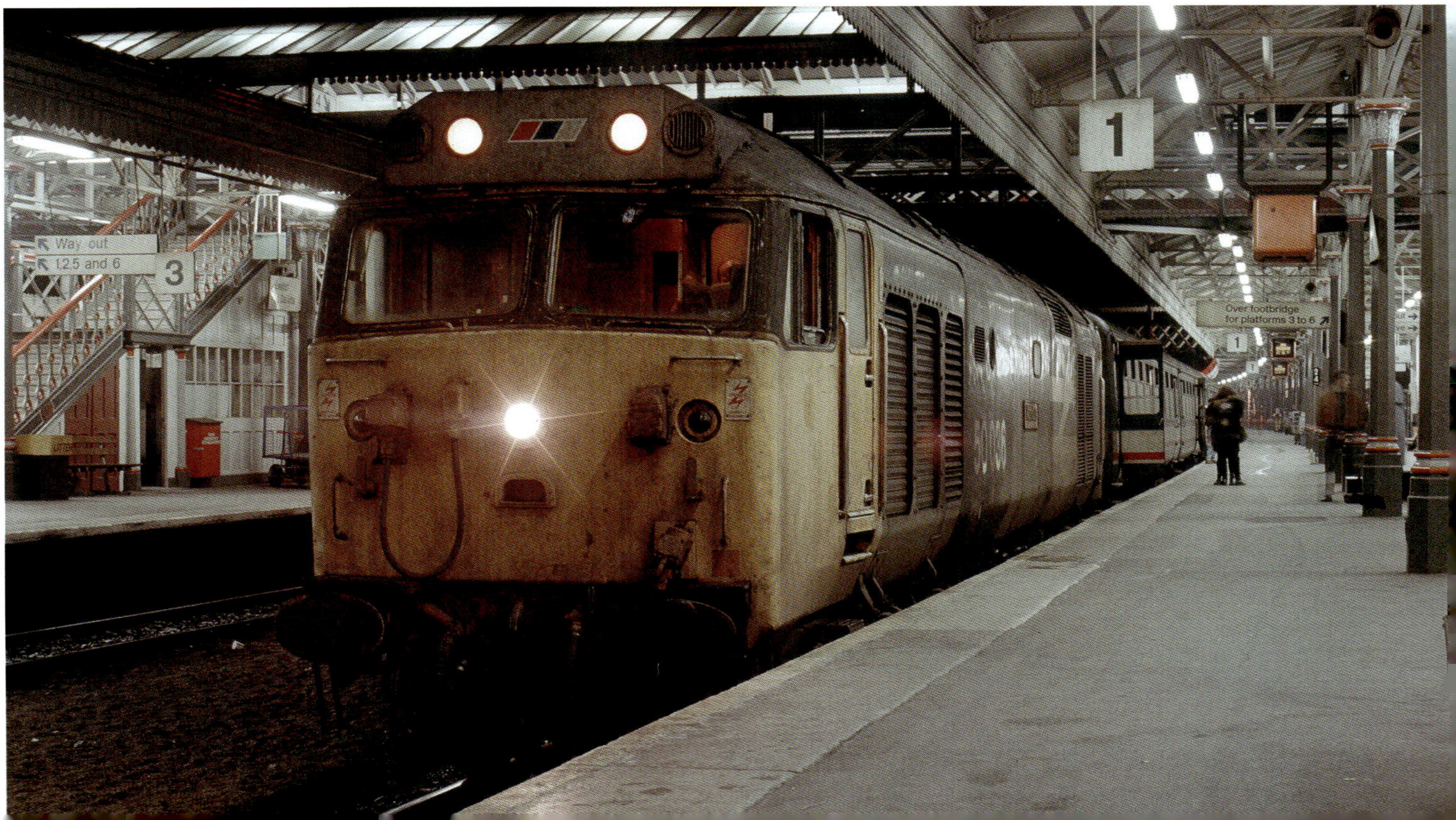

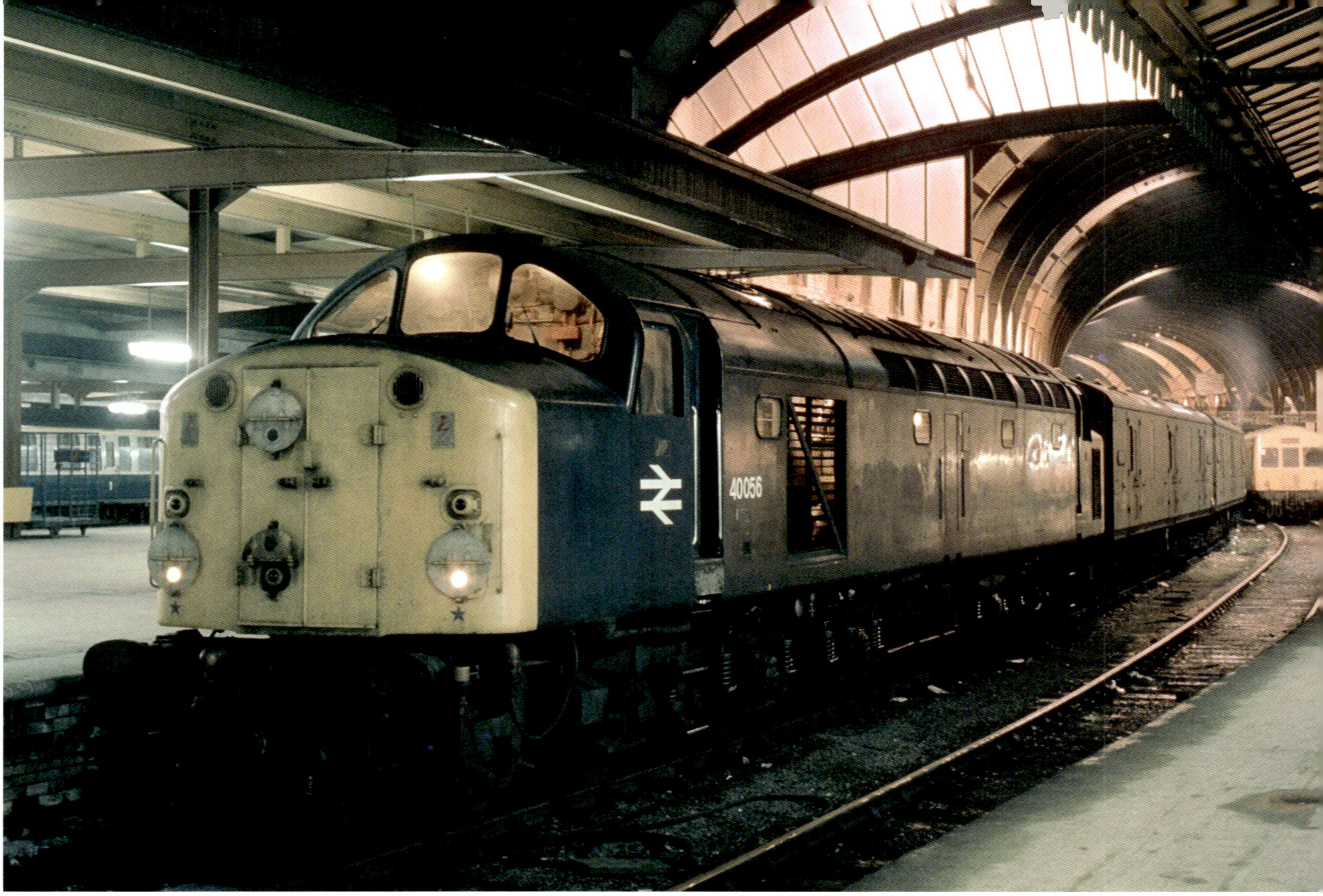

Even the engine room lights can be seen in this study of 40056 at York on 9 December 1980. ***Colin Whitbread***

Something to go for after the steam haulage has finished for the day with 55017 The Durham Light Infantry working the ecs off the Scarborough Spa Express at Leeds on Tuesday 11 August 1981. ***Colin Whitbread***

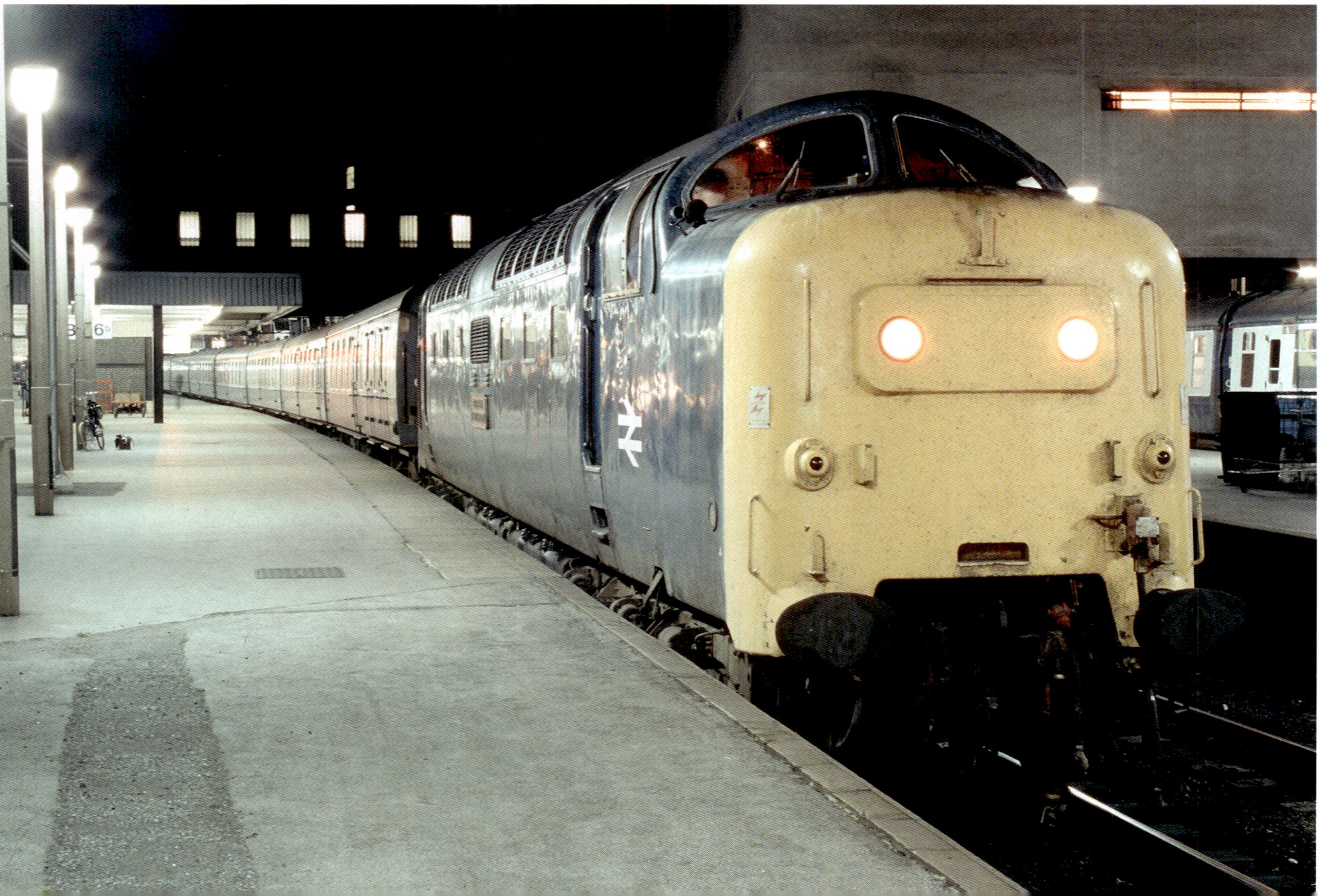

In Distress

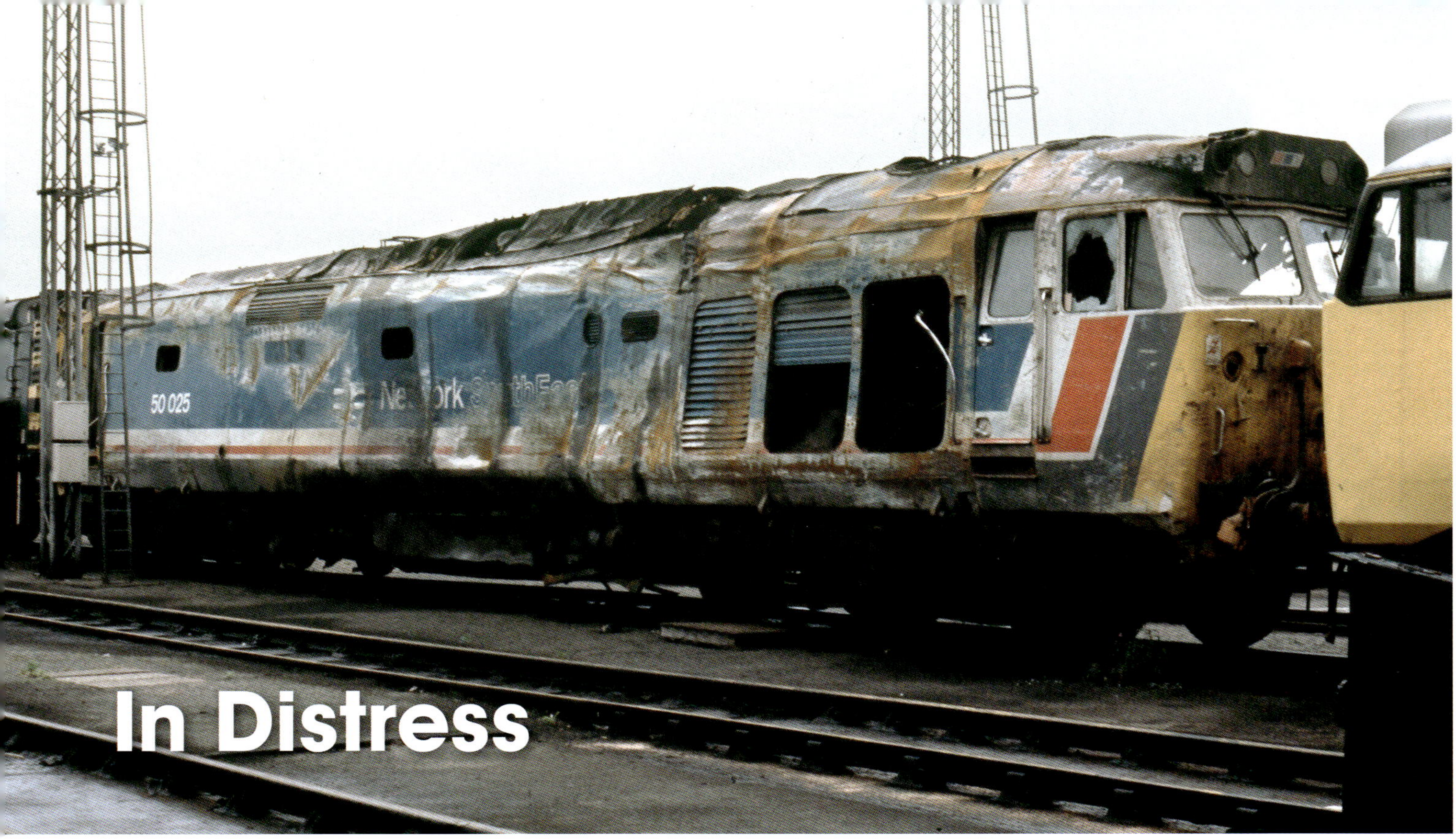

Standing at Old Oak Common in September 1989 is 50025 Invincible, which met with an untimely end in August 1989 when it was involved in a high-speed derailment due to vandals at West Ealing. Subsequently it was withdrawn due to the severity of the damage it sustained. ***Strathwood Library Collection***

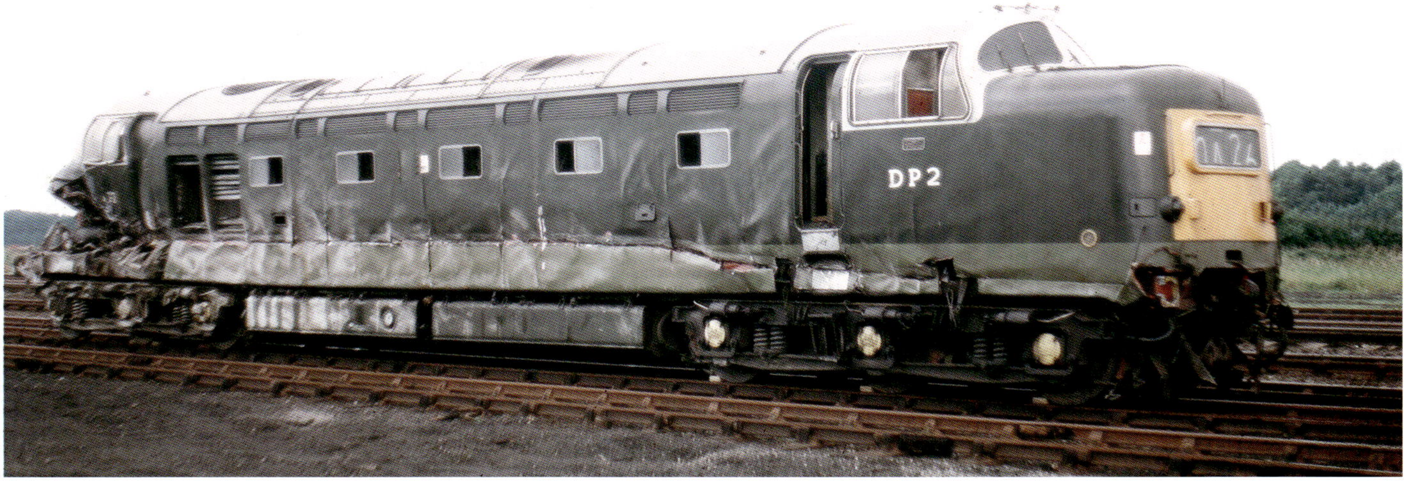

Even more violent an end for DP2 seen still at Thirsk after the tragic derailment on 30 July 1967. ***The Late John Bellwood/Strathwood Library collection***

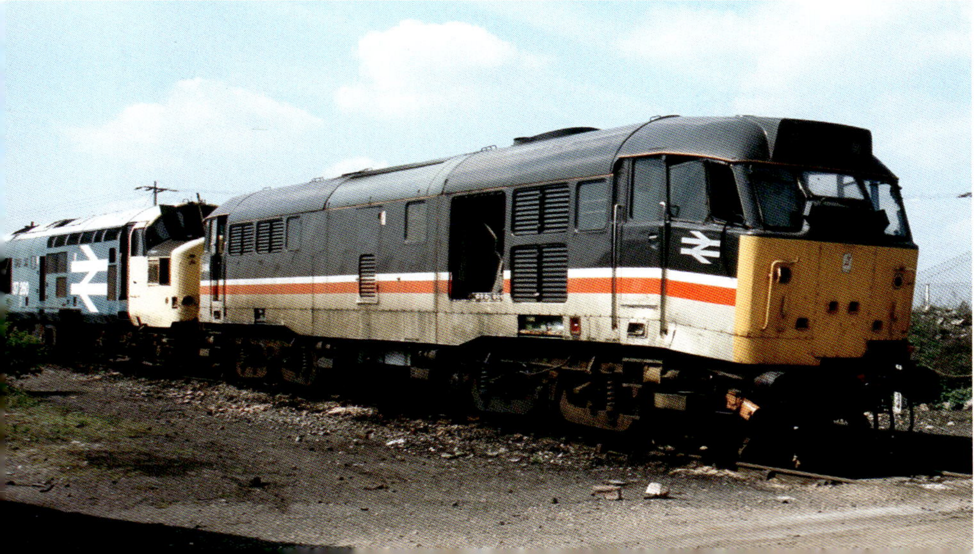

Class 31s are prone to droopy noses if rough shunted as typified by 31464 at Doncaster Works on 28 April 1991. ***Peter Robinson***

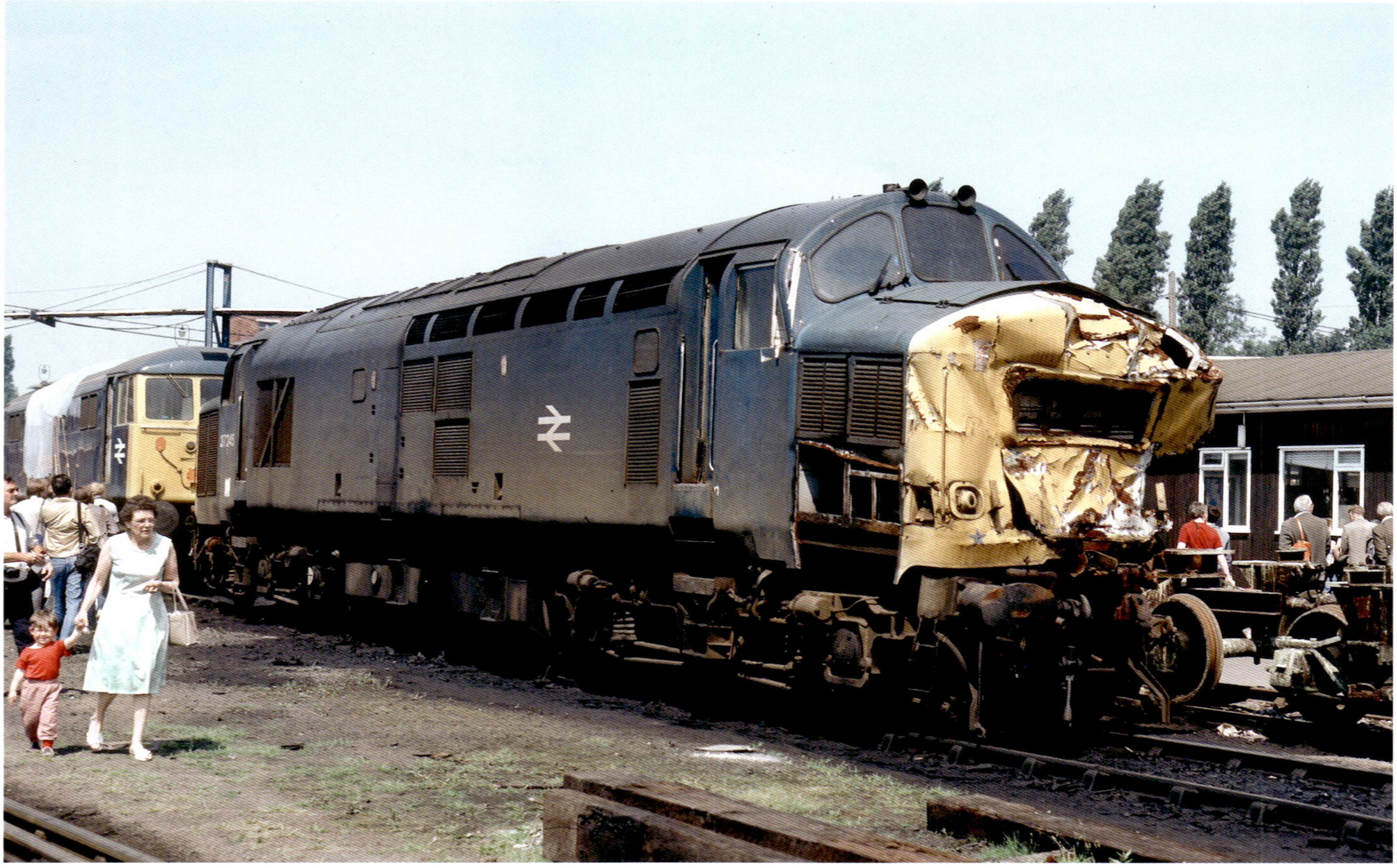

Not hidden away from public gaze for the Open Day at Crewe Works was the damaged sustained by 37245 earlier in 1987. ***David T Williams***

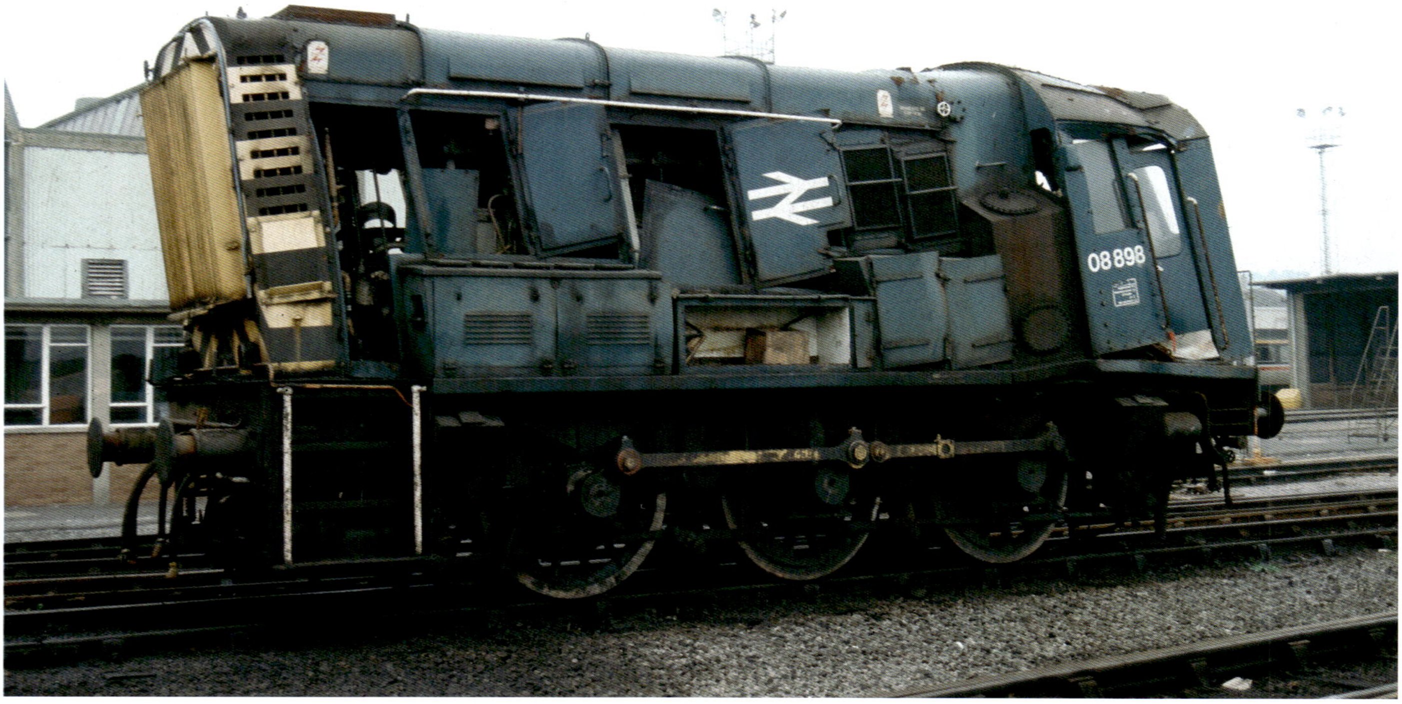

This is what happens if you take a standard Class 08 onto the Burry Port & Gwendreath Valley line and run it at speed into a low bridge on the route. The unfortunate shunter is seen at Landore awaiting a call to Doncaster for scrapping ten years later in 1998 by C. F. Booth. ***Strathwood Library Collection***

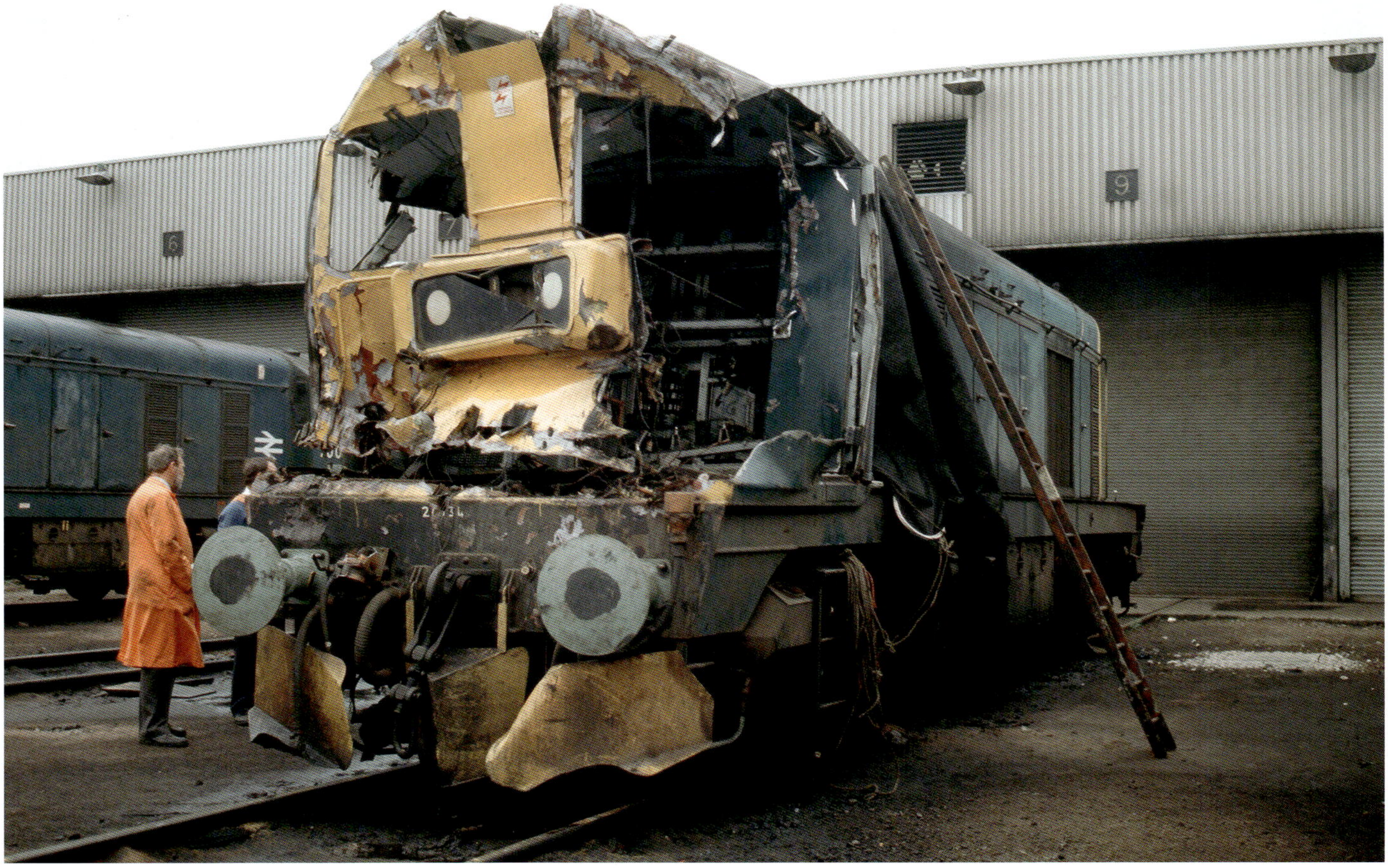

A grisly end for 20134 at Toton in May 1989 after a collision with a merry go round train. Two years later the locomotive was broken up in Glasgow by M. C. Metals. ***Stuart Broughton***

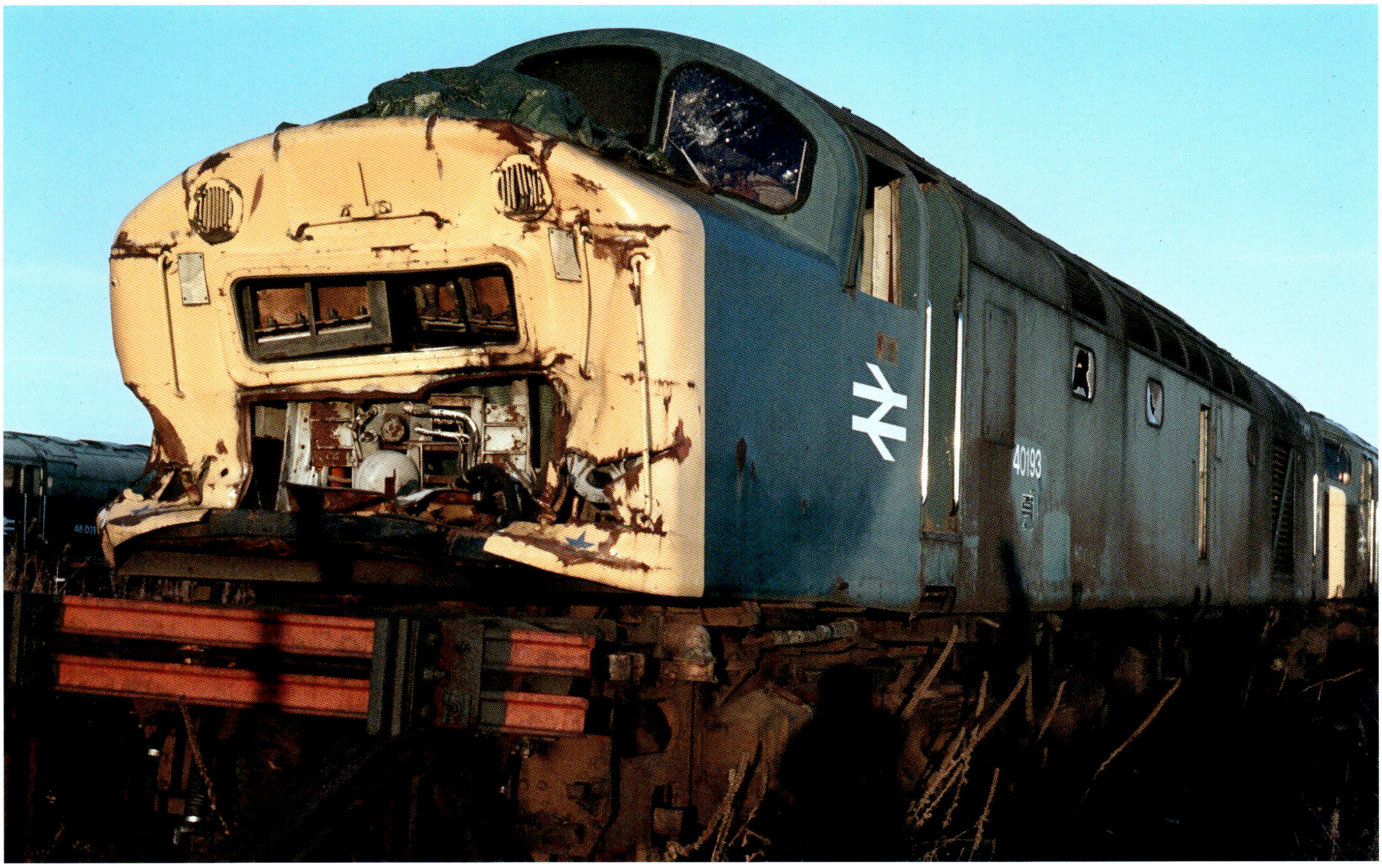

Although 40193 was withdrawn in October 1981 due to collision damage sustained at Lackenby Steel Works it arrived at Swindon Works for disposal in May 1982. This view shows the damage in a visit on a sunny day in November 1984 to the works. It was not until July of 1986 that the cutters got around picking on the unlucky Class 40. ***Steve Ireland***

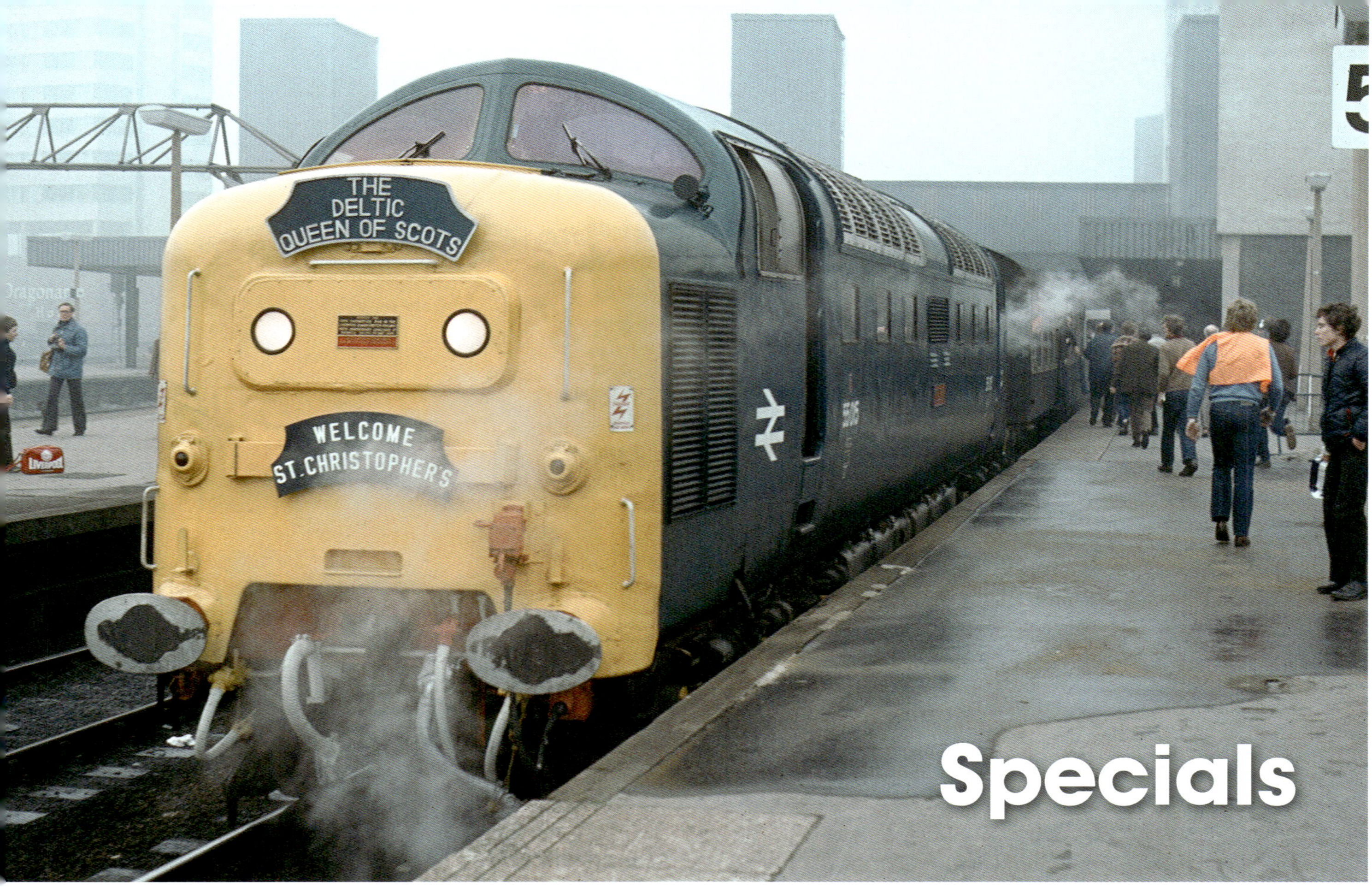

Specials

A stop at Leeds on route to Edinburgh Waverley for 55015 Tulyar on 7 November 1981. ***Steve Ireland***

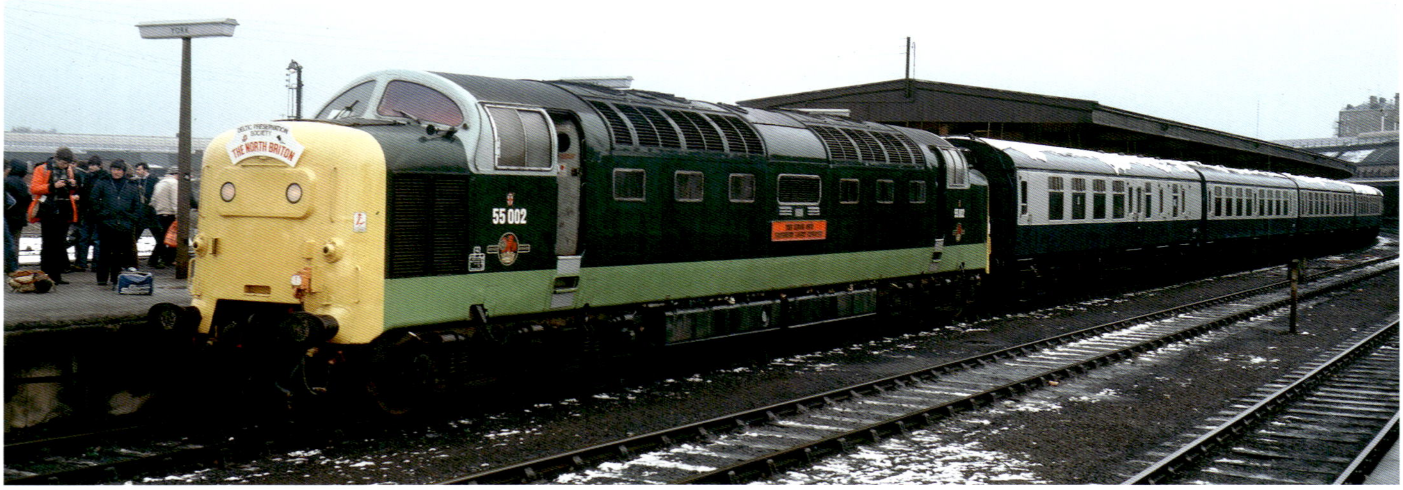

The North Briton tour on 25 April 1981 from York used 55002 The King's Own Yorkshire Light Infantry throughout. ***Strathwood Library Collection***

Below: On 26 March 1978, 55007 Pinza waits at Sittingbourne with The Man of Kent. ***Peter Simmonds***

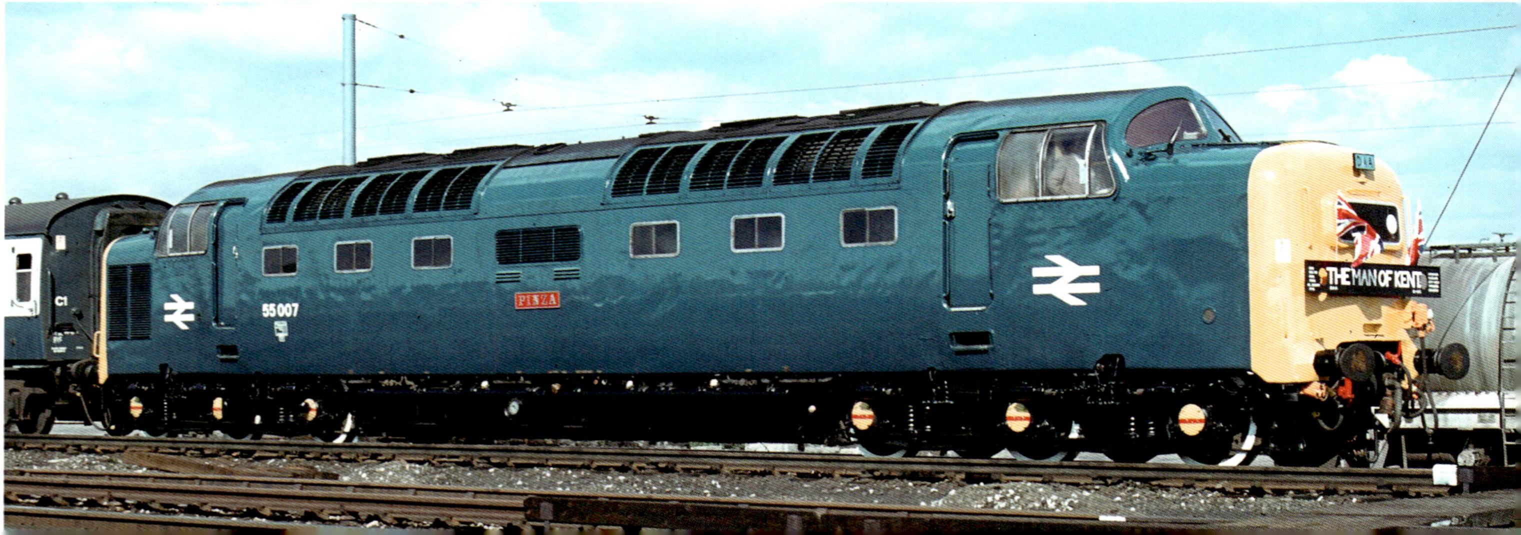

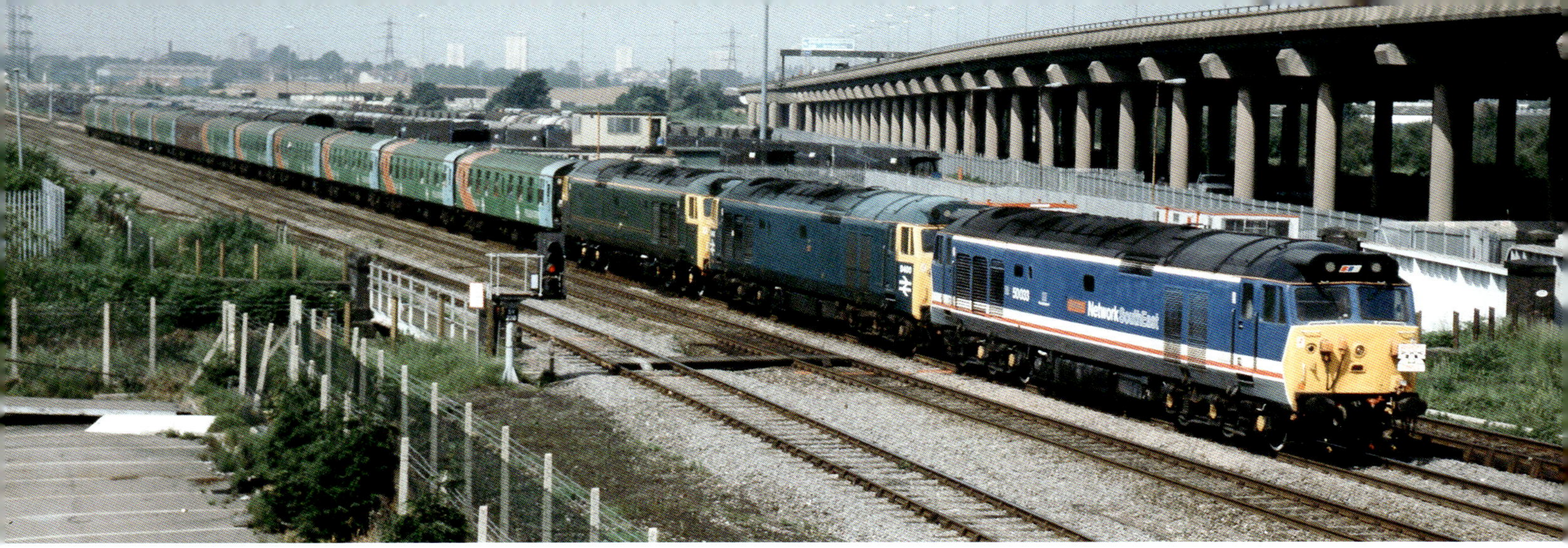

Ample power for The Bishops Triple with 50033 Glorious, D400 and 50007 Sir Edward Elgar at Washwood Heath on 5 June 1993. ***Steve Ireland***

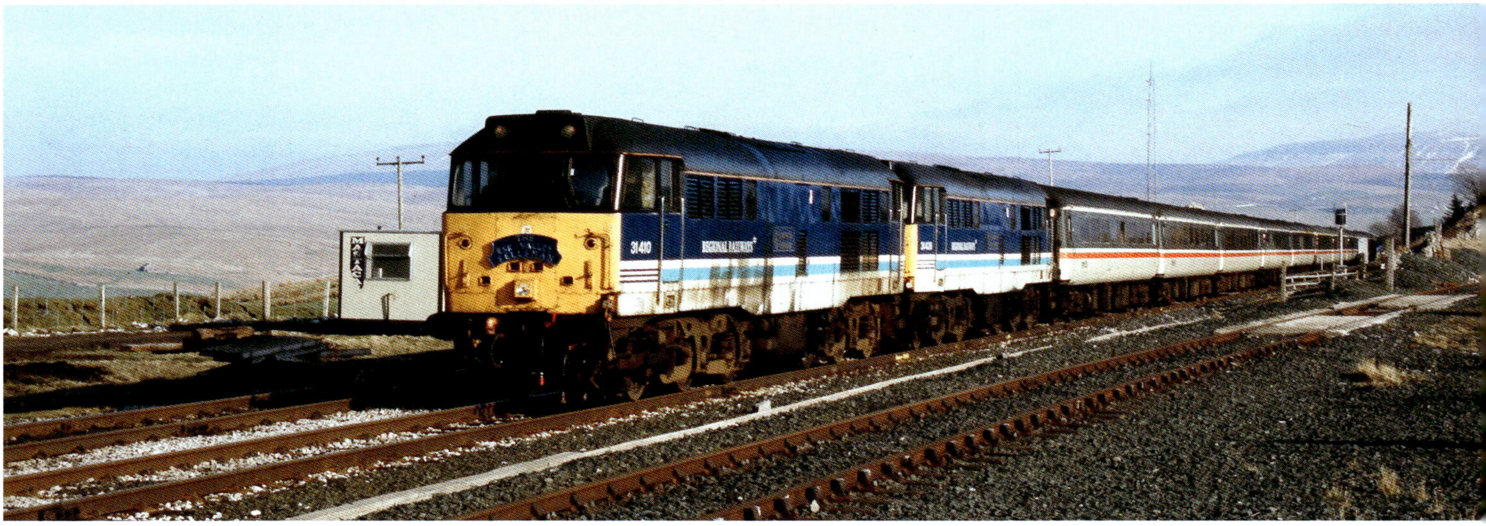

A Class 31 pairing of 31410 and 31439 on the Esk Valley Fellsman at Ribblehead on 6 March 1993. ***Peter Robinson***

Below: Type Ones 20210 and 20169 at Gloucester going to Kemble on 4 September 1991. ***Alister Betts***

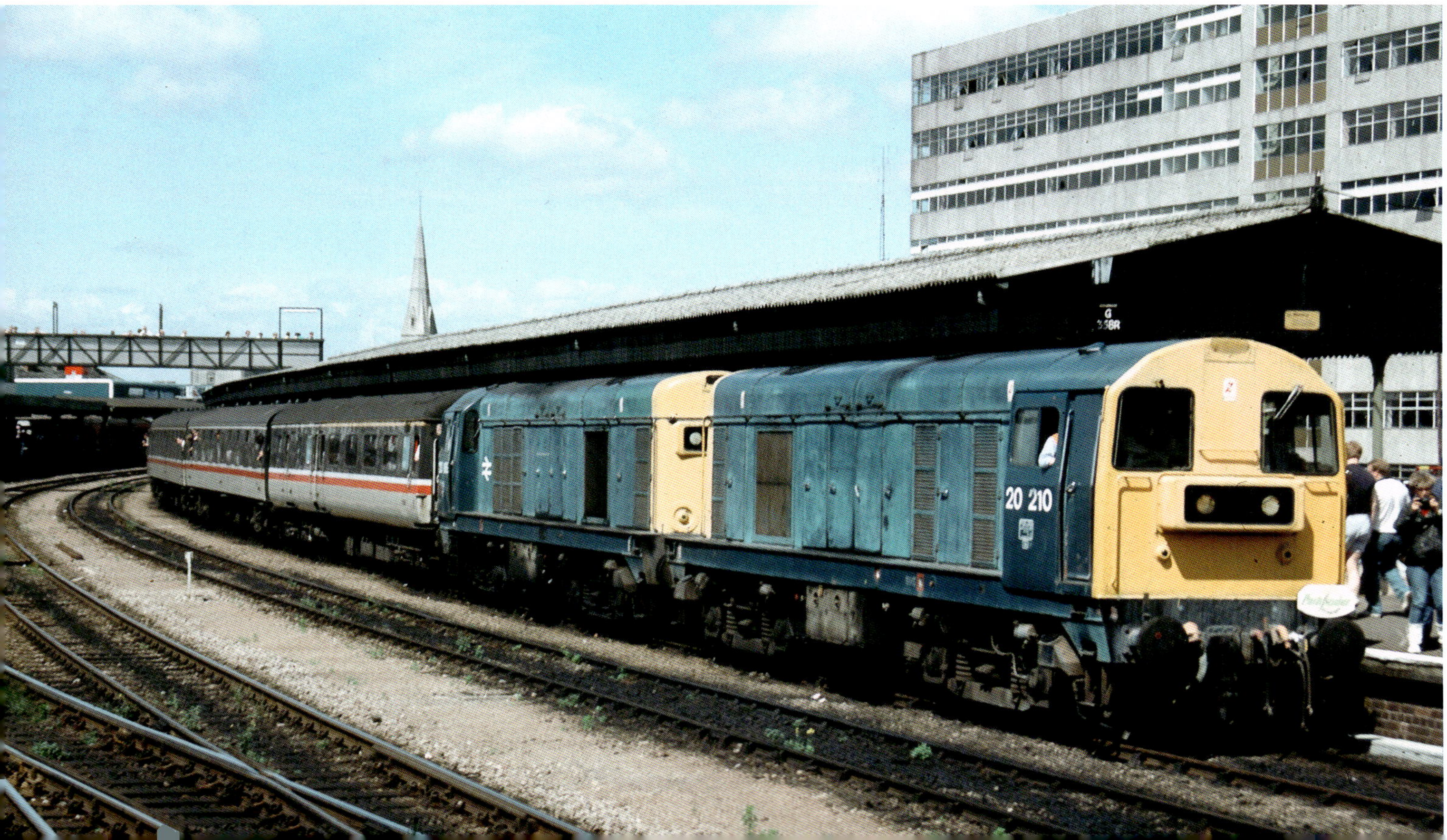

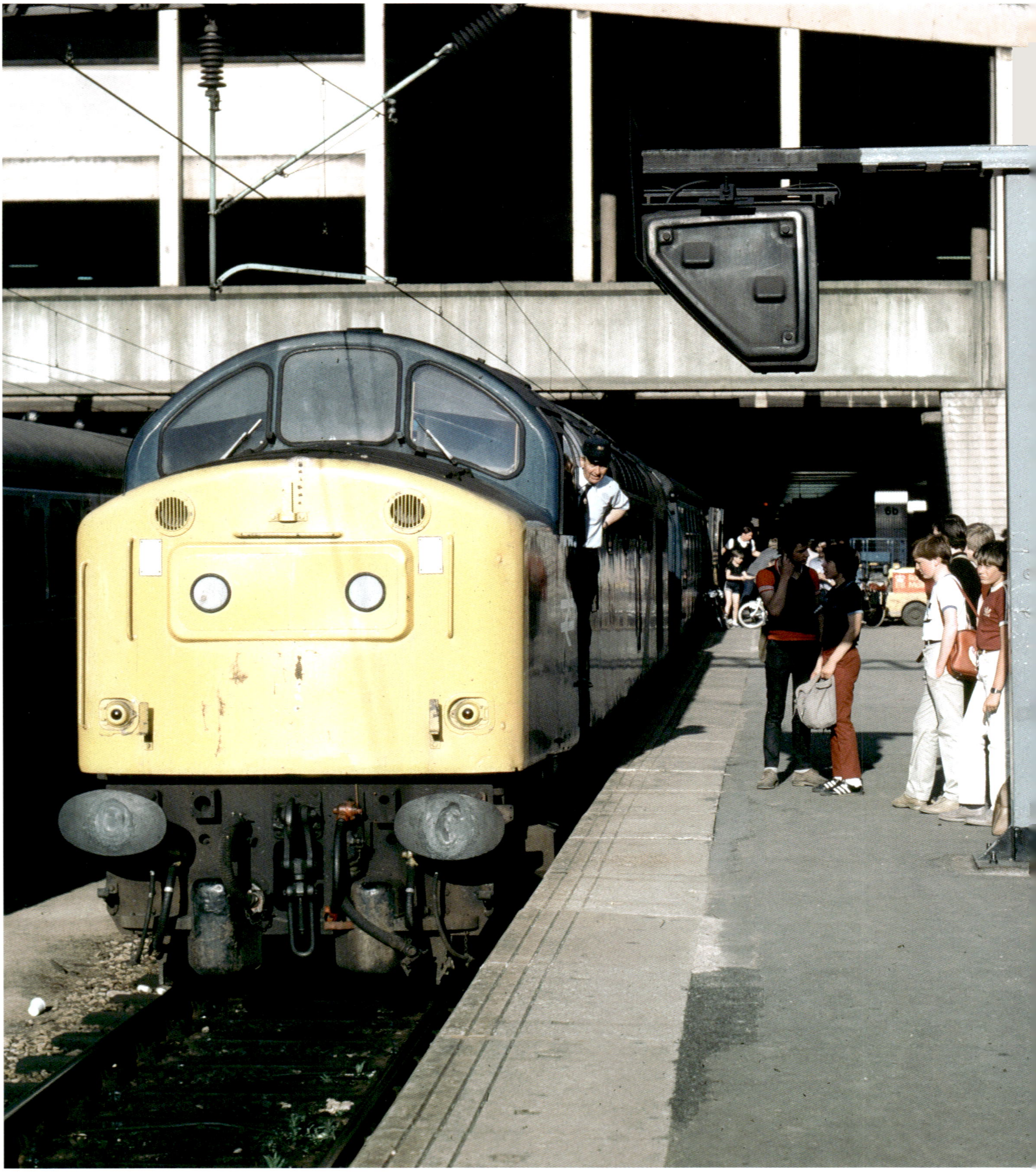

The distinctive No. 2 end of 40158 rebuilt with marker lights after a smash, waits with an unknown excursion from New Street in the late spring of 1983. By December this locomotive would be parked up and withdrawn, going to Doncaster for the formalities of breaking up during September 1984. ***David T Williams***

Mix and Match

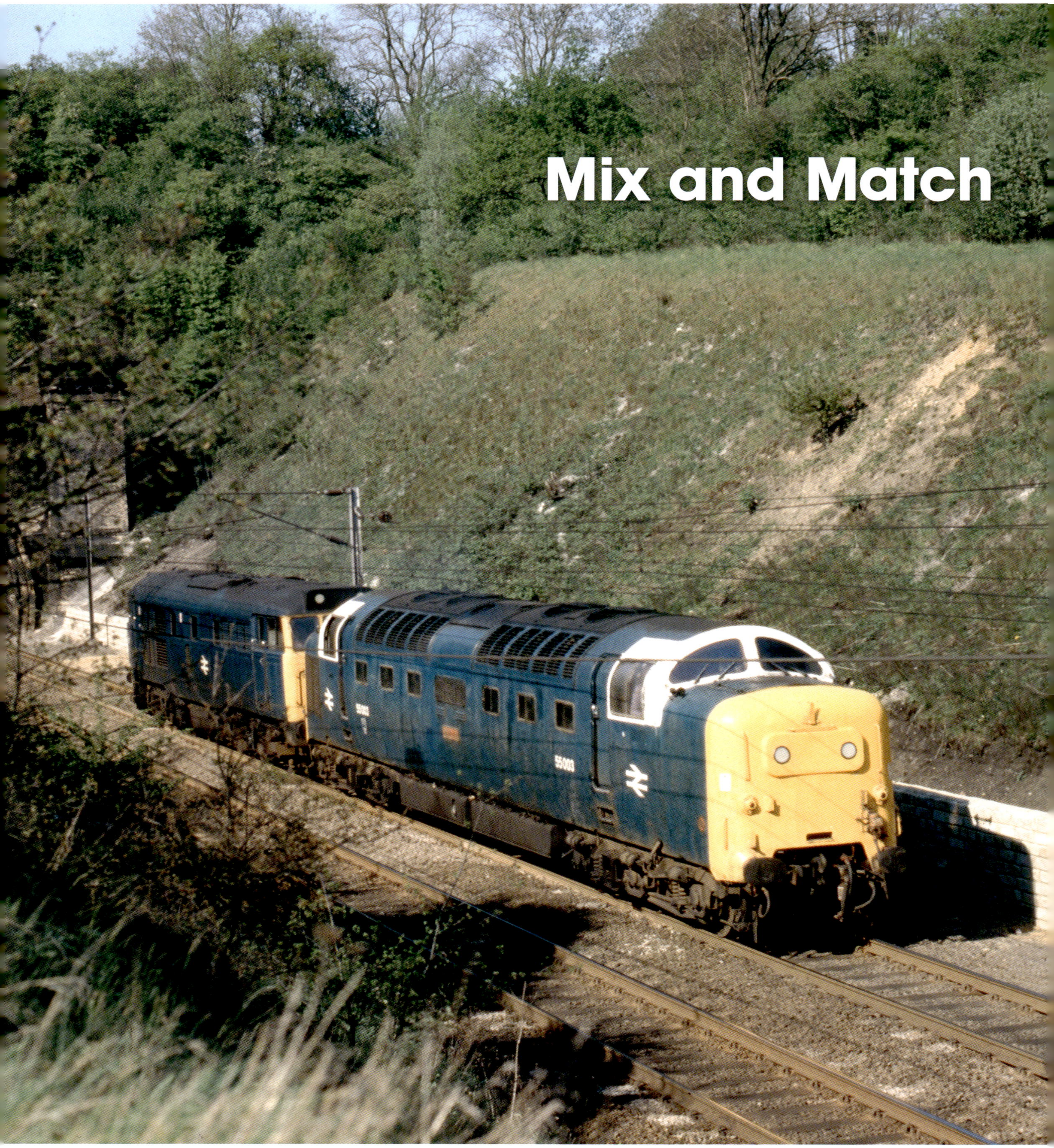

A light engine movement perhaps or has 55003 Meld rescued a failed 31217 as the pair exit the tunnel at Welwyn North on 15 May 1980. The racehorse Deltic looks a little shabby in this its last year of service, being stabled finally at Doncaster Works on the last day of the year to await the knackers who finished the Type Five off during the following March. ***Colin Whitbread***

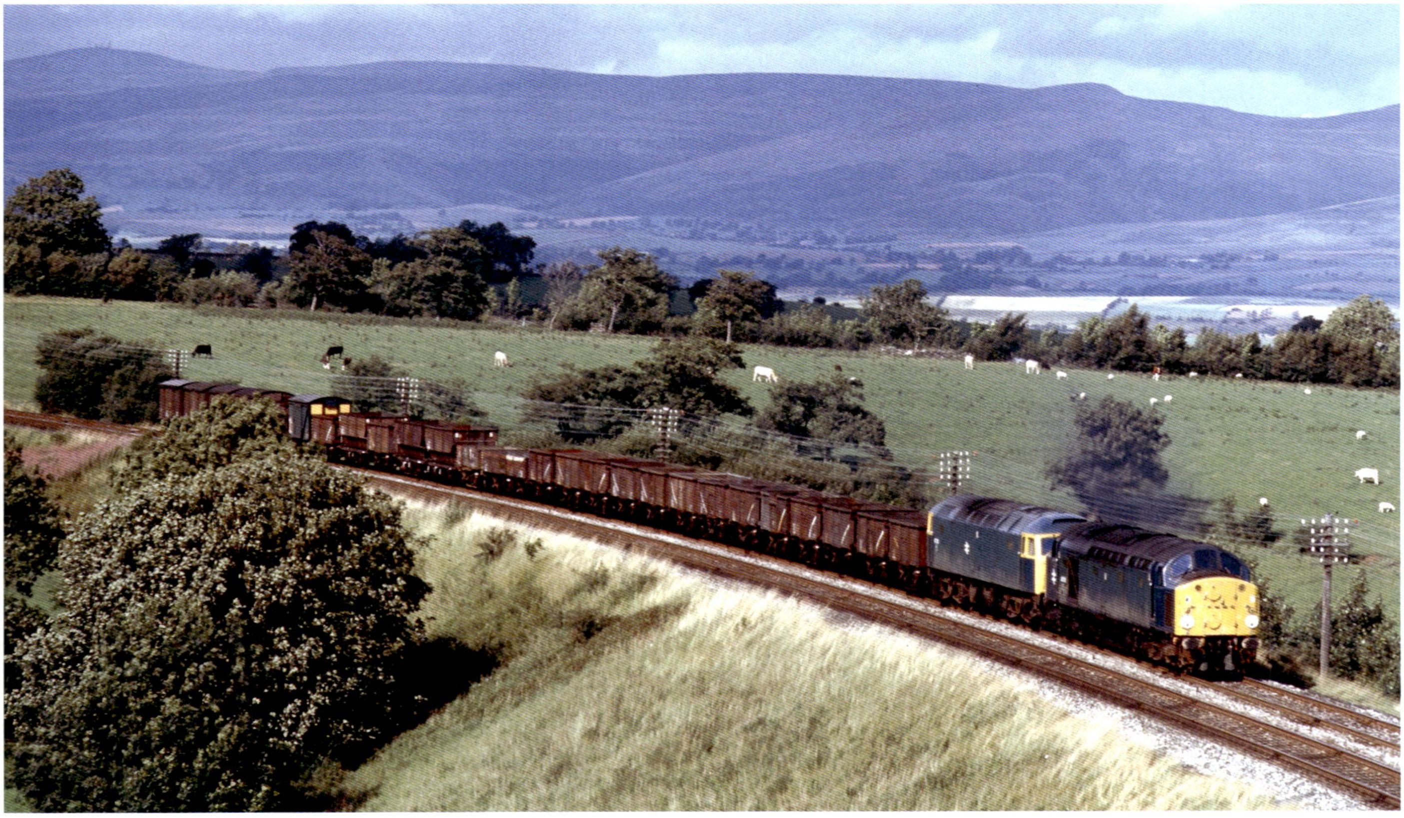

The Whistler is doing all the work as 40030 Scythia and 47370 head a short freight between Ormside and Kirkby Stephen on 26 August 1982. ***Late Pete Walton/Sid Steadman***

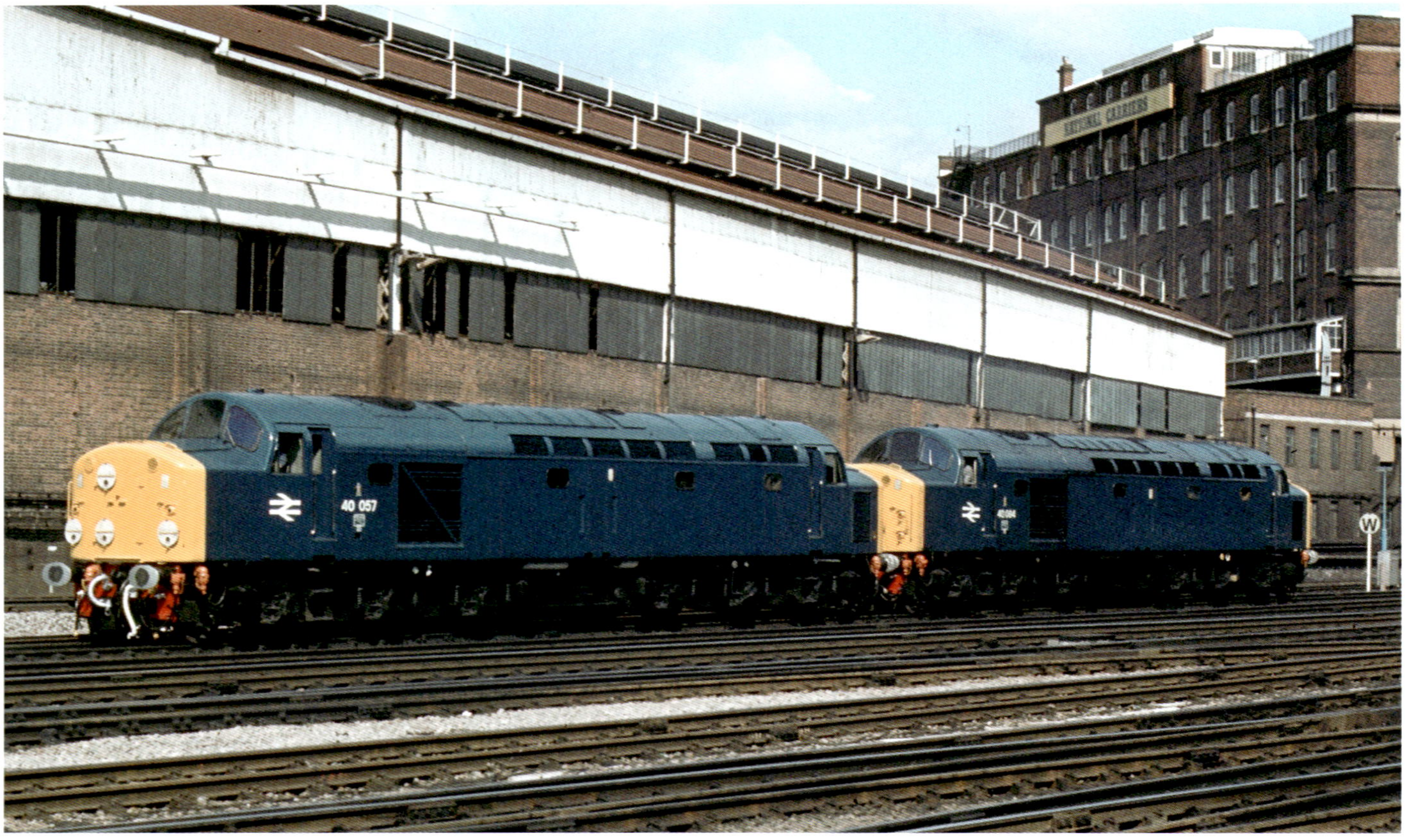

Paddington station enjoys the sound of a twin Class 40 working from the Capital, arranged by The Class Forty Preservation Society. Having arrived from York The Cotswold Venturer tour would be hauled throughout by 40057 and 40084 on 8 May 1982. ***Steve Ireland***

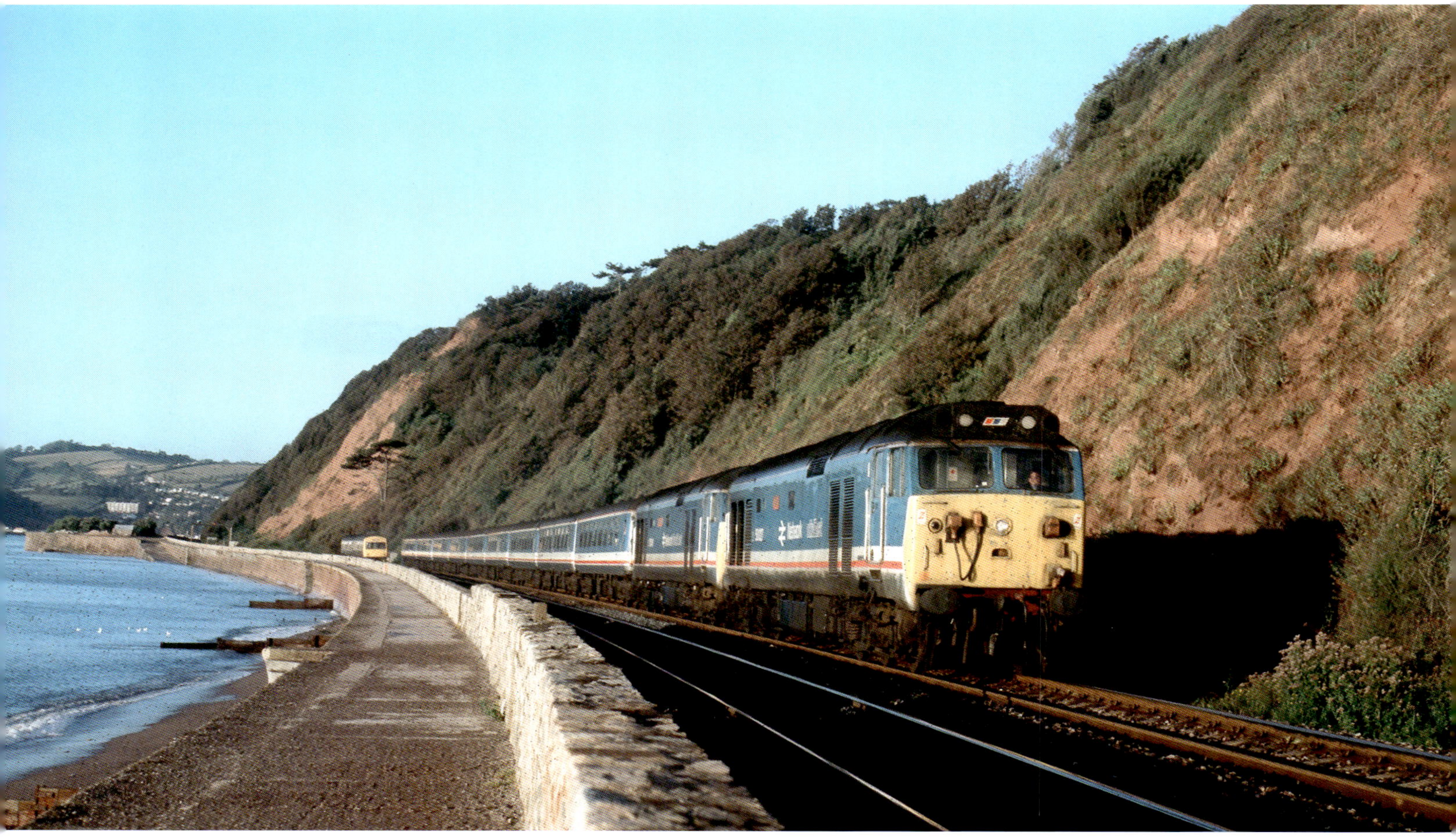

Double headed Fifties reminiscent of their early days from Crewe to Glasgow along the sea wall near Teignmouth on 6 September 1996 as 50027 Lion and 50049 Defiance make easy progress along the coastal section. ***Late Pete Walton/Sid Steadman***

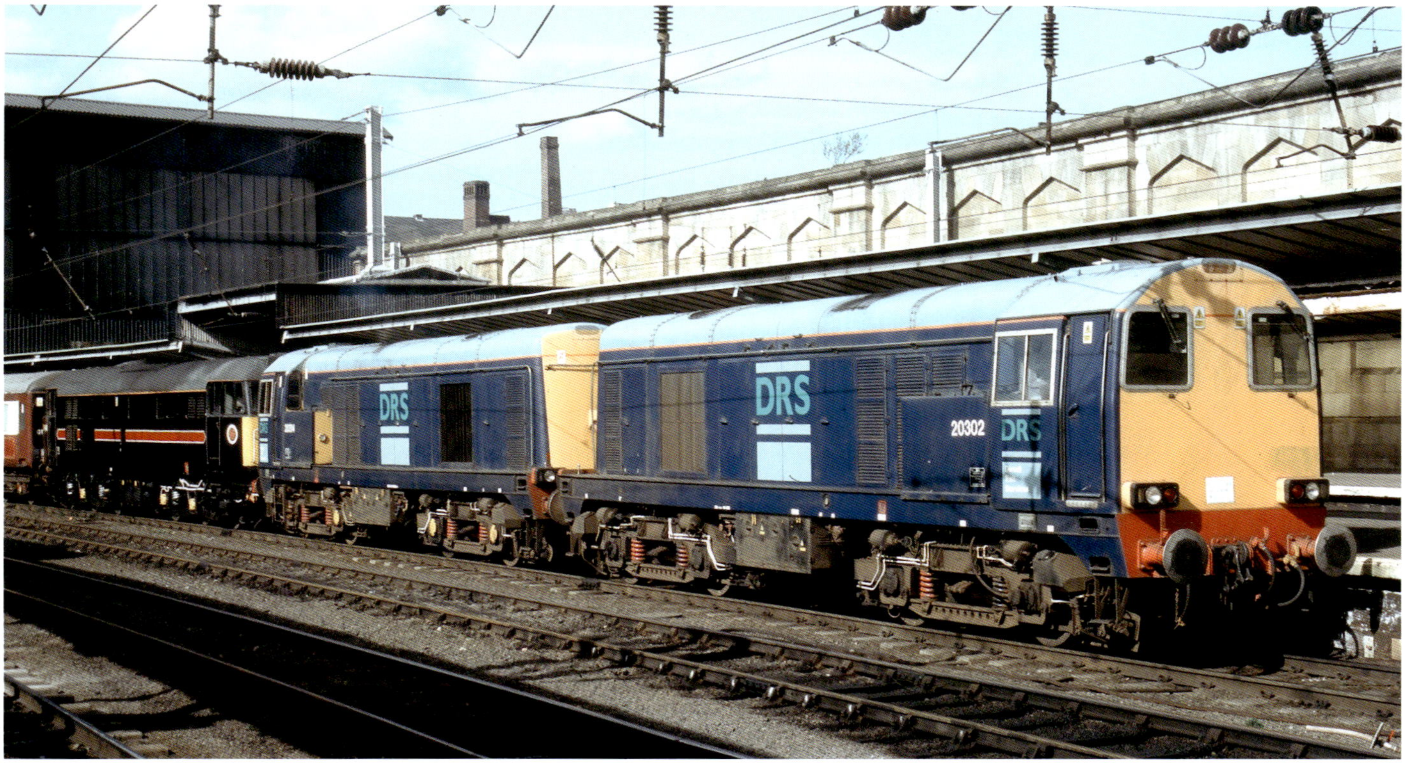

A Direct Rail Services Class 20 pairing of 20302 and 20302 lead an unknown Fragonset Railways Class 31 into Carlisle on 27 September 1998. ***Late Pete Walton/Sid Steadman***

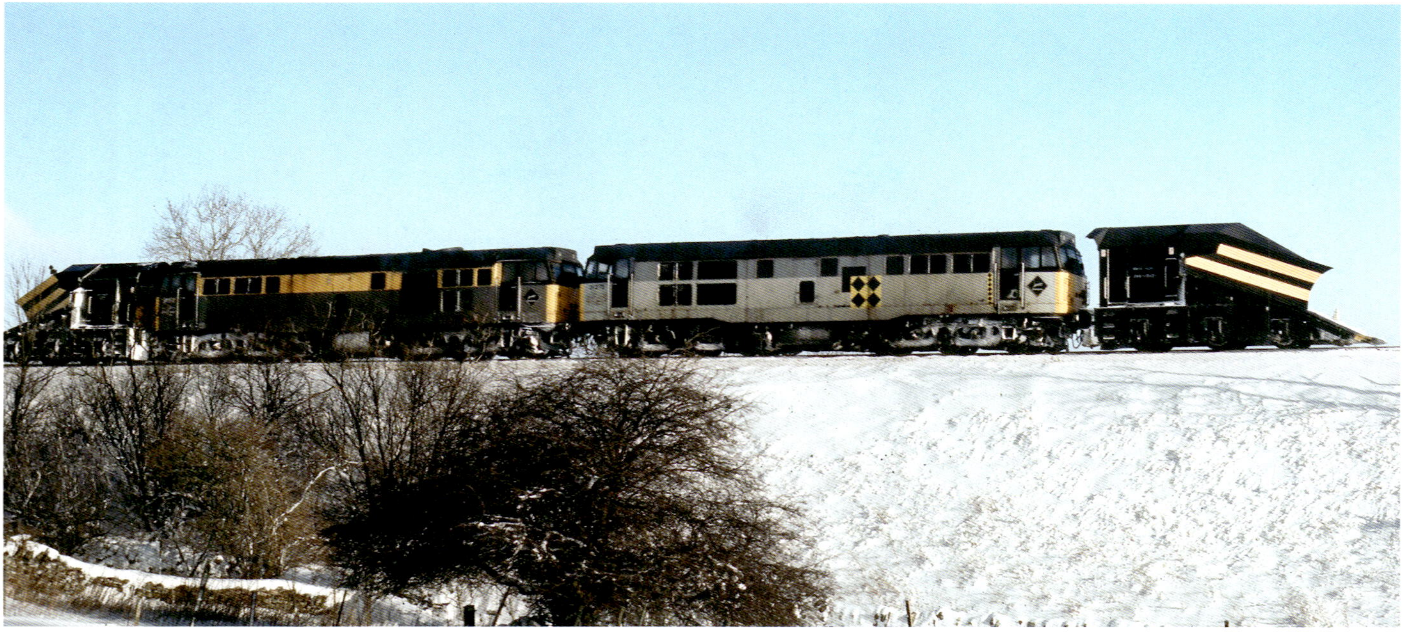

Snow plough duties for 31275 and another Class 31 near Ais Gill on 28 January 1996 in an attempt to keep the Settle and Carlisle open to traffic. ***Late Pete Walton/Sid Steadman***

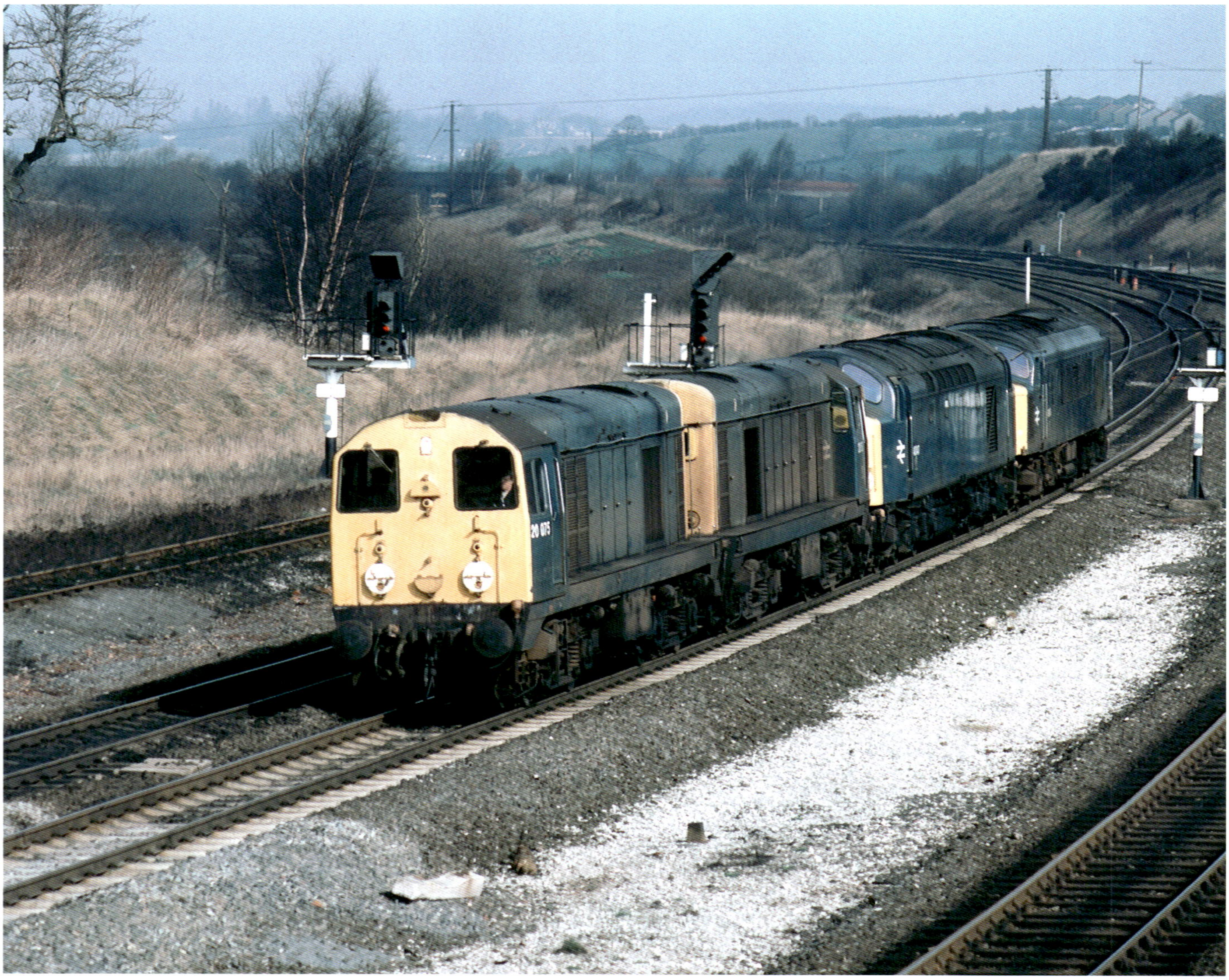

A heavyweight light engine movement of 420 tons comprising 20075, 20158, 40047 and 45054 at Clay Cross Junction in March 1984. ***David T Williams***

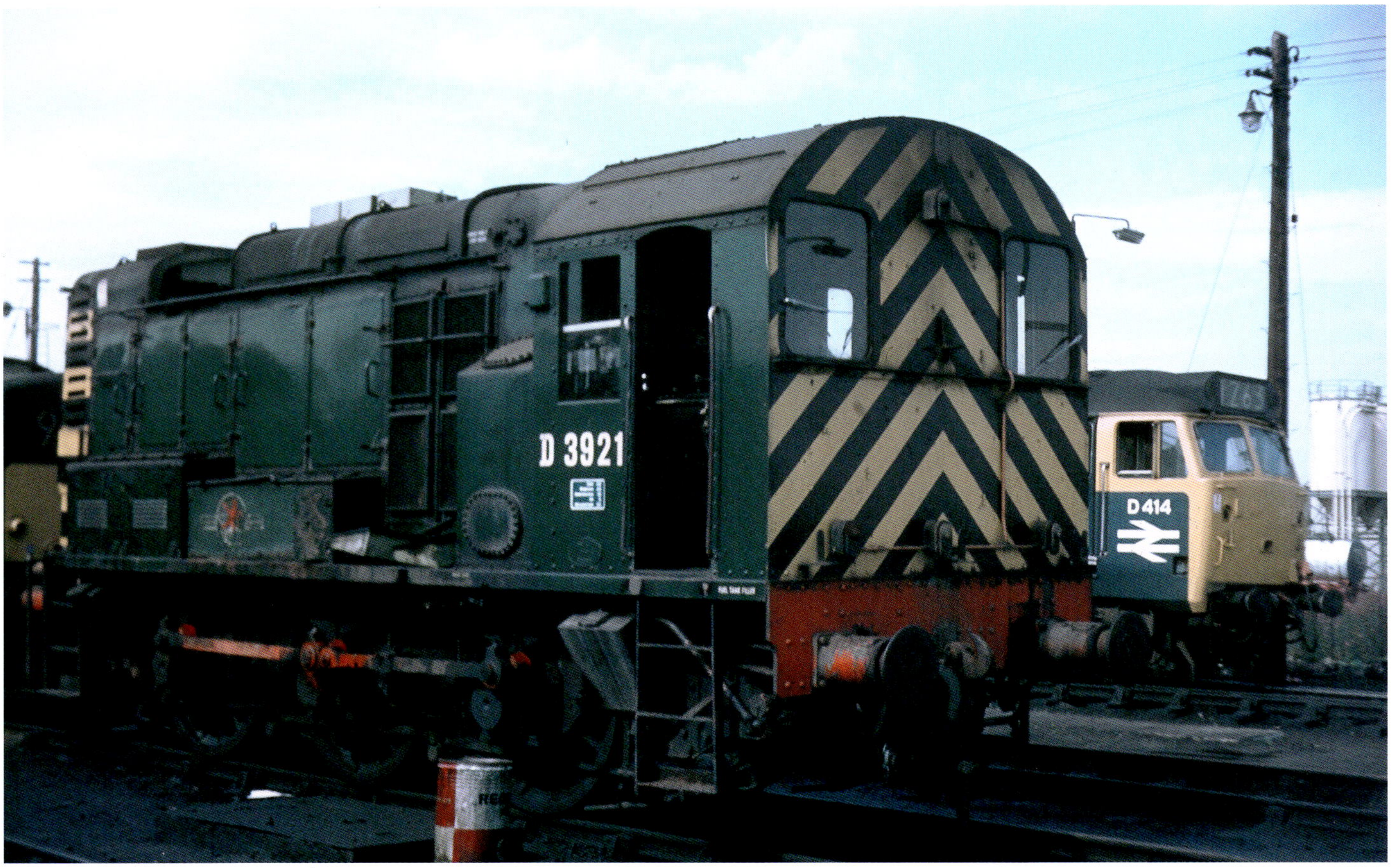

Work out in the open on 7 August 1969 within the engine compartment of D3921 whilst D414 awaits a call to arms again on the Anglo-Scottish traffic at Polmadie. ***Neil Snuggs***

Both styles of numerals can be seen on these green stable mates D5826 and D6802 resting in the sunshine outside the roundhouse at Barrow Hill on 24 August 1969. ***Frank Hornby***

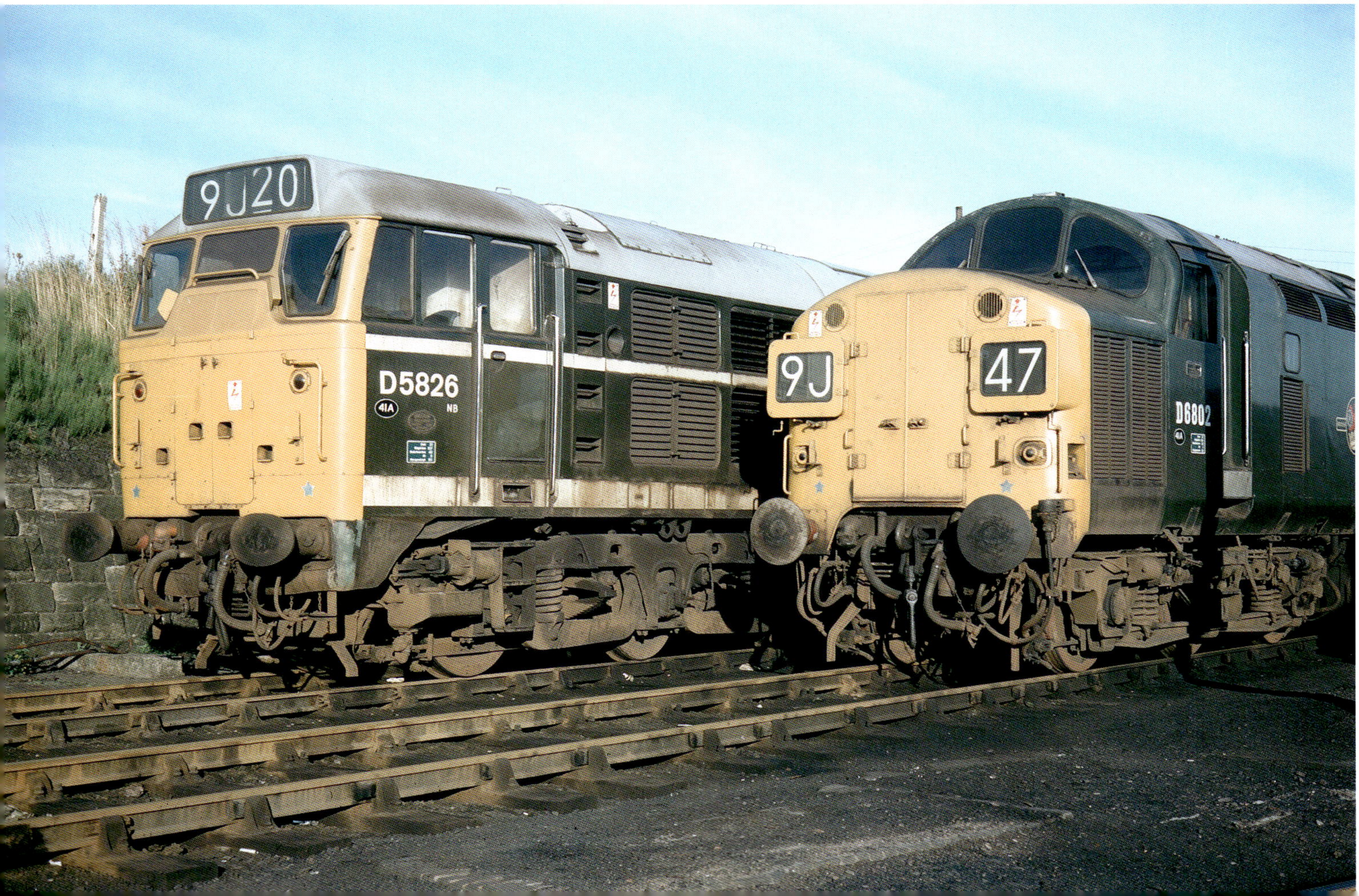

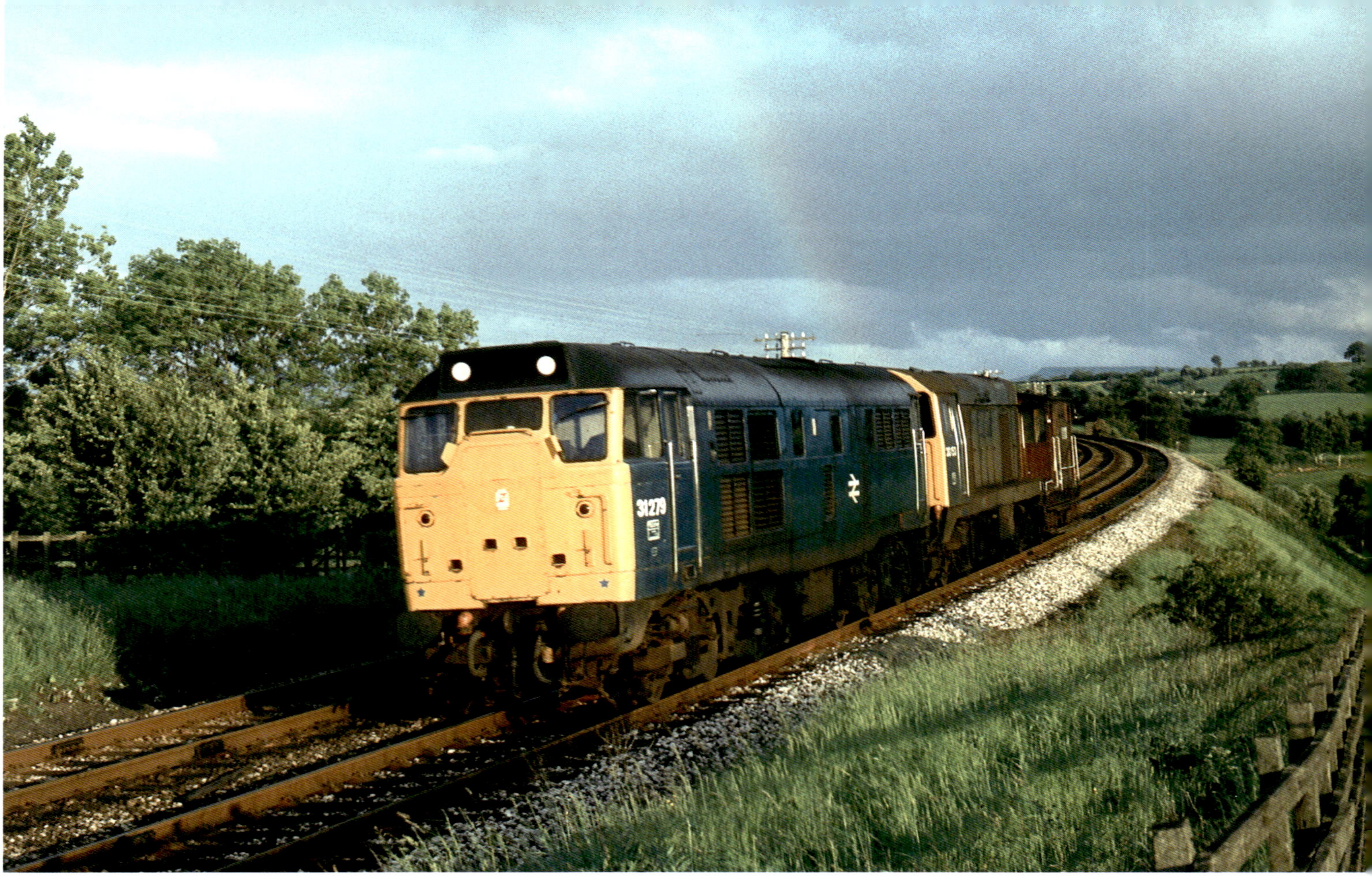

Not a pot of gold at the end of the rainbow at Ormside on 15 June 1981, just 20153 being hauled by 31279 light along the Cumbrian Fells. ***Sid Steadman***

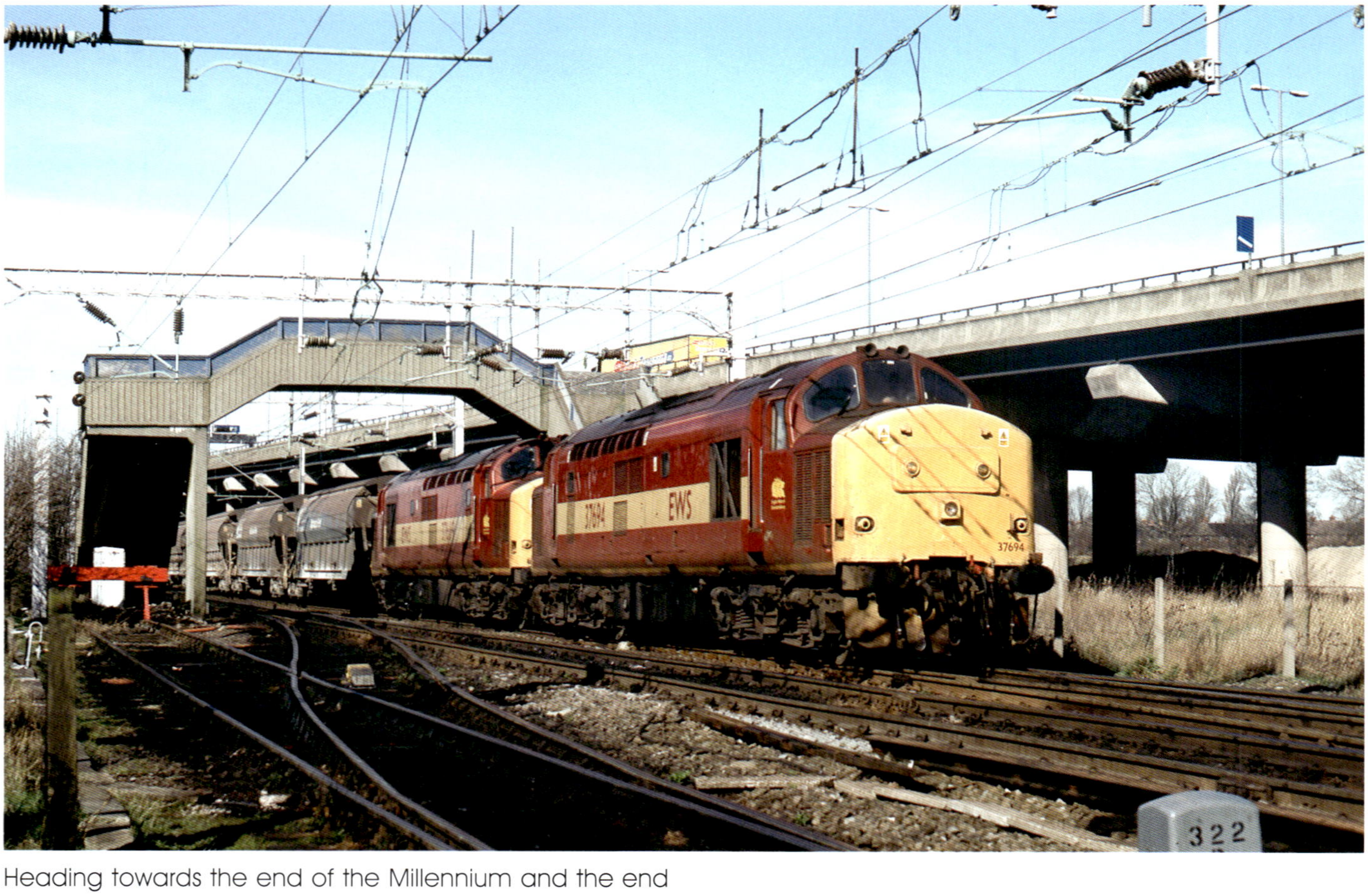

Heading towards the end of the Millennium and the end of this volume EWS liveried 37694 and 37669 double head through Bescot in 1999. ***David T Williams***

Help To Preserve Our Railway Heritage

Strathwood not only publish books on our railway heritage but have also set up the Railway Photographic Preservation Association as a Charitable Trust to house an archive of images comprising over 200,000 photographic negatives and slides.

The archive was established to not only preserve the collections of over one hundred photographers both living and deceased, but to also make their work available to a younger audience for the future. To achieve this aim, we have begun an energetic programme to publish a considerable number of books. Allied to this we are making as many as possible of the photographs and slides we hold, available as copies to interested enthusiasts, individuals, societies and other publishers.

Many photographers hcve chosen Strathwood to care for their collections and to publish the best examples of their work for posterity.

If you have negatives or colour slides of transport subjects then we would like to hear from you. We purchase, accept on loan, or welcome donations of material to the archive. Photographers always receive recognition for their work when it is used by publishers (A N Other/Strathwood Library). To answer why so many images are just credited as Strathwood Library Collection in this volume, the reason is we do not know who the original photographer was. This is usually because their collection gets split up via auctions or collectors upon their death with no record of the late photographer for us to credit. Please do not let this happen to your collection. Make contact with us today to discuss what can be done to ensure you work is fully credited and recognised for both today and the future.

Please call us today if you would like to see your work in print, perhaps in a similar fashion to this publication. We also undertake publications to benefit charities and societies on behalf of our contributors. In addition we can store, and catalogue collections on behalf of clubs and societies by way of loan, thereby releasing such groups to concentrate on other aspects of their activities.

Strathwood Ltd,
Glenavon House,
Kinchurdy Road,
Boat of Garten,
Inverness-shire,
PH24 3BP.

Telephone 01479 831139

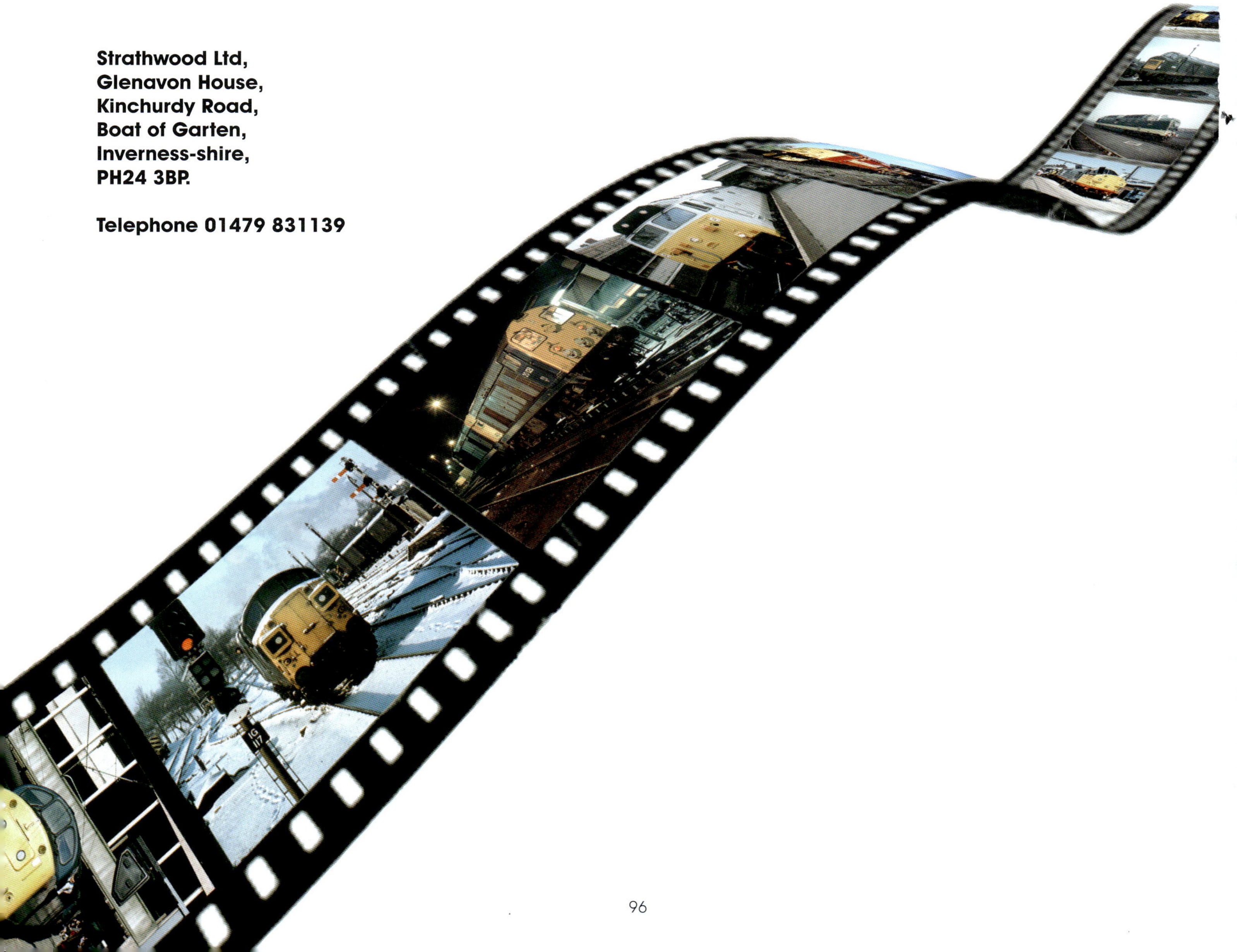